BECOMING A
Master
STUDENT

BECOMING A

Master

STUDENT

Tools, techniques, hints,
ideas, illustrations,
instructions, examples,
methods, procedures,
processes, skills,
resources, and suggestions
for success.

BY DAVID B. ELLIS

FIFTH • EDITION

College Survival, Inc., P.O. Box 8306, Rapid City, SD 57709

Library of Congress Number: 85-61906
ISBN: 0-942456-06-8
Fifth edition
Printed in the U.S.A.

Notice:
Becoming a Master Student was previously titled *Survival Tools for
Students,* and before that, *Survival Tools for College.*

Acknowledgments

Scores of people have contributed to this book.

I would like to acknowledge the staff of College Survival, Inc. for their personal and professional support. It is an honor to work with people I love.

Since the first edition of this text was published, hundreds of educators have provided valuable suggestions. In particular, I want to thank Judy Maisey, Bob Boyd, Sam Lanham, Russell Floyd, and Bill Norris.

For their contributions in writing and editing, I acknowledge Larry David, Tracy Grassby, Bill Harlan, Kay Horton, Bobbye Jones, Mary Maisey, Jody Severson, and Chris Stern. For his mastery in design I thank Bill Fleming. For their assistance in design and illustration I thank Laurie Ellis, Dan Jeziorski, Gregg Lee, Ben Leonard, Mike Speiser, and Susan Turnbull. I acknowledge Bruce Wagman and Jayne Erickson for photography and Linda Walters for her typesetting.

I thank the administration of National College in Rapid City, South Dakota and particularly John Hauer for assistance in the development of the student success course that led the way for this book; Lynn Ford, Jodi Melo, Leonard Running, and Susan Roe Kern for their work and dedication; and Karen Ellis, Barb Churchill, Trisha Waldron, and Stan Lankowitz for their contributions to my personal growth. I also treasure what I have learned from my children, Sara and Elizabeth, and the constant encouragement of my parents, Maryellen and Ken.

Several teachers have assisted me through their trainings or writings in my endeavor to support students to be successful. I thank Werner Erhard, Thomas Gordon, Ken Keyes, Albert Ellis, Carl Rogers, Virginia Satir, and Sid Simon.

I especially want to express my gratitude to the thousands of students who have taught me more than I ever imagined there was to learn. Their willingness to share personal experiences is a gift that I cherish.

Dave Ellis

REQUEST

I want your feedback. When you see ways to improve this book, please write to me.

I am always interested in new suggestions for being a successful student, new techniques for getting what you want in school, and feedback about what you use. If an idea in this book doesn't work at all for you, or is particularly effective, please let me know. Thank you.

David B. Ellis
College Survival, Inc.
P.O. Box 8306
Rapid City, SD 57709

Table of contents

Exercise #1

Textbook reconnaissance

Surveying a textbook can give you an idea of a course before you start. You get the general picture—the overview. The human brain works best when going from the general to the specific. When you inspect something in its entirety, you give your mind a framework in which to put the details. When you find something in the book that is interesting, you make the material meaningful.

Take a few minutes to look over this book. Start with the table of contents. Then, look at every page in the book. Do this quickly. Read some of the headlines. Look at the illustrations. Notice the forms, charts, and diagrams.

As you preview the book, look for ideas, techniques, and information you find interesting or possibly valuable. When you see something you like, write down the page number and a very brief description of the section (two or three words) in the space below. If you find five interesting things before you have completed your scan, stop writing and continue your survey. Look at every page. Do this quickly.

Page number   Description

1.

2.

3.

4.

5.

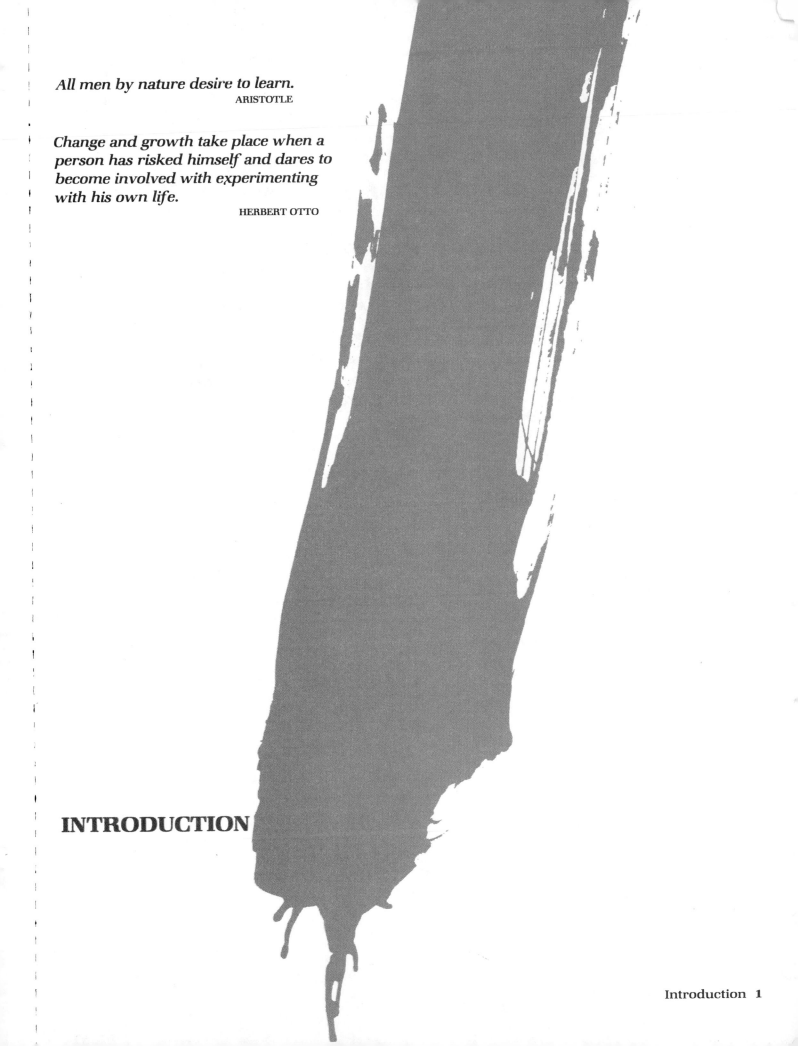

All men by nature desire to learn.
ARISTOTLE

Change and growth take place when a person has risked himself and dares to become involved with experimenting with his own life.
HERBERT OTTO

INTRODUCTION

This book is worthless.

The first edition of this book began with that sentence.

Many students interpreted it as a ploy to get their attention. That wasn't the case. Others thought it was reverse psychology. That wasn't the case, either. Still others thought it meant that the book was worthless if they didn't read it. It's more than that. The book is worthless even if it is read.

What was true of that first edition is also true of this edition. This book is worthless unless you actively use it to be successful in school.

You probably won't commit to using the ideas in this book until you are convinced that you have something to gain. The main purpose of this introduction is to sell you on the value of committing yourself to spend the energy to use this book actively.

Before you stiffen up and resist, the purpose of this sales pitch is not to separate you from your money. You already bought the book. Now you are being asked to commit yourself to having this book improve your performance in school.

Journal entry #1

Discovery statement

Write a description of a time in your life when you learned or did something well. This situation need not be related to school. Describe the details of the situation, including the place, time, and people involved. Describe how you felt about it, how it looked to you, how it sounded. Describe the physical feelings you associate with the event. Do the same for emotions.

Pitch #1: You can rediscover the natural learner in you.

As a child, you were a great natural learner. You learned complex skills such as language joyfully, without struggle. For children, learning is a high-energy process involving experiment, discovery, and broken dishes.

Later on, a different process was set in motion. Learning became associated with school, and since school is often a drag, learning got a bad image. It was connected with drudgery, or even mild torture. It was only natural your learning performance dropped off. After years of indifferent performance, you probably came to believe you couldn't do any better as a student even if you wanted.

This book can help you reverse the process and put you back in touch with the natural learner you really are.

Pitch #2: You can learn about you.

Throughout the book there are discovery and intention journals designed to give you the opportunity to see yourself more clearly. Using them, you can discover the master student who lives in your body.

Pitch #3: You can learn how to learn.

This book is about discovering what makes learning easier and more fun. It applies to learning anything anywhere anytime.

The world is changing fast. Your career is likely to change dramatically every few years. Your most valuable skill in the marketplace may well be knowing how to learn and to adapt to change. This book is designed to assist you to become that kind of student, not just for the short time that you are in school, but for your entire life.

Pitch #4: You can choose from hundreds of techniques.

The book is loaded with hundreds of nuts-and-bolts techniques to help you be a successful student. Whether you have a tendency to doze off in lectures, are a dyed-in-the-wool procrastinator, or have trouble remembering, taking tests, planning your time, or dealing with drugs and alcohol—for almost any difficulty you might face in school—this book offers effective solutions. You are invited to experiment and choose the ones that work for you.

Pitch #5: You get the best suggestions from thousands of students.

The concepts and techniques in this book did not come from learning theorists or psychologists. They came from tens of thousands of students in one-on-one counseling sessions, small groups, workshops, and large classes. The students came from all types of backgrounds, diverse parts of the country, and virtually every imaginable learning situation. Because the concepts and techniques have already been proven effective by students themselves, this book does not justify and explain its recommendations. It lays them out and lets you choose.

Key elements are continually reinforced throughout the book. The most effective methods for becoming a master student are reviewed in each chapter so that you learn to apply them to each topic area (time management, note-taking, test anxiety, creativity, etc.)

Pitch #6: You can use a proven product.

The first four editions of this work-text were successful for tens of thousands of students. In schools where it was widely used, the dropout rate decreased as much as 25 percent and in some cases, 50 percent. Student feedback has been very positive. In particular, students with successful histories have praised the techniques in this book.

This fifth edition is a further refinement. It takes into account thousands of suggestions made by students and teachers who used previous editions.

Pitch #7: You can save money now and make more later.

Being a master student can help you get the most of an expensive purchase— your education. There is an exercise in this book where you can figure out how much it costs you to attend one class. Most people figure that it is typical to spend about $30 an hour to sit through one class, but they often feel like they haven't gotten 30¢ worth of value. This book is about getting your money's worth.

Educated people, master students, typically earn more money than those who are not educated. During his career, an average college graduate makes $250,000 more than a less-educated person.

Wrap-up

Now, even if you are convinced this book can be of value, what makes it work is action. Through action, you create your own education.

There is no way to make you participate in this book. Your commitment to action is the last necessary ingredient to make it effective.

So, recognizing the power of commitment, here is an exercise to put you in touch with your intention to have *Becoming a Master Student* be of value to you.

Exercise #2

Commitment

Using this book actively, you can transform the way in which you approach learning. You are likely to be surprised by what you can learn in a short time and by what fun learning can be.

However, without your intention, without your commitment to get what you can, this book really will be worthless. Therefore, in the interest of saving your valuable time and energy, this exercise gives you a chance to declare your involvement up front. Choose the number from one to ten that reflects your level of commitment. Write the number below.

1. Lowest level of commitment—signified by, "Well, I'm reading this book right now, aren't I?"

2. "I will skim the whole book and actually read some of it."

3. "I will read the whole book and pay attention to some of what's being said."

4. "I will read this book and think about how some of the techniques might fit into my life as a student."

5. "I will read the entire book and even do the exercises that capture my attention."

6. "I will study this book and do almost all of the exercises."

7. "I will apply several of the suggestions in this book to my life as a student."

8. "I will experiment with most of the suggestions in this book and use the ideas that I like best."

9. "I will participate in this entire book vigorously, experimenting the whole way until I find what works best for me."

10. Highest level of commitment—"I promise to get value from this book even if I have to re-write the sections I don't like and even if I have to come up with new techniques of my own."

Enter your commitment level here:

If you selected commitment level 1 or 2, you might consider passing this book on to a friend.

If your commitment level is a 9 or 10, you are on your way to terrific success in school. If you are somewhere in between, experiment with the techniques and if you find they work, consider raising your level of commitment.

Journal entry #2

Discovery statement

Select a time and place when you know you will not be disturbed for at least twenty minutes. (The library is a good place to do this exercise.) Spend three or four minutes relaxing, letting go of your thoughts. Then write down in this space everything that you want to get out of your education. Write it all.

When you run out of things to write, stick with the exercise just a bit longer. This is important. To get what you want, you first have to know what you want.

To begin, complete the following sentences. Then keep writing.

The most important benefit I want from my education is . . .

I want to get this benefit because when I do, I expect to . . .

When I complete my education, I want to be able to . . .

I also want . . .

How to get the most out of this book

1. *Skip around.* Look for sections of this book that apply to your current situation. If you're having trouble listening to boring lectures, skip directly to Chapter 5. If you suspect that alcohol might be getting in the way of your progress, read Chapter 9. If there are sections of the book that don't apply to you at all, skip them. Be familiar with this book so that you can use it as a reference. Topics that aren't relevant now may be just what you want next year.

2. *Don't expect all the ideas to work.* Hundreds of ideas are presented that other students have found effective. Some of the ideas you experiment with won't work for you, and the tendency will be to think there's something wrong with the book or with you. Just know that not every technique works for every person.

3. *Do the exercises.* This book isn't finished until you complete the exercises. The suggestion is to do all the exercises, and if you don't, a more important suggestion is to not feel guilty because you skipped something.

4. *Participate.* Hundreds of examples are given to illustrate how suggestions can be applied to learning situations. These examples may not apply to you. Participate by continually considering how each suggestion could apply to your situation. If the topic is dealing with the stress of test-taking, and if you don't get stressed taking tests, apply the suggestions to other times in your life when you do experience stress.

5. *Apply the power processes.* Most of the techniques in this book are practical and down-to-earth. There are 12 exceptions to this nuts-and-bolts approach. Each chapter contains a power process which is a technique, sometimes a little unusual, that can be applied both in and out of school. Many students have proclaimed these power processes to be the best part of the book. See for yourself.

Review the textbook reconnaissance exercise. Consider the sections in this book that you thought might be valuable. Choose the one from which you think you can get the most immediate, practical benefit, and scan that section until you come to a specific technique you can use. Write an intention statement in this space concerning how you will use that technique within the next week. Include when you intend to use it.

For example, if you listed the section called "When reading is tough...", you could use any of the twelve techniques suggested for difficult reading assignments. If you have a tough computer science course, you might choose to form a support group to discuss reading assignments. In that case, you might write, "I intend to contact four other students after class tomorrow about forming a group to study computer science."

Journal entry #3

Intention statement

Look back

The study technique I choose is:

_____

_____

_____

The time(s) I intend to use it is (are):

_____

_____

_____

_____

After reviewing this chapter, complete the following sentence:
What I want from this chapter is...

_____

Journal entry #4

Discovery statement

_____

_____

_____

_____

CHAPTER ONE
FIRST STEP

In oneself lies the whole world, and if you know how to look and learn, then the door is there and the key is in your hand. Nobody on earth can give you either that key or the door to open, except yourself.

J. KRISHNAMURTI

The only man who is educated is the man who has learned to learn; the man who has learned how to adapt and change; the man who has realized that no knowledge is secure, that only the process of seeking knowledge gives a basis for security.

CARL ROGERS

In this chapter . . .

The first step in any journey is finding out where you are now and where you plan to go. The **First step** method shows how to get out of the same old rut.

The discovery and intention journal system lets you focus your energy so you can actually use less while getting more.

The discovery guide is like a camera pointed at you. You may see many parts of yourself in the picture of **The master student.**

Power process #1: Ideas are tools suggests that you not believe what you read in this book. You may bruise your philosophical knuckles.

This chapter also suggests: **Maybe it's your breath, Deface this book**, and that **"F" is for feedback, not failure**.

Exercises in this chapter are designed to put you in touch with where you are and where you want to be.

First Step

The first step opens the door to any value contained in this book. Without it, the other suggestions will remain just suggestions. They will never make a real difference in your life. This one technique, the first step, can enable you to increase your effectiveness as a student beyond all your expectations. No matter what kind of student you are, good or bad, you can use this method to tap resources you never imagined you had.

The first step technique is simpler to explain than it is to perform. It involves telling the truth about yourself, including the truth about your current abilities (which are not the same as capabilities) and the truth about what you want.

Admitting the truth about ourselves is hard to do. We don't like to admit our faults. It is equally difficult for most people to admit their strengths. Maybe they are embarrassed about what they want, but it could be they just don't know what they want.

Consider for a moment the success of Alcoholics Anonymous, a group founded by alcoholics to support people to live without drinking.

A fundamental principle of AA is that before an alcoholic can recover, she must tell the truth about her drinking, then declare her desire to stop. Doing this clears the path to learn new ways of coping with life's problems. This same concept is used by most self-help groups and by a majority of effective counselors.

Few learning situations are tougher than the one faced by the recovering alcoholic, who must learn to let go of a physical and emotional dependency on a chemical. In comparison, learning biology should be a snap.

The first step can be powerful in any learning situation. Its importance and difficulty increase as learning gets more complicated. Its power is the power of truth.

The closer you get to the truth, the greater the possibility for success. That's why it is important to be as specific as possible when taking the first step. Whether written or verbal, first steps work best when they cover observable, verifiable behavior.

If, for example, you want to improve your note-taking skills, do not write down as your first step, "I am an awful note-taker. My notes look like a three-year-old wrote them." Instead, write down objective data. You could write, "The notes I took for American Constitutional History were difficult to read. I couldn't tell which notes belonged to which class. Of seventy pages of notes, only eleven were useful to me."

In addition to telling the truth about your current abilities, be honest about what you want. And, again, be specific. In the case of improving your notes, you might write, "I want to take notes that will at least get me a passing grade on the exams" or, "I want to clearly label my notes and keep them in order."

The truth has a magical quality. It has power. The journal entries and exercises in this chapter and throughout the book are designed to give you an opportunity to experience that power.

A SALES PITCH FOR THE EXERCISES

You can't get something for nothing. You can, however, get nothing for something. That is what you get from this book, if your only investment in it is money.

Why exercises? Because learning works best when it involves action. People learn more effectively when, along with their brains, they can use their arms, legs, eyes, ears and noses in the process.

Again and again, you will be asked to observe, recall, ponder, search, breathe, touch, feel, move, see, hear, smell, and act. (The purpose is to make this book not like **going to** the movies but, instead, like **being in** the movies). You will find a lot of comment about creation in this book. True education is not about cramming material into your brain. True education is the process of expanding your capabilities, of bringing yourself out into the world.

There are no magic formulas in this book. All these study techniques have been around, in one form or another, for a long time. What will make them work is action. And there is no way to know whether a technique is right for you until you test it.

This book can't give you anything of significance, nor can your teachers, nor can your school. All they can do is set the stage to create learning through your own action.

Exercise #3

Taking the first step

The purpose of this exercise is to give you a chance to discover the positive as well as negative aspects of yourself. It is the most difficult exercise in this book. For the exercise to be worthwhile, it must be done with courage.

Some people suggest that looking at negative aspects is counter to positive thinking. Well, perhaps. Positive thinking is a great technique. So is seeing the truth, especially when we see the whole picture—even though a realistic picture of ourselves may include some extremely negative points.

If you admit that you can't read, and that's the truth, then you have taken a strong, positive first step to becoming a successful reader. On the other hand, if you say that you are a terrible math student, and that's not the truth, then you are programming yourself to accept unnecessary failure. The point is, tell the truth.

This exercise is similar to each *Journal entry—Discovery statement* appearing throughout this text. The difference is that in this case you don't write your discoveries in the book for reasons of confidentiality.

Be brave. If you approach this exercise courageously, you are likely to write down some things you don't want others to read. You may even write down some truths about yourself that could get you in trouble. Do this exercise on separate pieces of paper, then hide or destroy them.

For this exercise to work, follow these three suggestions:

1. Be specific. It is not effective to write, "I could improve my communication skills." Of course you can. Instead, write down precisely what you can do to improve your communication skills. For example, "I can spend more time really listening while the other person is talking, instead of thinking about what I'm going to say next."

2. Look beyond the classroom. What goes on outside of school often has the greatest impact on your ability to be an effective student.

3. Be courageous. This exercise is a waste of time if done half-heartedly. Be willing to risk. Sometimes you may open a door that reveals a part of yourself that you didn't want to admit was there. The power of this technique is that once you know "it" is there, you can do something about it.

Part 1

Time yourself, and for ten minutes, write as fast as you can and complete the following sentences with anything that comes to mind. Complete each sentence at least ten times. If you get stuck, don't stop; just write something—even if it's crazy.

> It is ineffective when I . . .
> It doesn't work when I . . .
> I could change . . .

Part 2

When you have completed the first part of the exercise, review what you have written and cross off things that don't make any sense. The sentences that remain represent possible goals for your experience as a master student.

Part 3

Here's the tough part. Time yourself, and for ten minutes, write as fast as you can. Complete the following sentences with anything that comes to mind. As in Part 1, complete each sentence at least ten times and just keep writing, even if it sounds silly.

> I am very good at . . .
> It is effective when I . . .
> Something that is very positive about me is . . .

Part 4

Review your list and circle the things that really fit. This is a good list to keep for those times when you question your own value and worth.

One way to become a better student is to grit your teeth, squint your eyes, set your jaw, grunt and try harder. There is another way. The journal system can enable you to increase your effectiveness with the least possible effort and struggle. It's a way to focus your energy.

Airplanes are seldom exactly on course. Human or automatic pilots are always checking and correcting the course. The resulting path looks like a zigzag. The plane is almost always flying in the wrong direction, yet because of constant observation and course correction, it arrives at the right place. The same system can be used by students.

It works this way: Throughout this book you will find exercises called "Journal entries." These will be labeled either "Discovery statement" or "Intention statement." Each journal entry will contain a short set of directions and a space in which you can write.

Through discovery statements, you can learn "where you are." They are a record of what you learn about yourself as a student (both strengths and weaknesses). Discovery statements are declarations of what you want, descriptions of your attitudes, pictures of your feelings, transcripts of your thoughts, and chronicles of your behavior.

Through intention statements, you can alter your course. They are statements of your commitment to do a specific thing, to take a certain action. An intention arises out of your choice to direct your energy toward a particular goal. The purpose of an intention statement is *not* to get you pumped up and excited to go out there and try harder. Intention statements are not about trying harder. The purpose of an

intention statement is to set your course, and to reset your course again and again, as often as necessary.

The process involves a cycle of writing discovery statements about where you are and intention statements about how to get where you want to go. Then you'll write discovery statements about whether you completed the intended action, followed by another intention statement, and so on. Sometimes the statements will be long and detailed. Usually they will be short—maybe just a line or two. With practice, the cycle becomes automatic.

There is no need for alarm when you fail to complete an intended task. Sometimes you will stray off course. The important thing is to make the necessary corrections. When you begin to use the Journal System, miraculous progress may not come immediately. Do not be concerned. Stay with the cycle. Use discovery statements to get clear about your world and what you want out of it. Then use intention statements to direct your actions. Do not worry if you don't do everything you intend. No one does. Simply return to the discovery phase and record your observations about not accomplishing what you intended. Dig a little deeper. Return to the intention phase and continue. When you notice progress, record it.

The following statement may strike you as being radical, but it is true: It takes the same amount of energy to get exactly what you want in school as it takes to get something you don't want. An airplane burns the same amount of fuel flying towards its destination as it does flying away from it. Test it for yourself. Use the discovery and intention journal system to get the education you want.

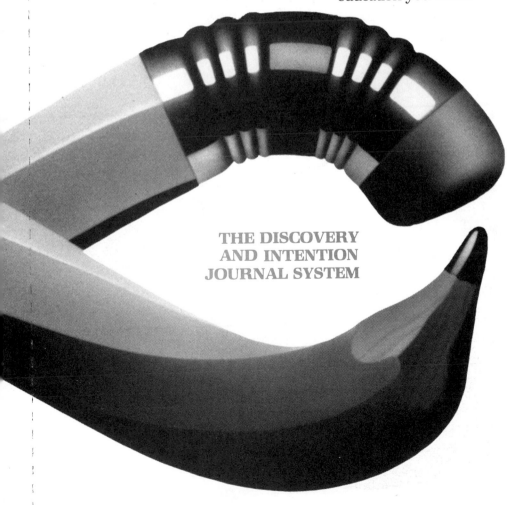

THE DISCOVERY
AND INTENTION
JOURNAL SYSTEM

DEFACE THIS BOOK!

There are valid reasons for not writing in any book. For one thing, it decreases the resale value. However, the benefit of writing in your books far outweighs that consideration.

Creating your own dialogue with a book is a way to make its knowledge yours. Something happens when you reach out and touch the book with your pen. You can hear yourself talking to the author. You can see before you a picture of your questions and responses.

This is especially true of *Becoming a Master Student.* The value you find in this book is the value you create in it for yourself.

When you have questions or disagreements or comments about what you find in *Becoming a Master Student,* write them down. Draw a picture of them. To demonstrate, turn the page and see how a student might have a dialogue with this book.

Find something with which you agree or disagree on this page. Write a short note in the margin about it. In Chapter Four, Reading, you will find suggestions on how to make effective notes in textbooks. For this exercise, however, let creativity be your guide. Get involved.

One way to become a better student is to grit your teeth, squint your eyes, set your jaw, grunt and try harder. There is another way. The journal system can enable you to increase your effectiveness with the least possible effort and struggle. It's a way to focus your energy.

Airplanes are seldom exactly on course. Human or automatic pilots are always checking and correcting the course. The resulting path looks like a zigzag. The plane is almost always flying in the wrong direction, yet because of constant observation and course correction, it arrives at the right place. The same system can be used by students.

It works this way: Throughout this book you will find exercises called "Journal entries." These will be labeled either "Discovery statement" or "Intention statement." Each journal entry will contain a short set of directions and a space in which you can write.

Through discovery statements, you can learn "where you are." They are a record of what you learn about yourself as a student (both strengths and weaknesses). Discovery statements are declarations of what you want, descriptions of your attitudes, pictures of your feelings, transcripts of your thoughts, and chronicles of your behavior.

Through intention statements, you can alter your course. They are statements of your commitment to do a specific thing, to take a certain action. An intention arises out of your choice to direct your energy toward a particular goal. The purpose of an intention statement is *not* to get you pumped up and excited to go out there and try harder. Intention statements are not about trying harder. The purpose of an

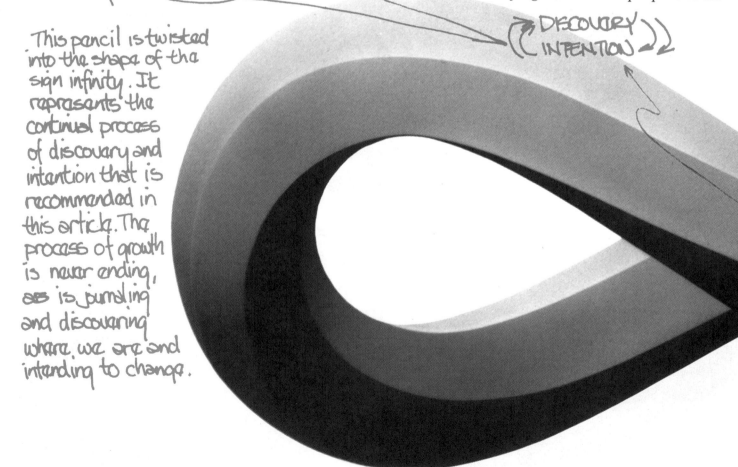

GOAL

This pencil is twisted into the shape of the sign infinity. It represents the continual process of discovery and intention that is recommended in this article. The process of growth is never ending, as is journaling and discovering where we are and intending to change.

DISCOVERY
INTENTION

intention statement is to set your course, and to reset your course again and again, as often as necessary.

The process involves a cycle of writing discovery statements about where you are and intention statements about how to get where you want to go. Then you'll write discovery statements about whether you completed the intended action, followed by another intention statement, and so on. Sometimes the statements will be long and detailed. Usually they will be short—maybe just a line or two. With practice, the cycle becomes automatic.

There is no need for alarm when you fail to complete an intended task. Sometimes you will stray off course. The important thing is to make the necessary corrections. When you begin to use the Journal System, miraculous progress may not come immediately. Do not be concerned. Stay with the cycle. Use discovery statements to get clear about your world and what you want out of it. Then use intention statements to direct your actions. Do not worry if you don't do everything you intend. No one does. Simply return to the discovery phase and record your observations about not accomplishing what you intended. Dig a little deeper. Return to the intention phase and continue. When you notice progress, record it.

The following statement may strike you as being radical, but it is true: It takes the same amount of energy to get exactly what you want in school as it takes to get something you don't want. An airplane burns the same amount of fuel flying towards its destination as it does flying away from it. Test it for yourself. Use the discovery and intention journal system to get the education you want.

But i'll feel guilty if i don't do what i wrote i would.

HELLO AUTHOR! sometimes i don't agree.

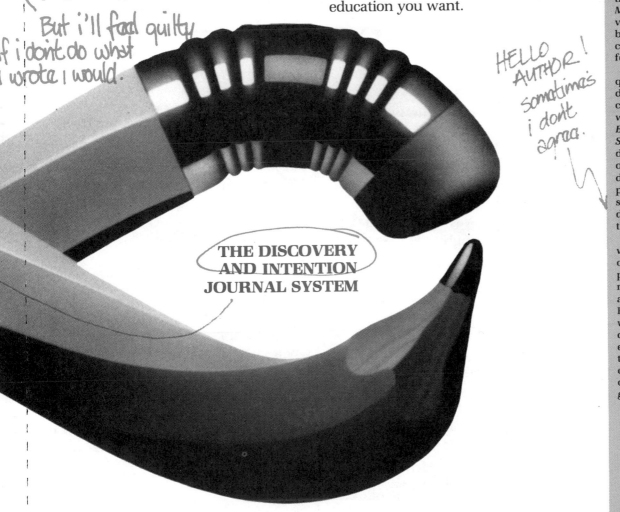

THE DISCOVERY AND INTENTION JOURNAL SYSTEM

THE POINT.

DEFACE THIS BOOK!

There are valid reasons for not writing in any book. For one thing, it decreases the resale value. However, the benefit of writing in your books far outweighs that consideration.

Creating your own dialogue with a book is a way to make its knowledge yours. Something happens when you reach out and touch the book with your pen. You can hear yourself talking to the author. You can see before you a picture of your questions and responses.

This is especially true of *Becoming a Master Student*. The value you find in this book is the value you create in it for yourself.

When you have questions or disagreements or comments about what you find in *Becoming a Master Student*, write them down. Draw a picture of them. To demonstrate, turn the page and see how a student might have a dialogue with this book.

Find something with which you agree or disagree on this page. Write a short note in the margin about it. In Chapter Four, Reading, you will find suggestions on how to make effective notes in textbooks. For this exercise, however, let creativity be your guide. Get involved.

Seven discovery statement guidelines

1. Discover what you want.

All of us have more energy doing something we want to do. Yet, many students are unclear about what they want from their education. Many students quit for that reason.

2. Record the specifics.

Observe your actions and record the objective facts of behavior. For instance, if the notes you take in a particular class are unsatisfactory, describe what they look like. You might write, "When I reread my notes, I was unable to decipher 14 scientific terms. I could not determine the main thrust of the lecture. The page was full of doodles."

Words and thoughts tell the story about life. Action tells the truth about life. Pay attention to details.

If you discover that you regularly avoid doing a certain kind of accounting problem, note the physical symptoms of your avoidance—how your stomach feels, how your breathing changes, whether you yawn. Notice what you do when you avoid studying accounting, right down to the smallest detail. For example, you might discover that when you avoid your accounting, you almost always eat a snack. Include that fact in a discovery statement.

Record these kinds of observations quickly, as soon as possible after you notice them.

3. Notice your inner voices.

Inner voices are internal chatter—the conversations that each one of us carries on in our head. We talk to ourselves constantly. Pay attention to these internal dialogues, and when you notice them getting in your way, write down their content. Be specific. If you can't pin them down, get as close as you can. Recreate them on paper.

This may seem difficult at first. Most people find, however, that the act of writing triggers the memory. If you are persistent, you can trigger a flood of thoughts.

You can explore yourself by noticing inner voices.

4. Notice feelings.

Be aware of physical sensations. Notice how you feel when you speak in class, for instance. Pay attention to what is happening in your stomach. Scan yourself for tension. If you are having difficulty reading a textbook, examine the accompanying feelings. Are you sleepy? Do you have butterflies in your stomach? Are your eyes burning?

Also notice how you feel when you function well. Identify the physical feelings you have when you are learning effectively. Some people feel best in the morning. If you notice that you can work math problems best when you are rested and alert, and you feel most rested and alert before lunch, you can set up your schedule so that you study math in the morning.

You can use discovery statements to pinpoint exactly where and when you learn most effectively.

5. Use discomfort as a signal.

It's natural to avoid discomfort, and for a student, discomfort is inevitable. The learning process often involves unpleasant sensations. All students experience boredom, fatigue, anger, and anxiety.

Some students are uneasy about keeping a journal. When you are writing a discovery statement and feel like quitting, when you start to feel uncomfortable, that is a signal that you are doing valuable work. Ernest Hemingway said that whenever he felt his writing was going too easily, he stopped. Stay with the uncomfortable feeling. Assure yourself that you can handle the discomfort a little while longer.

If you are uncomfortable about an upcoming test, do not try to stifle that feeling. Stay with it long enough to describe it to yourself.

This technique is especially valuable when you are bored. Boredom is almost never boredom. There is usually an underlying stress. When studying makes you yawn, take a moment to inventory your feelings.

If you are afraid, angry, distressed, or sad, write a discovery statement. Record your emotions.

6. Suspend self-judgment.

When you are discovering yourself, be gentle. If you continually judge yourself and evaluate your discoveries as either good or bad, sooner or later you will avoid discovering the kinds of experiences you label bad. The mind simply won't put up with that kind of abuse for very long.

Often the very qualities people tend to dislike and deny in themselves are qualities that can be turned into assets. For example, creative and imaginative students commonly have difficulty adjusting to the rigid structure of educational institutions. The qualities that get them into trouble are also the qualities that can make them powerful learners.

Be kind to yourself when you write discovery statements.

7. Tell the truth.

"The truth will set you free" is an idea that has become a cliché. It has been said so often that people use it without thinking about what it means. Use this idea and you will find out why the phrase is so frequently used.

Be truthful in your discovery statements. The closer you get to the truth, the more powerful your discovery statements will be.

Telling the truth requires courage and vigilance. Don't blame yourself when you notice that you avoid the truth. Be aware of your avoidance and tell the truth about it.

There is freedom in the truth.

Seven intention statement guidelines

tasks and be specific about what you intend to do about them. The most effective intention statements describe action you intend to take within 24 hours. If you want to get an A in biology, ask yourself, "What can I do today?" You might choose to study biology an extra hour. Make that your intention.

Challenge yourself, and be aware that if you always set goals that you cannot accomplish, soon you will stop setting goals. Give yourself a chance to experience success by choosing your intentions with care. Build a track record of accomplishment.

Success breeds success.

1. Make your intentions positive.
Tell yourself what you intend *to do*, rather than what you intend *not to do*. For example, instead of "I will not fall asleep while studying accounting," write, "I intend to stay awake when studying accounting."

As you do this, consider words like "try" and "hope" to be signals of failure. When you tell yourself that you are going to "try" to stay awake, you rob yourself of valuable information. If you fall asleep you can say, "Well, I tried." Trying is the same as not doing. It is absolutely all right to fail to accomplish what you intend. If, however, you deny that you failed to complete what you intended to do, your picture of your actions will become unclear. You will be less likely to change your behavior.

When you write intention statements, don't hedge your bets. Be positive about what you intend to do, and be willing to risk failure.

2. Make intentions small and keepable.
Give yourself the opportunity to succeed. Break large goals into small

3. Use observable criteria for success.
Set up goals that can be measured. Rather than writing, "I intend to work harder on my history assignments" write, "I intend to study history from 7 to 9 p.m. on Monday, Tuesday, and Thursday. I intend to spend one hour reviewing my class notes, and I intend to make summary sheets of my reading." Then, when you review your progress, you can determine exactly, without question, whether you accomplished what you intended.

4. Set deadlines.
You can use a deadline as a tool to accomplish a goal. If you are assigned a big project (a term paper for example), break the assignment into small tasks, and set a deadline for each task. You might write, "I intend to find a topic for my term paper by 9 a.m. Wednesday." To further divide the task, you could write down your intention to go to the library Tuesday evening and skim three books on the general subject.

Use deadlines to measure your progress. Remember that they are your creations, to be used for your benefit. Avoid the trap of being run by deadlines. Don't use them to make yourself feel guilty.

Set time limits on intentions. If you want to cut down on the number of carrots you eat, decide how long you will cut down. Keep it accomplishable. "I intend to eat less than three carrots a day for the next eight days."

5. Make intentions dependent on you alone.

If an intention depends on the actions of other people for completion, it is a setup for failure. If you write that you intend to get the highest mark in the class on your calculus exam, your success is dependent on the grades of other students as well as your own performance.

Likewise, avoid intentions which depend on external environmental factors. If you tell yourself that you intend to spend three hours sunbathing on Saturday, and it's cloudy, there is nothing you can do about it.

When you write an intention statement, be sure that the results depend solely on your actions.

6. Consider how you might sabotage your intentions.

You know yourself better than anyone. You know to what lengths you sometimes go to avoid something. Consider for a moment what you might consciously or unconsciously do to prevent this system from working. If your intention is to study differential equations at 9 p.m., and you get ultra-comfortable in your easy chair and fall asleep at 8:30 . . .

7. Identify your rewards.

People tend to work harder toward goals that have meaning for them, that lead to something they want. Rewards that are intrinsic to the goal are the most powerful. For example, your intention to complete a course of study leading to a particular career will be rewarded by the job you want.

In the short-term you might get value for external rewards—a movie or an afternoon in the park. Set up small rewards for small tasks. One such reward might be something like this: "I intend to study computer number systems from 7 p.m. until 10:30 p.m. I intend to read 35 pages and complete three exercises. For completing this assignment, I will reward myself with the late movie and a bowl of popcorn." Then, after you have finished the assignment, enjoy the reward.

Refer often to your intention statements. Plant them firmly in your consciousness. You can write them on 3x5 cards and carry them around with you. Read them just before you go to sleep at night. Make them a part of your daily routine.

Make mental pictures of what you intend to do. Take time during the day to relax and visualize yourself completing what you intend to accomplish.

Another effective way to reward yourself for accomplishing what you intended is to sit quietly after you have finished your task and savor the feeling. Pay attention to how your body feels when you have done a good job. You might even write a discovery statement about how you feel. One reason success breeds success is that it feels good.

The discovery guide

The discovery guide is a structured opportunity to tell the truth to yourself about the kind of student you are. This is not a test. There are no trick questions, and the answers will have meaning only for you.

The most important evaluations you can receive in your education are self-evaluations, the ones in which *you* determine the criteria for success. This discovery guide is intended to provide a framework for you to accomplish an honest self-evaluation.

A few suggestions. First, there is another Discovery Guide at the end of this book. You will have a chance to measure your progress, so as you answer these questions, keep in mind that there will be opportunities to change. Be frank about where you are right now.

Second, a little lightheartedness and good humor go a long way in self-evaluations. Lighten up. Be willing to laugh at yourself.

Here's how it works. By the end of this exercise, you will have filled in a circle similar to the one on this page. This circle is a picture of how you see yourself as student. The closer the shading comes to the edge of the circle, the higher the evaluation. In the example, the student has rated his reading skills low and his observation skills high. It is dangerous, however, to think of these evaluations in terms of "higher" and "lower" if those designations reflect a negative judgment. The purpose of shading in the circle is to create a visual representation, a shape. Remember, this shape is not what you are; it is a picture of what you think your abilities are.

To begin this exercise, read the statements on pages 21-23 and award yourself points for each one in the following way:

When you have finished, add up your point total for each section. Next, shade in the graph on page 24 to the appropriate point level.

5 points	This statement is always or almost always true of me.
4 points	This statement is often true of me.
3 points	This statement is sometimes true of me (about half the time).
2 points	This statement is seldom true of me.
1 point	This statement is never or almost never true of me.

1. __2__ I start each school term highly motivated, and I stay that way throughout the term.

2. __4__ I know what I want to get from my course of study.

3. __1__ I enjoy learning.

4. __4__ I have a clear idea of the benefits I expect to get from my education.

5. __2__ I have a clear idea of myself using what I am learning.

6. __2__ I study even when I'd rather be doing something else.

7. __1__ I get excited about the courses I take.

8. __4__ I put in long hours of studying when necessary.

__20__ Total score (1) Motivation

1. __4__ I am confident of my ability to remember.

2. __5__ I remember people's names.

3. __1__ At the end of a lecture, I could give a friend a short speech about what was presented.

4. __2__ I use a regular strategy to remember things.

5. __1__ I remember under pressure.

6. _____ Remembering lots of facts about one subject is easy for me.

7. _____ I can jog my memory when I'm stuck and can't recall.

8. _____ I remember formulas, equations and similar material.

_____ Total score (3) Memory

1. __4__ I set aside regular periods of time to review and refine my long-term goals.

2. __2__ I set aside regular periods of time to review and refine my short-term goals.

3. __1__ I assign priorities to each day's list of things to do.

4. __3__ I plan my review time so I don't have to cram at the end of a course.

5. __1__ I write a schedule for my week in advance.

6. __1__ I plan regular recreation time.

7. __2__ I decide for each course how much time I will devote to it.

8. __4__ I have enough time during the day to accomplish everything I want to.

__18__ Total score (2) Planning

1. _____ I feel comfortable reading textbooks.

2. _____ I generally need to read a textbook only once to get what I need.

3. _____ When I read, I ask questions about the reading.

4. _____ When I read textbooks, I am alert and awake.

5. _____ I relate what I read in textbooks to my life.

6. _____ I select my reading strategy to fit the kind of book I'm reading.

7. _____ I take effective notes when I read a textbook.

8. _____ When I don't understand a concept I'm reading, I make a note of my question and ask the instructor.

_____ Total score (4) Reading

IS FOR FEEDBACK, NOT FAILURE

From The Search for Solutions *by Horace Freeland Judson. Copyright 1980 by Playback Associates. Reprinted by permission of Holt, Rinehart and Winston, Publishers.*

Feedback is one of the fundamental facts of life and ideas of science, yet only in the last fifty years have we recognized its all-pervasive presence. The idea is simple: A feedback mechanism registers the actual state of a system, compares it to the desired state, then uses the comparison to correct the state of the system. Feedback is goal-oriented. Sometimes the goal is limited, definite. A feedback process tells living cells when to manufacture proteins and when to stop. Sometimes the goal is something as dynamic as an equilibrium. An explosion of the rabbit population is followed by a growth in the lynx population is followed by a collapse of the rabbit population is followed by a collapse of the lynx population—a feedback loop that maintains the balance of nature. In modern technology, feedback is the essence of automation. It runs lathes, lands airplanes, steers rockets. The economy is a huge, slow-moving, multiple feedback system. So is democracy. Fast or slow, movement is the essence of feedback. It implies purpose and progress. Like a walker on a high wire, it continually achieves and re-achieves balance in order to achieve something beyond balance. It can never rest.

5 points This statement is always or almost always true of me.

4 points This statement is often true of me.

3 points This statement is sometimes true of me (about half the time).

2 points This statement is seldom true of me.

1 point This statement is never or almost never true of me.

1. _____ When I am in class, I keep my attention in the room.

2. _____ I take notes in class.

3. _____ I can still read my notes a week after I take them.

4. _____ My notes are valuable for review.

5. _____ I review class notes within 24 hours.

6. _____ I notice when an instructor uses key phrases that might indicate later test questions.

7. _____ I copy material the instructor writes on the board.

8. _____ I take notes in my own words.

_____ Total score **(5) Observation**

1. _____ I feel confident and calm during an exam.

2. _____ I plan my time and work fast enough so that I answer every question I am capable of answering.

3. _____ I feel alive and energetic during exams.

4. _____ I feel secure about myself no matter what my grade on an exam.

5. _____ My test scores reflect my knowledge of a subject.

6. _____ I adapt my test-taking strategy to the kind of test I'm taking.

7. _____ I can examine essay questions in light of what I know and come to a new and original conclusion during a test.

8. _____ I receive the grades I want on tests.

_____ Total score **(6) Test taking**

1. _____ I have flashes of insight, and solutions to problems appear to me at unusual times.

2. _____ I find it easy to select a subject for a paper or speech.

3. _____ When I get stuck on a creative project, I have a way to get unstuck.

4. _____ When I get a great idea, I follow up on it and develop it.

5. _____ I am a good problem-solver in math and science.

6. _____ I am confident when I speak before others.

7. _____ I see problems as opportunities for learning and personal growth.

8. _____ I trust my intuition.

_____ Total score **(7) Creativity**

1. _____ I develop and maintain relationships which help me to get what I want.

2. _____ I say what I feel and let people know who I am when I talk to them.

3. _____ Other people have reported to me that I am a good listener.

4. _____ I value time alone.

5. _____ I enjoy contributing to the lives of others and do it regularly.

6. _____ I get along with my instructors.

7. _____ I have the ability to make friends and create valuable relationships in a new place.

8. _____ I am open to being with people I don't especially like in order to learn from them.

_____ Total score **(8) Relationships**

1. _____ At the end of the day, I have energy left to study.

2. _____ My physical health helps me to concentrate.

3. _____ My emotional health supports my ability to learn.

4. _____ If the situation calls for it, I have enough reserves to put in a very long day or a series of long days.

5. _____ I accept my body the way it is.

6. _____ I am responsible for the way I look.

7. _____ I am in control of the alcohol and drugs I put into my body.

8. _____ The food I eat contributes to my health.

_____ Total score **(9) Health**

1. _____ I have control of the money in my life.

2. _____ I have enough money to get the education I want.

3. _____ I have a clear picture of financial resources available to students.

4. _____ I have the ability to make a little money go a long way.

5. _____ My education supports my financial goals.

6. _____ I repay my debts.

7. _____ My sense of personal worth is independent of my financial condition.

8. _____ I know where my money goes.

_____ Total score **(10) Money**

1. _____ I feel comfortable and at home in libraries.

2. _____ I am involved in community activities.

3. _____ I use my job as a learning experience.

4. _____ I learn by contributing to others.

5. _____ I know where to get help in my community for a variety of problems.

6. _____ I have a group of friends with whom I meet for mutual support toward our educational goals.

7. _____ I use my own imagination as a resource.

8. _____ I see the world's problems as an opportunity for me to contribute.

_____ Total score **(11) Resources**

1. _____ I relate my learning process to what I plan to do for the rest of my life.

2. _____ I relate the subjects I study to my personal goals.

3. _____ I see learning as a lifelong process.

4. _____ I can experience myself growing every day through the learning process.

5. _____ I am clear about my purpose in life.

6. _____ I know that I am responsible for my own education.

7. _____ I am the creator of my experience.

8. _____ I recognize that I never stay the same, that I am always learning and growing.

_____ Total score **(12) Purpose**

MAYBE IT'S YOUR BREATH

The way you breathe affects the way you think, and the way you think affects the way you breathe. A good supply of oxygen to the brain is essential for focused concentration. Next time you find your mind wandering, take a short break and do the following exercise. Read all the directions, then take a moment to practice this technique.

1. Sit up in your chair in a relaxed position, head straight and hands uncrossed in your lap.

2. Close your eyes and take twenty or thirty seconds to relax. Let go of any tension in your face, neck, and shoulders.

3. Inhale, breathing deeply into your abdomen. Your belly will expand when you breathe deeply.

4. When you have filled your diaphragm with air, pause; purse your lips as if you were about to whistle; then exhale evenly and forcefully through the small hole between your lips.

5. At the end of your exhalation, pause, then push out the last bit of remaining air in three short, forceful puffs.

6. Repeat this process three to five times.

7. When finished, sit quietly for a minute, observing the rise and fall of your abdomen as you breathe naturally.

Filling in your discovery wheel

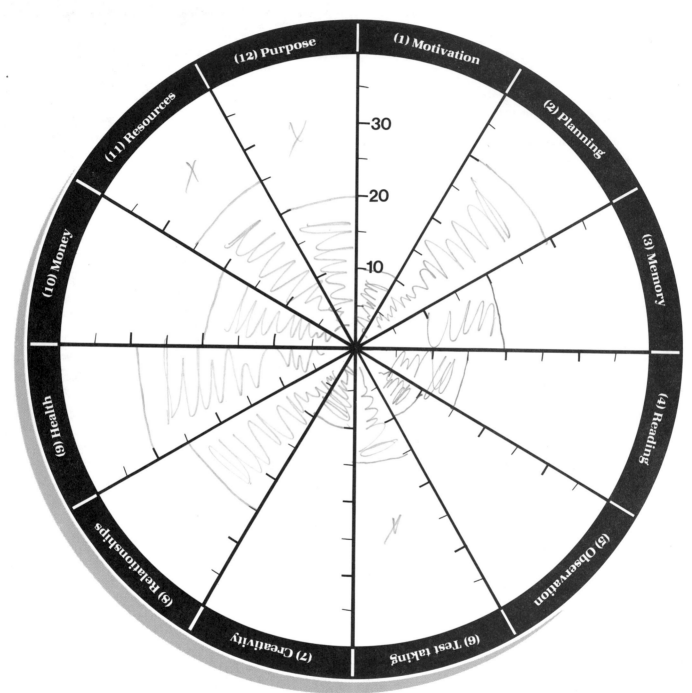

(12) Purpose | (1) Motivation
(11) Resources | (2) Planning
(10) Money | (3) Memory
(9) Health | (4) Reading
(8) Relationships | (5) Observation
(7) Creativity | (6) Test taking

30
20
10

Shade in each section's slice of the pie to the appropriate level. Use the scores from each section of the discovery guide.

Now that you have completed your wheel, spend some time with it. Make sure you are in a quiet and relaxing place, and take a few minutes to study the circle. Get a feel for the weight, shape, and balance. How would this wheel feel if you could run your hands around it? What would it sound like rolling down a hill? Would it roll at all? Is the wheel balanced?

Make your observations without judgment. Simply be with the picture you have created.

Journal entry #5

Discovery statement

This journal entry is part of the first step. If you have not read the section in this chapter entitled *The discovery and intention journal system,* please do so before you complete this exercise.

Return to the discovery guide wheel you created on page 24, take a moment to study it, then complete the following sentences. Don't be concerned if you have difficulty thinking of something to write. Just write what first comes to mind. Journal keeping requires practice. The more entries you make, the sharper your focus will become.

This wheel is an accurate picture of my ability as a student because . . .

My self-evaluation surprises me because . . .

The two areas in which I am strongest are related because . . .

The two areas in which I am weakest are related because . . .

The areas in which I want to improve are . . .

I want to concentrate on improving these areas because . . .

Ideas are

There are many ideas in this book. Don't believe any of them. Instead, think of them as tools.

When you pick up a hammer, for example, you do so with a purpose—to drive a nail. If you are using a new hammer you might notice its shape, its weight and its balance. However, you would probably not spend much time trying to figure whether or not the hammer is "right." You use it, and if it works, you use it again. If it doesn't work, you get a different hammer.

This is not the attitude most people adopt when they encounter new ideas. The first thing most people do with ideas is measure them against old ideas. If the new idea conflicts with the old, the new one is likely to be rejected. They say, "Oh, I don't believe that" or, "That's not right."

Interestingly, while people may have plenty of room in their lives for hammers of different shapes and weights, they tend to limit their capacity for ideas. Because they often identify ideas with who they are, a new idea, at some level, is a threat to their very being—unlike a new hammer, which is simply a new hammer.

As human beings, we have a built-in desire to be right. Our ideas, we think, represent ourselves, and when ideas become us they assume a new importance in our lives. We put them up on the mantle. We hang them up on our walls. We wear them on our T-shirts and display them on our bumpers. We join associations with other people who share the ideas. We make up rituals about ideas, compose songs about them, and write stories about them. We declare ourselves dedicated to these ideas, and sometimes become willing to give our lives for them. There is nothing "wrong" with

Tools

that for some ideas.

This book doesn't contain those kinds of ideas. These ideas are hammers. If you encounter one you don't think is "right," remember that the ideas in this book are for using, not believing.

Imagine someone defending a hammer. Picture this person holding up a hammer and declaring, "I hold this hammer to be self-evident. Give me this hammer or give me death. Those other hammers are the work of the devil. I really believe in this hammer. There are only two kinds of people in this world: people who believe in this hammer and infidels."

This book is not about being right. This book is a collection of ideas and techniques; you can choose the ones that work for you. When you encounter an idea that seems foreign or a bit crazy to you, note your reaction to it. Suspend your judgment. Give the idea a practical test and evaluate the results. If the idea works, use it. If an idea doesn't work for you, and you are satisfied you gave it a fair chance, discard it.

The Master Student

This book is about something that cannot be taught. It's about becoming a master student.

A master, in the sense of a master craftsman or a master artist, is a person who has attained a level of skill that goes beyond technique. For a master, methods and procedures become automatic responses to the needs of the task. Work becomes effortless; struggle evaporates. The master carpenter is one who is so familiar with her tools that they become part of her. To a master chef, utensils are like old friends. Because they don't have to think about the details of the process, masters bring more of themselves to their work.

Mastery can lead to flashy results—an incredible painting, for example. In basketball, mastery might result in an unbelievable shot at the buzzer; for a musician, it might be the performance of performances, the night when everything seems to come together.

More often, the result of mastery is a sense of profound satisfaction, well-being and timelessness. Work seems self-propelled. The master is in control by being out of control, as in the case of an athlete or musician about whom, after a spectacular performance, it is said that she was "playing out of her mind."

In that sense, the master student is a student who "learns out of his mind." Of course, that statement makes no sense. Mastery, in fact, doesn't make sense. It cannot be captured with words. It defies analysis. Mastery cannot be taught, only experienced.

Examine the following characteristics of master students in light of your own experience. This description of a master student is neither complete, nor is it the final word on the subject. It points in a direction. No one can teach us to be master students because we already are master students, by design. As students, we can discover that every day.

As you read, look for yourself.

In 1482, Leonardo Da Vinci wrote a letter applying for work from a wealthy baron. In excerpted form, he said, "I can contrive various and endless means of offense and defense...I have a sort of extremely light and strong bridges adapted to be most easily carried...I have methods for destroying every turret or other fortress...I will make covered chariots, safe and unassailable...In case of need I will make big guns, mortars, and light ordnance of fine and useful forms out of the common type..." and then, he added, almost as an afterthought, "In times of peace I believe I can give perfect satisfaction and to the equal of any other in architecture...I can carry out sculpture...and also I can do in painting whatever may be done." The Mona Lisa, for example.

Inquisitive

The master student is curious about everything and by posing questions can generate interest and aliveness in the most mundane, humdrum situations. When the master student becomes bored during a biology lecture, she thinks to herself, "I'm bored with this instructor, and I always get bored when I listen to this instructor. Why is that? Maybe it's because he reminds me of my boring Uncle Ralph who always told those endless fishing stories. He even looks like Uncle Ralph. Amazing! Boredom is certainly interesting."

Able to focus attention

The master student can become absorbed by a process or activity. His attention has a child-like quality. Watch a two-year-old at play. Pay attention to the eyes. That wide-eyed look reveals an energy and a capacity for amazement that keeps his attention absolutely focused in the here and now. The world, to the child, is always new. Because the master student can focus attention, to him the world is always new.

Willing to change

The master student is not afraid of the unknown and, in fact, welcomes it—even the unknown in herself. As we grow, we create pictures of who we think we are, and these pictures can be useful. They can also prevent learning and growth. The master student is open to changes in her environment and changes in herself.

Able to organize and sort

The master student can take a large body of information and sift through it to discover relationships. He can play with the information, organizing pieces of data by size, color, order, weight, and a hundred other categories.

Competent

The master student is a master of skills. When she learns mathematical formulas, she learns them so well that they become second nature. She practices until she knows them cold, then practices an extra few minutes.

Joyful

More often than not, the master student is seen with a smile on his face—sometimes a smile at nothing in particular other than amazement at the world and his experience of it.

Able to suspend judgment

The master student has opinions and positions, and she is able to let go of them when appropriate. She can quiet her internal dialogue and listen to an opposing viewpoint. She doesn't let judgment get in the way of learning.

Energetic

The master student has a spring in his step. He is enthusiastic and involved in class. When he reads, he often sits on the very edge of his chair. He brings energy to both work and play.

Well

The master student is healthy, not necessarily in the sense of being free of illness; rather, she values her body and treats it with respect. She is aware of her emotional and spiritual health, as well as her physical health.

Self-questioning

The master student is willing to evaluate himself and his behavior. He regularly examines his life.

Responsible

The master student is willing to take responsibility for everything in her life, including events that most people say she could appropriately blame on others. For example, if she is served cold eggs in the cafeteria, the master student chooses to take responsibility for getting cold eggs. This is not the same as blaming herself for cold eggs. Rather, she looks for ways to change the situation and get what she wants. Even if the cold eggs continue, by taking responsibility, she gives herself the power to choose her response to the situation.

Willing to risk

The master student often takes on projects where he is not sure he can succeed. He is willing to share himself in class dialogues at the risk of looking foolish. He welcomes risk.

Willing to participate

The master student does not sit on the sidelines. She can be counted on for something. She is a player. She can make a commitment and follow through.

Generalist

The master student is interested in everything around him. He has a broad base of knowledge in many fields and can find value in them that is applicable to his specialties.

Willing to accept paradox

The word "paradox" comes from two Greek words, para (beyond) and doxon (opinion). Thus, a paradox is something which is beyond opinion or, more accurately, something that may seem contradictory or absurd yet may actually have meaning, as in the Zen question, "What is the sound of one hand clapping?" The master student recognizes the limitations of the mind and is at home with paradox. She can have the experience of the sound of one hand clapping (as opposed to the thought or idea of it) and can accept the confusion associated with the concept.

Courageous

The master student will admit fear and is willing to experience it when appropriate. He looks forward, for example, to tough exams as an opportunity to explore feelings of anxiety and tension related to the pressure to perform. He does not deny fear; he faces it.

Self-directed

The master student's motivation comes from within. She doesn't need others to provide rewards (or punishment) in order to learn. The master student has an inner motivation.

Spontaneous

The master student is truly in the here and now. He is able to respond to the moment in fresh, surprising, and unplanned ways.

Maslow's "Qualities of a self-actualizing person"

Abraham Maslow is a psychologist who worked on a theory of psychological health rather than sickness. Maslow studied people whom he called "self-actualizing," which means, in part, healthy and creative. He listed traits he found in self-actualizing people (ranging from Abraham Lincoln to Albert Einstein). These characteristics also describe the master student.

The self-actualizing person:

Reality oriented
Accepting of himself and others
Spontaneous
Problem-centered rather than self-centered
Detached and needing privacy
Independent
Fresh, rather than stereotyped, appreciation of people
Had a mystical or spiritual experience
Identify with the human race as a whole
Has a few deep, intimate relationships
Democratic values
A philosophical rather than bitter sense of humor
Creative resources
Resistant to conformity
Transcendent of his environment

Relaxed about grades

The master student does not wind herself up over grades. She recognizes that in some situations they are important, and that grades are not the reason she studies. She does not attach her value as a human being to the grades she receives.

Intuitive

The master student has a sense that is beyond logic. He has learned to trust his feelings, and he works to develop that sense.

Creative

The master student is creative in every aspect of her life. She can gather pieces of knowledge from a wide range of subjects and put them together in a new way. Where others see dull and trivial elements, the master student sees opportunities to create.

Willing to be uncomfortable

The master student is not run by the desire for comfort. When discomfort is necessary to reach a goal, he is willing to experience it. He can endure personal discomfort and can look at unpleasant things with a detached frame of mind.

Willing to let go of ideas

The master student does not consider her thoughts and ideas to be herself. She does not hang on to them as if their survival were synonymous with her own. She is thus open to many more ideas than most of us.

Loving

The master student sees a correlation between loving and learning, and he gives meaning to life by combining the two.

Willing to laugh

The master student might laugh at any moment, and her sense of humor includes the ability to laugh at herself.

Hungry

The master student is hungry for knowledge. He approaches learning out of the desire for learning itself.

Willing to work

Once inspired, the master student is willing to follow through with sweat. Genius and creativity, she recognizes, are mostly the result of persistence and work. When she is in high gear, the master student works with the intensity of a child at play.

Epilogue

The master student is, of course, all of us and none of us. By design, human beings are learning machines. It is important to note the distinction between "learning" and "being taught." Human beings have a built-in capacity to resist being taught anything. Carl Rogers goes so far as to say that anything that can be "taught" to a human being is either inconsequential or plain harmful. What is important in education, Rogers asserts, is learning. And everyone has the ability to do that.

Unfortunately, people also learn to hide that ability. As they experience the pain associated with learning, they actually learn to shut down learning. If a child gets the experience of feeling foolish in front of a group of people, that child will learn to avoid those situations. In doing so, the child restricts his learning possibilities. As children, many people "learn" that they are slow learners. Some people learn it so well that all their behavior comes to match that of a slow learner. In a perverse way, perceived inability to learn is further evidence that the master student lives within all of us.

As people grow older, they accumulate an ever-growing body of ideas that must be defended, a fat catalog of experiences that tell them not to risk learning.

Yet, underneath all that, there remains a potential source of learning power. To tap it, you don't need to acquire anything. You already have everything you need. Instead, you need to uncover the ability you already have.

Journal entry #6

Discovery statement

After reading *The master student*, make a list of the qualities of a master student which you have observed in yourself.

This is no easy task. Most of us are competent self-critics, but we tend to discount our strong points. If you get stuck trying to complete this journal entry, warm up by brainstorming all your good points. On a separate sheet of paper, write down everything you can think of that is positive about yourself. Limit this brainstorming session to three minutes.

When you list the master student qualities you have observed in yourself, remember that not all learning takes place in school. Also draw on memories of those times you learned something outside the classroom (learning to drive, to fish, to fry hamburgers, etc.)

Master student qualities I have observed in myself:

Benjamin Franklin

In each chapter of this text there is an example of a person who serves as a model master student. None of these men and women have all the characteristics suggested in this book, but all of them are courageous and dedicated to the process of becoming a master student.

The following quote is from Benjamin Franklin's memoirs, available in L. Jesse Lemisch's Benjamin Franklin: the Autobiography and Other Writings *(New York: Signet Classic, 1961), 28-29, by permission of the Regents of the University of California, Berkeley. Reprinted by permission.*

A question was once somehow or other started between Collins and me on the propriety of educating the female sex in learning and their abilities for study. He was of opinion that it was improper and that they were naturally unequal to it. I took the contrary side, perhaps a little for dispute sake. He was naturally more eloquent, having a greater plenty of words, and sometimes, as I thought, I was vanquished more by his fluency than by the strength of his reasons. As we parted without settling the point and were not to see one another again for some time, I sat down to put my arguments in writing, which I copied fair and sent to him. He answered and I replied. Three or four letters on a side had passed, when my father happened to find my papers and read them. Without entering into the subject in dispute, he took occasion to talk with me about my manner of writing, observed that though I had the advantage of my antagonist in correct spelling and pointing (punctuation). . . I fell far short in elegance of expression, in method and in perspicuity—of which he convinced me by several instances. I saw the justice of his remarks and thence grew more attentive to my manner of writing, and determined to endeavor to improve my style.

About this time I met with an odd volume of the *Spectator.* It was the third. I had never before seen any of them. I bought it, read it over and over, and was much delighted with it. I thought the writing excellent and wished if possible to imitate it. With that view, I took some of the papers, and making short hints of the sentiment in each sentence, laid them by a few days, and then without looking at the book, tried to complete the papers again by expressing each hinted sentiment at length and as fully as it had been expressed before, in any suitable words that should occur to me. Then I compared my *Spectator* with the original, discovered some of my faults, and corrected them. But I found I wanted a stock of words or a readiness in recollecting and using them, which I thought I should have acquired before that time if I had gone on making verses; since the continual search for words of the same import but of different length to suit the measure, or of different sound for

the rhyme would have laid me under a constant necessity of searching for variety, and also have tended to fix that variety in my mind, and make me master of it. Therefore I took some of the tales in the *Spectator* and turned them into verse, and after a time, when I had pretty well forgotten the prose, turned them back again. I also sometimes jumbled my collections of hints into confusion, and after some weeks endeavored to reduce them into the best order before I began to form the full sentences and complete the paper. This was to teach me method in the arrangement of the thoughts. By comparing my work afterwards with the original, I discovered many faults and corrected them; but I sometimes had the pleasure of fancying that in certain particulars of small import I had been lucky enough to improve the method or the language, and this encouraged me to think that I might possibly in time come to be a tolerable English writer, of which I was extremely ambitious.

1. In order for the ideas in this book to work, you must believe in them. True or false.

2. What are the two elements of a first step?

3. What are two examples of first steps that Benjamin Franklin wrote about in his autobiographical excerpt?

4. Describe briefly the dilemma that a first step can resolve.

5. What is the purpose of this book?

6. Which of the following is *not* a characteristic of the master student?
    a. Creativity.
    b. Desire to be right.
    c. Acceptance of self.
    d. Willingness to take risks.
    e. All of the above are characteristics of the master student.

7. Write down three ways Franklin exhibited characteristics of the master student.

8. Review the two quotes on page 9 of this chapter, then explain briefly (three or four sentences) why this chapter comes first in this book.

9. Describe how an aircraft on autopilot takes a first step.

10. Explain how *The discovery and intention journal system* automatically creates first steps.

Journal entry #7

Discovery statement

Did you get what you wanted from this chapter? If you didn't, write down in the space provided everything you wanted to get and didn't.

Journal entry #8

Intention statement

Do you still want to get these things? If so, use this space to write the steps you intend to take to get them.

Journal entry #9

Intention statement

Choose two techniques from this chapter, and write an intention statement below about how you will use each of them.

I intend to. . .

I intend to. . .

Journal entry #10

Look back

In the introduction, you listed what you wanted to get from this book. Pick one of those and write it below. Then write at least three specific things you intend to do in the next 48 hours that could lead to the accomplishment of that goal. These actions need not, by themselves, actually accomplish the goal. They need only get you started in the right direction. Therefore, keep the tasks small. For this exercise, choose intentions you know you can accomplish.

One thing I want to get from this book is . . .

In order to get it, I intend to do the following in the next 48 hours:

1.

2.

3.

I want these things from this chapter:

Journal entry #11

Discovery statement

CHAPTER TWO
TIME

*Knowing how to use time effectively
is one of the greatest skills a manager
can possess, for improved time management
increases productivity.*

PETER DRUCKER

*Dost thou love life, then do not squander time, for that's
the stuff life is made of.*

BENJAMIN FRANKLIN

In this chapter . . .

Time is a resource like no other. **Time management** demonstrates how
to manage this unique resource to get jobs done quickly without
sacrificing the quality of your work.

Time management need not be an obsession. **Twenty-one ways to
get the most out of now** tells how to find the right time, the right
place, and right environment for learning.

The ABC "to do" daily priority system gives you a way to
evaluate and complete tasks in their order of importance.

You can develop the skill of staying in the moment with **Power
Process #2: Be here now.**

Exercises in this chapter are designed to allow you to experience the
satisfaction of realizing a goal. Among the selected shorts are **Studying
with children underfoot,** the **Seven-day procrastination plan** and
The polyphasic thinker.

TIME
MANAGEMENT

The picture on the right is the Andromeda galaxy. It is the most distant object that can be seen from earth with the unaided eye. It is over two million light years away from our planet; which means that the light reaching our eyes is over two million years old.

This shows us how elusive and unpredictable time really is. When looking at this object, we are literally seeing it as it was millions of years ago. Conversely, we would have to wait two million years to see this galaxy as it is today at this moment.

The idea of time management can call forth images of restriction and control. You might visualize a prune-faced Scrooge hunched over your shoulder, stopwatch in hand, telling you what to do every minute. In truth, however, time management is a blessing.

Time is an unusual commodity. It cannot be saved. You can't stockpile time like wood for your stove or food for the winter.

Time is a commodity that can't be seen, felt, touched, tasted, or smelled. You can't sense it directly. Even brilliant scientists and philosophers aren't sure how to describe it.

Because time is so elusive, it is an easy commodity to ignore. That doesn't bother time at all. Time is perfectly content to remain hidden until you are nearly out of it. And when you are out of it, you are out of it.

Time is a resource that you cannot renew. If you are out of wood, you can chop some more. If you're out of money, you can earn a little extra. If you're out of love, there is still hope. If you're out of health, sometimes it can be restored. But when you're out of time, that's it. When this minute is gone, it's gone.

Time is an equal opportunity resource. All people, regardless of race, creed, color, or national origin have exactly the same number of hours in a week. No matter how important you are, no matter how rich or poor, you get 168 hours to spend each week (no more, no less).

Time is an unpredictable commodity. There will come a week when you'll have fewer than 168 hours to spend, and you don't know which week that will be.

Time seems to be used up at varying speeds. Sometimes it's slow and sometimes faster than a speeding bullet. On Friday afternoons, classroom clocks can creep. After a hard day at work, the last few pages of an economics assignment can turn minutes into hours. A year in school can stretch out to an eternity. At the other end of the time spectrum, time flies. These are magic times when we are so absorbed by what we're doing that hours disappear in minutes.

You can manage this commodity so you won't waste it or feel regretful about it.

Approach time as if you are in control—even though it often seems you are not. Sure, sometimes it seems that a spouse controls your time; your boss controls your time; your teachers or your parents or your kids or somebody else controls your time. Maybe that is true. But maybe it isn't. When you say you don't have enough time, you may really be saying that you are not spending the time you do have in the way that *you* want.

Time management gives you a chance to spend your most valuable resource the way *you* want.

The product of this exercise is a detailed picture of how you spend one week of your life. To create this picture, you monitor your time in 15-minute increments, 24 hours a day, for seven days, recording how much time you spend sleeping, eating, studying, traveling to and from class, watching television, listening to music, sitting in lectures, taking care of the kids, running errands—everything.

If this sounds crazy, hang on for a minute. This is not about keeping track of the rest of your life in 15-minute intervals. Because most of us have little idea where our time really goes, this exercise is an opportunity to find out. When you know how your time is spent, you can find ways to adjust and manage it so that you spend your time doing things that are important to you. This exercise is an important first step toward putting you in control of your time.

How the Time Monitor works

Look at the Time Monitor form on page 43. The top row of the form represents a day's time, 24 hours, divided into 15-minute segments. The column on the left-hand side of the page labeled "categories" is for you to fill in. The categories are the general ways in which you spend time. If you have a part-time job, one category might be "work." Other categories might be "exercise" or "child care" or "driving."

The sample Time Monitor on page 42 shows some typical categories. Notice that some standard categories have been printed on each day. The categories you add will reflect your life style. (If you are a serious tuba player, for example, you will need a category labeled "tuba practice.") You can create additional categories as the week progresses.

Keep your Time Monitor with you every minute you are awake for one week. Record what you've done every two or three hours. Each small box on the Time Monitor represents 15 minutes. To record activity, use a pencil to darken appropriate squares. Estimate time spent to the nearest 15-minute interval. The sample Time Monitor illustrates a completed form.

How to remember to use your Time Monitor

It's easy to forget to fill out your monitor. One way to remember is to create a visual reminder for yourself. You can also use this technique for any activity you want to remember.

Relax for a moment, close your eyes, and imagine that you see your Time Monitor form, only imagine it with arms and legs, as big as a person. Imagine the form sitting at your desk at home. Picture it sitting in your car and sitting in one of your classrooms. Visualize the form sitting in your favorite chair at home. Picture it sitting wherever you're likely to sit.

When you sit down, the picture of the Time Monitor will come to you.

You can make this better by adding imaginary noise to accompany the act of sitting down. The Time Monitor might scream "Get off me!" Or, since time is money, the saying goes, you might associate the Time Monitor with the sound of a cash register. Imagine that every time you sit down, a cash register rings.

Analyzing the Time Monitor

When you have monitored a week's time, add up the number of shaded blocks in each category and divide by four. This will give the number of hours spent in each category. Make sure the grand total of all categories is 168.

Record your initial observations about these totals on the back of the Time Monitor, and then complete Journal Entry #12.

(An extra Time Monitor form is included in this book. In several months, you may want to take another detailed look at how you spend your life.)

By analyzing the results of one week of monitoring my time I discovered that:

I want to spend more time on:

Journal entry #12

Discovery statement

I want to spend less time on:

I was surprised that I spent so much time on:

I was surprised that I spent so little time on:

I had strong feelings about (describe the feeling—happy, sad, frustrated, confused, satisfied, and the situation):

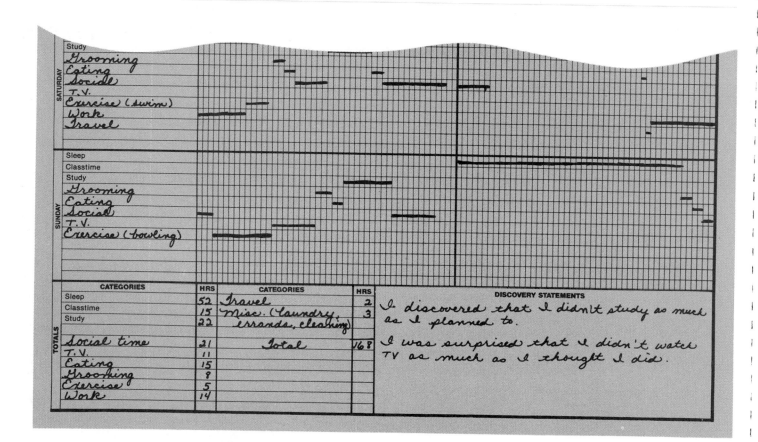

CATEGORIES	HRS	CATEGORIES	HRS	DISCOVERY STATEMENTS
Sleep	52	Travel	2	I discovered that I didn't study as much as I planned to.
Classtime	15	Misc. (laundry, errands, cleaning)	3	
Study	22			
Social time	21	Total	168	I was surprised that I didn't watch TV as much as I thought I did.
T.V.	11			
Eating	15			
Grooming	9			
Exercise	5			
Work	14			

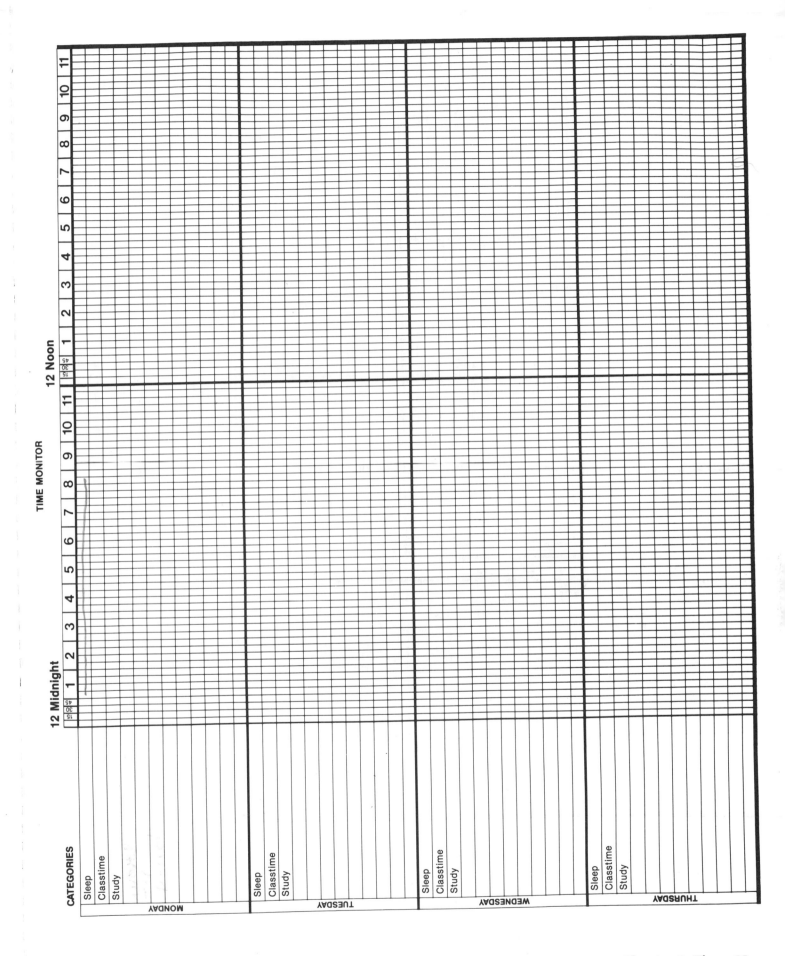

	TOTALS				SUNDAY				SATURDAY				FRIDAY	
			Study Classtime Sleep				Study Classtime Sleep				Study Classtime Sleep			Study Classtime Sleep

CATEGORIES

CATEGORIES

CATEGORIES

HRS

CATEGORIES

HRS

DISCOVERY STATEMENTS

TIME MONITOR

12 Midnight 15 30 45 1 2 3 4 5 6 7 8 9 10 11

12 Noon 15 30 45 1 2 3 4 5 6 7 8 9 10 11

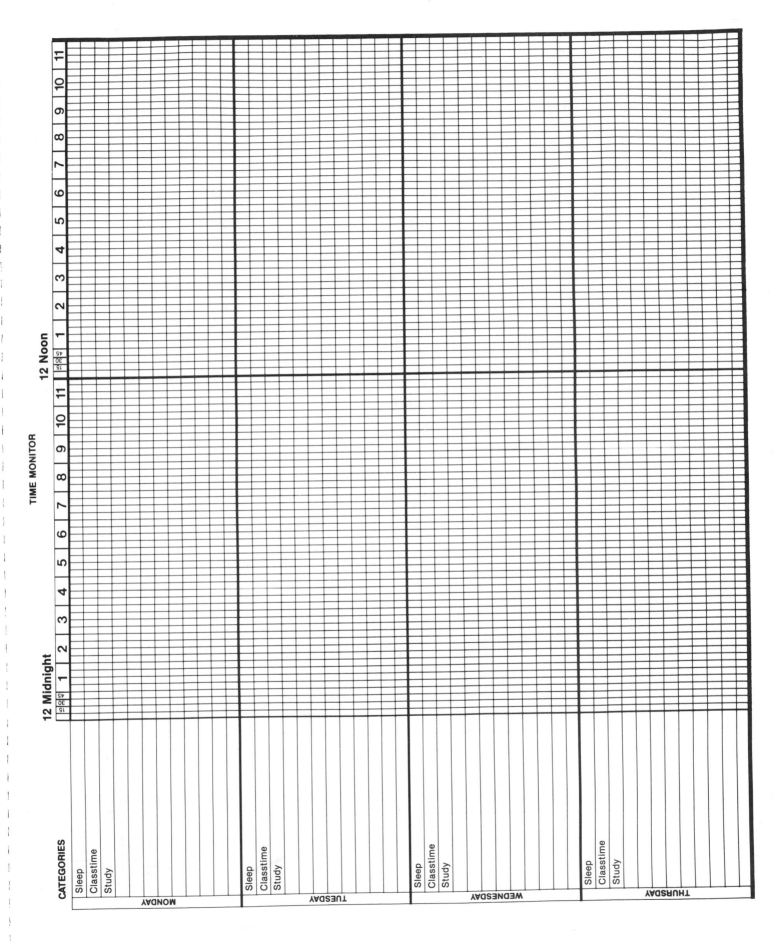

TIME MONITOR

12 Midnight 1 2 3 4 5 6 7 8 9 10 11

12 Noon 1 2 3 4 5 6 7 8 9 10 11

15 / 30 / 45

CATEGORIES

FRIDAY — Sleep, Classtime, Study

SATURDAY — Sleep, Classtime, Study

SUNDAY — Sleep, Classtime, Study

TOTALS — Sleep, Classtime, Study

CATEGORIES — HRS

CATEGORIES — HRS

DISCOVERY STATEMENTS

21 WAYS TO GET THE MOST OUT OF NOW

The following 21 time management techniques are about when to study, where to study, how to handle the rest of the world, and things you can ask yourself when you get stuck. As you read, underline, circle, or otherwise note the suggestions you think you can use.

Pick two or three techniques to use now. When they become habits and you do them automatically, come back to this article and pick a couple more.

When to study

1. Plan two hours study time for every hour you spend in class.

There are exceptions, but this is a good general rule. It's also one that few students follow. Students making the transition from high school to higher education are often unaware that more is expected of them. If you are taking 15 credit hours, plan to spend 30 hours per week studying. The benefits of following this rule will be apparent at exam time.

2. Study difficult (or boring) subjects first.

If your chemistry problems put you to sleep, get to them first, while you are fresh. Most of us tend to do what we like first, yet the courses we find most difficult often require the most creative energy. Save the subjects you enjoy for later. If you find yourself avoiding a particular subject, you might get up an hour early to study it before breakfast. With that chore out of the way, the rest of the day will be a breeze. (If you discover that you continually avoid a subject, that course might be a potential trouble area. Take a look at the circumstances of this behavior).

3. Avoid scheduling marathon study sessions.

When possible, study in shorter sessions. Three 3-hour sessions are far more productive for most people than one 9-hour session. In a 9- or 10-hour study marathon, the actual time on task can be depressingly small. With 10 hours of study ahead of you, the temptation is to tell yourself, "Well, it's going to be a *long* day. No sense getting in a rush. Better sharpen about a dozen of these pencils and change the lightbulbs." In the 10-hour sitting you might spend only 6 or 7 hours studying, whereas three shorter sessions might yield as much as 8 hours of productive time.

When you do study in long sessions, take a planned break every hour. Focus your attention for short periods, then give your brain a chance to take a break.

Finally, if you must study in a large block of time, work on several subjects and avoid studying similar subjects back to back. For example, if you plan to study sociology, psychology, and computer science, sandwich the computer course between psychology and sociology.

4. Be aware of your best time of day.

Many people learn best in daylight hours. Observe yourself, and if this is true for you, schedule study time for your most difficult subjects when the sun is up.

The roaring lion

Use this exercise to take a break and relax during long study sessions.

1. Draw in a deep breath; then exhale hard through your mouth.
2. As you force your breath out, open your eyes wide and stick out your tongue.
3. Spread your fingers apart and stretch your arms downward.
4. Hold your breath for a few seconds.
5. With your mouth closed, inhale deeply through your nostrils. Allow your abdomen to rise.
6. Breathe out slowly through your nostrils. Relax.

Repeat three times. Try it once now.

Many successful business people begin their day at 5 a.m. (or earlier!), while most of us sleep. Athletes and yogis use this time, too. Some writers complete their best work before 9 a.m.

Unless you grew up on a farm, the idea of being conscious at 4 a.m. might seem ridiculous. Getting up that early is like jumping in an icy mountain lake. After the initial shock, your body comes alive.

Very early morning is a beautiful time. The world is quiet. Inner voices are less insistent. Spiritual leaders of all persuasions have recommended predawn as a time of meditation and prayer. The mind is better able to focus before it is assaulted by the jangle of telephones, traffic, and top forty tunes.

If you aren't convinced to use this technique regularly, test it when you're in a time crunch. Even if it doesn't work for you, you might get to see a sunrise.

The key point is to determine your best learning time. If early morning doesn't work for you, find out what time is better.

5. Use waiting time.

Five minutes waiting for a bus, 20 minutes waiting for the dentist, 10 minutes between classes—waiting time adds up fast. Have short study tasks ready to do during these times. For example, you can carry 3x5 cards with equations, formulas, or definitions and pull them out anywhere.

Also, use time between classes or breaks during work to review class notes or notes on reading. A solid review of a lecture can be completed in 15 minutes, and even 5 minutes can be valuable if you are prepared.

Where to study

6. Use a regular study area.

Your body knows where you are. When you use the same place to study, day after day, your body becomes trained. When you arrive at that particular place, it will automatically sense that it's time to study. You will focus your concentration more quickly.

For that reason, don't sleep where you study. Just as you train your body to be alert at your desk, you also train it to slow down near your bed. Don't eat where you study. Don't watch television where you study. Use your study area for study and make it a ritual.

7. Don't get too comfortable.

In bed, your body gets a signal. For most students, it's more likely to be, "Time to sleep," rather than, "Time to study!" Easy chairs and sofas are also dangerous places to study. Learning requires energy. Give your body a message that energy is needed. Put yourself into a situation that supports that message.

8. Use a library.

Libraries are designed for learning. The lighting is perfect. The noise level is low. Materials are available. Entering a library is a signal to your body to quiet the mind and get to work. Most people can get more done in a shorter time at a library. Experiment for yourself.

How to handle the rest of the world

9. Pay attention to your attention.

Breaks in concentration are often caused by internal interruptions; your own thoughts jumping in to tell you another story about the world. When that happens, notice the thoughts and let them go.

10. Agree with living mates about study time.

This includes roommates, wives, husbands, and kids. (See the article in this chapter about studying with a toddler.) Make the rules clear, and be sure to follow them yourself. Make explicit agreements—even written contracts. One student always wears a colorful hat when he wants to study. When his wife and children see the hat, they respect his wish to be left alone.

11. Avoid noise distractions.

Don't study in front of the TV. Turn off the stereo. Many students insist that they study better with music, and that may be true. Some students have reported good results with carefully selected and controlled music. The overwhelming majority of research indicates that silence is the best form of music for study.

12. Notice how others misuse your time.

Be aware of repeat offenders. Ask yourself if there are certain friends or relatives who consistently interrupt your study time. If avoiding the interrupter is impractical, send a clear message. Sometimes others don't realize they are breaking your concentration. A gentle reminder should do it.

STUDYING WITH CHILDREN UNDERFOOT

Studying with young children in the house presents interesting challenges. It *is* possible to combine effective study time and quality time with children. Make the activity called "study" a game and have them join in.

Studying chemistry with a three-year-old is not as preposterous as it sounds. The secret is to choose the kind of studying that the child can participate in. For instance, use this time to recite. While studying chemistry, make funny faces as you say the properties of the transition elements in the periodic table. Talk in a weird voice as you repeat Faraday's laws. Draw pictures and make an exciting story about the process of titration. Use kids as an audience for a speech or for practicing any mnemonic device. If you have invented rhymes, poems, or songs to help you remember formulas or dates, children can learn them right along with you. Kids are attracted to energy, enthusiasm, and love. To them, the content of the conversation is less important.

The attention span of a young child may range from several seconds to maybe thirty minutes. Do not plan to read new and complex material in the presence of a conscious two-year-old. Most people require about twenty uninterrupted minutes to acclimate their brains to complicated reading assignments. Chances are a toddler will interrupt long before then. Instead, choose short review tasks, like going over previous class notes. You can set up the child with her own desk, just like yours, and even offer rewards for getting her "assignment" done. While she colors, you can work on your notes.

Tell the child how important studying is to you and how you appreciate her cooperation. Reward her with attention and praise when she is quiet. When they are included in the process, children are less likely to resent school work as something that takes you away from them. Rather, it becomes something you do together.

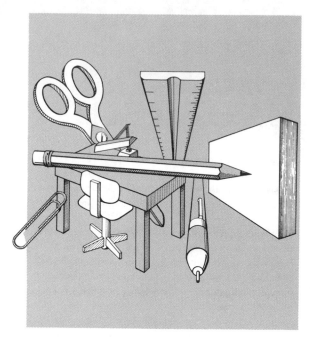

TOOLS OF THE TRADE

Useful items to a master student:

Buy these:
Ruler
Two pencils
Two pens
One ream of paper
5000 3x5 cards
Rubber bands
Two three-ring binders with tabs
Three-hole punch
Paper clips
Stapler
Tape dispenser
Scissors
Rubber cement
Bulletin board
Box of Kleenex
Two dozen push-pins
3x5 card file box with dividers

If your message doesn't work, there are ways to make it more effective. See page 212.

13. Get off the phone.

The telephone is the perfect interrupter. People who wouldn't think of distracting you when you are busy will call at the worst times because they can't see you. For your part, it is easy to rationalize interrupting your study for a phone call. After all, it wasn't your fault the phone rang, and besides, you don't want to be rude.

You don't have to be a telephone victim. If a simple, "I can't talk, I'm studying" doesn't work, use dead silence. It's a conversation killer. Or, short circuit the whole problem: You are unlikely to receive phone calls at the library.

If you assume that you are responsible for all the telephone calls you receive, you take control of the situation.

14. Learn to say no.

This is a valuable timesaver for students and a valuable life skill. Many people feel it is rude to refuse a request. Saying no can be done effectively and courteously. Others want you to succeed as a student. When you tell them that you can't comply with their request because you are busy educating yourself, 99% will understand.

15. Hang a "do not disturb" sign on your door.

Many hotels will give you one free, just for the advertising. Or you can make a creative one. They work. Using one will relieve you of making a decision about cutting off each interruption—a timesaver in itself.

Things you can ask yourself when you get stuck.

16. Ask: What is one task I can accomplish toward my goal?

This is a good technique to use on big, imposing jobs. Pick out one small accomplishment, preferably one you can complete in about five minutes, then do it. The satisfaction of getting one thing done often spurs you on to get one more thing done. Meanwhile the job gets smaller.

17. Ask: Am I beating myself up?

When you get frustrated with a reading assignment, or when you notice that your attention wanders repeatedly, or when you fall behind on problems due for tomorrow, take a minute to ask yourself how you feel about it. Are you scolding

SEVEN DAY PROCRASTINATION PLAN

A great introduction was planned about deadly procrastination and how it can strike a student when he least expects it. The author just didn't get around to writing it.

These are 7 strategies you can use to eliminate procrastination. The suggestions are tied to the days of the week to help your recall.

On Monday, Make it Meaningful.

Why is that job important? If you have been putting off something, take a minute to list all the benefits of completing the task. Look at the job in the perspective of your goals. Write down the task you have been avoiding, then below it, write your reason for doing it. Relate the task to your goals, and be specific about the payoff and rewards.

On Tuesday, Take it apart.

Break big jobs into small, manageable parts. Then be determined to complete one of those tasks. Make each task something you can accomplish in 15 minutes or less. Make the results measurable so you can see your progress. If a long reading assignment intimidates you, break it into two- or three-page sections, list the sections, then cross off each section as you complete it. Give yourself a visual experience of getting something done.

On Wednesday, Write an intention statement.

Use an intention statement in conjunction with a small task you have created. Write your statement on a 3x5 card, and carry it with you or post it in your study area where you can see it often.

For example, if you have a term paper to write and can't seem to get started, write yourself an intention statement that says, "I intend to write a list of at least ten possible topics for my term paper by 9 p.m. I will reward myself with an hour of guilt-free recreational reading."

On Thursday, Tell everyone.

Announce your intention publicly. Tell a friend. Tell your spouse, roommate, parents, or children. Telling the world of your intention is an excellent technique to ensure its completion. Make the world your support group.

On Friday, Find a reward.

Rewards can be difficult to construct. A reward must be something that you would genuinely withhold from yourself if you did not earn it. Don't pick a movie as a reward if you plan to go anyway. If you don't complete what you set out to do, and go to the movie anyway, the movie would be an ineffective reward.

And when you legitimately reap your reward, notice how it feels. You may find that movies, clothes, or an extra hour studying one of your favorite subjects are more enjoyable when you feel like you've earned it.

On Saturday, Settle it, now.

Do it now. The minute you notice yourself procrastinating, plunge into the task. Imagine yourself at a mountain lake, poised to dive. Gradual immersion would be slow torture. It's often less painful to leap.

Then be sure to savor the feeling of having the task behind you.

On Sunday, Say no.

Just say, "No!" When you notice yourself continually pushing a task into the low-priority category, re-examine the purpose for doing it at all. If you realize that you really don't intend to do something, quit telling yourself that you will. That's procrastinating. Tell the truth and drop it. Then you're not procrastinating, and you don't have to carry around the baggage of an undone task.

yourself too harshly? Lighten up. Allow yourself to feel a little foolish, recognize the feeling, and get on with it. Don't add to the problem by berating yourself.

18. Ask: Is this a piano?

Carpenters who build rough frames for buildings have a saying they use when they bend a nail or hack a chunk out of a two-by-four. They say, "Well, this ain't no piano." It means perfection is not necessary.

Ask yourself if what you are doing needs to be perfect. You don't have to apply the same standards of grammar to review notes that you apply to a term paper. The basketball player who refuses to shoot until the perfect shot is available may never shoot. If you can complete a job 95 percent perfect in two hours, and 100 percent perfect in four hours, ask yourself whether the additional five percent improvement is worth doubling the amount of time you spend.

Sometimes it is a piano. A tiny mistake can ruin an entire lab experiment. Computers are notorious for turning little errors into monsters.

Accept lower standards where appropriate, especially when time is short.

19. Ask: How did I just waste time?

Notice when time passes and you haven't accomplished what

you planned. Take a minute to review your actions and note the specific way you wasted time. We operate by habit and tend to waste time in the same ways over and over again. When you have noticed things you do that kill your time, you are more likely to catch yourself in the act next time. Observing one small quirk may save you hours.

20. Ask: Would I pay myself for what I'm doing right now?

If you were employed as a student, would you be earning your wages? Ask yourself this question when you notice that you've taken your third popcorn break in 30 minutes. Most students are, in fact, employed as students. They are investing in their own productivity and sometimes don't realize what a mediocre job may cost them.

21. Ask: Can I do just one more thing?

Ask yourself this question at the end of a long day. Almost always you may have enough energy to do just one more short task. If you get in the habit of working until you are done, then doing one more thing, those end-of-the-day tasks will soon add up. The overall increase in your productivity will surprise you.

Journal entry #13

Discovery statement

1. Spend five minutes brainstorming ways in which you waste time. Write down everything that comes to mind. Be sure to limit yourself to five minutes.

2. Take a few minutes to think about your list. Pick two time-wasting habits that you use most, and write a note to yourself about why these time wasters are so attractive to you. Write about the payoff for using them. Then write down what the cost is. Do this as if you were writing a note to someone else, and write it to yourself.

3. Take a few minutes to review your list from step one above and write down three time wasters that you are willing to give up.

The polyphasic thinker

The polyphasic thinker thinks he is getting lots done. What he is really doing is preparing himself for indigestion at best and a heart attack at worst.

He isn't really with the person on the other end of the phone line. He misses most of the newspaper. He is about to shave off his left ear. He is missing a great pleasure in life, corned beef on rye.

People know by instinct when your mind is not on the conversation you are sharing. You can read a whole page in a textbook and not remember a thing if your mind is somewhere else. Accidents happen when people don't pay attention to what their body is doing. Food is better digested in a relaxed setting.

The polyphasic thinker will get more accomplished by being in the moment, the here and now. And he may live longer.

Goal-Setting

This exercise will show you how to make goals as real as typewriters or chainsaws.

We all have vague, idealized notions of what we want out of life. They float among the clouds in our heads, nice and fuzzy and safe thoughts like, "I want to be a good person," "I want to be financially secure," and "I want to be happy." These are great thoughts. However, they aren't of much use to a student dealing with the choice between studying anatomy and going to the movies.

There is nothing vague or fuzzy about chainsaws. You can see them, feel them, and hear them. They have a clear function.

Goals can operate the same way—if you make them real. The way to do that is to examine them up close. Find out what they look like; listen to what they sound like. Pick them up and heft them. That's what this exercise is about. It's a chance to inspect the switches, valves, joints, cogs, and fastenings of one of your long-term goals. You do this by first finding a long-term goal, then by breaking it into smaller segments until you have it completely apart on the kitchen table.

Disassembled, a goal will look different. When you look at it closely, a goal you thought you wanted may not be something you want after all. You might see that you need to change directions to accomplish a goal you are sure you want. You will definitely be able to see how your education relates to your long-term goal.

This exercise is also an opportunity to test your brainstorming skills. You will need a pen, extra paper, and a watch with a second hand. Timing is an important part of the brainstorming process, so follow the time limits. The whole exercise takes about an hour.

Part one: long-term goals

Long-term goals represent major targets in your life. What are your major educational and career goals? What about your personal relationships? Do you want to travel? What do you want to accomplish in your life? Do you want your life to make a statement? What is it?

Section A

The first part of the exercise is an 8-minute brainstorm. For 8 minutes write down, as fast as you can, everything you think you want to do or be in your life. Leave no thought out. Don't worry about accuracy. The object is to generate as many ideas as possible. Use a separate sheet of paper for your brainstorm.

Section B

After you have completed section A, spend the next 8 minutes looking over your list. Think about what you wrote. Read the list aloud. Then, select 3 goals that are most important to you.

Write these goals in the space provided.

Goal _____

Goal _____

Goal _____

Part two: mid-term goals

Mid-term goals are objectives you can accomplish in two to five years. They include goals like completing a course of education or achieving a specific career level.

Section C

Read aloud the three long-term goals you selected in section B. Choose ONE long-term goal on which to focus your attention. Then brainstorm below a list of goals you might achieve in the next two to five years that would lead to the accomplishment of that one long-term goal. Spend 8 minutes on this brainstorm. Remember, neatness doesn't count. Go for quantity.

Section D

Review your list of mid-term goals in section C, then select three that you think would lead to the accomplishment of the long-term goal you picked. Allow yourself about 5 minutes for this part of the exercise.

Goal _____

Goal _____

Goal _____

Section F

Review your list of short-term goals in section E. Then cross out any that seem inappropriate. The most effective brainstorms are conducted non judgmentally, so you might find some bizarre ideas on your list. That's fine. Now is the time to weed them out.

Next, evaluate your short-term goals to determine which ones you can accomplish and are willing to accomplish. Select three of these and write them in the space provided.

Goal _____

Goal _____

Goal _____

Part four

Take a few minutes to reflect on all the goals you selected in sections B, D, and F during this process. Look for relationships. Think about what accomplishing these goals means to you. Think about how the process felt.

The more you practice, the more effective you will be at choosing goals that have meaning for you. You can repeat this exercise using the other long-term goals you generated, or create new ones. Use the process to make long-term goals real in the here and now.

Part three: short-term goals

Short-term goals are the ones you can accomplish in a year or less. These goals are specific. They can include goals about specific courses, financial goals that include exact dollar amounts, or personal goals requiring action now or in the very near future.

Section E

Review your mid-term goals in section D. Select one. In another 8-minute brainstorm, generate a list of goals you can reach in a year or less that will lead to the accomplishment of that mid-term goal. As always, in a brainstorm, write down everything that comes to mind. Do not evaluate or judge. The more ideas you write down, the better.

Be here now

This power process belongs in one of those late-night television ads—the ones in which hyperactive voices, shouting every sentence, describe "amazing," "fantastic," "revolutionary" new tools that chop, slice, dice, catch trout, and fit in your pocket.

The ad might sound like this:

BE HERE NOW! Yes, that's right friends. BE HERE NOW is a revolutionary tool for students. Carry it anywhere. Use it anytime. Get more out of lectures. Get more out of textbooks. Have more fun at parties! Solve problems faster. Take tests better. Can't stay awake in biology? No problem for BE HERE NOW. Order today! Send $399.99 to Power Process #2, P.O. Box 8306, Rapid City, South Dakota 57709. Offer limited.

If this power process were sold on late-night television, some people might even buy it. The problem is, being right here, right now, is such a simple idea. It sounds obvious. Where else can you be but where you are? When else can you be there but when you are there? The answer is you can be somewhere else at any time—in your head. It's human nature to live in our heads. When we do, we miss what's happening in the rest of the world.

Be here now means *do* what you're *doing* when you're doing it, and *be* where you *are* when you're there. It means focus your attention on the here and now. Nothing could be more simple, and sometimes nothing is more difficult.

Leaving the here and now

We all have a voice in our heads that hardly ever shuts up. If you don't believe it, conduct this experiment: Close your eyes for ten seconds and pay attention to what is going on in your head. Please do this right now.

Notice something? Perhaps your voice was saying, "Forget it. I'm in a hurry." Another might have said, "I wonder when ten seconds is up." Still another could have been saying, "What little voice? I don't hear a little voice."

That's the voice.

This voice can take you anywhere, anytime, especially when you are studying. When the voice takes you away, you may look like you are studying, but your brain is at the beach enjoying spring break.

All of us have experienced the voice, as well as the absence of it. When the voice is silent, we create. We expand our awareness. Time ceases to exist. We forget worries, aches, pains, reasons, excuses, and justifications. We are in the here and now. Life is magic.

The benefits of such a state of consciousness are many. It is easier to discover the world around us when we are not chattering away to ourselves about how we *think* it ought to be, has been, or will be. Letting go of inner voices and pictures, being totally in the moment, is a powerful tool for students, and there are techniques you can use to keep yourself closer to the here and now.

Do not expect to be rid of daydreams entirely. That is neither possible nor desirable. Inner voices serve a purpose. They enable us to analyze, predict, theorize, classify, and relate events in the world. Your stream of consciousness serves a purpose.

Letting go of these voices often, at appropriate times, can improve your effectiveness.

Returning to the here and now

The first step to return to the here and now is to notice when you leave it. Thoughts have a life of their own, which they seek to preserve at all times. It is useless to fight thoughts with force because the harder you fight them, the harder they fight back. Thoughts want to live. If you doubt this, for the next ten seconds do *NOT*, under any circumstance, think of a pink elephant. Please begin not thinking about one now.

Persistent image, isn't it? All ideas are this insistent when you try to deny them or force them out of your consciousness.

For example, during class you might notice yourself thinking about a test you took the previous day, or a party planned for the weekend, or a tape deck you want to buy for your car. You might look at someone else in the classroom and proceed to invent a story about them.

Don't try to force these thoughts out of your consciousness. Instead, when you notice a thought that seems to be interfering with the focus of your attention, just notice it. Accept it. Tell yourself, "There's that thought again." Then, gently return your attention to the task at hand. The thought will return again. Your mind will drift. Simply notice again where your thoughts take you, and gently return to the here and now.

Another way to return to the here and now is to notice physical sensations associated with your surroundings. Notice the way the room looks or smells. Notice how the chair feels. Notice the temperature in the room. And bring yourself back to here and now. Do this as often as necessary, calmly, without irritation.

Experiment with noticing and letting go of your inner voices. Let go of the ones that prevent you from focusing on learning. Practice the process. Be here now. And now. And now.

The here and now in your future
You can use power process #2 to keep yourself pointed toward your goals. In fact, the best way to get what you want in the future is to realize that you do not have a future. The only time you have is right now. The catch in this idea is that some students will think, "No future, huh? Terrific! Party time!" Being in the here and now, however, is not the same as living for today and forgetting about tomorrow.

Most students are pointed toward goals, and many of them have the idea that achieving those goals (and rewards) will make them happy. For these students, goals exist somewhere out there in the future. They think that when they get to that place out there called future, they will be satisfied. They rarely are. In fact, high numbers of students don't make it to graduation.

Examine this idea closely: Goals exist only in the present. Goals are tools we create to direct our actions right now. Goals, like our ideas of past and future, are useful creations of our minds. They are real only in the here and now. The power of this idea lies in the assertion that the only time to do anything is now. You can think about doing something next Wednesday. You can write about doing something next Wednesday. You can daydream, discuss, ruminate, speculate, fantasize, and speechify about what you will do next Wednesday.

But, you can't *do* anything on Wednesday until it is Wednesday.

The difference between looking at goals as things "out there" and recognizing them as existing in the here and now is important. When goals are shunted off to the misty future, action can be postponed. On the other hand, when goals are seen for what they are, tools of the present, immediate action makes more sense.

The word "goal" comes from the Anglo-Saxon *gaelan*, which means to hinder or impede, as in the case of a boundary. That's what a goal does. It restricts our activity in the here and now to acts that lead to the accomplishment of our purpose. Goals are useful only when directing action in the here and now.

Like goals, the process of time management exists only in the present. Using the Time Monitor in this chapter, you can see how you spent one week of your time. Then you can create a plan for the next week. The purpose of the plan is to enable you to direct your actions in the present. A time monitor is not a condemnation of past "time-wasting" activities, and a time plan is not a set of commandments. Each is a tool you can use right now.

When you plan for the future, plan for the future. When you listen to a lecture, listen to a lecture. When you read this book, read this book. To do that, use this handy power process you can take anywhere, use anytime. Be here now.

The 3 x 5 Time Plan

3x5 TIME PLAN

Goal generating from "Who am I?"

You will need a short stack of 3x5 cards, a watch, or a clock and a pen or pencil for this exercise.

Part one

As fast as you can, putting one idea or thought per 3x5 card, write down statements that begin with the phrases, "I am . . ." or "I have . . ." or "I can . . ." or "I like. . . ." You can also use other, similar phrases.

For example, you might write, "I am good at sports," "I can watch television for hours at a time," or "I like learning about people."

The objective of the first part of this exercise is to generate as many cards as possible. Volume is more important than accuracy. Give yourself 5 minutes for the first part of this exercise.

Part two

When you have finished, spread the 3x5 cards out on a large surface—a kitchen table, for instance. Take at least 10 minutes to look over the cards. Do this non judgmentally, as if you were examining the personality profile of someone you don't know. Do not draw conclusions about the person immediately. Simply look at each card. If you can see relationships between cards, rearrange the order so that related cards are near each other. Play with the cards. Experiment with relationships. Take time to look at each card three or four times.

When you are satisfied that you have examined each card thoroughly, put a rubber band around the stack and save it.

Part three

Step three is to do something else—preferably something you enjoy. Give yourself a break of at least 2 hours before going on to part four.

Part four

Take your card stack and spread the cards out on the table. Read them over again. Re-create in your mind the relationships you saw before. Be open to new ones. Then, play detective and ask yourself, as if you had never met the person behind the cards, "What kind of lifetime goals would this person probably have?"

Write down the goals you generate on several 3x5 cards.

Write an intention statement about when you plan to spend another 50-minute period reviewing your goals. Use a calendar and set a specific date and time.

Journal entry #14

Intention statement

I will review my goals on:

....

....

....

....

....

....

Exercise #8

Are you getting there?

The purpose of this exercise is to let you see how well you are focusing on long-term goals. It's easy to choose long-term goals, commit to them, then forget about them because they seem so far in the future. Yet big goals, like owning a farm, having your own business, or learning a profession, can be achieved only by stringing together hundreds of small daily goals.

Use your completed Time Monitor from Exercise #4 for this exercise. Pick three of your most important long-term goals. You can use the goals you generated in your Goal Setting Exercise, or you can use others. The first step of this exercise is to write those three long-term goals in the space provided below.

Next, go through the completed Time Monitor and circle everything you did that will eventually lead to the accomplishment of the long-term goals you chose.

Then, write down the activities and the time you spent on them under the appropriate goal.

The final step is your assessment of this data. Write this in the form of a discovery/intention statement. What have you learned about yourself by doing this exercise?

Goal:

Time Spent   Activity

....

....

....

Goal:

Time Spent   Activity

....

....

....

....

....

....

Goal:

Time Spent   Activity

....

....

....

....

Assessment of data:

....

....

....

By reviewing my Time Monitor and my long-term goals, I learned that . . .

....

....

Knowing that, I have decided to make the following intentions:

....

....

....

The Time Plan

The purpose of this exercise is to give you a tool to change the way you spend time. Do this exercise only after you have monitored your time for an entire week and have analyzed the results. (See Exercise #4 and Journal Entry #12.)

Look at the Time Plan form on page 61 and the sample Time Plan on this page. In the columns labeled "planned", you will block out activities for the coming week. Determine those tasks and projects you definitely want to accomplish, then be sure to schedule enough time for them first. You probably won't plan every minute of every day, but make your first Time Plan as detailed as possible. Like the Time Monitor, the purpose of this first Time Plan is to help you picture how you spend time.

Fill out the Time Plan at the beginning of the week, and as the week progresses, make notes in the column labeled "actual." This column is a record of how you *actually* spent your time. This record needn't be as thorough as the Time Monitor. Its purpose is to show where you deviated from your original plan so that next week's plan can be more effective. See the sample Time Plan for examples.

Please read these five suggestions before beginning your Time Plan.

FIVE TIME
PLANNING SUGGESTIONS

1. **Schedule fixed blocks of time first.** Start with class time or work time, for instance. These time periods are usually determined in advance. Other activities must be scheduled around them. Then schedule essential daily activities like sleeping and eating. No matter what else you do, you will sleep and eat. Be realistic about the time you need for these functions.

2. **Include time for errands.** The time we spend buying toothpaste, paying bills, and doing laundry is easy to ignore. These little errands, which are easy to overlook, can destroy a tight schedule and make us feel rushed and harried all week. Plan for them.

3. **Schedule time for fun.** Fun is important. Brains that are constantly assaulted with new ideas and new challenges need time off to digest them. Einstein went sailing or played the violin. Take time to do things you enjoy. Recreation deserves a place in your priorities.

4. **Set realistic goals.** Don't set yourself up for failure by telling yourself you can do a 4-hour job in 2 hours. There are only 168 hours in a week. If you schedule 169 hours, you lose before you begin.

5. **Allow flexibility in your schedule.** Recognize that unexpected things will happen, so plan for the unexpected. Don't schedule every hour. Give yourself time to get between places, etc.

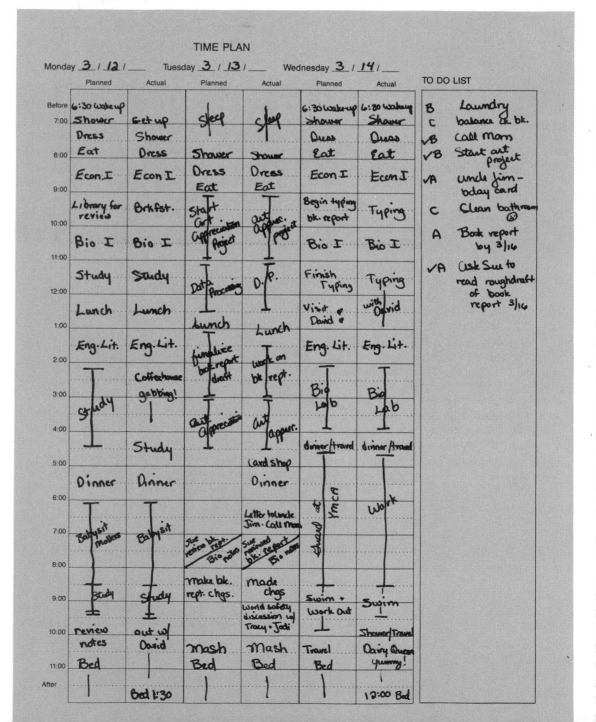

TIME PLAN

Monday ____ / ____ / ____   Tuesday ____ / ____ / ____   Wednesday ____ / ____ / ____

	Planned	Actual	Planned	Actual	Planned	Actual	TO DO LIST
Before							
7:00							
8:00							
9:00							
10:00							
11:00							
12:00							
1:00							
2:00							
3:00							
4:00							
5:00							
6:00							
7:00							
8:00							
9:00							
10:00							
11:00							
After							

TIME PLAN
page 2

	Thursday ___ / ___ / ___		Friday ___ / ___ / ___		Saturday ___ / ___ / ___		Sunday ___ / ___ / ___	
	Planned	Actual	Planned	Actual	Planned	Actual	Planned	Actual
Before								
7:00								
8:00								
9:00								
10:00								
11:00								
12:00								
1:00								
2:00								
3:00								
4:00								
5:00								
6:00								
7:00								
8:00								
9:00								
10:00								
11:00								
After								

THE
ABC
"TO DO"
DAILY PRIORITY SYSTEM
OR

"WORKING YOUR A'S OFF."

It's possible to look busy, even *be* busy, while accomplishing nothing.

One of the most effective ways to stay on track and actually get things done is to use a daily "to do" list. This is a simple list of things you want to accomplish during the day. Keep the list with you; cross out items when you complete them; add new items when you think of them. While the Time Plan is a general picture of the week, your daily "to do" list is a specific list of things you want to get done within 24 hours.

The advantage of keeping a daily list is that you don't have to remember what to do next. It's on the list. For students, this benefit alone makes the "to do" list worth the energy invested. A typical day in the life of a student is full of separate, unrelated tasks—reading, attending lectures, reviewing notes, working at a job, writing papers, doing special projects, research, errands, etc. It's easy to forget an important job in a busy day. When that job is written down, you don't have to trust your memory.

Keep a "to do" list *every day*. Write everything you want to accomplish on one sheet of paper, or on a daily planning calendar, a special notebook, or a 3x5 card. Cards work well because you can slip them into your pocket. It's important to keep your "to do" list with you. It's best to complete the daily "to do" list the night before the day you will use it.

Next, rate each task by priority. One way to do this is to label each task *A*, *B* or *C*.

A's on your list are those things that are most important. These are assignments that are due or jobs that need to be done immediately. *A* priorities also include activities that lead directly to your long-, mid-, or short-term goals.

The *B* tasks on your list are important, but less so than your *A*'s. *B*'s might become *A*'s

someday. These tasks are important, but not as urgent. They can be postponed if necessary.

C's do not require immediate attention. *C* items include things like "shop for a new blender" and "get brochures for next year's vacation." *C* priorities are often small, easy jobs.

Once you've labeled all the tasks on your list, schedule time for all of the *A*'s. The *B*'s and *C*'s, which usually include enjoyable, though not strictly necessary jobs, can be done in odd moments during the day when you are between tasks and don't have time to start the next *A*.

When you use the *ABC* priority method, you will discover a condition common to students: *C* fever. *C* fever is the uncontrollable urge to drop that *A* task and begin crossing *C*'s off the list. If your history paper is due tomorrow, you might feel compelled to vacuum the rug, call your third cousin in Tulsa, and make a trip to the store for shoelaces. The reason *C* fever is so common is that *A* tasks may be difficult, and the risk of failure is often high. Because they are the most important to us, *A*'s can be threatening.

If you notice symptoms of *C* fever, ask: "Does this job really need to be done now? Do I really need to alphabetize my record collection, or might I better use this time to study for tomorrow's data processing exam?"

Use your "to do" list to keep yourself on task and working on your *A*'s. Don't panic or berate yourself when you realize that in the last six hours, you have completed 11 *C*'s and not a single *A*. Calmly return to the *A*'s.

As you complete tasks, cross them off the list. Crossing off things can be fun. When you put a line through an item, it is physical evidence of progress, a visible reward for your diligence.

At the end of the day, evaluate your performance. Look for *A*'s you didn't complete. Look for tasks that repeatedly appear as *B*'s or *C*'s on your list and never seem to get done. Consider changing these to *A* priority or dropping them altogether. Similarly, you might consider changing an *A* that didn't get done to a *B* or *C* priority item.

Develop your own style. You might find that grouping tasks by categories like "errands" or "reading assignments" works best. Be creative.

And expect to make mistakes. You will assign *A* priority to some items that turn out to be true *C*'s. Some of the *C*'s that lurk at the bottom of your list day after day should have been *A*'s all along. When you keep a list every day, you are more likely to discover these errors before they become problems.

Make starting a "to do" list an *A* priority.

Malcolm X

From **The
Autobiography of
Malcolm X,** *by Malcolm
X, with the assistance of
Alex Haley. Copyright
1964 by Alex Haley and
Malcolm X. Copyright
1965 by Alex Haley and
Betty Shabazz.
Reprinted by permission
of Random House, Inc.*

I became increasingly frustrated at not being able to express what I wanted to convey in letters that I wrote, especially those to Mr. Elijah Muhammad. In the street, I had been the most articulate hustler out there—I had commanded attention when I said something. But now, trying to write simple English, I not only wasn't articulate, I wasn't even functional. How would I sound writing in slang, the way I would say it, something such as, "Look, daddy, let me pull your coat about a cat, Elijah Muhammad—"

Many who today hear me somewhere in person, or on television, or those who read something I've said, will think I went to school far beyond the eighth grade. This impression is due entirely to my prison studies.

It had really begun back in the Charlestown Prison, when Bimbi first made me feel envy of his stock of knowledge. Bimbi had always taken charge of any conversation he was in, and I had tried to emulate him. But every book I picked up had few sentences which didn't contain anywhere from one to nearly all of the words that might as well have been in Chinese. When I just skipped those words, of course, I really ended up with little idea of what the book said. So I had come to the Norfolk Prison Colony still going through only book-reading motions. Pretty soon, I would have quit even these motions, unless I had received the motivation that I did.

I saw that the best thing I could do was get hold of a dictionary—to study, to learn some words. I was lucky enough to reason also that I should try to improve my penmanship. It was sad. I couldn't even write in a straight line. It was both ideas together that moved me to request a dictionary along with some tablets and pencils from the Norfolk Prison Colony school.

I spent two days just riffling uncertainly through the dictionary's pages. I'd never realized so many words existed! I didn't know which words I needed to learn. Finally, just to start some kind of action, I began copying.

In my slow, painstaking, ragged handwriting, I copied into my tablet everything printed on that first page, down to the punctuation marks.

I believe it took me a day. Then, aloud, I read, back to myself, everything I'd written on the tablet. Over and over, aloud, to myself, I read my own handwriting.

I woke up the next morning, thinking about those words—immensely proud to realize that not only had I written so much at one time, but I'd written words that I never knew were in the world. Moreover, with a little effort, I also could remember what many of these words meant. I reviewed the words whose meanings I didn't remember. Funny thing, from the dictionary first page right now, that "aardvark" springs to my mind. The dictionary had a picture of it, a long-tailed, long-eared, burrowing African mammal, which lives off termites caught by sticking out its tongue as an anteater does for ants.

I was so fascinated that I went on—I copied the dictionary's next page. And the same experience came when I studied that. With every succeeding page, I also learned of people and places and events from history. Actually the dictionary is like a miniature encyclopedia. Finally the dictionary's A section had filled a whole tablet—and I went on into the B's. That was the way I started copying what eventually became the entire dictionary. It went a lot faster after so much practice helped me to pick up handwriting speed. Between what I wrote in my tablet, and writing letters, during the rest of my time in prison I would guess I wrote a million words.

I suppose it was inevitable that as my word base broadened, I could for the first time pick up a book and read and now begin to understand what the book was saying. Anyone who has read a great deal can imagine the new world that opened. Let me tell you something: From then until I left that prison, in every free moment I had, if I was not reading in the library, I was reading on my bunk. You couldn't have gotten me out of books with a wedge. Between Mr. Muhammad's teachings, my correspondence, my visitors—usually Ella and Reginald—and my reading of books, months passed without my even thinking about being imprisoned. In fact, up to then, I never had been so truly free in my life.

. . . I have often reflected upon the new vistas that reading opened to me. I knew right there in prison that reading had changed forever the course of my life. As I see it today, the ability to read awoke inside me some long dormant craving to be mentally alive. I certainly wasn't seeking any degree, the way a college confers a status symbol upon its students. My homemade education gave me, with every additional book that I read, a little bit more sensitivity to the deafness, dumbness, and blindness that was afflicting the black race in America. Not long ago, an English writer telephoned me from London, asking questions. One was, "What's your alma mater?" I told him, "Books."

1. When do your goals for the future exist?

2. List three ways you can control interruptions when you study.

3. The objective of time management is to enable students to avoid frustration and discomfort. True or false

4. "A" items on your "to do" list should be worked on within the next week or so. True or false

5. The best way to be in the here and now is to force daydreams and other thoughts out of your head. True or false

6. How many study hours are recommended for every hour in class?

7. Why set up one or two regular study areas?

8. Imagine that you have 30 problems assigned for a math course. You finish the problems and notice that answer #17 is incorrect. Should you cross out the wrong answer or redo the entire page? Why is it important to stop and ask yourself, "Is this a piano?"

9. Name a time when you can accomplish your educational goals.

10. If you have a time plan for the week, you can forget about keeping "to do" lists. True or false

Journal entry #15

Discovery statement

The following is a list of things I wanted to get from this chapter and didn't.

_____

_____

_____

_____

_____

_____

_____

_____

_____

_____

_____

Journal entry #16

Intention statement

In order to get what I want (but didn't get) from this chapter, I will . . .

_____

_____

_____

_____

_____

_____

_____

_____

_____

_____

Journal entry #17

Intention statement

Pick three time management techniques and write a short, one-sentence intention statement about how you plan to use each one in the next 72 hours.

1. I intend to use technique #_____ in order to

2. I intend to use technique #_____ in order to

3. I intend to use technique #_____ in order to

Also write about two other techniques you will use from this chapter.

1. I intend to . . .

2. I intend to . . .

After thoroughly previewing this chapter, list what you want to learn. Write down several things you want from this chapter.

I want...

Journal entry #18

Discovery statement

I want...

I want...

Review the Time Monitor exercise in chapter 2, *Time*. Describe below something that you learned about yourself when doing that exercise.

I learned that I...

Journal entry #19

Look back

CHAPTER THREE
MEMORY

Memory is the mother of imagination, reason and skill. . . This is the companion, this is the tutor, the poet, the library with which you travel.

MARK VAN DOREN

The true art of memory is the art of attention.

SAMUEL JOHNSON

In this chapter . . .

You already have a powerful memory. The unconscious mechanisms you use to recall the names of relatives, how to drive a car, and the meaning of words on this page are the same mechanisms you can use to remember chemistry formulas, economic principles, or medical procedures. This chapter will give you an opportunity to discover your powerful memory and then develop methods to tap it.

You never forget gives you a picture of how your memory works and shows that memory is a built-in skill. Your mind is structured to remember.

You can take the guesswork out of memory development by using a combination of the powerful memory strategies outlined in *Twelve memory techniques.*

Love your problems, experience your barriers is an unusual suggestion demonstrating how you can turn problems into opportunities, have fun with anxiety, and handle barriers that seem insurmountable.

Mnemonic devices are memory tricks that you can use effectively if you know the pitfalls. Learn how to make up new words, create sentences, use rhymes and songs, and apply other proven systems to improve recall.

Also in this chapter are exercises that allow you to discover memory skills that you already use: *Finding your car keys, Remembering names,* and *Be a poet.* You also can practice self-hypnotism and be introduced to the most powerful memory aid available, *The 3x5 memory tool.*

You never forget

The key to using your memory more effectively is to realize that—short of injury, disease or death—your brain never loses anything. Once a thought or perception has been input to your memory, it stays there for the rest of your life. What we call "forgetting" is either the inability to recall stored information or the failure to store information in the first place.

For example, during certain kinds of brain surgery, the patient remains conscious. When sections of the brain are stimulated with a mild electrical current, the patient will often remember events of his childhood with absolute clarity. He can recall details he thought were long forgotten—like the smell of his father's starched shirts or the feel of sunlight warming his face through the window of his first grade classroom.

People under hypnosis have reported similar experiences. Some people have been able to recall events that took place shortly after their birth. Working with police, hypnotists have enabled witnesses of crimes to remember vital information, such as license plate numbers.

Once information is stored in memory, it is never forgotten. Sometimes, however, we do have difficulty *recalling* a piece of information from our memory. The data is still in our heads. We simply can't find it.

Just as often, when we think we have forgotten something, the truth is that we never stored it in our memory in the first place.

Think of your memory as a vast, overgrown forest. This memory-forest is thick with wild plants, exotic shrubs, twisted trees, and creeping vines. It spreads over thousands of square miles—dense, tangled, forbidding. Imagine that the forest is bounded on all sides by impassable mountains. There is only one entrance to the forest, a narrow pass through the mountains that opens into a small meadow.

In the forest there are animals, millions of them. The animals represent all the information in your memory. Imagine that every thought, picture, or perception you ever had is represented by an animal in this forest. Every single event ever perceived by any of your five senses—sight, touch, hearing, smell, or taste—is also in the forest. Some of the thought animals, like your picture of the color of your seventh grade teacher's eyes, are well-hidden. Other thoughts, like your telephone number or the position of the reverse gear in your car, are easier to find.

There are two rules of the jungle. Each thought animal must pass through the meadow at the entrance to the memory forest; and once an animal enters the forest, it never leaves.

The meadow represents short-term memory. It's the kind of memory that you use when you look up a telephone number. You can look at seven digits and hold them in your short-term memory long enough to dial them.

Short-term memory appears to have a limited capacity (the meadow is small), and short-term memory disappears fast (animals pass through the meadow quickly.)

The forest itself represents long-term memory. This is the kind of memory that allows us to recall information from day to day, week to week, and year to year. Remember that animals never leave the long-term memory forest.

The following visualizations can help you recall useful concepts about memory.

Visualization #1: *A well-worn path*
Imagine what happens as a thought, in this case we'll call it a deer, bounds across short-term memory and into the forest. The deer leaves a trail of broken twigs and hoof prints which you can follow. Brain research suggests that thoughts also wear paths in the memory. These paths are called neural traces. The more well-worn the neural trace, the easier it is to retrieve (find) the thought. In other words, the more often the deer retraces the path, the clearer the path becomes. The more often you recall information, and the more often you put the same information into your memory, the easier it is to find.

When you buy a new car, for example, the first few times you try to find reverse you have to think for a moment. After you have found reverse every day for a week, the path is worn

into your memory. After a year, the path is so well-worn that when you dream about driving your car backwards you even dream the correct motion for finding reverse.

Visualization #2: *A herd of thoughts*
The second picture you can use to advantage is the picture of many animals gathering at a clearing—like thoughts gathering at a central location in the memory. It is easier to retrieve thoughts that are grouped together, just as it is easier to find a herd of animals gathered in a clearing than it is to find one deer.

Pieces of information are easier to recall if you can associate them with other similar information. For example, it is easier to remember a particular player's batting average if you associate it with other baseball statistics.

Visualization #3: *Turning your back*
Imagine releasing the deer into the forest, turning your back on it, and counting to ten. When you turn around, the deer is gone. This is exactly what happens to most of the information we receive. Generally, people cannot remember 50% of the material they have just read. Within 24 hours, most people can only recall about 20%. That means that 80% of the material is

The fourth picture is one with you in it. You are standing at the entrance to the short-term memory meadow, directing herds of animals as they file through the pass, across the meadow, and into your long-term memory. You are taking an active role in the learning process. You are paying attention. You are doing more than sitting on a rock and watching the animal traffic file into your brain. You become part of the process, and as you do, you take control of your memory.

wandering around lost in the memory forest.

The remedy is simple: Review quickly. Do not take your eyes off the animal as it crosses the short-term memory meadow; and review it soon after it enters the long-term memory forest. Wear a path in your memory immediately.

Visualization #4: *You are directing the animal traffic*

Exercise #10

Use a tool

In the first two chapters, two power processes were suggested for being more effective in school. One was entitled *Ideas are tools* and the other one, *Be here now*. Most examples used for these methods were related to the chapter in which they were presented.

Pick one of these ideas and show how it would apply to all or part of this chapter on memory.

MEMORY AND JOBS

Memory is more than a handy tool to help you get through exams.

More than ever, the ability to process new information quickly, in a way that makes it available for recall, is an essential job skill. The information explosion is leaving no field untouched. The only certainty about any career is that learning on the job will be continuous.

Information now increases at a rate of 13% per year. That rate will soon jump to as much as 40% per year. That means the volume of available information will double every 20 months.

In the immediate future, adaptable employees, people who can learn, will be the ones who prosper. An effective memory is essential to learning, and does more than enable you to recall data. An effective memory will assist you in finding relationships between new information and what you already know. An effective memory will enhance your adaptability and creativity.

Use the memory techniques in this chapter to create the kind of memory you can use on the job.

Twelve memory techniques

Effective memory does not mean the ability to memorize the phone book, although there are people who can. For a master student, effective memory means the ability to produce the right information at the right time.

Make your memory system flexible. The following techniques can be used in various combinations and applied to a variety of learning situations.

The twelve memory techniques are divided into four categories. Each category represents a basic principle for improving your memory. Briefly, these are:

1. *Be organized.* Information that is organized is easier to find.

2. *Be physical.* Learning is an active process. Get all your senses involved.

3. *Be clear.* You can reduce the background noise that your own brain produces and improve your ability to recall.

4. *Be smart.* Intelligent application of memory techniques can save work. You can work with your memory, not against it.

Survey the twelve techniques by reading each title. Then read the techniques. Next, skim them again looking for the ones you like best. Mark those.

BE ORGANIZED

1. *Learn from the general to the specific.* If, when looking at a painting for the first time you backed up to it, swirled around with your eyes closed, pulled out your magnifying glass, and began by examining the microscopic details, you wouldn't get much of an idea of it. Yet many students do just that. They feel a need to jump right into the thick of things in order to get through quickly. Take a deep breath and use a different approach.

   Get a broad overview of a subject before you begin to learn the details. Skim your entire textbook at the beginning of a term. Ask someone who has taken the class to quickly review the entire class with you. Look over the reading assignment before you begin. Take time to get to know the big picture. The details will be easier to recall.

2. *Make it meaningful.* Relate what you learn to your goals, to what you want to get from your education. We all learn more effectively when it has meaning to our lives. A skydiver will not become bored learning to pack her own parachute. Her reward for learning the skill is too important. Know what your rewards are, then connect those rewards to your studies. When you

elve

want something, you can remember it. So be specific about what you want.

Also, relate new material to what you have previously learned.

3. *Create associations.* Your memory forest is already arranged according to a scheme that makes sense to you. When new data is introduced, you will be able to recall it more effectively if it is stored near similar or related data. Fit new material in with what you already know.

For example, if you are introduced to someone named Greg, one way to remember his name would be to call up an image of another person you know named Greg. Visualize these two people together. Then in the future, when you see the new Greg, your mind will immediately associate him with a Greg you already know.

Any time you have to remember many details, you can gather them all together and create a common association. One way to do that is to create an extended metaphor, or story, like the story of the memory forest. That story holds together several details in one image.

BE PHYSICAL

4. *Learn it once, actively.* Learning consumes energy. The major reason that people "forget" is that they

never really learned in the first place. To be able to recall something from memory, you must first put it into memory.

The learning process can be deceptive. Most learning, especially in higher education, takes place in a passive setting. The environment is quiet and subdued. Students are sitting down. Don't be fooled. When you learn effectively, you are burning calories. If you are not, you probably aren't learning much.

Create an atmosphere of activity where you study. When you sit at your desk, sit up. Experiment with sitting up on the edge of your chair, as if you were about to spring out of your chair and sprint across the room. Consider standing up when you study. It's harder to fall asleep in this position, and some people insist that the brain works better when we stand. Also, don't be afraid to make gestures when you recite material. Pace back and forth as you study. Draw pictures of concepts in the air. Use your hands. Get your whole body involved in studying. This technique is especially valuable when you are getting bored. It's pretty tough to remember things you tried to learn when you were bored. Keep yourself active and interested, especially when you

Twelve memory techniques

mem

Exercise #11

A LITTLE SELF-HYPNOTISM

One of the best ways to remember something is to tell youself that you will remember it. The intention to remember is more powerful than any memory technique.

When you are learning something that you want to be able to recall, tell yourself that you *will* remember. This message is most effective if you do it in a state similar to hypnosis. Here's how.

Right before you learn something, or right after, take a moment to affirm your ability to remember. Close your eyes or focus on a point several feet away. Take three slow, deep breaths, paying attention to each breath. Then take three more breaths while consciously relaxing your entire body.

Once your body is relaxed and your mind is stilled, say to yourself, "At any time I choose, I will be able to recall . . ." Insert a brief description of what you want to remember at the end of the sentence. Repeat the entire experience three times.

(continued on page 79)

think the material itself is boring.

Active learning is a critical skill in an information-intensive society. Data is everywhere. Every day we are bombarded with thousands of messages. Because much of this information is not important to us, we develop the tendency to be passive receivers. To learn information that is important to you, be physical while you learn it.

5. *Visualize relationships.* Create pictures about things you want to learn. Draw diagrams. Make cartoons. Use mental visualizations to connect a series of facts, as you did when you read about the memory forest. Visual information is associated with a different part of the brain than verbal information. For right-handed people, most visual information is processed in the right hemisphere of the brain, while verbal information is generally processed in the left hemisphere. When you make up a picture to go with a concept or a fact, you are anchoring the information in two separate parts of the brain, thus doubling your chances of being able to recall it.

Relationships within abstract concepts can be "seen" and recalled easily when they are visualized. The key is to use your imagination. For example, Boyle's Law in physics states that the pressure of a quantity of gas is inversely proportional to the volume the gas occupies. That is, if you cut the volume in half, you double the pressure. To remember this concept, you might visualize a picture of a man and a bicycle pump. As he doubles the pressure by halving the volume in the pump cylinder, he seems to be getting angrier. By the time he has doubled the pressure, he is boiling mad. Why this visualization? Because you want to remember that the name of the law that defines this relationship is Boyle's Law.

Use the following three techniques:

(a) Create action. Make something happen. The man with the bicycle pump is working hard. He is compressing the air inside the pump.

(b) Make pictures vivid. The clearer the picture, the better. Create an unusual picture with the elements detailed and exaggerated. The man with the pump is "boiling" mad.

(c) Turn abstract ideas into concrete actions. Boyle's Law is an

ory te

abstract concept.
The man with the pump is concrete.

Bizarre or unusual images help some people remember. Others find them hard to conjure up. Experiment for yourself. See what kind of images work for you.

6. *Recite and repeat*. Of all memory techniques, recitation works the best for most people. When you want to remember something, repeat it aloud.

The aloud part is important. When you repeat something aloud, you anchor the concept in two different senses. First, you get the physical sensation in your throat when voicing the concept. Second, you hear the concept. The combined result is synergistic. That is, the effect of using two different senses is greater than the sum of their individual effects.

If all you do is recite silently in your head, your mind can play tricks on you. A concept might lodge itself in your short-term memory for a few minutes, leaving you with the idea that the concept is available for recall when, in fact, it isn't. When you review information only in your head, you are in danger of overlooking gaps in your recall. Get

some other senses into the act when you recite and repeat.

Recitation works best when you put concepts you want to remember into your own words. For example, if you want to remember, "The acceleration of a falling body due to gravity at sea level equals 32 feet per second per second," you might reword this to say, "Gravity makes a thing accelerate 32 feet per second faster each second that it's in the air at sea level," or, "For every second an object falls at sea level, it picks up an additional 32 feet per second in velocity."

Recite and repeat. It's a technique you can use anywhere. When you repeat and recite, you are making the neural trace in your memory forest wider and deeper and easier to find.

BE CLEAR

7. *Reduce interference*. Turn off the stereo when you study. Find a quiet place that is free from distraction. If you have a strong attraction to food, don't torture yourself by studying next to your refrigerator.

Study your most difficult subjects during daylight hours. Most people are able to concentrate more effectively during the day.

Allow yourself time to tune into a subject. The most efficient learning

(continued from page 78)

The description needs to be short. The sentence you would repeat might be, "At any time I choose, I will be able to recall what the instructor is going to tell me today about data organization on a computer disc." Or the sentence might be, "At any time I choose, I will be able to recall what I just read about the culture of Native Americans in the 17th century."

It is also a good idea to state your intentions out loud or to tell a friend. When all is said and done, it is the intention to remember that activates your recall.

Twelve memory techniques

Exercise #12

Finding your car keys (or anything else)

Pick something you frequently forget. Some people are chronic car key losers. Others forget to write down checks in their check register. Others forget anniversaries and birthdays.

Pick your forgettable item or task. Then, design a strategy for remembering it. You are on your own, and you are your own best expert. Use any of the techniques in this chapter, research other techniques, or design your own from scratch.

Record your technique design and the results below. In this exercise, as in most of the exercises in this book, a failure is also a success. Don't be concerned with whether your technique will work. Design it, then find out.

The technique:

The results:

begins 15 to 20 minutes after you begin studying. Your brain needs to warm up, so plan accordingly.

Take a break. For most of us, the brain needs a rest every 40 or 50 minutes. If you don't take a break, your ability to recall will suffer. After studying an especially difficult subject, do something enjoyable that requires little mental energy. Take in a movie. Go for a walk.

8. *Overlearn.* One way to fight mental fuzziness is to learn more about a subject than you have to. Students often stop studying when they know the material well enough to pass a test. A master student will pick a subject apart, examine it, add to it, and go over it until it becomes second nature.

This technique is especially effective for problem solving. Do assigned problems, then do more problems. Find another text and work similar problems. Make up your own problems and work those. When you pretest yourself this way, the reward will be speed and accuracy.

One effect of overlearning is that overlearned material acts as a magnet for other material. Knowledge begins to grow. Information attaches itself to related

information. You feel smarter.

Overlearning does not mean adding more facts at random or staying up all night rehashing the same material. Instead, learn what is required, then take time to explore what others say about the subject. Read other texts. Talk with other students. Immerse yourself.

9. *Be aware of attitudes.* Your attitudes about a subject can affect your ability to recall. If you have the attitude that history is boring, you may find it quite difficult to recall history. If you have an attitude that math is difficult, you will probably have trouble remembering math.

We tend to forget information that contradicts our opinions. A student who believes that federal deficits cause unemployment will likely discount and forget facts that don't support that idea. On the other hand, a student who believes that federal spending reduces unemployment will remember facts to support that position.

Even when you are bored, consider the possibility that you are creating your boredom. When you are anxious about a subject, consider the possibility that you are creating your anxiety. Take responsibility for your attitudes. Notice them.

You will find concepts repeated in this book. Some of the most repeated concepts seem, on the surface, to be the simplest. There is a reason for this repetition. Through repetition, learning takes place on a deep level. When concepts become second nature, they are more readily available for use in any situation. So, the book repeats itself. Consider doing the same.

ues

Remembering names

This does not mean to fight your attitudes or struggle to give them up. Simply acknowledge them; notice them. You can unlock your recall by being aware that an attitude is blocking your memory.

BE SMART

10. *Distribute learning.* Marathon study sessions are not effective. You can get far more done in three 2-hour sessions than in one 6-hour session. Two-hour sessions work even better if they are divided into shorter sessions of 40 to 50 minutes.

For example, when you are studying for your American History exam, study for an hour, and then wash the dishes. While you are washing the dishes, part of your mind will automatically review what you studied. Return to studying for a while, and then call your mother. Even while you are deep in conversation, part of your mind will be reviewing history.

Take regular breaks. Use breaks as mini-rewards. You can actually get more done if you give your brain a break every hour or so.

The exception to this rule is when you catch fire and can't put a book down, or are deep in the creation of a term paper, or engrossed in programming a computer. During these times, truly significant learning can take place. If you're on a roll, go for it.

11. *Remember something else.* When you are stuck and can't remember something that you *know* you know, remember something else that is related. If you can't remember your great aunt's name, remember your great uncle's name. If your memory is blocked during an exam, recall facts that are related to the one you are having trouble with. Similar information is stored in the same area of the brain. You can unblock your recall by stimulating that area of your memory.

A brainstorm is a good memory jog. When you are stumped in a test, start writing down lots of answers to related questions and—pop—the answer you need is likely to appear.

12. *Combine memory techniques.* All of these memory techniques work, and all of them work even better in combination with other techniques. Choose two or three techniques to use on a particular assignment. Experiment for yourself.

For example, repetition (#6) and reflection (#11) combine naturally. They can be accomplished at the same time. After you have repeated a math formula to yourself, think

Most of us have trouble remembering names. When we meet someone new, generally we don't really hear the name. Our minds are most often occupied with thoughts about ourselves. During the introduction, we hear our own name quite well. Then we pay attention to thoughts like, "I wonder what she thinks of me?" or, "What will I say next?" or even, "When am I going to get my shopping done?"

This exercise will allow you to see how your mind works when you meet someone new. The exercise involves meeting three new people. If you think you might not meet three new people in the next three days, take control of the situation. Introduce yourself to a classmate, to someone at work, or maybe to a neighbor.

Find three people you don't know and introduce yourself. Each time you meet a new person, watch yourself. Pay attention to what you are paying attention to.

This exercise can also be used to test some memory devices. When you hear the person's name, repeat it. Immediately say it to yourself several times. In the conversation that follows, make a point of repeating the person's name at least twice. Respond to an introduction with the

(continued on page 82)

(continued from page 81)

name, "I'm pleased to meet you, Greg." After the conversation, construct a brief visual image of the person, or find a way to connect the person to someone you know with a similar name. Or use any of the memory techniques from this chapter.

At the end of three days, record your discoveries in the following journal entry.

about how you will apply it or how it relates to other specific problems.

If you have an attitude that math is difficult, distribute your math study time in such a way that the sessions are short and easy to handle. Plan several short sessions during a day.

Make a subject meaningful to you by visualizing your reward for learning the material.

And, remember . . . you never forget. You know this already. You haven't forgotten the deer in the forest. That deer is still in

your memory.

Even though you remember the deer, you may not believe that an idea or thought never leaves your memory. That's OK. In fact, it doesn't matter whether you agree with the idea at all. The idea can work anyway.

Try it out.

Develop an attitude that says, "I never forget anything. I may have difficulty recalling something from my memory, but I never really forget it. All I have to do is find where I stored it."

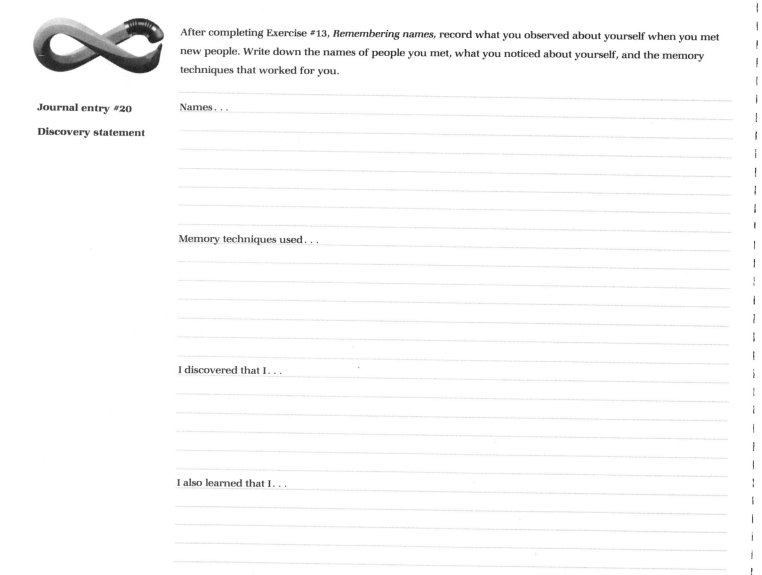

After completing Exercise #13, *Remembering names*, record what you observed about yourself when you met new people. Write down the names of people you met, what you noticed about yourself, and the memory techniques that worked for you.

Journal entry #20

Discovery statement

Names . . .

Memory techniques used . . .

I discovered that I . . .

I also learned that I . . .

mnemonic devices

It's pronounced *ni-mon-ik*. These tricks can profoundly increase your ability to recall everything from speeches to grocery lists. Some entertainers use mnemonics to perform "impossible" feats of memory like recalling the names of everyone in a large audience after hearing them just once. Waitresses can use them to take orders from a dozen people without the aid of pad and pencil, then serve food correctly without asking. Using mnemonic devices, speakers can go for hours without looking at their notes. The possibilities for students are endless. But there is a catch.

Mnemonic devices have three serious limitations. First, they don't help you understand or digest material. Mnemonics only assist rote memorization. Second, the mnemonic device itself is sometimes complicated to learn and time-consuming to develop. It may take more energy to create a mnemonic than to memorize something by using a more traditional memory technique such as repetition. Third, they can be forgotten. Recalling the mnemonic device might be as hard as recalling the material itself.

In spite of the limitations, mnemonic devices are powerful. There are four general categories: new words, creative sentences, rhymes and songs, and special systems including the loci system, the peg system, and the phonetic system. If you experiment with each, you can impress your mother-in-law by remembering her birthday and favorite color at just the right moment.

New words

Acronyms are words created by the first letters of a series of words. Examples include: NASA (**N**ational **A**eronautics and **S**pace **A**dministration), radar (**ra**dio **d**etecting **a**nd **r**anging), scuba (**s**elf-**c**ontained **u**nderwater **b**reathing **a**pparatus), and laser (**l**ight **a**mplification by **s**timulated **e**mission of **r**adiation). You can make up your own words to recall series of facts. Each letter in the word or series of words can stand for items you want to remember. A common mnemonic acronym is Roy G. Biv, which has helped thousands of students to remember the colors of the visible spectrum (red, orange, yellow, green, blue, indigo, violet.)

Possible Uses for 3x5 Cards

"to do" lists
coasters
fireplace starters
paper planes
card house
guitar pick
replace address books
confetti
food lists
noisemaker on spokes of
  bikes
office check-out
recipe cards
messages
shim desk legs
vocabulary lists
baby toys
flashcards
bookmarks
generic card deck
ink blotter
drop from planes as ad
  pamphlets
note-taking
write affirmations
doodle sheets
appointment keeper
bend, fold and multilate
  to release tension
fan
poor man's business card
pick teeth
clean combs

Be a poet

Construct your own mnemonic device for remembering the 12 memory techniques in this chapter. Make up a poem, a jingle, acronym or acrostic, or use a mnemonic system. Describe your mnemonic device in the space below.

Creative sentences

Acrostics are sentences created by words that begin with the first letters of a series of words. For example, "Every good boy does fine," is the music student's acrostic for recalling the notes associated with the lines of a treble clef staff: E, G, B, D, F. "George Elliott's old grandfather rode a pig home yesterday," is a way to remember how to spell geography.

Medical students and law students have developed some classic acrostics including "On old Olympus' towering top, a Finn and German viewed some hops." The first letter in each word helps the medical student remember the cranial nerves—olfactory, optic, oculomotor, trochlear, trigeminal, abducens, facial, auditory, glossopharyngeal, vagus, spinal accessory, and hypoglossal.

Rhymes and songs

Madison Avenue advertising executives spend billions of dollars a year on commercials that will burn their message in your memory. "Nobody can do it like _____ can," is a jingle that instantly brings the name "McDonald's" to the mind of almost every American. McDonald's song, "We do it all for you," practically stands for McDonald's, despite the fact that its customers do everything from standing in line for their food and carrying it to their tables, to cleaning up the mess when they are finished.

Rhymes have been used for centuries to teach children basic facts. "In fourteen hundred and ninety-two, Columbus sailed the ocean blue," or "Thirty days hath September. . . ."

Systems—loci, peg, phonetic

The loci system is an old one. Ancient Greek orators used it to remember long speeches. Use the loci system to create visual associations with locations you already know. It also helps you to remember things in a particular order. The Marvelous Memory Car article in this chapter is an example using the loci system for recalling memory techniques. The Greek orator didn't have a memory car to help him remember items in his speech, but he did have a house. He decided to remember his speech by visually placing its key elements in various rooms of his house. If his topic was that road taxes be raised to pay for school equipment, his loci visualizations might have looked like these:

First, as he walked in the door, he imagined a large **porpoise** jumping through a hoop. This was to remind him to begin by telling the audience the **purpose** of his speech. Next, he visualized his living room floor covered with paving stones forming a road leading into his kitchen. In the kitchen, he pictured dozens of school children sitting on the floor because they have no desks.

Now the day of the big speech. The Greek politician is nervous. He is perspiring so much that his toga sticks to his body. He has cold feet (no socks.) He stands up to give his speech and his mind goes blank. "No problem," he thinks to himself. "I am so nervous that I can hardly remember my name. But, I can remember the rooms in my house. Let's see, I'm walking in the front door and, Wow! I see the porpoise. Oh, yeah, that reminds me to talk about the purpose of my speech. . . ."

Unusual associations are the easiest to remember. This system can also be adapted to locations in your body. You visually link things you want to remember with places inside your skin. The shopping list is remembered when you recall the visualization of a loaf of bread stuck in your brain cavity, a large can of frozen orange juice in your larynx, a bunch of broccoli tucked under your collar bone. . . .

The *peg system* employs key words represented by numbers. For example, one-bun, two-shoe, three-tree, four-door, five-hive, six-sticks, seven-heaven, eight-gate, nine-wine, and ten-hen. In order for this system to be effective, these peg words need to be learned well.

You might use the peg system to remember that the speed of light is 186,000 miles per second. Imagine a hotdog bun (1) entering a gate (8) made of sticks (6). Since we tend to remember pictures longer than we do words, it may be easier to recall this weird scene than the numbers one, eight, and six in order.

The *phonetic system* is similar to the peg system, but instead of words representing numbers, sounds represent numbers. Thus, zero is represented by the sound of "s," one by "t" or "d," two by "l," three by "m," four by "r," five by "n," six by "sh," seven by "k," eight by "f," and nine by "b." To remember the number 186, you would form a word using those consonant sounds. (Vowel sounds don't count, and neither do any letters except those associated with the numbers 1-9.) The speed of light could be remembered by remembering the phrase, "two fish"—t(1)wo f(8)ish(6).

While this system is cumbersome in recalling a three digit number, it can be valuable with long strings of numbers. Most people can remember words better than numbers.

Journal entry #21

Discovery statement

Describe one or two barriers you have in your life that keep you from getting what you want. (First read about barriers as discussed in Power process #3: *Love your problems* on page 86.) If you have trouble identifying a barrier, review the Discovery Guide you completed in Chapter 1.

A barrier I have is . . .

Another block to my growth is . . .

Journal entry #22

Intention statement

The following intention statement is in three parts.

1. Describe how you could set up circumstances that would allow you to experience (be with) the barrier (or problem) you discovered. What could you do to put yourself right up against the barrier?

To experience the barrier, I could . . .

Also, I could . . .

2. Brainstorm a list of possible benefits or rewards you could enjoy if you let yourself experience away (love to death) the barrier. Do this on 3x5 cards or a separate sheet of paper.

3. This is for the courageous. Pick *just one* circumstance that you intend to set up in order to be with the barrier or problem you have written about. This will be your opportunity to love it to death. Choose a circumstance that you can arrange within the next three days. (For example, if your barrier is fear of speaking in front of a group, the circumstance you could arrange would be giving a speech.)

Love your problems, experience your barriers

We all have barriers that block our going forward, our moving into new areas of our universe. We put boundaries on our experience. We limit what we allow ourselves to be, to do, to have.

It's like we walk around in life and bump—we're up against something—some barrier that prevents us from progressing on that particular path. Usually we turn around to avoid the barrier and start walking along a different path. And all of a sudden, Bump! We've struck another barrier. Barriers could be the fear of speaking in front of a group, hesitancy about looking silly when trying something new, or even anxiety about being successful.

There is nothing wrong with barriers, but sometimes they limit our experience so much that we get bored with life. There are three ways to deal with a barrier.

One way is to pretend that it doesn't exist. It's like turning your head the other way, putting on a fake grin, and saying, "See, there's really no problem at all. Everything is fine. Oh, that problem. That's not a problem, it's not really there." Besides looking foolish, this approach leaves the barrier intact, and we keep bumping into it. And because of our denial, we may not even be aware that we're bumping into it. For example, a student who avoids math may find himself avoiding a whole realm of life situations in which math is essential.

The second approach is to fight the barrier, to struggle against it. This usually makes the barrier grow. It increases the barrier's magnitude. It's like the person who is obsessed with weight. He continues to think about how overweight he is, continues to worry about it, struggle with it, go on diet after diet after diet. The more he struggles, the bigger the problem gets.

The third alternative is to love the barrier. Totally experience it. Get involved with it. Tell the truth about it. Describe it in detail. When you do this, the barrier loses its power. You can literally love it to death.

For example, suppose one of your barriers is being afraid to speak in front of a group. You can ignore it by refusing to speak in front of groups, or you can approach it one of three ways. First, you can get up in front of the group and pretend you're not afraid. You fake a smile, not admitting to yourself, and for sure not to the group, that you have any concerns about speaking, even though your legs have turned to rubber bands and your mind feels like jello. The problem is that everyone in the room will know you're scared and you will too, when you suddenly pitch forward or lose your voice.

The second way to approach this barrier is to fight it. You could say, "I'm not going to be scared," and then try to keep your knees from knocking and force your teeth to stop clicking. Generally, this doesn't work. They click and shake even more.

The third approach is to get up in front of the room, look out into the audience, and say to yourself, "I am scared. I notice that my knees are shaking, my mouth feels dry, and I'm having a rush of thoughts about what might happen if I say the wrong thing. Yup, I'm scared and that's OK. As a matter of fact, it's just part of me, so I accept it, and I'm not going to try and change it. I'm going to give this speech even though I'm scared."

In this example, you may not actually eliminate the fear. It's just that the fear barrier (something that stops you) disappears. Often you will find that if you examine the fear, love it, accept it, and totally experience it, the fear itself will disappear.

Loving in this sense does not imply enjoyment. We don't always enjoy our problems. Love in this sense means total

and unconditional acceptance.

P.S. This technique can also be effective for minor physical ailments. Next time you have a headache, try the experiment of loving your headache. Totally accept and experience the headache that you have.

Take a few minutes to look at the headache as if it were an object. Describe its color, shape, weight, volume (if it could hold water), its density, and even its smell. As you describe it, continue to experience it and look at it. You will notice that your visualization of your headache will change. Allow it to change, and continue to describe it. Most people who try the technique for three or four minutes find that the headache disappears.

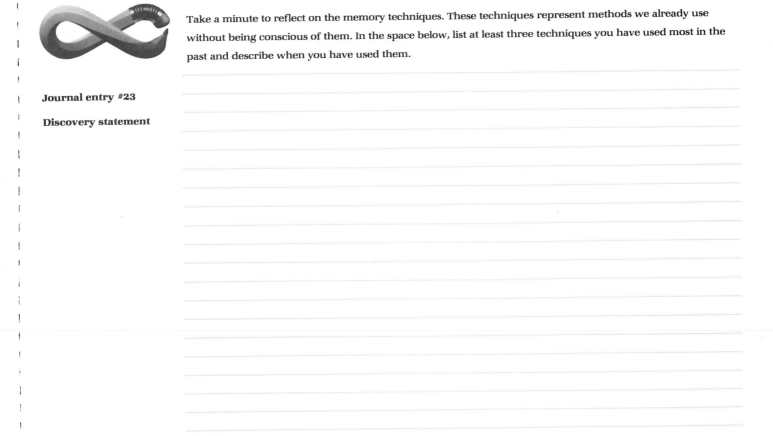

Take a minute to reflect on the memory techniques. These techniques represent methods we already use without being conscious of them. In the space below, list at least three techniques you have used most in the past and describe when you have used them.

Journal entry #23

Discovery statement

The marvelous memory car

You are about to become the owner of a powerful memory tool. If you have gone through life believing that you have a poor memory, stop right here. The marvelous memory car can help you remember up to 12 things in correct order.

First, spend a few minutes studying the drawing of the memory car. It is a fancy, powerful, luxurious sports sedan. Look at the side view. Notice that it is a four-door. See the exhaust ports which serve a thunderous V-8 engine. Observe the classic hood ornament. Now look at the front view. See the two headlamps and the broad grill? Now look at the drawing of the cockpit with its nine-spoked steering wheel, 10-instrument cluster and roomy glove box. What a car!

The next step is to associate the numbers 1-12 with certain parts of the car, and write the appropriate number on the drawing next to each item:

1. *Grill*—there is only one grill.
2. *Headlamps*—there are two headlamps.
3. *Hood Ornament*—there are three segments in this hood ornament.
4. *Doors*—this is a four-door sedan.
5. *Wheels*—there are five wheels (remember the spare).

6. *Windows*—there are six windows.
7. *Antenna*—this antenna will tune in seven channels.
8. *Engine*—this engine is a big V-8.
9. *Steering wheel*—there are nine spokes in the steering wheel.
10. *Instrument panel*—there are 10 instruments in this powerful car.
11. *Glove box*—this roomy glove box has 11 stripes.
12. You, the driver! You can easily remember a dozen (12) things.

Review the numbers associated with each part of the car one more time while looking at the drawings. Put your list and drawings aside, and recite the list in order. If you had any doubts about certain ones, review them again. Now recite the list backwards. Then recite all the odd numbers and their parts. Then all the even ones. Call out items at random and give their correct numbers. Now you are ready to use your marvelous memory car to learn any list of up to 12 items in order.

For example, here's how to use the memory car to help recall the 12 memory techniques in this chapter. It is important to mentally attach each item to a particular part of the car. The following list shows one possible way to do the

attention among all ten dials, or you may run out of gas, overheat the engine, or get stopped for speeding.

11. *Remember something else.* Point 11 goes in the glove box. You might remember that gloves aren't the only things you keep in the glove box.

12. *Combine techniques.* Point 12 is the driver—you. You might remember that the only way to be an effective driver is to combine several of the car's functions at once. To turn a corner, you will use your turn signal while applying the brakes and watching the road around you.

This car can be used for any list. You've just seen how to use it to remember 12 memory techniques. Next time you need to remember 12 things in order, get your memory car out of the garage and start with the grill. You can add more parts to your car to enlarge your list. Be creative.

Exercise #15

The recharger

Actively storing and recalling information requires energy. Use this exercise when you are slowing down.

1. Stand straight, hands at your side.

2. Inhale deeply and hold it.

3. Raise your arms out in front of you. Relax as you hold them up.

4. Slowly make fists as you bring your hands to your shoulders.

5. Keeping fists tightly clenched, slowly extend your arms in front of you.

6. Keeping your fists tight, pull them to your shoulders again. Do this as fast as you can.

7. Relax, hands at your sides, and exhale forcefully through your mouth.

8. Repeat these steps again.

attaching—and it's just an example. If you can find a better way to do the attaching, use it:

1. *General to specific.* It's number one, so attach it to the grill. You might tell yourself that this car is so fancy it must belong to a General.

2. *Make it meaningful.* It's number two, so put it on the headlamps. There are two M's in this phrase and there are two headlamps. Perhaps you could visualize an M on each headlamp.

3. *Create associations.* It's number three, so it goes on the hood ornament, and hood ornaments are often *associated* with fancy cars.

4. *Learn once, actively.* Four goes on doors. You might use the memory hook that this phrase applies to the doors because to get in or out, you must do it actively.

5. *Visualize relationships.* Five goes on wheels, and in this case, you might remember that all five wheels are alike. They are related.

6. *Recite and repeat.* Six goes on the windows, and you might remember rolling the windows up and down, over and over.

7. *Reduce interference.* Seven goes on the antenna. Using an antenna with the radio will reduce static and help you stay tuned to one station.

8. *Overlearn.* Eight is the motor, and this particular V-8 engine probably has more power than you will need, and extra power may be useful at times.

9. *Be aware of attitudes.* Point nine goes on the steering wheel, and you might remember that your attitudes steer you.

10. *Distribute learning.* Point 10 goes on the instrument panel. You must distribute your

Helen Keller

*The Story of My Life, by
Helen Keller, 22-24, 1905*

The morning after my teacher came she led me into her room and gave me a doll. The little blind children at the Perkins Institution had sent it and Laura Bridgman had dressed it; but I did not know this until afterward. When I had played with it a little while, Miss Sullivan slowly spelled into my hand the word "d-o-l-l." I was at once interested in this finger play and tried to imitate it. When I finally succeeded in making the letters correctly I was flushed with childish pleasure and pride. Running downstairs to my mother I held up my hand and made the letters for doll. I did not know that I was spelling a word or even that words existed; I was simply making my fingers go in monkey-like imitation. In the days that followed I learned to spell in this uncomprehending way a great many words, among them *pin, hat, cup,* and a few verbs like *sit, stand,* and *walk.* But my teacher had been with me several weeks before I understood that everything has a name.

One day, while I was playing with my new doll, Miss Sullivan put my big rag doll into my lap also, spelled "d-o-l-l" and tried to make me understand that "d-o-l-l" applied to both. Earlier in the day we had had a tussle over the words "m-u-g" and "w-a-t-e-r." Miss Sullivan had tried to impress it upon me that "m-u-g" is *mug* and that "w-a-t-e-r" is *water,* but I persisted in confounding the two. In despair she had dropped the subject for the time, only to renew it at the first opportunity. I became impatient at her repeated attempts and, seizing the new doll, I dashed it upon the floor. I was keenly delighted when I felt the fragments of the broken doll at my feet. Neither sorrow nor regret followed my passionate outburst. I had not loved the doll. In the still, dark world in which I lived there was no strong sentiment or tenderness. I felt my teacher sweep the fragments to one side of the hearth, and I had a sense of satisfaction that the cause of my discomfort was removed. She brought me my hat, and I knew I was going out into the warm sunshine. This thought, if a wordless sensation may be called a thought, made me hop and skip with pleasure.

We walked down the path to the well house, attracted by the fragrance of the honeysuckle with which it was covered. Someone was drawing water and my teacher placed my hand under the spout. As the cool stream gushed over one hand she spelled into the other the word *water,* first slowly, then rapidly. I stood still, my whole attention fixed upon the motions of her fingers. Suddenly I felt a misty consciousness as of something forgotten—a thrill of returning thought; and somehow the mystery of language was revealed to me. I knew then that "w-a-t-e-r" meant the wonderful cool something that was flowing over my hand. That living word awakened my soul, gave it light, hope, joy, set it free! There were barriers still, it is true, but barriers that could in time be swept away.

I left the well house eager to learn. Everything had a name, and each name gave birth to a new thought. As we returned to the house every object which I touched seemed to quiver with life. That was because I saw everything with the strange, new sight that had come to me. On entering the door I remembered the doll I had broken. I felt my way to the hearth and picked up the pieces. I tried vainly to put them together. Then my eyes filled with tears; for I realized what I had done, and for the first time I felt repentance and sorrow.

I learned a great many new words that day. I do not remember what they all were; but I do know that *mother, father, sister, teacher* were among them—words that were to make the world blossom for me, "like Aaron's rod, with flowers." It would have been difficult to find a happier child than I was as I lay in my crib at the close of that eventful day and lived over the joys it had brought me, and for the first time longed for a new day to come.

1. What are the two main purposes of this chapter?

2. List two limitations of short-term memory.

3. What law governing the behavior of animals in the memory forest analogy represents the theory that our brains store all perceptions?

4. List the four categories of memory techniques.

5. Describe the Boyle's Law visualization.

6. List at least three characteristics of an effective visualization.

7. Why is reciting aloud such an effective memory technique?

8. Describe how reciting material aloud is a suggestion that is difficult for most people.

9. In what learning situation can the loci system be of most value?

10. Why can't we remember names?

List what things you wanted to get from this chapter but didn't.

I didn't get, but I wanted . . .

Journal entry #24

Discovery statement

Describe steps you intend to take to get whatever you listed in Journal entry #24.

I intend to . . .

Journal entry #25

Intention statement

Pick three memory techniques and write an intention statement about how you will use them in the next week. Be specific in your description of your intention and include a reward.

Journal entry #26

Intention statement

Think about how reading skills relate to your educational goals. Preview this chapter. Review your discovery guide, especially the section on reading then list below what you want to learn from this chapter.

I want to learn . . .

Journal entry #27

Discovery statement

Consider your attitude about memory. How have your ideas changed since reading the article, *You never forget?*

Concerning my memory attitudes, I learned that . . .

Journal Entry #28

Look back

CHAPTER FOUR
READING

Reading furnishes our mind only with materials of knowledge; it is thinking that makes what we read ours.
JOHN LOCKE

I have read on subways, trains and buses for 40 years . . . approximately 10 hours of reading a week for 2,000 weeks. Those 20,000 hours add up to at least five college degrees.
CORNELIUS HIRSCHBERG

. . . there would seem to be almost no limit to what people can and will misunderstand when they are not doing their utmost to get at a writer's meaning.
EZRA POUND

In this chapter . . .

This chapter is for students who have the thought, "I can read well" as well as students who have the thought, "I can't read well." Those of you in the first category may discover how reading textbooks differs from reading newspapers or novels. The discovery can cut your reading time in half. Students in the second group can discover how, when combined with your present reading skills, techniques in this chapter can result in surprising reading effectiveness.

Muscle reading shows you that you have everything you need, right now, to bring to a textbook the same energy and aliveness that master musicians bring to their instruments. The true masters of music do more than reproduce the composer's notes. They add themselves to the composition. They create music. The master student does the same with a textbook.

When your reading slows to the speed of a glacier, use the techniques in **When reading is tough.**

Your mental pictures of the world can sabotage your studies before you begin. **Notice your pictures and let them go** suggests a way to deal with frustration.

Also in this chapter you can learn about **Reading fast**, using your secret brain, making movies, relaxing with black, and the dreaded disease, **Mumpsimus.**

MUSCLE
R E A D I N G

Picture yourself sitting in front of a book, facing the page, eyes open. Suddenly your head jerks up. You look around the room, realize that your eyes have been scanning the page for 10 minutes, and you can't remember a single thing you have read.

Or, picture this: You've had a hard day. You were up at 6 a.m. to get the kids ready for school. A co-worker called in sick and you missed your lunch trying to do your job and his. You picked up the kids, then had to shop for dinner. Dinner is late, of course, and the kids are grumpy. Finally, you get to your books at 8 p.m., and you begin plodding through something called "The equity method of accounting for common stock investments." "I am preparing for the future," you tell yourself, as you claw your way through two paragraphs and begin the third. Suddenly, everything in the room looks different. Your head is resting on your elbow, which is resting on the equity method of accounting. The clock reads 11:30. Say goodbye to three hours.

Sometimes, the only difference between a sleeping pill and a textbook is that the textbook doesn't have a warning on the label about not operating heavy machinery.

Muscle reading is a technique you can use to avoid those mental trips to Zzz'sville and reduce the number of unscheduled naps during study time, even after a hard day. More than that, muscle reading is a way to decrease effort and struggle by increasing energy and skill. You can actually spend less time on your reading and get more out of it.

Of course, you cannot avoid all work and still challenge yourself in your education. Muscle reading, at first glance, might even seem to entail more work. Effective textbook reading is an active, edge-of-your-seat business. That's why this strategy is called muscle reading.

How muscle reading works

The key idea behind muscle reading is that your textbooks have something you want. They have knowledge and valuable information. Sometimes the value is so buried that extracting it will require skill and energy.

Muscle reading is a three-phase technique you can use to accomplish that extraction. Each of the three phases has three steps. To assist your recall of all nine steps, we suggest you memorize three short sentences:

Pry out questions.

Root up answers.

Recite, review, and review again.

Take a moment to invent images for each of those sentences. First, visualize yourself prying questions out of a text. These are questions you want answered, based upon your brief survey of the assignment. Make a mental picture of yourself scanning the territory, spotting a question, and reaching into the text to pry it out.

Then root up the answers to your questions. Get your muscles involved. Flex. Feel the ends of your fingers digging into the text to root up the answers to your questions.

Finally, hear your voice reciting what you have learned. Hear yourself making a speech about the material. Hear yourself singing it. Picture yourself on a stage, waving your arms dramatically as you sing what you have learned to an audience. Know that this is your repeat performance.

These sentences form an acrostic. The first letter of each word stands for a muscle reading procedure. Thus:

Pry out questions.			**Root up answers.**		
r	u	u	e	n	n
e	t	e	a	d	s
v	l	s	d	e	w
i	i	t	r		e
e	n	i	l		r
w	e	o	i		
		n			n
		s			e

Recite,	**review,**	and **review** again.			
e	e	e			
c	v	v			
i	i	i			
t	e	e			
e	w	w			

Configured another way, the three phases and nine steps look like this:

Phase one: Pry out questions.
Step 1: Preview
Step 2: Outline
Step 3: Question

Phase two: Root up answers.
Step 4: Read
Step 5: Underline
Step 6: Answer

Phase three: Recite, review, and review again.
Step 7: Recite
Step 8: Review
Step 9: Review again

A nine-step reading strategy might seem cumbersome and unnecessary for a two-page reading assignment. It is. However, once you've used muscle reading several times, you can automatically use the steps appropriate to the reading.

Phase one

Step 1: Preview
Before you begin to read, look over the entire assignment. If you are starting a new book, look over the table of contents and flip through the text page by page. Even if your assignment is merely a few pages in a book, you can benefit from a brief preview of the table of contents.

Keep the preview short. If the entire reading assignment will take less than an hour, your preview might take five minutes. Previewing longer assignments can take as much as 15 minutes. Spend more time previewing books you will use for an entire term. (Previewing is also a good way to get yourself started when an assignment looks too big to handle. It is an easy way to step into the material.)

When previewing, look for familiar concepts, facts, or ideas. These items can help cluster new information around previously learned material. Look for ideas that spark your imagination or curiosity. Ask yourself how the material can relate to your long-range goals.

Inspect drawings, diagrams, charts, tables, graphs, and photographs. These images register quickly, and they

THE
UNIVERSAL
LAW OF
READING

First corollary:
To read effectively, always wear a face mask, snorkel and flippers, and sit in a canoe.

Second corollary:
Don't believe everything you read.

become reference points when you get into actual reading.

Keep an eye out for summary statements. If the assignment is long or complex, read the summary first. Many textbooks have summaries in the introductions or at the end of each chapter. Read all chapter headlines, section titles, and paragraph headlines. These are often brief summaries in themselves.

If you expect to use a book extensively, read the preface. The author often includes a personal perspective in a preface. A subjective picture of the person behind the words can remove barriers to understanding.

Look for lists of recommended books and articles. If you have difficulty with a concept, sometimes another viewpoint will nail it down for you.

Before you begin reading, take a few moments to reflect upon what you already know about this subject, even if you think you know nothing. This technique prepares your brain to accept the information that follows.

Finally, determine your strategy. Some assignments are appropriately skimmed. Ask yourself how you will be tested on the material. "How will knowing this be useful later? How much time can I afford for this?" Choose a strategy based on these considerations.

You might write the first letters of the muscle reading acrostic in a margin or at the top of your notes and check off the steps you intend to follow. Another idea: Write the muscle reading steps on 3x5 cards and use them for bookmarks.

Remember that you never forget anything. You don't have to make a conscious effort to memorize what you preview to get value from this step. Previewing sets the stage for incoming information by warming up a space in

your mental storage area.

Step 2: Outline
The amount of time you spend on this step will vary according to the kind of reading. For some assignments, fiction and poetry for example, skip this step. For other assignments, a 10-second mental outline is all you need.

With complex material, take time to understand the structure of what you are about to read. If your textbook provides chapter outlines, spend some time studying them.

If a text does not provide an outline, sketch a brief one in the margin of your book or at the beginning of your notes. Then, as you take notes on the chapter, you can fill in your outline.

Section titles and paragraph headlines are useful major and minor topics for your outline. If assigned reading does not contain section titles or headlines, you can outline the material as you read. In this case, outlining actively organizes your thoughts about the assignment.

Outlining can make complex information meaningful. The more detailed the material, the more power this step will add to your reading. It provides a structure for what you read. For techniques on outlining, check out pages 122 and 123 in chapter five, *Notes*.

Step 3: Question
Ask yourself what you want from an assignment before you begin reading. Your preview might suggest some questions. Imagine the author is in the room with you. What would you ask her? How can she help you to get what you want from your education? Create a dialogue. Begin your active participation in the book before you start to read.

Write down a list of questions. Be

tough. Demand your money's worth from your textbooks. If you do not understand a concept, write down specific questions about it. The more detailed your questions, the more powerful you will find this technique. Knowledge is born of questions.

If a reading assignment seems irrelevant, sit back for a minute and think about what it is you want from your time in school. Check to see if your education will be complete without this piece of the puzzle.

Learning to ask effective questions takes practice. Another useful technique is to turn chapter headings and section titles into questions. For example, if a subtitle is "Transference and Suggestion" you can ask yourself, "What are transference and suggestion?" If you know more about the subject, you might ask, "How does transference relate to the psychology of suggestion?" Make up a quiz as if you were teaching this subject to your classmates.

Make the questions playful or creative; enjoy the technique. You don't need to get an answer to every question you ask. The point of making up questions is to stimulate your interest and mental activity. Don't feel discouraged if your questions are not answered by the assignment. Take your unanswered questions to class where they can be springboards for class discussion.

The questions you formulate will help you stay awake through complicated reading. (At the end of a hard day, you may need all the help you can get.) Boredom and fatigue tend to disappear when you work to answer a question, especially one that means something to you.

When you do find an answer to one of your questions, expect to feel a burst of energy. This burst may be small or large, depending on how important the question is. Whatever boost you get will reinforce the process and help you stay alert. If you answer a series of questions and generate new ones in the process, you may feel less tired than when you began.

You may often spend considerable time on phase one before you start the actual reading. It's worth it. The first phase is critical to reading comprehension and will save you time in the long run.

Phase two

Step 4: Read

At last! You have previewed the assignment, organized it in your mind, and formulated questions. Now you are ready to begin reading.

Be conscious of where you are and what you are doing. Practice Power

Journal entry #29

Discovery statement

Check off the muscle reading techniques you already use.

	Preview	Outline	Question	Read	Underline	Answer	Recite	Review	Review again
Always									
Often									
Sometimes									
Seldom									
Never									

process #2: *Be here now.* When you notice your attention wandering, gently bring it back to the present.

One way to stay in the here and now is to make tick marks on scrap paper whenever you notice your attention flagging. Expect many tick marks at first. In fact, the more marks you make in the beginning, the greater the resulting benefit. The marks actually signify your attentiveness, so don't be discouraged by lots of marks. Most students notice that as they pay attention to their attention, the number of tick marks decreases.

If a personal problem or something else is interfering with your concentration, try this idea. Write down the problem along with a commitment to a future course of action. You may wish to follow the seven guidelines for intention statements listed on page 18. Getting the problem down on paper, with a commitment to take action, can free your mind for the present task.

Another way to focus is to schedule breaks. Don't force yourself through reading marathons. Set a reasonable goal for reading, then reward yourself with an enjoyable activity for five to ten minutes every hour. With practice, some students find they can read up to two hours without a break. It's easy, however, to fool yourself about the quality of your reading. Just moving your eyes across a page doesn't make it.

For difficult reading, set shorter goals. Tell yourself that you are going to read for a half hour, then break. Most students find that shorter periods of reading distributed throughout the day and week are more effective than long sessions.

Reading textbooks requires energy. One study revealed that corporation presidents usually wear out the front of their chairs first. We suggest you approach your reading assignment like the company president. Sit up. Keep your spine straight. Don't read in bed, except for fun.

There are a number of ways you can approach the actual reading.

One way is to visualize the material as you read. Form mental pictures of the concepts as they are presented. If you read that a voucher system can help control cash disbursements, picture a voucher handing out dollar bills. Use the visualization techniques presented in chapter three, *Memory*.

You can read out loud. Get the sound of a concept right away. Some of us remember better and understand more quickly by hearing the idea.

A third way is to get the feel of a subject, literally. Imagine what it would be like if you could reach out and touch a concept. Ask yourself how it would feel. For example, let's say you are reading about a micro-organism, a paramecium, in a biology text. Imagine what it would feel like to run your finger around the long, cigar-shaped body of the animal. Imagine feeling the large fold of its gullet on one side, and feel the hairy little cilia as they wiggle in your hand.

Finally, watch for answers to your questions as you read. Review your questions if you get stuck or bored. Stop from time to time to ask new questions based more directly on what you've just read. Talk to the author. Be involved.

Step 5: Underline

Deface your books. Use them up. Keeping them clean and neat will not contribute to your learning from them. Have fun writing and coloring in them. Indulge yourself as you never could with your parent's books.

The purpose of underlining and making other marks in a text is to create signals for reviewing. Underlining can save lots of time when you study for tests.

A secondary benefit of underlining is that when you read with a pen in your hand, you are involving another mode of perception, your kinesthetic (touch and motion) sense. Being physical with your books can help build strong neural traces in your memory.

Do not underline as you read. Wait until you have completed a section or concept to make sure you know what is important. Then underline. Sometimes stopping after each paragraph works best. In some cases you will want to wait until you have read a larger section before deciding what to underline.

Buy a colored highlighter for underlining. Use a pen only for making marginal notes and circling important sections. Underlining with a pen doesn't work very well. You can end up making the important parts harder to read than the rest of the book. With highlighters you needn't worry about making the text illegible.

Do not underline too much of the text or the purpose is lost. Underlining less than 10% allows more effective review of most material.

Write in the margins of your texts. Write summary statements and questions. Mark passages that you don't understand. If you find a list or series of elements in a paragraph, you can circle and number them.

A sales pitch for owning and keeping your textbooks might sound something like this:

Yes, my friends, textbooks are expensive and money is tight. However, the cost of your textbooks, when compared to the real value of education, is ridiculously small. College graduates earn a lifetime average of $250,000 more than their less educated friends. So put your economics in perspective and do the smart thing. Start with a clean textbook and make it yours! Use it for everything it's worth!

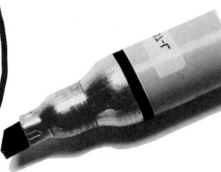

Exercise #16
It's hard to know
what's going on . . .

. . . until you have
the big picture

Read the following paragraph and then summarize it in one sentence.

"With hocked gems financing him, our hero bravely defied all scornful laughter that tried to prevent his scheme. 'Your eyes deceive.' 'It is like an egg, not a table.' Now three sturdy sisters sought truth. Forging along, sometimes through calm vastness, yet more often over turbulent peaks and valleys, days become weeks as many doubters spread fearful rumors about the edge. At last, from nowhere, winged creatures appeared, signifying momentous success."

Summarize the previous paragraph now.

Most people have difficulty knowing what in the world the previous paragraph was about. If it was part of a reading assignment you had previewed, and noticed it was about Christopher Columbus, then it would have made more sense. Read it again while thinking about that famous world traveler.

Step 6: Answer

This step is simple. As you read, get the answers to your questions and write them down. Fill your outline. Write down new questions and note when you don't get the answers you wanted to find. Use these notes to ask questions in class, or you can see your instructor personally.

When you read, create an image of yourself as a person in search of the answers. You are a detective, watching for every clue, sitting erect in your straight-back chair, alert as a Zen master, curious as Sherlock Holmes, demanding that your textbook give you what you want: the answers.

Phase three

Step 7: Recite

This is similar to the suggestion in the memory chapter. Talk to yourself. When you finish reading an assignment, make a speech about it.

One way to get yourself to recite is to go over your reading and look at each underlined point. Note what you marked, then put the book down, and

recite as much as you can about that particular point.

For an even greater effect, do this in front of a mirror. It's not easy, and the benefits can be enormous, particularly at exam time.

Another good technique is to find a friend or group of friends and practice teaching each other what you have learned. There is a secret buried in this suggestion. That secret is: Have someone else do the work. Your instructors might not appreciate this suggestion, but it can be a salvation when you are pressed for time. Find a friend you trust and split up the reading assignment. Then, each of you can teach half the assignment to the other. One of the best ways to learn anything is to teach someone else. (Warning: You will be far better versed in the part you read and taught.) Talk about what you read whenever you can.

Step 8: Review

Plan your first review within 24 hours of reading the material. Sound the trumpets, this is critical: A review within 24 hours can save you hours

Make your textbook a movie

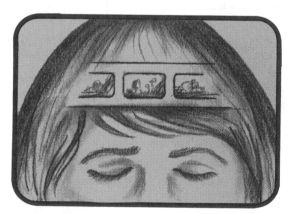

Film makers, television directors, and the people who produce commercials use storyboards like this to plan scenes. Using a storyboard helps them picture each scene.

When reading a text, you can mentally construct your own storyboard or you can draw one. The benefit of this technique lies in adding action to a dry concept.

Suppose, for example, that you are studying the function of market analysis. You read that market research is a market analysis function

performed to determine the need for a product or service. This concept may be important, but the screenplay isn't ready for the Academy Awards.

later on. Review within one day. If you read it on Wednesday, review it on Thursday.

During this process, look over your notes and clear up anything you don't understand. Recite some of the main points again.

In a sense, you will be learning some of the material over again during this review. At first, you might get discouraged by how much you think you forgot from the previous day. Don't worry. Notice how quickly you pick up the material the second time. One of the characteristics of memory is that even when something cannot be recalled, if it has been learned once, the relearning process is much quicker. And relearning wears a deeper path into your memory.

This review period need not be time-consuming. You might spend as little as fifteen minutes reviewing a two-hour reading assignment. That time will save you hours when you study for exams.

Step 9: Review again

The final review step is the weekly and monthly review. This step can be very short—perhaps only four or five minutes per assignment. Simply go over your notes. Read the highlighted parts of your text. Recite one or two of the more complicated points.

The purpose of these review periods is to make the path in your memory forest more visible. You can accomplish these short reviews anytime, anywhere, if you are prepared. Take your text to the dentist's office, and if you don't have time to read a whole assignment, review last week's assignment or the previous week's assignment. Conduct a five-minute review when you are waiting for a bus, for your socks to dry, or for water to boil.

Three-by-five cards work well for review. Write ideas, formulas, concepts, and facts on cards and carry them with you. These short review periods can be effortless and fun.

Sometimes longer review periods are appropriate. For example, if you found an assignment difficult, consider rereading it. Start over as if you had never seen the material. Sometimes a second reading will provide you with

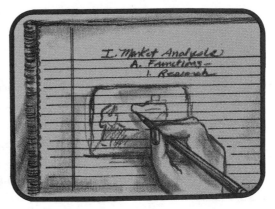

Add some drama. Your storyboard might picture an ice cream salesman walking up and down Main Street asking people if they would buy a new flavor of ice cream called tomato cashew.

Sometimes a short, mental visualization works. If you are stuck, or if you want to ensure that you remember a complex idea, draw boxes in your notes like the storybook panels on this page and create your own movie.

surprising insights. Your previous experience acts as a platform from which you can see aspects that didn't appear the first time through.

Schedule some review periods well in advance. You might set aside one hour on a Saturday or a Sunday to review several subjects. Keep your reviews short and do them often. You will notice a payoff during exams.

Finally, take some time to reflect on what you read. As you walk to and from class, in your discussions with other students, or before you go to bed at night, turn over new ideas in your mind. Take time to play with them. Develop a habit of regular review.

Journal entry #30

Discovery statement

Now that you have read about muscle reading, review your assessment of your reading skills in the discovery guide in chapter one, *First Step.* Do you still think that evaluation was accurate? What new insights have you had about the way you read textbooks? Are you a more effective reader than you thought? Less effective? Record observations here.

_____

_____

_____

_____

_____

_____

_____

_____

_____

_____

_____

_____

_____

_____

_____

_____

_____

_____

Exercise #17

Relax with black

Eye strain is the result of continuous stress. You can use this exercise to take a break from your reading.

1. **Sit on a chair or lie down** and take a few moments to breathe deeply.

2. **Close your eyes**, place your palms over your eyes, and visualize a perfect field of black.

3. **Continue to be aware** of the blackness for two or three minutes while you breathe deeply.

4. **Now remove your hands** from your eyes and open your eyes slowly.

5. **Relax for a minute**, then continue reading.

Exercise #18

Make it a habit

Changing our reading style is as complicated as changing how we tie our shoes. We've been doing both since we started school.

This chapter suggests a significant change in how you read. This exercise can help that change become automatic. During the next week, fill out the assignment section of this page, listing pages and book titles that you intend to read within a week or two. As you read each of those assignments, check off the muscle reading techniques as you apply them. By the time you have used this technique ten times, you'll have a new habit.

Assignment: Pages ____ to ____ in book ____ actually completed / to be completed

Preview

Outline

Question

Read

Underline

Answer

Recite

Review

Review again

Reading Fast

A saccade (pronounced sack-Aid) is a sharp jerk on the reins of a horse—one violent pull to stop the animal quickly. The movements of your eyes when you read are also called saccades for their stop-and-start nature; this resembles a horse being pulled up short every few feet. You can observe these movements by watching a friend read.

Although we experience the illusion that we read by continuously scanning each line, our eyes really take in groups of words, usually about three at a time. Between every saccade is a fixation, a time when the eye stops. More than 90% of reading time is consumed by these fixations. The third kind of movement the eye makes is regression. You re-read words. Ineffective readers and beginning readers have many regressions.

There are two ways to increase your reading speed. Discover which one works best for you. First, you can reduce regressions by improving concentration and/or by raising your awareness of the regressions themselves.

To increase awareness, read with a 3x5 card in one hand, and use the card to cover words and lines you have read. You will soon notice how often you have to stop and move the card back. Don't be discouraged if at first you have to stop often. Be aware of it and you'll naturally begin to regress less frequently.

To improve concentration, take extra time on step 3 of muscle reading where you create questions that have meaning for you. Then actively search for answers as you read.

Second, move your eyes faster. Your eyes can move faster if, instead of taking in three words per fixation, they take in, say, six. Do this by following your fingers as you read. The faster your finger moves, the faster your eyes move. You can also use a pen, pencil, or 3x5 card as a guide.

MUMPSIMUS

Beware of the dread disease, mumpsimus. Mumpsimus is dangerous. It has caused the downfall of more than one dictator, more than one nation, and countless individuals. Mumpsimus is as old as mankind.

According to Webster's Dictionary, mumpsimus is an error obstinately clung to. The word comes from the story of an old priest who, for thirty years, had conducted services using the word *mumpsimus* as a substitute for the correct Latin word *sumpsimus*. One day, when his error was finally pointed out to him, he replied, "I will not change my old *mumpsimus* for your new *sumpsimus*." Mumpsimus is blind adherence to a principle or concept. It's a mistake we continue to repeat, even after we know it's a mistake.

In other words, if you have been shown that a drug is harmful, that it can cause pain or illness, and yet continue to use that drug, then you have a case of mumpsimus.

Another example of mumpsimus is the student who reads the techniques in this chapter, finds the logic behind them solid, recognizes their value, and yet continues to use her old methods. That's the danger of mumpsimus. The afflicted student knows the old concepts haven't worked very well, yet continues to act as if they did.

Mumpsimus is nothing to feel guilty about; it's just a disease.

WHEN READING IS TOUGH

Sometimes ordinary methods are not enough. You can use the following techniques to drain the swamp when you are up to your neck trying to understand conceptual alligators. When a textbook is unclear, use these suggestions:

1. *Read it again, Sam.* This is not always a waste of time, especially with highly technical writing as found in the sciences. If you read an assignment and are completely lost, do not despair. Admit your confusion.

    After reading, leave it alone. Sleep on it. Your mind will work on those concepts while you rest or play.

    When you return to the assignment, regard it with fresh eyes.

2. *Look for essential words.* If you are stuck on a paragraph, mentally cross out all the adjectives and adverbs, and read the sentence without them. Find the important words. These will usually be verbs and nouns.

3. *Hold a mini-review.* Stop at the end of each paragraph and recite, in your own words, what you have read. Or write a short summary. You can write these in the margin of your text.

4. *Read it aloud.* Make some noise. This slows you down, but speed isn't everything. Read a passage aloud several times, each time using a different inflection, emphasizing a different part of the sentence. Be creative. Imagine that you are the author talking.

5. *Use your instructor.* Admit when you are absolutely stuck and make an appointment with your instructor. Most teachers welcome the opportunity to work individually with students. Be specific about your confusion. Point out the paragraph that you found toughest to understand.

6. *Find a tutor.* Many schools provide free tutoring services. Often a tutor is a student who was in your position not long ago. Tutors can give you a new perspective on a problem. If tutoring services are not provided by your school, other students who have completed the course can assist you.

7. *Use an alternate text.* Find one in the library. Sometimes the same concept can be understood better if you find it expressed another way. Even children's books, especially

children's encyclopedias, provide useful overviews of baffling subjects.

8. *Pretend you understand, then explain it.* We often understand more than we think we do. To get in touch with this ability, pretend it's clear as a bell and explain it to yourself. Write your explanation and be amazed at what you know.

9. *Stand up.* Changing positions periodically can combat fatigue. Try standing when you read, especially if you get stuck on a tough passage and decide to read it aloud. Sometimes hearing the words makes them more understandable, and pacing back and forth can help to focus concentration.

For some people, getting up on their feet works wonders.

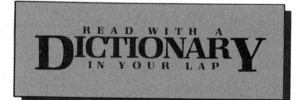

Malcolm X demonstrated one way to improve vocabulary. While in prison, he read and copied the entire dictionary. Few of us have such single-minded sense of purpose with regard to vocabulary building. Yet we all share the ability and desire to learn. You can use that natural ability to strengthen your vocabulary by concentrating on words that interest you.

When you are reading, look up all unfamiliar words. Pay special attention to words that arouse your curiosity.

You can regularly use two kinds of dictionaries: the desk dictionary and the unabridged dictionary. A desk dictionary is the one you use several times a day, the one you own. Keep this book within reach (maybe in your lap) so that you can look up every

unfamiliar word as you read. You can find the large unabridged dictionary in the library. It provides more complete information on words, definitions not included in your desk dictionary, and a history of each word.

Construct a word stack

When you find unfamiliar words in your reading, write them down. Put each one on a separate 3x5 card. Also, copy below the word the sentence where it occurred. Now, look up the word. Add the diacritical marks (the symbols which tell you how to pronounce the word.) Write the definition on the back of the 3x5 card.

When you have accumulated a stack of these cards, you can take them to the unabridged dictionary. Look up the words to expand your definitions and find the history behind the word. As you find related words in the dictionary, add them to your stack.

These cards become another portable study aid which you can review in your spare moments.

When your dictionary is across town

When you are listening to a lecture and find an unfamiliar word, or when you are reading on the bus and run across a word you don't know, you can still build your word stack. Pull out a 3x5 card and write down the word and its sentence. Later you can look up the word and put the definition on the back of the card.

Scenario #1: You go to accounting class, pay attention, take good notes, and receive an assignment. After the lecture, you go to the student center and put a roll of quarters into Star Invaders from the Monkey Planet. Your score is 26,789,988—not bad, but short of your record—and you quit for dinner. After dinner you watch television for an hour, start feeling guilty, and finally you read your accounting assignment. You complete the assignment and go to bed. You have done well.

Scenario #2: You go to accounting class, pay attention, take good notes, and receive an assignment. After class you go straight to the library. With the sound of your instructor's voice still echoing in your head, you open your book. The neurons in your brain labeled "accounting" are already warmed up, so you can start reading immediately. You study until dinner, eat, then head to the student center with your roll of quarters. This time, as you blast away at apes from space, your brain is simmering with accounting. You are also enjoying Star Invaders from the Monkey Planet more because accounting isn't hanging over your head. You are so "here now" that you wipe out three entire Monkey Planets and score 36,879,999—a personal best. To end a perfect day, you conduct a five-minute review of your accounting before you go to bed.

By reading your assignment immediately, you have saved yourself some review time. It takes just as much energy to read an assignment earlier as it does later. Accounting class made your reading session more powerful, while galactic gorillas provided a relaxing background for some subconscious brain activity. You then capped off your efforts by reinforcing your long-term memory with a quick review.

Amazingly, you did not spend more time studying. The time you saved by beginning your reading assignment right after accounting class more than made up for your five-minute review. Smart cookie.

Notice your pictures and let them go

The brain's job is to manufacture pictures. We use mental pictures to make predictions about the world, and we base much of our behavior on those predictions. When a cook adds chopped onions, mushrooms, and garlic to the spaghetti sauce, he has a picture of how the sauce will taste and measures each ingredient according to that picture.

Pictures are not strictly visual images. Mental pictures are thoughts. They can involve any of the senses. When you buy a record album, you have a picture of how it will sound. When you buy a sweater, you have a picture of how it will feel.

The pictures we make in our heads are survival mechanisms. Without them we couldn't get from one end of town to the other. We couldn't feed or clothe ourselves. Without a picture of a socket, we couldn't screw in a lightbulb.

Pictures can also get in our way. For example, take the case of a student who plans to attend a college she hasn't visited. She chose this school for its strong curriculum and good academic standing, but her brain can't stop there. In her mind, the campus is a Shangri-la, ivy-covered walls, and tree-lined avenues. The professors, she imagines, will be combinations of Johnny Carson and Jane Fonda; her roommate will be the best friend she'll ever have. The cafeteria will be a cozy nook serving

delicate quiche and fragrant teas. She will gather there with fellow students for hours of stimulating, intellectual conversation. The library will have every book, the dorm every luxury.

Then she arrives on a campus which turns out to be four grey buildings downtown, next to the bus station. The first class she attends is taught by an overweight, balding professor who is wearing a purple and orange bird of paradise tie and has a bad case of the sniffles. The cafeteria is a nondescript hall with machine food, and her dorm room is barely large enough to accommodate her roommate's tuba.

Our hypothetical student gets depressed. She begins to think about dropping out of school.

The problem with pictures is that they sometimes prevent us from seeing what is really there. Pictures act as a filter to the rest of the world. The picture our student carried with her prevented her from noticing that the campus is at the heart of a culturally vital city—close to theaters, museums, government offices, clubs, and all kinds of stores. The professor with the weird tie is not only an expert in his field, he is a superior teacher. The school cafeteria is skimpy because it can't compete with the variety of inexpensive restaurants in the area. There may even be hope for a tuba-playing roommate.

Anger and disappointment are often the result of our pictures. We set up expectations of events before they occur. These can then lead to disappointment. Sometimes we don't even realize that we had the expectation.

Next time you discover you are angry, disappointed, or frustrated, look to see which of your pictures aren't being fulfilled.

Often there is disappointment even if the event that you had pictured turns out to be better than you had imagined. For instance, you might have expected the "Philosophy of Logic" class you're taking as a graduation requirement to be hopelessly boring. You get to class and find that the professor has a great sense of humor and relates logic processes to practical examples in your life. Disappointment results partly because you maintained a position (or idea) that philosophy is boring. And now there is a conflict between your position about philosophy and your experience in the class.

What to do

Having pictures is unavoidable. Having these pictures run your life is avoidable. Awareness is the key. The technique for dealing with pictures is so simple, so effortless, that you may be tempted to discount it as silly nonsense.

The way to deal with pictures is to notice them. Be aware of them. Then, in the most gentle manner possible, let them go. Let them drift away as if they were wisps of smoke picked up by a gentle wind.

Pictures are persistent. They come back over and over again. Don't fight them when they return. Notice them again and let them go again. At first, a picture might return repeatedly and

insistently. Pictures are like independent beings. They want to live.

Visualize an expectation as if it were an animal scurrying around in your head. If you can see the picture as a thought independent from you, you will find it easier to let it go. You have separated the thought or the picture from yourself, and so you are not giving up a part of yourself.

If your pictures are interfering with your education, visualize yourself tying them to a brightly colored helium balloon and letting them go. Let them float away again and again.

Barbara Jordan

Excerpt from Barbara Jordan, A Self-Portrait, by Barbara Jordan. Copyright 1978 by Barbara Jordan and Shelby Hearon. Reprinted by permission of Doubleday & Company, Inc.

So I was at Boston University in this new and strange and different world, and it occurred to me that if I was going to succeed at this strange new adventure, I would have to read longer and more thoroughly than my colleagues at law school had to read. I felt that in order to compensate for what I had missed in earlier years, I would have to work harder, and study longer, than anybody else. I still had this feeling that I did not want my colleagues to know what a tough time I was having understanding the concepts, the words, the ideas, the process. I didn't want them to know that. So I did my reading not in the law library, but in a library at the graduate dorm, upstairs where it was very quiet, because apparently nobody else there studied. So I would go there at night after dinner. I would load my books under my arm and go to the library, and I would read until the wee hours of the morning and then go to bed. I didn't get much sleep during those years. I was lucky if I got three or four hours a night, because I had to stay up. I had to. The professors would assign cases for the next day, and these cases had to be read and understood or I would be behind, further behind than I was.

I was always delighted when I would get called upon to recite in class. But the professors did not call on the "ladies" very much. There were certain favored people who always got called on, and then on some rare occasions a professor would come in and would announce: "We're going to have Ladies Day today." And he would call on the ladies. We were just tolerated. We weren't considered really top drawer when it came to the study of law.

At some time in the spring, Bill Gibson, who was dating my new roommate, Norma Walker, organized a black study group, as we blacks had to form our own. This was because we were not invited into any of the other study groups. There were six or seven in our group—Bill, and Issie, and I think Maynard Jackson—and we would just gather and talk it out and hear ourselves do that. One thing I learned was that you had to talk out the issues, the facts, the cases, the decisions, the process. You couldn't just read the cases and study alone in your library as I had been doing; and you couldn't get it all in the classroom. But once you had talked it out in the study group, it flowed

more easily and made a lot more sense . . .

Finally I felt I was really learning things, really going to school. I felt that I was getting educated, whatever that was. I became familiar with the process of thinking. I learned to think things out and reach conclusions and defend what I had said.

In the past I had got along by spouting off. Whether you talked about debates or oratory, you dealt with speechifying. Even in debate it was pretty much canned because you had, in your little three-by-five box, a response for whatever issue might be raised by the opposition. The format was structured so that there was no opportunity for independent thinking. (I really had not had my ideas challenged ever.) But I could no longer orate and let that pass for reasoning. Because there was not any demand for an orator in Boston University Law School. You had to think and read and understand and reason. I had learned at twenty-one that you couldn't just say a thing is so because it might not be so, and somebody brighter, smarter, and more thoughtful would come out and tell you it wasn't so. Then, if you still thought it was, you had to prove it. Well, that was a new thing for me. I cannot, I really cannot describe what that did to my insides and to my head. I thought: I'm being educated finally.

1. Write the initial letters of the muscle reading acronym.

2. In chapter three, the twelve memory techniques were divided into four categories. List those four categories and assign a muscle reading step to each one. Then assign any other techniques you learned in this chapter to a category you think is most appropriate.

3. To be an effective reader, a student must have a good vocabulary and a strong working knowledge of grammar. True or false.

4. List five elements of a textbook you can look for when you preview.

5. One way to focus your attention on a reading assignment is to formulate questions to be answered before you begin reading. Describe three techniques you can use to create effective questions.

6. Describe how recitation is a synergistic study technique.

7. Explain the value of a 24-hour review of reading material.

8. List at least five ways to deal with reading difficult material.

9. What are two ways to increase your reading speed?

10. How did Malcolm X build his vocabulary?

Review Journal entry #27. Did you get what you wanted? If you got exactly what you wanted, just write yes. If you didn't get what you wanted, write what you didn't get. If you got something unexpected, write that too.

Journal entry #31

Discovery statement

If there was something you wanted from this chapter and didn't get, write a strategy you intend to use to get it.

Journal entry #32

Intention statement

There are dozens of suggestions presented in this chapter on how to read most effectively with the least amount of effort and time. Quickly review the chapter and then choose two or three techniques that you will put into practice.

I intend to . . .

Journal entry #33

Intention statement

Describe one or two times in your life when you have been (or still are) afflicted with mumpsimus. Include the payoffs and costs of your behavior in your description.

Journal entry #34

Look back

How do you want to improve your note-taking skills? Do you want to be able to write faster? More clearly? Do you want notes that are easier to review? Write here what you want to get from this chapter.

Journal entry #35

Discovery statement

CHAPTER FIVE
NOTES

Rather than try to gauge your note-taking skill by quantity, think in this way: am I simply doing clerk's work or am I assimilating new knowledge and putting down my own thoughts? To put down your own thoughts you must put down your own words. . . . If the note taken shows signs of having passed through a mind, it is a good test of its relevance and adequacy.

JACQUES BARZUN AND HENRY GRAFF

I did not start out to be an educational heretic, and I was inwardly astonished at the fact that when I tried honestly to review my experience, teaching seemed of such little importance, and learning so vastly important.

CARL ROGERS

In this chapter . . .

Observe, record and review makes the note-taking process flow. There are 21 note-taking techniques to choose from so you can observe more carefully, record more accurately, and review to save hours of study time. **Mind mapping** is a powerful technique to organize notes and create works of art that look more like spider webs rather than structured notes in an outline form.

Take responsibility for boring classes, tests, and irritating people when you apply **Power Process #5, You create it all.**

Learn how to cope **When instructors talk fast.** Experiment with these techniques in the exercise **Television note-taking practice.**

Observe, & record & review:

The note-taking process flows.

Note-taking is a three-part process of observing, recording, and reviewing. In class, the process looks like this: First, you observe an event—most often a statement by the instructor; then you record your observations of that event; finally, you review what you have recorded. What you observe, obviously, determines what you record, which in turn determines what you review.

Less obviously, what you review and how you review it will affect your ability to observe information, because learning is sequential. It is difficult to learn (observe) division unless multiplication is thoroughly understood (reviewed).

Of the three activities in the note-taking process (observing, recording and reviewing), the first and the last are by far the most important. Accurate observation and regular review can turn pages of disorganized chicken scratches into a valuable tool.

Observe

A doctor can save lives by observing suspicious moles. A motorist can save miles of walking by observing the location of a service station prior to her car breaking down. A student can save hours of study time by observing that he can get twice as much done at a particular time of day.

The best scientists are good observers. The best writers are good observers. The best counselors, cooks, policemen, engineers, painters, mechanics, and accountants are good observers. The keen observer is open to every detail, can focus her attention on a minute point, and follow her observations with persistent work. Out of what she observes, she creates new relationships.

In the classroom, you can be a Sherlock Holmes. Sherlock could track a villain by analyzing the wrinkles in his hat. You can track down important information by keenly observing what goes on in a classroom.

To sharpen your classroom observation skills, experiment with the following techniques and continue to use the ones that you find most valuable.

Set the stage

1. Complete outside assignments. Instructors usually assume that students complete assignments, and then construct their lectures accordingly. Nothing is more discouraging (or boring) than sitting through a lecture on the relationship of the Le Chatelier principle to the principle of kinetics if you have never heard of Le Chatelier or kinetics.

The more familiar you are with a subject, the better you can observe what happens in class. You have opened a space in your memory into which you

can fit new details. If the structure already exists in your mind, you can focus all your energy on observation. For example, a knowledgeable football fan will see more of what goes on at a football game than will a person who knows nothing of the game. A seasoned birdwatcher will see more birds than someone who knows nothing about birds.

Open your mind to the subject before you get to class. Complete the reading assignments and work the assigned problems.

2. Bring the right materials. Make sure you have pen, pencil, notebook, and any other materials you will need.

Being unprepared can create enough distraction to take the fine edge off your concentration.

If you are consistently unprepared for class, that may be a message about your intentions concerning the course. Find out if it is. The next time you're in a frantic scramble to borrow pen and paper 37 seconds before class begins, notice the cost. Use the borrowed pen and paper to write yourself a discovery statement about the circumstances surrounding your lack of preparation. Consider your intention to be successful in the class.

3. Sit front and center. Students who get as close as possible to the front and center of the classroom do better on tests, for several reasons. The closer you sit to the lecturer, the harder it is to fall asleep. The closer you sit to the front, the fewer interesting heads there are to watch between you and the instructor. Material on the board is easier to read. The instructor can see you more easily when you have a question. Each time you pick the front-most center chair available, it will be a different chair than you had before. This movement gives a new perspective and freshness to each lecture. By moving around, you are less likely to sit near people you know well, and this can cut down on distracting side conversations. Finally, instructors are usually not trained as actors or performers. While some may be able to project their energy to a large audience, many may not. A professor who sounds boring from the back of the room may sound more interesting if you're closer. Get close to the energy.

4. Conduct a short pre-class review. Arrive early, then put your brain in gear by reviewing your notes from the previous class. Scan your reading assignment. Look at parts you have underlined. Review assigned problems and exercises. Note questions you intend to ask. Depending on the type of material, the mind can take from two or three minutes to ten minutes to truly warm up to a subject. Give yourself a head start.

5. Clarify your intentions. Write a short intention statement about what you plan to get out of the class, your intended level of participation, or the quality of attention you will bring to the subject. Be specific. If you found previous class notes to be inadequate, write down things you intend to do to make your notes from this class more useful.

Be here now in class
1. Accept your wandering mind. Don't fight daydreaming. When you catch yourself with your head in the clouds, look at it as an opportunity to re-focus your attention. Whenever you notice that your attention is wandering from thermodynamics class to beach parties,

let go of the beach. Every time you bring your mind back to the here and now, you strengthen your observer consciousness. Eventually you will increase your ability to stay on task. Trust the process.

Be gentle with yourself about daydreaming. Let each daydreaming episode become opportunity to return to the task.

2. Be with the instructor. In your mind, put yourself right up front with the instructor. Imagine that the lecture is a personal talk with you. Pay attention to the instructor's body language and facial expressions. Look the instructor in the eye. (This is a good reason to sit as close to the front and center of the classroom as you can get.)

3. Notice your environment. When you become aware of yourself daydreaming, bring yourself back to class by paying attention to the temperature in the room, the feel of your chair, or the quality of light in the room. Run your hand along the surface of your desk. Be with that environment.

4. Postpone debate. When you hear something with which you disagree, note your disagreement and let it go. Don't allow your internal dialogue to drown out subsequent material. If your disagreement is persistent and strong, write down the point and move on. Internal debate can prevent you from absorbing new information. It is OK to absorb information you don't believe. Just absorb it with the thought tag, "I don't believe this and my instructor says . . ."

5. Let go of judgments about lecture styles. Instructors have idiosyncrasies—like using the same phrases over and over ("You know," "OK, OK," "Well, my Aunt Clara . . . ," "Six of one, half a dozen of the other"), wearing strange clothes, or talking too softly or too loudly.

Human beings are judgment machines. We evaluate everything, especially other people, automatically. If another person's eyebrows are too close together (or too far apart), if he walks a certain way, or combs his hair a certain way, we instantly make up a story about him. We do this so quickly that the process is usually not a conscious one.

The problem is, these judgments and evaluations filter our perceptions. They screen out information that doesn't fit with our pictures. This process can be deadly during a lecture. It can prevent you from getting what you want from your education.

Don't let your attitude about an instructor's habits or appearance get in the way of your education. You can decrease the power of your judgments if you pay attention to them and let them go.

6. Participate in class activities. Ask questions. Volunteer for demonstrations. Join in class discussions. Be willing to be a fool. When you risk looking foolish, you let go of being self-conscious about saying the wrong thing or asking a dumb question.

7. Relate what is going on in class to your goals. If you are having trouble staying awake in a particular class, at the top of your notes write how that class relates to a specific goal. Write the reward or payoff for reaching that goal.

Watch for clues

1. Be alert to repetition. When an instructor repeats a phrase or idea, make a note of it. Repetition is a signal that the instructor thinks the information is important.

2. Listen for introductory, concluding and transition words and phrases like "the following three factors . . . ," "in conclusion . . . ," "the most important consideration . . . ," "in addition to . . . ," and "on the other hand . . . ." These phrases signal relationships, definitions, new subjects, conclusions, cause and effect, and examples. In other words, they reveal the structure of the lecture. You can use these phrases to organize your notes.

Think about the way you have conducted reviews of your notes in the past. Answer the following questions by writing "always," "often," "sometimes," "seldom," or "never" after the question.

Journal entry #36

Discovery statement

I review my notes immediately after class. *often*

I conduct weekly reviews of my notes. *often*

I make summary sheets of my notes. *sometimes*

I edit my notes within 24 hours. *sometimes*

Before class, I conduct a brief review of the notes I took in the previous class. *always*

3. *Watch the board.* If an instructor takes time to write something down, consider that another signal that the material is important. Copy all diagrams and drawings, equations, names, places, dates, statistics, and definitions.

4. *Watch the instructor's eyes.* If an instructor glances at her notes and then makes a point, it is probably a signal that the information is especially important. Anything she brought to a lecture in note form is likely to come up later as a test question.

5. *Don't ignore obvious clues.* Instructors will often tell students pointblank that certain information is likely to appear on an exam. Make stars in your notes beside this kind of information. Instructors are not trying to hide what's important.

6. *Notice the instructor's interest level.* If the instructor is excited about something, that something is likely to appear on any exam the instructor creates. Pay attention if he seems more animated or alive than usual.

Record

The format and structure of your notes are more important than writing speed or pretty handwriting. The following techniques can improve the effectiveness of your notes.

1. Use the Cornell format of note-taking. On each page of your notes, draw a vertical line, top to bottom, 1½ inches from the left edge of the paper. Write your notes to the right of the line. Reserve the area to the left of the line for key word clues and sample questions. Fill in the left-hand column when you review your notes.

Metal Conductive	Hard, shiny, malleable (roll into sheets), ductile (pulled into wires). Conducts electric current & heat. 3 or fewer electrons in outer level so good conductors because electrons can move thru.
Metallic Bond	Outer electrons distributed as common electric cloud. Electrons shared equally by all ions which explains properties (conductive, malleable, ductile) → ions slide by each other & can be displaced w/o shattering.
Alkali Metals	Soft metals. Most reactive — kept under oil so won't react directly w/oxygen or H_2O. Forms compound by ionic bonding. Can identify alkalis by flame test. Electrons gain energy when heated. When cooling, lose energy as light. Ex: Ca = red, Cu = green, K = blue

2. Create mind maps. This system can be used in conjunction with the Cornell system, although in some circumstances you might want to use mind maps exclusively.

Mind mapping involves starting in the middle of the page instead of at the top. Write the main subject on a line in the center of the page. Record points subordinate to the main topic on lines branching out from the central subject, as shown in the illustration on page 128. In turn, each subordinate point can have its own branches. Mind maps spread out from the center of the page, and each mind map takes on its own shape as it develops.

At the center of a mind map might be the general subject of the lecture, or it could be a key word relating to the subject of the lecture.

Mind maps present a picture of the whole subject and show immediately how each separate point is related to the main point. By connecting various branches with arrows or enclosing them in circles or boxes, you can illustrate relationships quickly and accurately. Drawings, diagrams, or references to other mind maps may also be included.

Mind maps can be used in conjunction with Cornell format notes in a number of ways. You can divide your note paper in half, reserving one half for mind maps and the other for information more suited to the traditional paragraph method (equations, long explanations, word-for-word definitions). You can also incorporate a mind map into your paragraph-style notes wherever you feel one is appropriate.

Another way to use mind maps is to abandon the Cornell format, draw a line down the center of the page, and use the left-hand side for mind mapping and the right-hand side for more linear information (lists, graphs, paragraphs).

> Bio I
> 9/27
>
> I. Bones - living organs, 206 in body, 18% of weight
>   A. Marrow - in center of bones. Contains nerves + blood vessels
>   1. Red
>   a. in flat bones (ribs) + ends of long bones
>   b. produces red blood cells in adults
>   2. Yellow - mostly flat tissue
>   a. in center of long bones
>   b. might make red blood cells if great blood loss or w/ certain blood diseases
>   B. Haversian canals - carry blood thru bones (for oxygen, food + waste)
>   C. Periostium - protective membrane covers bone
>   D. Composed of:
>   1. Minerals, organic matter, H_2O
>   a. Calcium + phosphorus present as calcium phosphate $(Ca_3(PO_4)_3)$ + calcium carbonate $(CaCO_3)$
>   b. Hardness depends on how much mineral
>   2. Embryo - skeleton is cartilage Ossification - formation of bone tissue

3. Write notes in outline form. You can use a standard Roman numeral outline or a more free-form indented outline to organize the information in a lecture. The outline form graphically demonstrates major points and supporting ideas that are presented in a

lecture. The main advantage to taking notes in outline form is that it can totally occupy your attention. You are organizing information that at times is presented in a disorganized way.

4. Write notes in paragraphs. When it is difficult to follow the organization of a lecture or to put information into outline form, create a series of informal paragraphs. These paragraphs will contain few complete sentences. Reserve complete sentences for precise definitions, direct quotes, and important points that the instructor emphasizes by repetition or other signals (such as, "This is an important point"). For other material, use key words and phrases, as explained in this section.

During your review process, you can organize your notes. During class, write related thoughts in a paragraph and leave a space when the lecturer moves to another point.

5. Use key words. An easy way to sort out all the extraneous material from the important points is to take notes using key words.

Key words (or phrases) are those words which contain the essence of communication. They include technical terms, names, numbers, equations, and words of degree (most, least, faster, slower).

Key words are laden with associations; they call forth images of other words. Key words trigger your memory. They are powerful review tools precisely because they evoke associations with other facts and ideas. One key word can initiate the recall of a whole cluster of ideas. A few key words can form a chain from which you can reconstruct an entire lecture.

In order to see how key words work, take yourself to an imaginary

Exercise #19

Television note-taking practice

You can use evening news broadcasts to practice listening for key words, writing quickly, focusing your attention, and reviewing.

Next time you watch the news, do it with pen and paper. During the commercials, review and revise your notes. At the end of the broadcast, spend five minutes reviewing your notes. Create a mind map of a few news stories, then recreate the news of the day for a friend.

This exercise will help you develop an ear for key words. Since you can't ask questions or ask the speaker to slow down, you train yourself to stay totally in the moment. If you get behind, you learn not to panic, but to leave a space and get back into the rest of the broadcast.

Don't be discouraged if you don't get much the first time around. Do this exercise several times. Observe how your brain works.

You can also ask a friend to do the same exercise. Compare notes the next day.

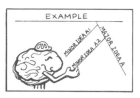

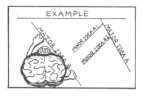

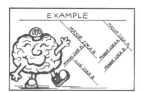

classroom. You are now in the middle of an anatomy lecture. Picture what the room looks like, what it feels like, how it smells. You hear the instructor say:

OK, what happens when we look directly over our heads and see a piano falling out of the sky? How do we take that signal and translate it into the action of getting out of the way? The first thing that happens is that a stimulus is generated in the neurons—receptor neurons—of the eye. Light reflected from the piano reaches our eyes. In other words, we see the piano. The receptor neurons in the eye transmit that sensory signal, the sight of the piano, to the body's nervous system. That's all they can do, pass on information. So, we've got a sensory signal coming into the nervous system. But the neurons that initiate movement in our legs are effector neurons. The information from the sensory neurons must be transmitted to effector neurons or we will get squashed by the piano. There must be some kind of interconnection between receptor and effector neurons. What happens between the two? What is the connection?

Key words you might note in this example include "stimulus," "generated," "receptor neurons," "transmit," "sensory signals," "nervous system," "effector neurons," and "connection." Out of 148 words, you choose twelve key words.

Note the last key word, "connection." This word is part of the instructor's question, which leads to the

next point in the lecture. Be alert for questions like this. They can help you organize your notes, and they are often clues for test questions.

Your notes, with a minimum number of connecting words, might look like this:

> Stimulus (piano) generated in receptor neurons (eye).
> Sensory signals transmitted by nervous system to effector neurons (legs).
> What connects receptor to effector?

6. Use pictures and diagrams. Make relationships visual. Copy all diagrams from the board and also invent your own.

The picture of a piano falling on someone who is looking up, for example, might be used to demonstrate the relationship of receptor neurons to effector neurons. That picture implies that some action must be taken. The sight of the piano must be translated into a motor response. By connecting the explanation of the process with the unusual picture of the piano falling, you can link the elements of the process together.

7. *Copy material from the board.* Record all formulas, diagrams, and problems. Copy dates, numbers, names, places, and other facts. If it's on the board, put it in your notes.

8. *Use a three-ring binder.* Three-ring binders have several advantages over other kinds of notebooks. First, pages can be removed and spread out when you review. This way you can get the whole picture of a lecture. Second, the three-ring binder format will easily allow you to insert handouts right into your notes. Third, you can insert your own out-of-class notes in the correct order. You can make additions, corrections, and revisions easily.

9. *Use only one side of a piece of paper.* When you use one side of a page, you can review and organize all your notes by spreading them out side by side. Most students find the benefit well worth the cost of paper.

10. *Use 3x5 cards.* As an alternative to notebook paper, use 3x5 cards to take lecture notes (copy each new concept on a separate 3x5 card). Later these cards can be organized in an outline form, and they can be used as pocket flash cards.

11. *Keep your own thoughts separate.* For the most part, avoid making editorial comments in your lecture notes. The danger is that when you return to your notes, you may mistake your own idea for that of the instructor. If you must make a comment—either a question to be asked later or a strong disagreement—clearly label it as your own.

12. *Use a "lost" signal.* No matter how attentive and alert you are, sooner or later you will get lost and confused in a lecture. If it is inappropriate to ask a question, record in your notes that you were lost. Invent your own signal for this, like a circled question mark. Later, when you review, you will know you missed something. Then, you can call your instructor or ask to see a fellow student's notes. As long as you are honest with yourself when you don't understand, you can stay on top of the course.

13. *Label, number, and date all notes.* Record the name of the class and the date on all your notes and number the pages. Sometimes the sequence of material in a lecture is important. Write your name and phone number in each notebook. Class notes become more and more valuable as a term proceeds.

14. *Use standard abbreviations.* Be consistent with your abbreviations. If you make up your own abbreviations or symbols, write a key explaining them in your notes.

Avoid vague abbreviations. When you use an abbreviation like "comm." for, say, "committee", you run the risk of not being able to remember whether you meant committee, commission, common, commit, community, communicate, or communist.

15. Use white space. White space is simply that—space on the page where there is no writing.

Notes tightly crammed into every corner of the page are hard to read and difficult to use for review. Give your eyes a break by leaving plenty of space.

Later, when you review, you can use the white space in your notes to clarify points, write questions, or add other material. Often, instructors return to material covered earlier in the lecture. If you have left adequate space, you can add information.

Advertising designers know the value of white space. It is their business to get you to read ad copy. Next time you read a magazine, notice how white space is used in advertisements. See which ones are easiest to read. Chances are those ads use plenty of white space.

16. Avoid tape recorders. In most cases, tape recorders hinder rather than help students. There is a strong temptation to relax mentally when you tape a lecture. After all, whatever you miss you can listen to again. The problem is it takes too much time to listen to a lecture a second time, and you might not understand the lecture the second time. Tape recorders don't answer questions.

17. Use graphic signals. Brackets, parentheses, circles, and squares can be used to group information that belongs together.

Use stars, arrows, and underlines to indicate important points. Flag the most important points with double stars, double arrows, or double underlines.

Use arrows and connecting lines to link related groups, to show causation, and to replace words like "leads to," "becomes," "produces."

Use equal signs and greater- and less-than signs to indicate compared quantities.

Use question marks for their obvious purpose. Use double question marks to signal tough questions or especially confusing points.

[ ], ( ), ○, □ = info that belongs together

*, ↘, = = important

**, ↘↘, ≡, !!! = extra important

> = greater than   < = less than

= = equal to

⟶ = leads to, becomes
Ex: school → job → money

? = huh?, lost

?? = big trouble, clear up immediately

18. Use complete sentences when material is important. Sometimes key words aren't enough. When an instructor repeats a sentence using exactly the same words, she might be sending you a signal. Technical definitions are often worded precisely because even a slightly different word will render the definition useless.

Review

Think of reviewing as an integral part of note-taking rather than an added task. In order for information to be useful, it needs to be available to your recall.

1. Review within 24 hours. This suggestion can save you hours. It's critical. Short-term memory decays fast. A quick review can save that

Journal entry #37

Discovery statement

For this journal entry, you will need a few pages of your old notes—the older the better. If possible, use notes from last year. If you have some notes you took several years ago, they will work perfectly.

Look over those notes as if you were to be tested on them tomorrow. Then, in the space provided here, write down a one-paragraph summary of what those notes tell you today.

Next, put on your critic's hat and evaluate your notes. And remember, critics look for the positive as well as the negative. Write down what works in your notes and what doesn't. Be specific about strengths and weaknesses of your old note-taking techniques.

information. The sooner you review your notes the better. This review can be as short as ten minutes or less

Think of the day's unreviewed notes as leaky faucets, constantly dripping, losing precious information until you shut them off with a quick review.

This system can salvage even sloppy and garbled notes. If a lecture has been difficult, get to those notes within an hour. You will be amazed at what you can remember and understand, and your review will put the information in long-term memory. Remember, 24 hours after learning, most students are unable to recall even 20% of the content—*unless they have reviewed the material.*

2. Edit notes. During your first review, fix words that are illegible. Write out abbreviated words that might be unclear to you later. Go over your notes and make sure that you can read everything. Check to see that your notes are labeled and the pages are numbered.

3. Fill in key words in left-hand column. This task is important if you are to gain the full benefit from using the Cornell format. Using the key word principles described earlier in this chapter, go through your notes and write key words or phrases in the left-hand column. (See sample notes on page 122.)

These key words will speed the review process later. Also, when you read your notes and focus on extracting key concepts, your understanding of the lecture is further reinforced.

4. Organize your notes with graphic signals. During your immediate review, add arrows, brackets, and other signals that aid the organization of your notes.

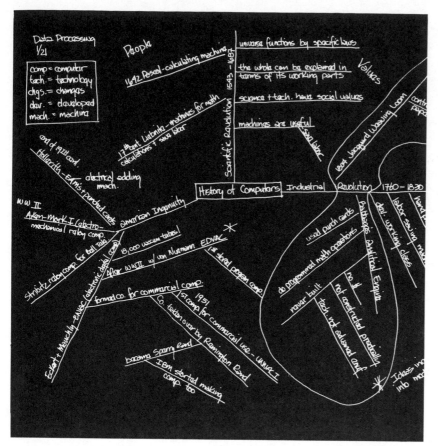

Circle related concepts. Fill out diagrams. Illustrate important points.

5. Conduct short weekly review periods. Once a week, review all your notes again. This will be a second refinement of the information and will assist recall. The review sessions don't need to take a lot of time. Even a 20-minute weekly review period is valuable.

6. Use your key words as cues to recite. With a blank sheet of paper, cover your notes, leaving only the key words in the left-hand margin showing. Take each key word in order and recite as much as you can about the point. Then, uncover your notes and look for important points you missed.

7. Create "mind map" summaries. Mind mapping is an excellent way to make summary sheets.

Start with the main subject to be reviewed. Write down the topic in the center of a page; then, on lines branching out from the starting point, write everything you can think of concerning that subject. Use key words. Write each word on a line and write related words on lines branching out from the original. Continue this process until you can't think of anything else to write.

When you are sure you have exhausted your ability to recall, look at your original notes and fill in anything you missed. This system is fun to use, it's quick, and it gives your brain a hook on which to fasten the material.

8. Conduct pre-class reviews. We return to the first step of observation. This process is part of setting the stage for clear observation. Link information from each lecture to the preceding lecture.

Exercise #20

The in-class oxygenator

When you become sleepy in class, the problem might be lack of oxygen. You can run through the following process in 30 seconds.

1. Straighten your spine. Put both feet on the floor, uncross your arms and legs, sit up straight, and hold your head up straight.

2. Tense all muscles. Take a deep breath and while you're holding it, tense the muscles in your body. Start with the muscles in your feet, then the legs, thighs, stomach, chest, shoulders, neck, jaw, forehead, arms, and hands. Hold these tense muscles for the count of five and then relax.

3. Breathe deeply three times. Inhale slowly and deeply, breathing into your belly as well as your chest. Pause momentarily at the top of the breath and then exhale completely. When you have exhaled as much as your can, force out more air by contracting the muscles of your stomach. Do this breathing three times.

4. Repeat step #2. You've now activated all of your muscles and filled your body with oxygen. You are ready to return your attention to the task at hand.

Practice this exercise now by completing it twice. Then make a mental note so that next time you're sleepy in class, or when you're studying, you can use this exercise. With a little practice, it can be very subtle and your instructor and classmates won't even notice you're doing it.

Taking notes on reading

Taking notes from reading requires the same skills that apply to class notes: observation, recording, and review. Almost all techniques in this chapter can be applied to notes on reading. Reading also requires some special considerations.

There are two kinds of notes on reading: review notes and research notes.

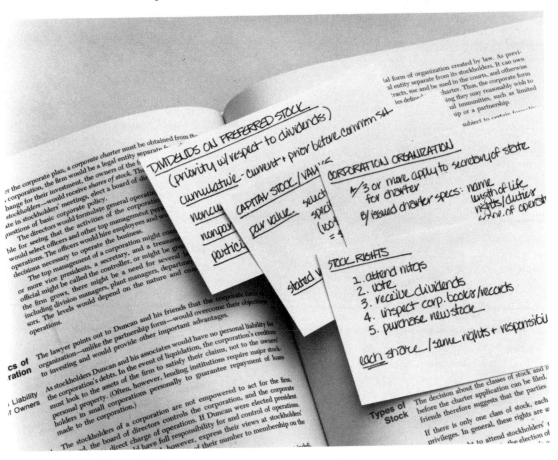

Review notes

Review notes will look like the ones you take in class—a combination of the Cornell format and mind mapping. You can't underline or make marginal notes in library books, so you need to make separate notes when you use these sources. Sometimes you will want more extensive notes than you can write in a margin of your text.

Mind map summaries of textbook material are particularly useful for review. You can outline the material in the text or take notes in paragraph form. You can also single out a particularly difficult section of a text and make

separate notes. Or make mind map summaries of overlapping lecture and text material.

Use the left-hand column for key words and questions, just as you do in your class notes.

Research notes

Research notes—the ones you make for papers and speeches—follow a different format. Creating papers and speeches is a special challenge, and the way you take notes can help you face those challenges.

Use the mighty 3x5 card. There are two kinds of research cards: source cards and

(continued from page 129)

information cards. Source cards identify where information is found. For example, a source card on a book will show the title, author, publisher, date, and place of publication. Source cards are written for magazine articles, interviews, tapes, or any other research material.

When you write source cards, give each one a code—either the initials of the author, a number, or a combination of numbers and letters.

The beauty of using source cards is that you are creating your bibliography as you do the research. When you are done, simply alphabetize the cards and voila!—instant bibliography.

Write the actual notes on information cards. At the top of each information card, write the code for the source from which you got the information.

The most important point to remember about information cards: write only one piece of information on each card. You can use your information cards to construct an outline of the paper by sorting the cards. Placing more than one fact on each card creates a barrier to organizing your outline.

Thinking about notes

Whether you are making review notes or research notes, use your own words as much as possible. When you paraphrase what an author is saying, you must think about what you are reading.

Special cases

The style of your notes can vary according to the material.

If you are assigned a short story or poem, read the entire work once without taking any notes. On your first reading, enjoy the piece. When you finish, write down your immediate impressions. Then go over the item and make brief notes on characters, images, symbols, settings, plot, point of view, or other aspects of the work.

Normally, you would ask yourself questions before you read an assignment. When you read fiction or poetry, however, ask yourself questions after you have read the piece. Then reread (or skim if it's long) to get answers. Your notes can reflect this question-and-answer process.

When you read scientific or other technical material, copy important formulas. Write down data that might appear on an exam. Recreate important diagrams and draw your own visual representations of concepts.

"I can't do anything about it. That's just the way I write."

Most people are resigned to writing the way they write for the rest of their lives. They feel they have no control over penmanship. They see their handwriting as part of their personality, and that's the way it is. Handwriting is a reflection of personality. Graphologists make remarkable predictions about people by analyzing handwriting.

Yet everyone's handwriting does change. Notice how your own handwriting changes when you are angry or depressed. Your signature, when you're on top of the world, is not the same as when you are down in the dumps. Handwriting also changes as we mature.

If handwriting changes unconsciously, you can change it consciously.

The prerequisite for improving your handwriting is the desire to change it. Good handwriting in itself, while pleasant to look at, doesn't mean much. After all, doctors often have notoriously bad handwriting, and they are usually successful, respected members of the community. Many people take a kind of perverse pride in their bad handwriting. They use it as a running joke, a conversation piece of their personality. ("Oh, you know silly old me and my chicken scratching. Half the time I can't read what I write!")

Many people live productive, fulfilling, happy lives and never write legibly. And as long as they don't care about how they write, their writing will never change. For these people, none of the following 12 techniques will work.

1. Use the "first step" technique. Take a first step by telling the truth about the problem. Admit it and acknowledge your desire to improve.

The problem, by the way, is not bad handwriting. The problem is, "I can't read my notes and therefore have difficulty studying," or "The people I work with are always getting upset because they can't read what I write."

2. Intend to improve. Use the power of your intentions. Write an intention statement about your handwriting. Be specific about the results you intend to achieve.

This suggestion might sound a bit like, "How do you improve handwriting? Well, you do it by improving your handwriting." That advice doesn't sound very useful until you follow it a few times and discover the power inherent in your will.

3. Use creative visualizations. Find a quiet spot to sit, relax your whole body, close your eyes, and see yourself writing clearly. Feel the pen as it moves over the page, and picture neat, legible letters as you write them.

Practice visualizations for a few minutes every day. Be patient about the results. They will come. Simply see yourself writing the way you want to write.

4. Keep your eye on the ballpoint. Watch the way you write. Don't "try" to change. Focus all your attention on the tip of the pen, right where it meets the paper. When you do this, let go of judgments or evaluations about how you write. Simply observe closely. See the tiny details of each stroke of the pen.

Writing is an unconscious kind of activity, like dancing or playing guitar. The minute you stop to think about what you are doing, you can't do it. By focusing your attention on the tip of your pen, you are giving your brain something else to do, thereby letting your body do the writing.

5. Demonstrate your excellence. At least once a day, write something as clearly as you can. Write it as if it were going to appear on the front page of the *New York Times.*

Take your time, and write with painstaking care. You will be programming your body to write clearly.

6. Revise sloppy writing immediately. Use an erasable pen or pencil and when you write something sloppy, fix it immediately. At first, you might find yourself rewriting almost everything. As you use this technique, you will naturally learn to write it right the first time.

The advantage of this technique is that your short-term memory can tell you what your chicken scratching means; whereas if you wait to revise, the thought might be lost.

7. Practice with the best materials. Practice with an expensive pen and high quality paper. When you use the leaky pen you lifted from the Starlight Motor Hotel and write on your little sister's Big Giant tablet (the kind with wood chunks floating around in it), you are not likely to take pains to be legible.

When you put a quality pen to fancy paper, there is incentive to produce clean, crisp, pleasing lines. Practice with these fine materials by writing letters to people you care about.

Try using a fountain pen rather than a ballpoint. Fountain pens require much less pressure and "cramp." Words flow from the pen rather than having to be engraved on the paper. Some people find them faster and smoother.

Impeccable tools encourage craftsmanship.

8. Take a calligraphy course. Improve your eye-hand coordination with calligraphy. Of course, you can't take notes in Gothic script, but the practice you get working with a calligraphy pen can improve your overall writing.

9. Dot all "i's" and cross all "t's." A well-placed dot can make all the difference. An undotted "i" can resemble an "r," an "e", or the tail of any letter. "T's" uncrossed look like "l's" or even "f's."

    The time you spend dotting and crossing will eliminate time spent scratching your head.

10. Notice problem letters. Go through your notes and circle letters you have difficulty deciphering. Practice writing these letters. Simply knowing that your "n's" look like "r's" can improve your note-taking ability.

11. When understanding is critical, print. When you record an important idea that must be letter-perfect, avoid any possibility of misunderstanding by printing. Printing will stand out from your other notes. And you can read printing faster when you review.

12. Appreciate the value of legible writing. Notice how you feel when you read a legible note from someone else. Jot a legible note to yourself about the specific ways you appreciate and admire other people's ability to write clearly.

    Notice how you feel when your own handwriting works well for you. Give yourself a pat on the back. Write a discovery statement when you become aware that you have improved your handwriting, and list the benefits of the improvement.

When instructors talk fast

1. Leave large empty spaces in your notes. Leave plenty of room for filling in information you missed. Use a signal or symbol that means you missed something so you'll remember to come back to it. Make the space obvious.

2. Be willing to make choices. When an instructor talks fast, focus your attention on key points. Don't try to write everything down. Choose what you think is important and don't panic. Sometimes students paralyze themselves with fear that they are missing something important. Occasionally you will make a wrong choice and neglect an important point. Worse things could happen. Stay with the lecture, write down key words, and revise your notes immediately after class.

3. Exchange photocopies of notes with classmates. Your fellow students might write down something you missed, and your notes might help them. Compare notes, and if this is the case, make an agreement to exchange notes regularly.

4. Take more time to prepare for class. Familiarity with a subject increases your ability to pick out key points. If an instructor lectures quickly or is difficult to understand, make a point of conducting a thorough preview of material to be covered. Set the stage for the lecture.

5. See the instructor after class. Take your class notes with you and show the instructor what you missed. Most instructors appreciate visits from students. You can also ask questions you didn't get to ask in class.

6. Ask the instructor to slow down. We saved the obvious for last. You can simply ask him to slow down or, if that seems inappropriate, ask him to repeat what you missed.

You creat

This is a very powerful tool in times of trouble. When something is going wrong in your life, power process #5 can be particularly effective.

"You create it all" is probably the most unusual and bizzare suggestion in this book. It is certainly not something to be believed. In fact, believing it can get you in trouble. When you use power process #5, be sure to have power process #1 handy (*Ideas are tools*).

"You create it all" means just what it says. Nothing in the world exists at all except as you create it in your head. You create everything. You are 100% responsible for your job. You create all the lectures you attend, you create your textbooks, you create your instructors, classrooms, and classmates. You create the campus and the town that it is in. You create your relatives and you create your grades. Your creations don't

stop there. All those things that you are absolutely certain you do not control—the weather, wars, world hunger, the planets—you create those, too.

When the dog has just tracked fresh tar on the white shag carpet, when the teacher has just announced a pop quiz on the material you haven't read, when your lover reveals an affair with someone else, when you discover an unpleasant truth about a friend (or about yourself)—those are the times to tell yourself, "I create it all."

Some people don't like to hear this. As a matter of fact, they get angry when exposed to this concept, this tool. It's the worst news for people who are locked into the idea that they are victims of life. Some of us are certain that we don't have any control or influence over what happens to us.

Consider the student who says,

e it all

"That instructor is boring, and I don't get anything in her class. She really is dull. She fumbles with her notes. She stutters. She talks too softly. She recites word for word from the text. Besides, everybody else thinks she's boring, too." These reasons sound reasonable. (Funny thing how *reasons* always sound *reasonable*.) This student has great justification for being bored. Here is a perfect place to apply power process #5.

When you accept the notion that you create parts of your life you don't like, you can become very uncomfortable. For example, if for years you have found your Aunt Hildegard to be terribly irritating, consider that maybe you have something to do with what makes her so irritating. Bad news.

Good news. If indeed you create your aunt as "irritating," and if indeed you create it all, then you have the power to recreate your Aunt Hildegard.

Poof, you have a new aunt. Well, almost. You *do* have the power to handle the irritation that you have been creating (and putting up with) for years. You *can* create thoughts and make choices that allow for pleasant experiences to happen with your aunt.

(The real problem is imagining that you've been needlessly enduring the irritation for so long. People sometimes continue to create their irritation, just so they don't have to admit they could have done something about it long ago.)

This example illustrates two distinct positions that you can take in your approach to living. One is called "being at effect," and the other is called "being at cause." Being at effect means operating as though you are controlled by things outside you, a victim of circumstance. Being at cause means operating as though what is going on inside you affects what goes on "out there." Being at cause means that you are the creator of your experience.

Being at effect

Some students approach grades from the position of being at effect. The student who is at effect, and acting like a victim, gets an F and reacts something like this:

"Oh, no!" (slaps forehead)

"Rats!" (slaps forehead again)

(Students who get lots of F's often have flat foreheads.)

"Another F! Well, sure I got an F. That teacher couldn't teach his way out of a wet paper bag. He can't teach English for nothing."

Or, "Of course I got an F. Have you seen that textbook? Talk about boring! If the author knows what he's talking about, he sure can't explain it."

Or, "Heck, yes, I got an F. Do you realize how hard it is to study around my kids? You couldn't study, either. They run all over the house, even past the dining room table where I have to study."

Or, "Of course I couldn't pass this test. My friends made me go out last night and get drunk."

The problem with being at effect is that while the student is defending himself with rationalizations and justifications, he's robbing himself of the power to get anything but an F. He's giving all the power to a "boring teacher," a "bad textbook," "noisy children," or "friends."

There is another way.

Being at cause

Some students approach grades from the position of being at cause. They choose to be the source, rather than the receptacle, of things that happen in their lives. The student who is being at cause can still get an F and he might react like this:

"Oh, no!" (slaps forehead)

"Rats!" (slaps forehead again)

"Another F. Darn. Oh, shoot, well, hmmm. I see I chose an F. I created an F. I don't like it, but I must have chosen it because I've got it. Let's see. How did I choose this grade?"

Now, that's power. When you ask, "How did I choose it?", that's the power of this process. That's when you start looking for internal motivations and things that you know you can control.

The student who is operating at cause might continue with, "Well, let's see. I didn't review my notes after class. That might have done it."

Or, "I studied in the same room with my children while they watched TV. Then I went out with my buddies right before the test. Well, that probably helped me fulfill some of the requirements for getting an F."

The strength in this position is that if you can choose the F, you can also choose not to have another F. When the F is the result of your kids, your roommate, the book, or the teacher, then you probably can't do anything about it. When the F is the result of your own actions and choices (I create it) and no one else's, you get to be in charge.

If you are skeptical about "You create it all," consider this: Your thoughts and behavior totally control what you experience. You create it all.

Thoughts

Your thoughts specifically affect your experiences by controlling your perceptions. Every bit of your experience results from input through your five senses. You know something exists only because of your ability to see it, smell it, feel it, taste it, or hear it.

For example, you know about the

chair you're sitting on right now only because of your senses. To experience the chair, you must collect information about it through one or more of your senses. You can feel the chair with your hands or your bottom. You can see the chair and hear it scrape against the floor. If you have a freshly oiled wooden chair, you can smell it. Your senses are what make the world real. They are your only connection with everything outside you.

We do not sense everything in our environment. If we did, we'd go crazy very quickly because of sensory overload. We filter out much of the sensation available to us. For example, when you're talking to someone at a party, you generally don't hear details of other conversations in the room. You're aware that conversations exist, but you don't hear anything in particular until someone (even someone across the room) mentions your name. You immediately shift your attention to different sensations and notice the content of that other conversation. Your senses are selective. That selectivity is primarily controlled by your thoughts.

Imagine for a moment that the universe is whole and complete. It is filled with everything you would ever want, including happiness, love, friends, and all the material wealth you would want. Most people have no experience of that concept of the universe. Maybe it is because their thoughts limit what they see.

On the other hand, if you think the world is unfriendly, you are much more likely to see things that justify that thought. If you consider the world to be unsafe, you notice all of those news stories which justify your notion that the world is unsafe. There may be just as much evidence to demonstrate that the world *is* safe, but because of your thought, "The world is unsafe," you notice only those sensations that verify the correctness of your thought.

Our behaviors

The way we act is a reflection of our choices. Moment by moment we are continually making choices about what we will do and where we will go. The resulting sum total of these choices is where we are in life. All those choices provide us with our current circumstance. People who are in car accidents seldom see their role in the "accident." "Well, it just happened. The other car came out of nowhere and hit me. It wasn't my fault."

Our behaviors are often subtle, and our choices are made at a rate of thousands per hour. We are not always conscious of how our choices led us to our current situation. Power process #5 allows us to take a look at how we create our experiences through our thoughts and choices.

Caution #1: This power process is not suggesting that you physically create the chair in which you're sitting. Of course, you didn't manufacture it. The point, however, is that you *do* create your *experience* of the chair, including how comfortable it is, and how you feel in it. And *you* made a choice to sit in that chair.

Caution #2: This process is not to be used to make other people feel wrong or guilty. If someone confronts you about an aspect of your behavior that annoys them, this is not the time to suggest to them, "You create it all." Rather, this is the time to use the process to see how you created their finding you to be irritating. Remember, *you* create it all.

Caution #3: Accepting total responsibility for your experience is not the same as making yourself wrong.

Blaming yourself is just as much being at effect as when you blame another. Blaming yourself or feeling guilty is not the objective of power process #5. Be gentle with yourself.

Caution #4: This is not a religion. It is not something to believe or disbelieve. It is a tool. In no way does this concept need to conflict with your religious beliefs. Acting as if you create it all does not mean denying God. It means only that you have taken responsibility for what happens in your life.

Caution #5: This concept is easy to refute, to deny, or to negate. People often discount the power of this tool by coming up with arguments such as, "But what about world hunger? I didn't cause that," "What if I'm locked up in prison? I wouldn't have the power to create anything," or, "What about people that get cancer? Did they create that?"

There *are* people in the world who approach world hunger with the attitude, "I am responsible for this. What will I do about it?" These people look at their role in a global problem and see choices that others may be blind to.

Viktor Frankl, a famous psychiatrist and concentration camp survivor, created dignity out of incredible humiliation.

Malcolm X created education in jail.

Sidney Rittenberg spent nine years in solitary confinement in China and emerged without bitterness, still a friend of the Chinese people.

Thousands of people are living productive lives and creating positive experiences out of a circumstance called cancer.

Whenever education isn't working for you, especially when it looks like you have no responsibility in the situation, experiment with the notion that you create it all. See if this process doesn't wake you up when you start getting sleepy, fidgety, resentful, or frustrated in class. Give yourself the power to create your own experience.

P.S. Power process #5 also works when life is going great. Often we give responsibility to others for our good fortune, when in fact, it's time to pat ourselves on the back for making the right choices and holding on to effective thoughts. By being conscious of our choices and our thoughts, we can create A's, interesting classes, enjoyable relationships, material wealth, and contributions to a better world.

Exercise #21

Apply a process

Love your problems was the power process presented in chapter three, Memory, and this chapter introduced the power process, *You create it all.* Below, write how you can apply the idea of loving your problem to the problem of note-taking or list 10 ways you create it all in your notes.

Of the classes in which you are presently enrolled, pick the one you find least interesting. In this space, write all the ways you make the class uninteresting (or less interesting than other classes.)

Journal entry #38

Discovery statement

Rudolfo Anaya

From **Chicano Authors: Inquiry by Interview** *by Juan D. Bruce-Novoa. Copyright 1980. Reprinted by permission of University of Texas Press.*

I read a great deal when I was a child, in grade school. I not only ran in a gang and did everything that normal, red-blooded Chicano boys do as they grow up, but I also used to spend a lot of time reading. I was the only one in the gang that used to go to the library on Saturday mornings. It was a decrepit, old building, run by one of the teachers, who volunteered to open it on Saturdays. Many Saturday mornings she and I were the only ones at the library. I sat there and read and leafed through books, and took some home. I read a lot of comic books and saw a lot of movies. I think all of that was important, in some respect, to the question of what influenced me when I was young. I also heard stories. Any time that people gathered, family or friends, they told stories, cuentos [tales], anecdotes, dichos [sayings], adivinanzas [riddles]. So I was always in a milieu of words, whether they were printed or in the oral tradition.

Later, I read a great deal in American literature when I was at the university, and it was as formative a period for me as my childhood, because both were very full and alive with the mystery of discovery in literature. Through formal education, I was exposed to many writers, not only to American literature and contemporary writers, but world literature. I think it's very important for Chicano students, whether or not they're going to be writers, to engage in some kind of educational process. There are those who say that education will change who you are, how you think, destroy your culture, assimilate you—I think that's nonsense. Those are people who are afraid of change. We cannot hide our heads in the sand and pretend that everything that is important and good and of value will come only out of our culture. We live in a small world where many other cultures have a great deal to offer us. This is very important for the writer—to read as much as he possibly can, to learn a bit of the analytical study of literature. That's important.

Both my father and my mother spoke Spanish, and I was raised speaking Spanish in an almost completely Spanish background. I did not learn English until I started first grade. Now I speak more fluently in English. The thrust of my education has been in English literature and I wrote in English when I began to write, so I am more fluent and more comfortable with English.

There are some of us who have had, at one time, a great disadvantage. We came from poor families, poor in the sense that we had no money, but we were rich with love and culture and a sense of sharing and imagination. We had to face a school system that very often told us we couldn't write. It did not teach us our own works, and we had nothing to emulate, to read of our own. So of course we were very disadvantaged in that way. For example, when I began to write I had a hard time to find those models that would click, that had a relevance to my internal being. But I kept at it, I kept at it. You can call it what you want; it's something you know you have to do, and eventually you find the rhythm and you find what you want to say and you say it and you keep practicing the skills and the elements. I don't think they become any easier, to tell you the truth. After ten or fifteen years now, I'm still in the process of learning about writing; a process that never finishes. That's exciting!

Even today Chicano children are being told they are at a disadvantage because they don't have command of the English language. The sooner you begin to tell children that, the more they begin to believe it; you build in a self-fulfilling prophecy. That is not right! We have, as I have stated before, a rich culture, rich tradition, a rich oral tradition, and we have, through part of our roots, a rich literary tradition. So we have to change that around y en vez de decir que no tenemos el talento [and instead of saying that we don't have the talent], say, "You can write! You do have talent! You can produce literature that is valuable!" We have to go out and tell the kids in high school and grade school, cuando estan chiquitos [when they are little], "You can write, you can write about what you know, your experience is valuable, who you are is valuable, and how you view the world and society and the cosmos is valuable. Put it down on paper, paint a picture, make a drawing, write music!"

1. List four ways to prepare yourself to be a good observer in class.

2. In order to focus on what is being said, students should concentrate hard on not daydreaming. True or false.

3. Describe how you can use your chair as a device to keep you awake and alert in class.

4. Describe how judgments might interfere with note-taking.

5. List at least five ways in which you can create an interesting lecture in a circumstance where there is a lot of justification for "this is boring."

6. Describe three ways to improve handwriting.

7. List at least two reasons for sitting toward the front of class.

8. Why is the review session you conduct within 24 hours the most important review?

9. List the nine steps of muscle reading.

10. Think of a circumstance in your life that you think is impossible to change. Discuss ways that you could create your experience of the situation differently.

In this space, write techniques you wanted to get from this chapter and did not get.

Journal entry #39

Discovery statement

In this space, write an intention statement about how you now plan to get what you wanted to get from this chapter but didn't.

Journal entry #40

Intention statement

In this space, write an intention statement declaring how you will use the techniques in this chapter.

I intend to . . .

Journal entry #41

Intention statement

I intend to . . .

Describe a time in your life when something happened that you blamed on someone or something else. Switch your perception and write how you see that *you created it all.*

Journal Entry #42

Discovery Statement

Look Back

What I want to get out of this chapter is . . .

Journal Entry #43

Discovery Statement

CHAPTER SIX
TESTS

In this chapter...

Prepare for a test the way a performer prepares for a concert. Tests are performances. They are brief opportunities to demonstrate the mastery you have attained. Handle **Test anxiety** (stage fright) by using proven methods that can turn nervous energy into an asset. Learn how to welcome exam jitters.

See how to make study sessions (rehearsals) more effective. Rehearsals for theatrical productions run like clockwork. Energy is focused. A good director knows exactly what is to be accomplished every minute. You can teach yourself to be your director, working toward a successful exam (the opening night).

Coordinate your body and brain using them the way they were designed to be used, so studying can be satisfying and enlivening. Have some fun during exam week. Release yourself from negative emotions with **Power process #6, Detach yourself.**

What to do during the test gives you a system for getting what you know out of your head and on to the exam. You can learn how to know what's on the test before you take it—without cheating. Exercises in this chapter demonstrate how you can **Relax with a sigh,** develop a **Master review schedule** and **Rehearse for success.**

D

On the surface, tests don't look dangerous, but we treat them like they're land mines.

Suppose a man walks up to you on the street and asks, "Does a finite abelian P-group have a basis?" Will you break out in a cold sweat? Will your muscles tense up? Will your breathing become shallow?

Probably not. Even if you have never heard of a finite abelian P-group you are likely to remain coolly detached. However, if you find that same question on a test, and if you have never heard of a finite abelian P-group, then your hands might get clammy.

Grades (A to F) are what gives power to tests. And there are lots of misconceptions about what grades are.

Grades are not a measure of intelligence. Grades don't measure creativity. They are not an indication of your ability to contribute to

sarm tests

society. Grades are simply a measure of how well you did on one test on one particular day.

Some people think that a test score measures what a student accomplished in a course. This is false. A test score is a measure of what a student scored on a test. If you are anxious about a test and blank out, then the grade cannot measure what you learned. The reverse is also true; if you are good at taking tests and a lucky guesser, the score won't be accurate.

Grades are not a measure of self-worth; yet we tend to give test scores the power to determine how we feel about ourselves. Common thoughts are, "If I fail the test, I'm a failure," or "If I do badly on a test, I'm a bad person." The truth is that if you do badly on a test you are a person who did badly on a test. That's all.

Carrying around misconceptions about tests and grades can put undue pressure on your performance. It's like walking on a railroad track. Most people can stay balanced and find it fairly easy to walk 10 feet down a rail. Yet the task seems entirely different if the rail is placed between two buildings, ten stories up.

It is easier to do well on exams if you don't exaggerate the pressure on yourself. Don't give the test some magical power over your worth as a human being. Academic tests are usually not a matter of life or death. Even scoring low on important tests—entrance tests for college or medical school, law boards, CPA exams— usually only means a delay.

The real risk (10 story fall) or the imagined risk (F means personal failure) of a performance can reach a point where it is paralyzing. The way to deal with tests is to keep the risk in perspective. Keep the railroad track on the ground.

What to do before the test

MANAGE REVIEW TIME.

A key to successful test preparation is managing review time.

The biggest benefit of early review is that facts will have time to roam around in your head. A lot of learning takes place when you are not "studying." Your brain will have time to create relationships that can show up when you need them—like during a test. Use short daily review sessions to prepare the way for major review sessions. Also, be specific about your intention to review from the beginning of the term.

Daily reviews

Daily reviews include the short pre- and post-class reviews of lecture notes. You can also conduct brief daily reviews when you read. Before you begin a new reading assignment, scan your notes and the sections you underlined in the previous assignment. Use the time you spend waiting for the bus or the laundry to conduct short reviews.

Concentrate daily reviews on two kinds of material: material you have just learned, either in class or in your reading, and material that involves simple memorization (equations, formulas, dates, definitions).

Conduct short daily reviews several times throughout the day. To make sure you do, include them on your daily "to do" list. Write down, "5 min. review of biology," or "10 min. review of economics," and give yourself the satisfaction of crossing them off.

Regular daily reviews will pay off during exam week.

Begin to review the first day of class. The first day, in fact, is important for review. Most instructors outline the whole course at that time.

Weekly reviews

Weekly reviews are longer—about an hour per subject. These review periods are also more structured than short daily reviews. When a subject is complex, the brain requires time to dig into the material; don't skip from subject to subject too quickly. Review each subject at least once a week.

The content of these weekly review sessions includes review of assigned reading, review of lecture notes and practice answering questions in the questions section of your notes. Look over any mind map summaries or flashcards you have created.

Major reviews

Major reviews are usually conducted the week before finals or other major exams. They integrate concepts and deepen understanding of the material presented throughout the term. These are longer review periods, two to five hours at a stretch, punctuated by sufficient breaks. Remember that the effectiveness of your review begins to drop after an hour or so unless you give yourself a short rest.

After a certain point, short breaks every hour will not be enough to refresh you. That's when it's time to quit. Each of us has our own limit. In a marathon 10-hour review session, a student might typically accomplish only a half hour's worth of review in the last two or three hours of that session. In other words, he might as well be at the movies. Learn what your limits are by being conscious of the quality of your concentration.

During long sessions, study the most difficult subjects when you are the most alert: at the beginning of the session.

Of course, it's easy to write (or read) about reviewing regularly from the very first day of class. Actually doing it is something else. Reviewing is easy to postpone.

To combat procrastination, set aside time in the future to plan how you will quit putting things off. Do this for sure within three days or at least within a week or two.

Create a system of rewards for time spent reviewing.

Clarify your intentions about reviewing. Use the intention statements in this chapter, or invent your own, to draw a detailed picture of your plans for review time.

Your commitment to review is your most powerful ally.

CREATE REVIEW TOOLS

Study checklists, mind map summaries, and flash cards take the guesswork and, just as important, much of the worry out of studying. When you use these tools on a daily and weekly basis, you are dividing a big job into small, manageable parts. Your confidence will increase and you will probably sleep better at night.

Study checklists

Study checklists are used the way a pilot uses a pre-flight checklist. Pilots go through a standard routine before they take off. They physically mark off each item: test flaps, check magneto, check fuel tanks, adjust instruments, check rudder. They use a written list to be absolutely certain they don't miss anything. Once they are in the air, it's too late, and the consequences of failing to check the fuel tanks could be drastic.

Taking an exam is like flying a plane. Once the test begins, it's too late to memorize that one equation you forgot. And the consequences could be unpleasant.

Make a list for each subject. List reading assignments by chapters or page numbers. List dates of lecture notes. Write down various types of problems you will need to be able to solve. Write down other skills you must master. Include major ideas, definitions, theories, formulas, equations, and other information you might need.

A study checklist is not a review sheet. It contains the briefest possible description of each item.

Keep a study checklist beginning the very first day of class. Add to it as the term progresses. Then, when you conduct your final major review sessions, check items off the list as you review them.

A study checklist for a history course might look like this:

Study Checklist—Amer. History

Materials:
Text pages: 190-323
Lecture notes: 9/14 - 10/29
The Federalist: 1, 3, 14, 18, 26, 41
C.A. Beard, Ec. Interpr. Const.
    pgs. 56-81, 114-117
Rossiter: pgs. 314-336
Hill: pgs. 175-183, 214-226

Subjects:
Hamilton + bank
Frontier crisis
Jay's treaty + foreign policy
Election 1796
Alien & Sedition Acts
Pinckney's Treaty
John Adams' presidency:
    domestic policy, foreign policy
Jefferson's presidency:
    domestic policy, foreign policy
Louisiana Purchase

Mind map summary sheets

Mind mapping is an effective system for note-taking and it's also a great way to make summary sheets for tests. Mind maps let you work with your brain rather than against it.

Traditional, Roman numeral/capital letter outlines contain main topics which are followed by minor topics which, in turn, are subdivided further. They organize a subject in a sequential, linear way. This kind of organization, however, doesn't reflect some very natural aspects of brain function, specifically "right brain" activities.

Right brain function refers to creative, pattern-making, visual, intuitive brain activity. Left brain function refers to the orderly, logical, step-by-step characteristics of thought. Left brain is words. Right brain is pictures. (The reverse is sometimes true for left-handed people). A mind map uses both kinds of brain functions. Mind maps can contain lists and sequences and show causes (left brain functions), but they also provide a picture of a subject. Mind maps are visual patterns (right brain functions) that can provide a framework for recall. They work on both verbal and nonverbal levels.

Further, the mind mapping process directs you toward thinking from the general to the specific. By choosing a main topic, you focus first on the big picture, then zero in on subordinate ideas.

By using key words, you can condense a large subject into a small area on a mind map. You review more quickly by looking at the key words on a mind map than by reading notes word for word.

Making a mind map is simple. Write the main subject in the center of a sheet of paper. Write related subjects on lines branching out from the main subject.

(See the illustration of a mind map on page 128).

Indicate relationships between elements of a subject by drawing arrows between them, enclosing related ideas in circles, boxes, or other shapes, or by color coding them. Use symbols, graphic signals, and pictures for emphasis.

There are several ways to begin a mind map as you study for tests. You can start by creating a map totally from memory. When you use this technique, you might be surprised by how much you already know. Mind maps release floods of information from the brain because the mind works by association. Each idea is linked to many other ideas. When you think of one, other associations come to mind. An advantage of mind mapping is that you don't have to stifle any of these associations just because they don't come next in a sequential outline. Everything fits in a mind map. Let the associations flow, and if one seems to go someplace else, simply start another branch on your map. After you have gone as far as you can using recall alone, go over your notes and text and fill in the rest of the map.

Another way to create a mind map summary is to go through your notes and pick out key words. Then, without looking at your notes, create a mind map of everything you can recall about each key word. Finally, go back to your notes and fill in material you left out.

You can also start a mind map with underlined sections from your text.

Make mind maps for small, detailed subjects, as well as for large ones. You can mind map a whole course, or a single lecture, or a single point from a lecture.

As you build a mind map on paper, you are also constructing a map in your

(continued on page 152)

Use this exercise when you are studying or during an exam. It releases tensions before they build.

The sigh is the body's natural mechanism for tension reduction, so there is nothing to "learn" in this technique. Your body already knows how.

Put your spine straight and sigh deeply. Simply let the air flow out of your body. Focus on the sigh and then inhale naturally.

Relax with a sigh

HOW TO
PREDICT
TEST QUESTIONS

It's no mystery: Test questions come from assigned reading and lectures. The format of test questions can help you predict what the question will be.

Ask your instructor to describe the test format—how long it will be, and what kind of questions to expect (essay, multiple choice, problems). Get an accurate picture of what the test will be like early in the term so you can be alert for possible test questions during lectures and in your reading. Have a separate section in your notebook labeled "Test Questions." Add several questions to this section after every lecture and after you read assignments for the course.

In lectures you can watch for test questions by observing not only *what* the instructor says but *how* he says it. Instructors give clues. They might repeat a point several times, or write it on the board, or return to it in subsequent classes. Pay attention to questions the instructor poses to students. Note questions other students ask. When material from reading assignments is also covered extensively in class, it is likely to be on the test.

Put yourself in your instructor's head. What kind of question would you ask? Make practice test questions. Use the essay question words in this chapter as a guide; turn the key words in your notes into questions.

Save all quizzes, papers, lab sheets, and graded material of any kind. Quiz questions have a way of appearing, in slightly altered form, on final exams. Sometimes instructors make old exams available. (Also check libraries, residence halls, and fraternity or sorority houses.) If copies of previous exams are available, use those to predict questions.

For science courses and other courses involving problem solving, practice working problems using different variables. Make up and solve problems with slightly different forms.

You can also brainstorm test questions with other students.

(continued from page 150)

mind. When you are finished, the picture of the map will be firmly implanted in your memory. You could throw away your paper mind map and still retain most of the benefit of making it.

Flashcards

Three-by-five flashcards are like portable test questions. You can take them with you anywhere and use them anytime.

On one side of the card, write the question. On the other, the answer. It's that simple.

Use flashcards for equations, formulas, definitions, theories, key words from your notes, axioms, dates, foreign language phrases, hypotheses, sample problems, and more.

Create flashcards regularly as the term progresses. You can buy an inexpensive card file to keep your flashcards arranged by subject.

Carry a pack of flashcards with you whenever you think you might have a spare minute to review them. Keep a few blank cards with you too. That way you can make new flashcards whenever the need arises.

What to do during the test

AS YOU BEGIN

Prepare yourself for the test by arriving early so you have time to do a breathing or relaxation exercise.

Pay particular attention to verbal directions given as the test is distributed. Ask about the general rules of the exam room, such as the procedure for asking questions, materials allowed in the room, etc. Knowing the rules will ensure that you don't create the impression of cheating.

Scan the whole test immediately. Evaluate the importance of each section. Notice how many points each part of the test is worth and estimate how much time you will need for each section; use its point value as your guide. For example, don't budget 20% of your time for a section that is worth only 10% of the points. Then jot down a short time plan to keep you on track during the test.

Read the directions *slowly*. Then reread them. Nothing is more agonizing than to discover you have lost points on a test not because you didn't know the material, but because you failed to follow the directions. If the directions call for short answers, give short answers. Sometimes you will be asked to answer two out of three questions. Oh, the frustration of finding that out as you finish your third answer!

Jot down memory aids, formulas, equations, facts, or other material you know you'll need and might forget. Do this in the margins.

Now you are ready to begin.

IN GENERAL

Answer easiest, shortest questions first. This gives you the experience of success and stimulates associations, thus preparing your mind for more difficult questions.

Next answer multiple-choice, true-false, and fill-in-the-blank questions. Proceed to short-answer questions and finally the essay questions.

Use memory techniques when you're stuck. If your recall on a certain point is blocked, remember something else that's related. Start from the general and go to the specific. Use a small mind map in the test margin to stimulate your memory.

Pace yourself. Watch the time; if you are stuck, move on. Follow your time plan.

Leave plenty of space between answers. The space makes it easier on the person who grades your test, and you can use the extra space if there's time for additional information.

Look for answers in other test questions. A term, name, date, or other fact that escapes you might appear in the test itself. You can also use other questions to stimulate your memory.

In quick-answer questions (multiple-choice, true-false), your first instinct is usually best. Don't change your answer unless you are sure the second choice is correct. If you think your first answer is wrong because you misread the question, do change your answer.

Multiple-choice questions

Check the directions to see if the questions call for more than one answer.

Answer each question in your head before you look at the possible answers. If you can come up with the answer before you look at the choices, you eliminate the possibility of being confused by those choices.

Mark questions you can't answer immediately and come back to them if you have time.

If you have no clue as to what the answer is, and if incorrect answers are not deducted from your score, use the following guidelines to guess:

1. If two answers are similar, except for one or two words, choose one of these answers.

2. If two answers have similar sounding or looking words (intermediate—intermittent), choose one of these answers.

3. If the answer calls for a sentence completion, eliminate the answers that would not form grammatically correct sentences.

4. If two quantities are almost the same, choose one.

5. If answers cover a wide range (4.5, 66.7, 88.7, 90.1, 500.11), choose one in the middle.

6. If there is no penalty for guessing and none of the above techniques work, close your eyes and go for it.

True-false questions

Answer true-false questions quickly. Generally, these questions will not be worth many points individually. Don't invest a lot of time to get two points on a 100-point exam.

If any part of the true-false statement is false, the statement is false.

Look for qualifiers like "all," "most," "sometimes," "never," or "rarely." These are the key words upon which the question depends. Absolute qualifiers such as "always" or "never" generally indicate a false statement.

Machine-graded tests

You must be certain the answer you mark corresponds to the question you are answering. Check the test booklet against the answer sheet whenever you switch sections and again at the top of each column. Watch for stray marks. These can look like answers.

Open-book tests

When studying for the test, write down

any formulas you will need on a separate sheet. Tape tabs onto important pages of the book (tables, for instance) so you don't have to waste time flipping through the pages. (You could also use paper clips.)

If you plan to use your notes, number them and write a short table of contents.

Prepare thoroughly for open-book exams. They are almost always the most difficult tests.

Short-answer/fill-in-the-blank questions

These questions often ask for definitions or short descriptions. Pick up points fast when you work the fill-in-the-blank section of a test. Concentrate on key words and facts. Be brief.

Here's where overlearning, as discussed in chapter three, really pays off. When you know a subject backwards and forwards, you can answer this type of question almost as fast as you can write.

Essay questions

When you set out to answer an essay question, your first task is to find out what the question is asking—*precisely*. If a question asks that you *compare* Gestalt and Reichian therapies, no matter how eloquently you *explain* them, you are on a one-way trip to No Credit City.

Standard essay question words are defined in this chapter on page 159. Learn them well.

Before you begin to write, make a quick outline. There are three reasons for doing this. First, you will be able to write faster. Second, you will be less likely to leave out important facts. Third, if you don't have time to finish your answer, your outline might win you some points.

When you start to write, get to the point. Forget introductions. Sentences such as, "There are many interesting facets to this difficult question," cause acute pain in teachers grading tests. One way to get to the point is to include part of the question in your answer. For example, if the question asks, "Discuss how increasing the city police budget may or may not contribute to a decrease in street crime," your first sentence might read, "An increase in police expenditures will not have a significant effect on street crime for the following reasons." Your position is clear. You are on your way to the answer.

When you expand your answer with supporting ideas and facts, bring out your big guns immediately. Don't try for drama by saving the best for last.

Some final points in regard to style:

1. Write clearly. Grading essay questions is in large part a subjective process. Sloppy, difficult to read handwriting might actually lower your grade.

2. Be brief. Avoid filler sentences that say nothing. ("The question certainly bears careful deliberation in order to take into account all the many interesting facts pertaining to this important period in the history of our great nation.") Write as if you expect the person grading your test to be tired, bored, and overworked. This might not be the case; but even a well-rested instructor doesn't like to wade through a swamp of murky writing in order to trap an occasional lonely fact.

3. Use a pen. Many instructors will require this because pencil is difficult to read.

4. When possible, write on one side of the page only. Writing will show through and obscure writing on the other side. If necessary, you can use the blank side to add points you missed. Leave a generous left-hand margin with plenty of space between your answers, in case you need to add to them later.

Finally, if you have time, review your answers for grammatical errors, clarity, and legibility.

NOTABLE FAILURES

Dr. Milton E. Larson, "Humbling Cases for Career Counselors," Phi Delta Kappan, February 1983, Volume LIV, No. 6; 374.

Creative and imaginative people are often not recognized by their contemporaries. Even more often, they are not recognized in school by their teachers. History is full of examples.

Einstein was four years old before he could speak and seven before he could read. *Isaac Newton* did poorly in grade school, and *Beethoven's* music teacher once said of him, "As a composer he is hopeless." When *Thomas Edison* was a boy, his teachers told him he was too stupid to learn anything. *F. W. Woolworth* got a job in a dry goods store when he was 21, but his employers would not let him wait on a customer because he "didn't have enough sense." A newspaper editor fired *Walt Disney* because he had "no good ideas." *Caruso's* music teacher told him, "You can't sing. You have no voice at all." The director of the Imperial Opera in Vienna told *Madame Schumann-Heink* that she would never be a singer and advised her to buy a sewing machine. *Leo Tolstoy* flunked out of college; *Werner von Braun* flunked ninth-grade algebra. *Admiral Richard E. Byrd* had been retired from the Navy as "unfit for service" until he flew over both Poles. *Louis Pasteur* was rated as "mediocre" in chemistry when he attended the Royal College. *Abraham Lincoln* entered the Black Hawk War as a captain and came out as a private. *Louisa May Alcott* was told by an editor that she could never write anything that had popular appeal. *Fred Waring* was once rejected for high school chorus. *Winston Churchill* failed the sixth grade.

Master review schedule

Schedule review time on this one month calendar. Mark the appropriate dates of the month in the upper left-hand corner of every square, then schedule weekly review periods for each subject. Write down the name of the subject, what time of day you intend to conduct the review, and how long the review will be.

Also schedule at least two major review periods. The length of these review periods will range from two to five hours depending on your needs.

The more difficult it is for you to find time for review, the greater the benefit of this exercise. Use your imagination and skill to create extra time to review.

If you regularly use a Time Plan for the week, or if you use a different system of time management (daily appointment calendars or "to do" lists), incorporate these review periods into that system.

The purpose of this exercise is to give you an opportunity to step back and look at your overall review habits. For a longer view, photocopy this calendar and make a review plan for two or three months.

Priming

Before you begin each study session, take a moment to organize the task. Survey the territory ahead. Ask yourself several questions about your purpose:

1. How will I be tested on this material?

2. How will what I am studying relate to what I do beyond school?

3. How important is this information to the rest of my education?

4. How does this material relate to what I already know?

5. How much time shall I spend on this?

Monday	Tuesday	Wednesday	Thursday	Friday	Saturday	Sunday

Month _____

Month _____

Monday	Tuesday	Wednesday	Thursday	Friday	Saturday	Sunday

KEY WORDS
F O R • E S S A Y • Q U E S T I O N S

The following words are commonly found in essay test questions. Understanding them is essential to success on these kinds of questions. Study this sheet thoroughly. Know these words backwards and forwards.

Analyze

Break into separate parts and discuss, examine, or interpret each part.

Compare

Examine two or more things. Identify similarities and differences. Comparisons generally ask for similarities more than differences. (See Contrast.)

Contrast

Show differences. Set in opposition.

Criticize

Make judgments. Evaluate comparative worth. Criticism often involves analysis.

Define

Give the meaning; usually a meaning specific to the course or subject. Determine the precise limits of the term to be defined. Explain the exact meaning. Definitions are usually short.

Describe

Give a detailed account. Make a picture with words. List characteristics, qualities, and parts.

Discuss

Consider and debate or argue the pros and cons of an issue. Write about any conflict. Compare and contrast.

Enumerate

List several ideas, aspects, events, things, qualities, reasons, etc.

Evaluate

Give your opinion or cite the opinion of an expert. Include evidence to support the evaluation.

Illustrate

Give concrete examples. Explain clearly by using comparisons or examples.

Interpret

Comment upon, give examples, describe relationships. Explain the meaning. Describe, then evaluate.

Outline

Describe main ideas, characteristics, or events. (Does not necessarily mean "write a Roman numeral/letter outline.")

Prove

Support with facts (especially facts presented in class or in the text).

State

Explain precisely.

Summarize

Give a brief, condensed account. Include conclusions. Avoid unnecessary details.

Trace

Show the order of events or progress of a subject or event.

If any of these terms is still unclear to you, go to your unabridged dictionary. Thorough knowledge of these words will enable you to give the teacher what she is requesting.

Detach yourself

Process #6 will allow you to release the powerful, natural student within you during times of stress. Use power process #6 whenever negative emotions or feelings are getting in the way of your education.

Attachments are addictions: we think we cannot live without them, just as a drug addict feels she cannot live without drugs. We all have attachments. We can be attached to just about anything . . . ideas, objects, people, results, rewards—the list is endless.

The most important quality of an attachment is that we clutch it for dear life. A drowning man, for example, is so attached to being rescued that he will often foil his rescuer. The more he resists drowning, the more difficult he is to rescue. Ironically, as he becomes literally "attached" to his would-be rescuer, grasping and grabbing, they both sink.

Addictions and attachments can be recognized by the emotions they evoke. They give rise to irritation, anger, jealousy, confusion, fatigue, boredom, fear, and resentment.

Suppose you are attached to the idea of getting an "A" on your physics test. You are holding on to this idea tightly because you really want that "A." In fact, you don't just want that "A". You must have it. You need it.

So, during the exam, with the thought "I must get an 'A'" in the back of your mind, you begin to work a problem. And the problem is difficult. You've studied hard, spent hours working practice problems, but this problem is a killer. The first time you read it you have no idea how to solve it, and the second time you read it you aren't even sure what it's asking. The more you read and reread it, the more confused you get. To top it all off, this problem is worth 40% of your score. And you are stuck!

The harder you work, the more stuck you get and the louder the thought in the back of your head: "I must get an 'A'; I Must Get An 'A'; I MUST GET AN 'A'!"

Your hands begin to sweat and shake. Your knees feel weak. You become nauseous. You are unable to concentrate. Thoughts zip in and out of your head uncontrollably. You flail about for the answer like a drowning man. Panic. Total confusion.

You look up at the clock, sickened by the inexorable sweep of the second hand. You are doomed.

Now is the time to reach for power process #6. When you notice that you are in a state of panic, detach yourself.

The first step in detachment is to recognize the symptoms of attachment. Pay attention to how you feel. If you are confused and feeling stuck, tell yourself, "Here I am, confused and stuck." If your palms are sweaty and your stomach is one big knot, admit it. Focus on the physical symptoms of your negative emotions.

When you have identified the negative emotions and thoughts, detach yourself from them by placing yourself in your "observer consciousness."

Observer consciousness
Observer consciousness is the quiet

state above and beyond your usual thoughts, the place in your consciousness that can *be aware of being aware.* It's a tranquil place, apart from your emotions. Reading about this place, of course, is not the same as getting there; and unfortunately, no one can tell you exactly how to get there. Yet we all share this observer consciousness.

There are techniques you can use in your search. For instance, during your physics exam, once you have identified your attachment to getting an "A", you might simply tell yourself to "let go." Or, you might take a moment to consider the worst thing that could happen if you didn't get an "A". Or, you might calm your mind with a breathing or relaxation technique.

Observe yourself as if you were outside yourself. Gently let go of your addiction to an "A". Accept your negative emotions and if you can't accept your emotions, accept that you can't accept them. Let go of attachment.

Don't try to force attachments out of your consciousness. The harder you fight them, the harder they fight back. That's because the force behind attachments is survival. The stronger the attachment, the more we think we cannot survive without the object of our attachment.

Some people, for example, are so attached to their cars that an attack on the car is seen as a personal attack on the driver. Pity the poor unfortunate who backs into the car of an addicted owner. He might as well have backed into the owner himself.

Other people are addicted and attached to their jobs. Their minds have made up a story that who they are is their job. These people can become suicidally depressed if they get fired or laid off.

Most of us are addicted, to some

extent, to identifications. We identify ourselves as Americans, Blacks, veterans, feminists, industrialists, athletes, Elks, bowlers, Episcopalians, parents, dancers, hockey fans, or birdwatchers. Our minds invest our very beings into these identities, and when we think these identities are in danger, we fight to survive. The more addicted we are to the identity, the harder we fight.

Although we have used the example of a student attached to a good grade, many students are attached to bad grades, odd as this seems. The attachment to failure can be just as strong as the attachment to success. When these students approach success their anxiety is just as real. Their minds have identified them as bad students and the mind wants to be "right." These students will create diabolically clever ways to fail.

We can be addicted to our emotions as well as our thoughts. We can identify with our anger so strongly that we are unable to let go of it. We can also be addicted to depression. Extremely depressed people are often reluctant to give up their depression.

Not all negative emotions are inappropriate. If you are being chased by a bear, do not stop to ask yourself, "I wonder why I am so afraid and attached to not being eaten by a bear?" (Instead, run.) Use power process #6 when you notice that negative emotions resulting from addictions or identifications are preventing you from getting what you want.

Giving up the addiction to (or identification with) being an "A" student does not mean giving up being an "A" student. Nor does giving up the addiction to a car mean giving up the car. Rather, it means not holding on to the grade or the automobile so tightly

Exercise #24

Rehearse for success

Sit up in a chair, legs and arms uncrossed. Close your eyes, let go of all thoughts, and focus on your breathing for a minute or two.

Then tell yourself to relax, beginning with your feet. Relax your toes, your feet, and your ankles. Move up to your calves and thighs. Relax your buttocks. Tell yourself to relax the muscles of your lower back, abdomen, and chest. Relax your hands, arms, and shoulders. Relax your neck, jaw, face, and scalp.

When you are completely relaxed, imagine yourself in an exam room. It's the day of the test. See the test being handed out. Hear the other students shuffle in their seats. Feel the desk, the pencil in your hand and the exam in front of you. See yourself looking over the exam calmly and confidently.

Create an image of yourself previewing the exam, budgeting your time, and beginning the test. You feel confident as you answer the questions. Stay with this image for a few minutes.

See yourself complete the test and hand it in, confident of your grade.

Finally, imagine receiving the test grade. It is an "A."

(continued from page 161) that either one drags you down like an anchor.

Detach yourself. Notice your anger, fear, and frustration from the observer's point of view. The observer consciousness is that part of you that can be aware of being aware. As you assume that level of consciousness, you will experience a certain calm, even as you remain anxious. You can observe yourself becoming tired and bored while studying for a test, and, remaining tired and bored, gently detach yourself from those feelings. When you do this, you take away much of the power of negative feelings.

Behind your attachments is a master student. By detaching yourself, you release that master student.

Detach yourself.

Special Techniques for Math and Science Tests

1. Translate problems into English. Putting problems into words will help you understand what is asked. When you study equations and formulas, put those into words too. The words will help you see a variety of applications for each formula. For example, the Pythagorean Theorem, $C^2 = A^2 + B^2$, would be translated as "The square of the hypotenuse of a right triangle is equal to the sum of the square of the other two sides."

2. Perform opposite operations. If a problem involves multiplication, check your work by dividing; add, then subtract; factor, multiply; square root, square; differentiate, integrate.

3. Use time drills. Practice working problems fast. Time yourself. Exchange problems with a friend and time each other. You can also do this in a study group.

4. Analyze before you compute. Set up the problem before you begin to solve it. When a problem is worth a lot of points, read it twice, slowly. Analyze it carefully. When you take time to analyze a problem you will often see ways to take computational short-cuts. By canceling or combining factors, for example, you may save time.

5. Make a picture. Draw a picture or a diagram if you are stuck. Sometimes a visual representation will clear a blocked mind.

6. Estimate first. An estimation is a good way to double-check your work. When you estimate first you will notice if your computations go awry and you can correct the error quickly.

7. Check your work systematically. When you check your work, ask yourself: "Did I read the problem correctly?", "Did I use the correct formula or equation?", "Is my arithmetic correct?" and "Is my answer in the proper form?"

HOW TO CRAM

Even Though You Shouldn't

Know the limits of cramming. If you haven't cracked a book in any of your courses and have daydreamed through all the lectures, cramming will not help.

It might help raise a grade if you have been reasonably attentive in class, taken fair notes, and have read or skimmed most of the material for the course. It will not work if you try to cram for several courses.

Also recognize that cramming is not really the same as learning. When you rely on cramming, you cheat yourself of true education because you won't remember what you cram. This point is important to know when you cram for mid-term exams. Some students think they have then learned this material and will be able to recall it on the final. They will be unpleasantly surprised. Material learned in cramming sessions is generally unavailable to recall after one or two days.

Cramming is also more work. It takes longer to learn material when you do it under pressure. You can't save time by cramming.

The purpose of cramming, therefore, is only to make the best of a bad situation. Cram to get by in a course so that you can do better next time.

Having been warned of the limitations and costs of cramming, you still might use this four-step cramming process:

1. Make choices. Don't try to learn it all when you cram. You can't. Instead, pick out a few of the most important elements of the course and learn those backwards, forwards, and upside down. Sometimes these choices will be difficult. You may be tempted to go over everything lightly. Resist this temptation. If you cover a lot of material lightly, chances are you will recall none of it during the exam. Be courageous and choose a few important items. A good rule is to spend 25% of cramming time learning new material and 75% of cramming time drilling yourself on that material.

2. Use mind map review sheets and flashcards. Condense the material you have chosen to learn into mind maps. Choose several elements of the mind maps to put on 3x5 flashcards. Practice recreating the mind maps, complete with illustrations. Drill yourself with the flashcards.

3. Recite ad nauseam. The key to cramming is recitation. Recitation will burn facts into your brain like no other study method. Go over your material again and again and again.

Repeat out loud what you have chosen to study until you are confident that you will be able to recall it.

4. Relax. Since material studied while cramming is not learned well, you are more likely to freeze or forget it under pressure. Use relaxation techniques to reduce test anxiety.

During the test, don't beat yourself up about being unprepared. Give yourself permission to do the best that you can.

Study with people

Education often looks like competition. We compete for entrance to school, for grades when we're in school, and for jobs when we leave school. In that climate, it's easy to overlook the power of cooperation.

Study support groups feed you energy. People are social animals and we draw strength from groups. Aside from the camaraderie, the fellowship, and the fun, support groups can assist you by elevating your spirit. There will be days when you just don't want to work at your education. Other members of a study support group can give you encouragement. You are more likely to keep an appointment to study with a group than to study by yourself. If you skip the solo study session, no one will know. If you declare your intention to study to others and know they are depending on you, your intention will gain strength.

In addition to drawing strength from the group when you're down, you can give support to others when they need it. A study support group is also a good place to build rewarding relationships with people.

How to form a group

When you form a support group, look for dedicated students. Find people you are comfortable with and who share some of your academic goals.

You can look for people who face similar academic or personal challenges. For example, if you are divorced and have two toddlers at home, you might look for other single parents who have returned to school.

Studying with friends is fine, but if your common interest is beer and jokes, beware of getting together to work.

The challenge of forming a study group is in making the first contacts and asking others to participate. You can get members by approaching people directly or by advertising.

Watch for people who remain conscious, ask questions, and take notes during class. Ask these students if they want to participate in a study group.

Suggest to two or three others that you meet for coffee and talk about group goals, meeting times, and other logistics. You don't have to make an immediate commitment.

Limit groups to five or six people. Larger groups are unwieldly. Test the group first by planning a one-time-only session. If that session works, plan another. After several successful sessions, you can schedule regular meetings.

Another way to get into a group is to write a note on the blackboard asking interested students to contact you, or pass around a sign-up sheet before class. Most schools have bulletin boards where similar messages can be posted. The advantage of this method is you don't have to face rejection. The disadvantage is that this method takes more time and you don't get to choose who applies.

Conducting a study group

You've formed your support group. Now what do you do? You have many options.

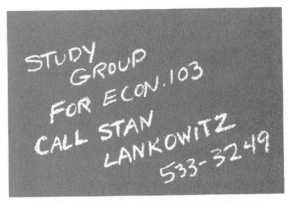

1. Test each other by asking questions. Each group member can agree to bring four or five test questions to each meeting, then you can all take the test made from these questions.

2. Practice teaching each other. Teaching is a great way to learn something. When you teach something you naturally take on a teacher's attitude of, "I know this," as opposed to a student's attitude of, "I still have to learn this." Also, the vocalization involved in teaching further reinforces your memory.

3. Compare notes to make sure you all heard the same thing in class and that you all recorded the important information. Ask other students about material in your notes that is confusing to you.

4. Set aside five or ten minutes to conduct a group brainstorm of possible test questions. You can add these to the "Test Questions" section of your notebook.

5. Conduct open-ended discussions and debates designed to produce understanding and insight.

6. Take advantage of group support in personal areas. Other people can often have insight into your problems involving transportation, child care, finances, time scheduling, or other barriers you may experience in getting what you want from school.

7. Set an agenda for each meeting. Select the items from the above list or create other activities that you will do as a group. Set approximate times for each agenda item and determine a quitting time. End each meeting with assignments for each member.

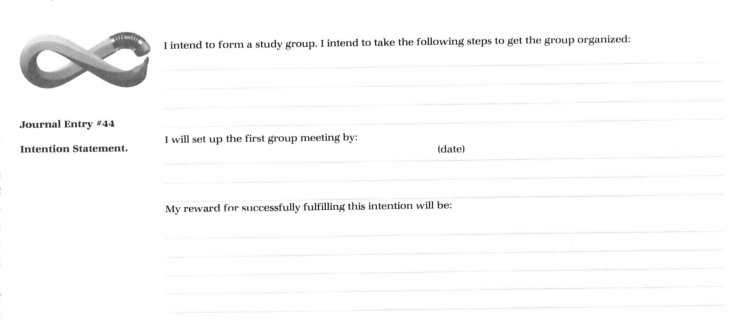

I intend to form a study group. I intend to take the following steps to get the group organized:

Journal Entry #44

Intention Statement.

I will set up the first group meeting by:

(date)

My reward for successfully fulfilling this intention will be:

Test anxiety

If you sometimes flub questions when you know the answer, if you freeze during tests, if you have difficulty sleeping as exams approach, if you tend to weep uncontrollably during finals week, if you keep a rope and a chair in your closet for after the exam—then you might be suffering from test anxiety.

A little tension before a test is good. That tingly, butterflies-in-the-stomach feeling you get from extra adrenalin can sharpen your awareness and keep you alert. Sometimes, however, the tension is damaging. When it is, you are suffering test anxiety, a condition that prevents you from doing your best on exams.

The condition is characterized by feelings of nervousness, fear, or dread. Specific symptoms can include insomnia, loss (or increase) of appetite, an inability to concentrate. Boredom is also a symptom of anxiety. A surface lack of interest in a subject may mask a deep-seated anxiety about future test performance.

During an exam, symptoms include confusion, panic, mental blocks, fainting, or nausea. Frequent yawning immediately before a test is a common reaction. Yawning looks like boredom but it's usually a sign of tension. Oxygen is not getting to the brain because the body is tense, and a yawn is one way our body increases its supply of oxygen. Symptoms after the test include mock indifference, ("I answered all the multiple-choice questions as 'None of the above' because I was bored"), guilt ("Why didn't I study more. . ."), anger ("The teacher never wanted me to pass this stupid course anyway"), blame ("If only the textbook wasn't so dull"), or depression ("Excuse me, could I borrow a rope and a chair?").

The rope and the chair isn't always a kidding matter. Students really have committed suicide over test scores. Stress can be excessive. It can also be managed.

Stress management: two components

Text anxiety has two components, mental and physical. The mental component of stress includes all your thoughts and worries about tests. The

physical component includes feelings, sensations, and tension.

The following techniques deal with both the physical and the mental components of stress in any situation, whether it be test anxiety or stage fright.

Dealing with thoughts

1. Yell stop! When you are aware that your thoughts are racing, your mind is cluttered with worries and fears, and your thoughts are spinning out of control, mentally yell "Stop!".

If you're in a situation that allows it, yell it out loud.

This action is likely to momentarily break the cycle of worry. Once you've stopped it for a moment, you can use any one of the following techniques:

2. Daydream. When you fill your mind with pleasant thoughts, there is no room left for anxiety. If you are worried about an upcoming test, substitute those worry thoughts with visions of what you like to do. Dream about being with a special friend or lying in the sun.

3. Visualize success. Most of us live up to our own expectations, good or bad. If you spend a lot of time mentally rehearsing what you will do when you fail, you increase your chances for failure.

Once you've stopped the cycle of worry, take time to rehearse what it will be like to succeed. Be very specific.

Visualize taking the test successfully. The key to successfully using this tip is detail. Think of yourself in the classroom. Notice your surroundings. When you get the test, see yourself previewing it, looking at each question in every section. You discover that you know all the answers. Imagine yourself writing quickly and confidently. In your mind, watch yourself hand in the paper with confidence. Visualize your celebration when you find out you got an A. As soon as you realize you are feeling anxious about an upcoming test, begin using this technique. The more you do this visualization, the better it will work.

4. Focus. Focus your attention on a specific object. Examine details of a painting, study the branches on a tree, observe the face of your watch including the tiny scratches in the glass, listen to the sound of the lights in the room, listen to the air conditioner or the heating system, listen to the sounds made by other students or by yourself sitting at the desk. Touch the surface of your desk, rub your hand across the material of your shirt.

Concentrate all of your attention on one point. Don't leave room in your

Reprinted by permission of United Feature Syndicate.

mind for anxiety-related thoughts.

This focusing is very similar to meditation techniques. The idea is to occupy your mind with some sensation (sight, hearing, touch) or a mantra. A mantra is a word or syllable that is continually repeated in meditation, (om, love, yes, etc).

5. *Praise yourself.* Talk to yourself in a positive way. Many of us take the first opportunity to say, "Way to go, dummy, you don't even know the answer to the first question on the test." The alternative is to give yourself some loving encouragement.

Consider phrases like, "I am very relaxed," "I am doing a great job on this test," "I'm answering these questions very well," "I'm writing very neatly," "I never forget anything and I have a lot of tools that will help me recall".

With positive self-talk, it is possible to feel that you are lying to yourself. An alternative is to consider that you're just prematurely telling the truth. Or, as the old saying goes, "Fake it until you make it".

6. *Consider the worst.* When you are worrying about something, rather than trying to stop worrying about it, consider the very worst thing that could happen. Expand on your fear. Take the fear to the limit of absurdity.

For example, if you're sitting in a test worrying about whether or not you're going to be successful, stop for a moment (consider yelling "Stop!" under your breath without moving your lips). Imagine the catastrophic problems that might occur if you fail the test. You might say to yourself, "Well, if I fail this test, I might fail the course. And if I fail the course, I might take it over again and then I might fail it again. And then,

Journal Entry #45

Discovery Statement

Explore your feelings about tests. Complete the following sentences.

As exam time gets closer one thing I notice I do is . . .

When it comes to taking tests, I have trouble . . .

The night before a test I usually feel . . .

The morning of a test I usually feel . . .

During a test I usually feel . . .

After the test I usually feel . . .

When I get my score I usually feel . . .

I might lose my financial aid or I might get kicked out of school for academic problems. And if I get kicked out of school, I couldn't get a job so I'd start drinking and pretty soon I'd be a bum on skid row."

Generally you start to chuckle when you see the absurdity. It's at this point that you can backtrack and find out what is a reasonable fear. In the testing situation, your worry that you might fail the entire class if you fail this test might be justified. That's probably as far as rational fear will take you. At that point ask yourself, "Can I live with the worst, with what's rationally possible?" The answer is usually yes. If it's not, use another technique.

This method works because when you consider the worst that could happen, the cold facts are hardly ever as bad as those undefined fears. Shine a light on your fears and they become more manageable.

Dealing with feelings.

1. Breathe. You can calm physical sensations within your body by focusing your attention on your breathing. Concentrate on the air going in and out of your lungs. Experience it as it passes through your nose and mouth. Do this for two to five minutes. If you notice that you are taking short, shallow breaths, begin to take longer and deeper breaths. Fill your lungs and your abdomen, then release all the air.

A visualization that can be effective when you are focusing on your breathing, is to imagine yourself standing on the tip of your nose. Watch the breath pass in and out of your nose as if it were a huge ventilation fan for an underground mine.

2. Scan your body. Simple awareness is

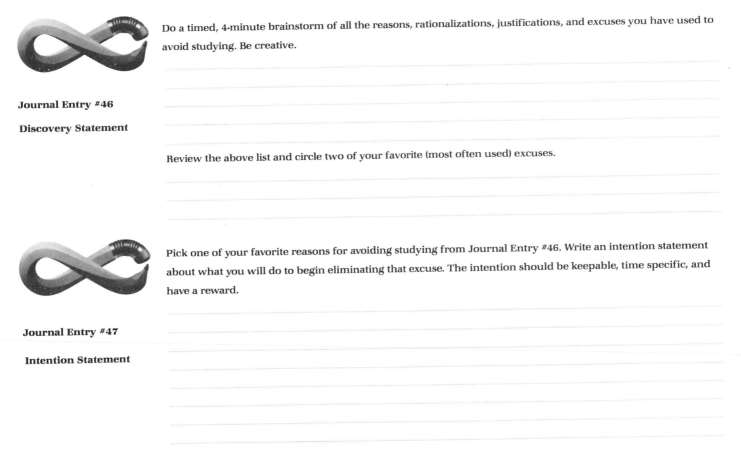

Do a timed, 4-minute brainstorm of all the reasons, rationalizations, justifications, and excuses you have used to avoid studying. Be creative.

Journal Entry #46

Discovery Statement

Review the above list and circle two of your favorite (most often used) excuses.

Pick one of your favorite reasons for avoiding studying from Journal Entry #46. Write an intention statement about what you will do to begin eliminating that excuse. The intention should be keepable, time specific, and have a reward.

Journal Entry #47

Intention Statement

an effective technique to reduce the tension in your body.

Sit comfortably and close your eyes. Start at your feet. Focus your attention on the muscles in your feet and notice if they are relaxed. Tell the muscles in your feet that they can relax. Move up to your ankles and repeat the procedure. Next go to your calves and thighs and buttocks, telling each group of muscles to relax. Do the same for your lower back, diaphragm, chest, upper back, neck, shoulders, jaw, face, upper arms, lower arms, fingers, and scalp.

3. Tense and relax. If you are aware of a particularly tense part of your body, or if you discover tension when you're scanning your body, you can release this with the tense-relax method. To do this, find a muscle that is tense and make it even more tense. For example, if your shoulders are tense, pull them back, arch your back, and tense your shoulder muscles even more tightly, then relax. The net result is that you'll be aware of the relaxation and allow yourself to relax more. You can do the same thing with your legs, arms, abdomen, chest, face, and neck. Clench your fists, squinch your eyebrows, straighten your legs, tense your abdomen and then relax.

4. Use guided imagery. Relax completely and take a quick fantasy trip. Close your eyes, relax your body, and imagine yourself in a beautiful, peaceful, natural setting. Create as much of the scene as you can. Be specific. Use all your senses.

For example, you might imagine yourself at a beach. Hear the surf rolling in and the seagulls calling to each other. Feel the sun on your face and the cool sand between your toes. Smell the sea breeze. Feel the mist from the surf on your face. Notice the ships on the horizon and the rolling sand dunes.

Some people find that a mountain scene or a lush meadow scene works well. You can take yourself to a place you've never been or recreate an experience out of your past. Find a place that works for you and practice getting there. When you become proficient you can return to it quickly for trips that may only last a minute,

Exercise #25

**Twenty things
I like to do**

One way to relieve tension is to mentally yell "Stop!" and substitute a pleasant image (daydream) for the negative thoughts and emotions you are experiencing.

In order to create a supply of pleasant images you can call up during times of stress, conduct an 8-minute brainstorm on things you like to do. Before you begin, tell yourself your goal is to generate 20 ideas. Time yourself, and write as fast as you can. Use the space below for your brainstorm.

When you have completed your list, study it. Pick out two activities that seem especially pleasant, and elaborate on them by creating a mind map of each one. Write the activity in the center of a piece of paper, then using the mind mapping technique, write down all the memories you have about that activity.

You can use these images to calm yourself in stressful situations.

even while you are taking a test.

5. *Describe it.* Focus your attention on your anxiety. If you are feeling nauseous, or have a headache or pain in your abdomen, concentrate on that feeling. Describe it to yourself. Tell yourself how large it is, where it is located in your body, what color it is, what shape it is, what texture it is, how much water it might hold if it had volume, and how heavy it is. Be with it. Describe it in detail and don't resist it.

Oddly enough, if you can completely experience a physical sensation it will often disappear. This is a technique used by people suffering from severe and untreatable pain.

6. *Exercise aerobically.* This is one technique that won't work in the classroom or while you're taking a test, but it's an excellent way to reduce body tension. Do some kind of exercise that will get your heart beating at twice your normal rate and keep it beating at that rate for 15 or 20 minutes. Aerobic exercises include rapid walking, jogging,

swimming, tennis, handball, tag football, basketball, or anything that gets your heart beating very quickly.

When these techniques don't work, when anxiety is serious, get help. If you become withdrawn, have frequent thoughts about death, get depressed and stay depressed for more than a few days, or have feelings of hopelessness, see a counselor.

Depression and anxiety are common among students. Suicide is the second leading cause of student deaths. This is a tragedy because the conditions are treatable. Many schools have counselors available or they can refer you to community agencies where inexpensive counseling is available.

Have Some Fun During Exam Week.

Contrary to popular belief, finals' week does not have to be a drag. Fun actually contributes to performance by releasing anxiety.

A fun week can be your reward for regular study throughout the term.

Golda Meir

Reprinted by permission of G.P. Putnam's Sons from My Life *by Golda Meir. Copyright 1975 by Golda Meir.*

I started school in a huge, fortresslike building on Fourth Street near Milwaukee's famous Schlitz beer factory, and I loved it. I can't remember how long it took me to learn English (at home, of course, we spoke Yiddish, and luckily, so did almost everyone else on Walnut Street), but I have no recollection of the language ever being a real problem for me, so I must have picked it up quickly. I made friends quickly, too. Two of those early first- or second- grade friends remained friends all my life, and both live in Israel now. One was Regina Hamburger (today Medzini), who lived on our street and who was to leave America when I did; the other was Sarah Feder, who became one of the leaders of Labor Zionism in the United States. Anyhow, coming late to class almost every day was awful, and I used to cry all the way to school. Once a policeman even came to the shop to explain to my mother about truancy. She listened attentively but barely understood anything he said, so I went on being late for school and sometimes never got there at all—an ever greater disgrace. My mother—not that she had much alternative—didn't seem to be moved by my bitter resentment of the shop. "We have to live, don't we?" she claimed, and if my father and Sheyna—each for his and her own reasons—would not help, that didn't mean I was absolved of the task. "So it will take you a little longer to become a *rebbetzin* [a bluestocking]," she added. I never became a bluestocking, of course, but I learned a lot at that school.

More than fifty years later—when I was seventy-one and a prime minister—I went back to that school for a few hours. It had not changed very much in all those years except that the vast majority of its pupils were now black, not Jewish, as in 1906. They welcomed me as though I were a queen. Standing in rows on the creaky old stage I remembered so well, freshly scrubbed and neat as pins, they serenaded me with Yiddish and Hebrew songs and raised their voices to peal out the Israeli anthem "Hatikvah" which made my eyes fill with tears. Each one of the classrooms had been beautifully decorated with posters about Israel and signs reading SHALOM (one of the children thought it was my family name), and when I entered the school, two little girls wearing headbands with Stars of David on them solemnly presented me with an enormous white rose made of tissue paper and pipe cleaners, which I wore all day and carefully carried back to Israel with me.

Another of the gifts I got that day in 1971 from the Fourth Street School was a record of my grades for one of the years I had spent there: 95 in reading, 90 in spelling, 95 in arithmetic, 85 in music, and a mysterious 90 in something called manual arts, which I cannot remember at all. But when the children asked me to talk to them for a few minutes, it was not about book learning that I chose to speak. I had learned a lot more than fractions or how to spell at Fourth Street, and I decided to tell those eager, attentive children—born, as I myself had been, into a minority and living, as I myself had lived, without much extravagance (to put it mildly)—what the gist of that learning had been. "It isn't really important to decide when you are very young just exactly what you want to become when you grow up," I told them. "It is much more important to decide on the way you want to live. If you are going to be honest with yourself and honest with your friends, if you are going to get involved with causes which are good for others, not only for yourselves, then it seems to me that that is sufficient, and maybe what you will be is only a matter of chance." I had a feeling that they understood me.

1. Describe briefly three kinds of reviews. Include in your description the purpose for each.

2. Compare the mind map sheet to the traditional outlined review.

3. Mind map ways to cram, even though you shouldn't.

4. List at least five uses for flashcards.

5. Explain the value of conducting major review periods well before the exam.

6. List three ways an instructor might give clues about test questions.

7. List some qualities to look for in a candidate for your study group.

8. Trace the steps a student might take from the time she finds her seat in the exam room to the time she answers the first question.

9. The way to eliminate addictions is to stop wanting things. True or false. Please explain answer.

10. Discuss briefly how it might decrease anxiety during a test if you consider the worst that can happen.

Journal Entry #48

Discovery Statement

Review Journal Entry #43. Did you get what you wanted? If you got exactly what you wanted, just write yes. If you didn't get what you wanted, write what you didn't get. If you got something unexpected, write that down, too.

Journal Entry #49

Intention Statement

If there was something you wanted from this chapter and didn't get, write down a strategy you intend to use to get it.

Journal Entry #50

Intention Statement

Write a statement about your intention to practice one of the relaxation techniques and to use one of the test-taking hints.

Since reading *How to predict test questions* in chapter 6, *Tests*, have you heard many potential test questions during class lectures? Which instructor do you see as giving the best clues about what will be tested?

Journal entry #51

Look back

I want these things from this chapter:

Journal entry #52

Discovery statement

CHAPTER SEVEN
CREATIVITY

> Man's mind once stretched by a new idea
> never regains its original dimension.
>
> OLIVER WENDELL HOLMES

> In most lives insight has been accidental. We wait for it as
> primitive man awaited lightning for a fire. But making mental
> connections is our most crucial learning tool, the essense of human
> intelligence is to forge links; to go beyond the given; to see pattern,
> relationships, context.
>
> MARILYN FERGUSON

> This is the sort of English up with which I will not put.
>
> WINSTON CHURCHILL

In this chapter...

People who don't think they are creative can discover how to tap
creative resources they might not have known they had.

People who think they are creative can learn some new tricks.

Anyone can be creative if they know how to set the stage for it. That
know-how can be handy when the deadline for a term paper
looms ominously.

Creativity techniques will show you how to set the stage.
*Brainstorm, Focus attention, Let go, Expect the Aha!, Play with
data, Use chance,* and *Refine ideas* will show you what to do once
the stage is set.

Become your creative best with techniques illustrated in *Creating
papers and speeches from nothing.* Find out what it takes to whip
out dynamite research papers in *Writing papers*, and hear how to
come out on top with speech opportunities in *Preparing speeches*.
Getting started is tough. Handle it by reading *Choosing a subject* and
Collecting data.

See how math and science problems are like climbing rocks in
Solving math and science problems. Don't put it off—*Writing
letters* will get you going. Other suggestions await you in *The cheap
word processor, Idea files, Creative serendipity,* and *Learn
to type.*

Power Process #7 suggests that you may not be a fool often
enough. *Be a fool* is a path to growth.

Exercises in this chapter, *Eschew verbosity, Fix the world
brainstorm, Working titles, Meditation with white light, Master
mind map, A creative approach,* and *Contra-lateral movement* are
designed to unlock your creativity.

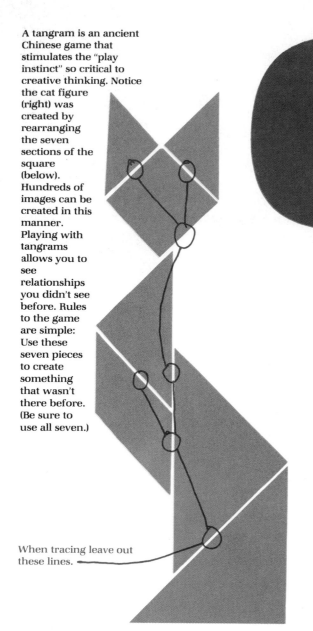

A tangram is an ancient Chinese game that stimulates the "play instinct" so critical to creative thinking. Notice the cat figure (right) was created by rearranging the seven sections of the square (below). Hundreds of images can be created in this manner. Playing with tangrams allows you to see relationships you didn't see before. Rules to the game are simple: Use these seven pieces to create something that wasn't there before. (Be sure to use all seven.)

When tracing leave out these lines.

Make your own tangram by cutting pieces like these out of cheap poster board. When you make a pattern you like, trace around the edges of it and see if a friend can discover how you did it. If you leave out the connecting lines, it's not as easy as it looks.

CREA
TECH

The techniques in this section can increase the probability that you will have an Aha! experience when you need one.

The Aha! is the idea, the creative spark, that pops into your brain unexpectedly. It is the sudden emergence of a new pattern, a previously undetected relationship, an unusual new combination of familiar elements.

These techniques can be used for everything from term papers and math problems to remodeling a house or rewriting the Constitution. The techniques presented here all use the logical, sequential left side of the brain in a way that enhances function in the intuitive, creative right side of the brain.

These techniques will enable you to use logical, step-by-step processes to set the stage for creative leaps to occur.

Brainstorm

The brainstorming process is described briefly in earlier chapters. Brainstorming is a technique for finding solutions to specific problems. For example: If you run out of money two days before payday every week, you could brainstorm ways to make your money last longer. You can brainstorm ways to solve scheduling problems. You can brainstorm ways to get home for Thanksgiving. You can brainstorm ways

TIVITY

IQUES

to pay for your education.

The purpose of brainstorming is to generate as many solutions as possible. Sometimes the craziest, most outlandish solutions, while unworkable in themselves, lead to new ways to solve problems.

The brainstorming process works like this:

1. Formulate the question or problem precisely.

2. Let go of the need for a particular solution.

3. Relax.

4. Set a time limit for the brainstorming session.

5. Set a quota or goal for the number of solutions you want to generate. (Optional)

6. Use 3x5 cards for each possible solution. (Optional)

7. Brainstorm in a group. (Optional and powerful)

8. Write down solutions or suggestions as fast as you can think of them.

9. Avoid making judgments and evaluations during the brainstorming session.

10. After the session, review, evaluate, and edit.

Focus attention

Focusing attention means being in the here and now.

In order to focus your attention on a project, notice when your attention wanders. Involve all your senses.

For example, when you are composing at a typewriter and the writing is going well, listen to how the machine sounds as you type. Pay attention to the feel of the keys as you strike them. When you know the sights, sounds, and sensations of being truly in focus, you'll be able to get into focus more easily.

You can change your body position to increase focus. Some people concentrate better lying down. Others focus more easily if they pace back and forth. Still others need to have something in their hands.

It is difficult, if not impossible, to let go of your left brain (the logical, analytical side) for long periods of time. If you give your left brain something to do, like watching the spin on the tennis ball or listening to the sound of the typewriter, the left brain will be still so that your right brain (the creative, intuitive side) can take over.

Don't expect to be focused all the time. Periods of inspiration may last only seconds. Be gentle with yourself when you notice your concentration has flagged.

Be willing to accept conflict, tension, and discomfort. Notice them and allow them to be rather than fighting with them.

Exercise #26

Fix the world brainstorm

This exercise works best with four to six people. Pick a major world problem (hunger, disarmament, poverty, totalitarianism, pollution). Then conduct a ten-minute brainstorm on all the things that an individual can do to contribute to solving the problem. Use the brainstorming techniques described on page 179. Remember, do not evaluate or judge the solutions during the process. The purpose of a brainstorm is to generate a flow of ideas.

After the brainstorming session, discuss the process and the solutions that it generated. Did you feel any energy from the group? Were any new or exciting ideas created? Are any of the ideas you created worth pursuing?

Creative serendipity

Serendipity comes from an 18th century story by Horace Walpole, "The Three Princes of Serendip." The princes had a knack for making lucky discoveries. Serendipity is more than just luck. It is the "gift" of finding something valuable or agreeable that you're not looking for. By remaining open to the world around you, expecting to make lucky discoveries, and developing your creative powers, you can make your own creative "luck."

History is full of serendipitous events. Pasteur noticed "by accident" that milkmaids seldom got smallpox. The result was his discovery that mild cases of cowpox immunized them.

Penicillin was discovered by accident. Alexander Fleming was growing bacteria in a laboratory. A spore of Penicillium notatum, which is a kind of mold, apparently blew in the window and landed in the dish. It killed the bacteria. Fleming isolated the active ingredient, and a few years later, during World War II, it saved thousands of lives. Had Fleming not been alert to the possibility, the discovery might never have been made.

Serendipity is most likely to occur in the course of work.

Serendipity will flow into your life when you keep your eyes open. Multiply your contacts with the world. Keep pumping the world into your brain.

Let go

Letting go is the other side of focusing. They are inseparable parts of the same process.

"Letting go" means not forcing yourself to be creative.

Practice focusing for short periods at first, then give yourself a break. Phone a friend. Take a walk. This part of the creative process is essential. It gives the subconscious time to work on the problem. Movies, music, walks in the park, and other pleasant activities are good ways to stir up the creative soup that's simmering in our right brains.

Intersperse periods of focused concentration with occasional stretches. Do sit-ups or push-ups. Use relaxation and breathing exercises between periods of focused activity. Muscle tension and the lack of oxygen can inhibit self-expression.

Take a nap when you are tired. Edison napped frequently during the day.

Trust this process. Creativity will happen if you let it.

Expect the Aha!

Learn to trust your creative process—even when no answers are in sight. Often people are reluctant to look at problems if no immediate solution is apparent. They are impatient. If the answer isn't quickly apparent, they resist frustration by giving up. Most of us do this to some degree with personal problems. We have difficulty with a relationship, for example, and don't see an immediate solution; so rather than face the problem, we deny its existence.

Trust that a solution will show up. Recognize the fact that frustration and being stuck are part of the solution.

Sometimes solutions break through in a giant AHA! More often they come in a series of little Aha's. Be aware of what your Aha's look, feel, and sound like.

Play with data

At a seminar on creativity a few years ago, one of Johnny Carson's writers was asked how he could create so many new jokes day after day for years at a stretch.

"Stuff your brain," he replied. "Keep pumping information into it. Read anything you can get your hands on. Read anything that interests you. Don't worry about whether you can use it or how you will use it, just pump it in there. Give your brain lots of raw material. Then give it a chance to 'cook'."

Creativity works the same way for students.

Look at data from all sides. Collect lots of it. Switch your attention from one aspect to another. Spend time examining each fact. Avoid getting stuck on one particular part of a problem.

Stand the problem on its head. Assume a solution, even if it looks wrong, then work backwards.

Ask other people to look at the data. Solicit opinions.

Live with the problem. Write down data, possible solutions, or a formulation of the problem on 3x5 cards and carry them with you. Look at them before you go to bed at night. Review them when you are waiting for the bus. Make them part of your life. Think about them constantly.

Look for the obvious solution or the obvious "truths" about the problem, then dump them. Ask yourself, "Well, I know X is true, but if X were not true, then what would happen?"

Put unrelated facts next to each other and invent a relationship, even if it seems absurd at first.

Make imaginary pictures with facts.

Condense the data.

Look for opposites.

Put the data in chronological order.

Put the data in alphabetical order.

Put the data in order from most complex to least complex, or the reverse.

It's been said that there are no new ideas, and that creative genius is merely the process of finding new ways to combine old ideas. That's all it took for Henry Ford. He merely combined a motor and a carriage. He didn't invent either one.

Use chance

The world works in strange ways. Be sensitive to happy coincidences. You might find a solution to an accounting problem in a Saturday morning cartoon, if you are open to it.

When you're stuck, pick out solutions at random and test them.

To use chance more effectively, look at every situation as a learning situation. What you learn from a plumber on the bus in the morning may be applicable to your economics class in the afternoon.

Keep a journal.

Keep a scrapbook of interesting newspaper and magazine articles.

Keep a 3x5 card file of ideas that randomly pop into your head.

Follow your random hunches. If you get an idea when you are studying, take some time to develop it.

Refine ideas

Most people ignore this part of the process. How many great moneymaking schemes have we all had that were never followed up? How many good ideas for short stories? How many times have we said to ourselves, "You know, what they ought to do is attach two handles to one of those things, paint it orange, and sell it to police departments.

They'd make a fortune."

And we never get it that we are they.

True genius resides in the follow-through. Ideas usually appear in rough form. They need tuning. The right brain imagines a whole concept, complete and ready to use. The left brain must then bring logic, order, and a system of implementation to the idea; then, concept becomes reality.

Almost always, refinement means simplification. If there is any law about good ideas, it is "Keep it simple."

Idea files

We all have ideas. People who are labeled "creative" are the people who keep their ideas.

One way to keep ideas is to write them on 3x5 cards. Make up your own categories and number the cards so that they can be cross-referenced. For example, if you have an idea about making a new kind of bookshelf, you might file it under "Remodeling." The card might also be filed under "Marketable ideas." On one card, you can write your idea, and on the other you can write, "see card #132—Remodeling."

You can include powerful quotes in your files. Write down jokes.

Keep a journal. Journals don't have to be exclusively about your thoughts and feelings. You can also include your observations of the world around you, observations others pass on to you, important ideas—anything.

Keep letter-size files of important correspondence, magazine and newspaper articles, and other material.

Review your files from time to time. Something that was an amusing thought in November might be the perfect solution to a problem the following March.

A creative approach

Step one
Choose a situation or condition in your life that isn't working or that you want to change.

Using 3x5 cards, one idea per card, conduct a seven-minute brainstorm on possible solutions. Use the brainstorming guidelines on page 179.

After the brainstorm, evaluate your solutions. Spread them out on a table and focus on each one. Discard the obviously unacceptable solutions. Practice putting the remaining solutions into categories. Look for relationships between solutions. Study them. Do this until your mind begins to wander. Continue to concentrate on them for two more minutes, then put them away.

Step two
Wait 24 hours, then conduct another brainstorm. This time, instead of solutions, brainstorm problems. For seven minutes, on separate 3x5 cards, write down everything that doesn't work in your life. Do this as quickly as you can.

Step three
Take out the solutions you generated the day before. See how many of those solutions apply to other problems you brainstormed. Spread out all the 3x5 cards and match solutions to problems.

(continued on page 183)

Creating papers and speeches from nothing

Perhaps you are one of those folks who has the idea that preparing a speech or term paper is an exercise in misery that will prove once again that you are not the creative type.

If that's so, consider this alternative approach to the problem. Rather than trying to be Ernest Hemingway, picture yourself as the manager of a factory. You have been assigned to start from nothing and build something from the ground up.

The factory is located immediately adjacent to and above your shoulders. You are the boss. You choose the goal. You devise the system of data collection. You write production schedules, make internal deadlines, institute quality controls, monitor progress, adjust for contingencies, and create a final product. You decide whether to meet (or miss) deadlines, work under pressure, direct the factory, and take risks.

Choosing a subject

It's easy to put off starting work on papers or speeches if you have a hard time choosing a topic. Selecting a topic is easy when you use a strategy.

It is virtually impossible to make a wrong choice at this stage of the game. The best way to choose is to just do it.

Using your instructor's guidelines for the paper or speech, sit down and make a list of topics that interest you or that you know something about. Write as many of these as you can think of in two minutes. Choose one. If you can't decide, use scissors to cut your list into single items, put them in a hat or box, and draw out your topic. To avoid getting stuck on this first step, set a precise deadline for yourself. Write an intention statement, "I will have a topic chosen for my term paper by 4 p.m. on Wednesday."

The most common pitfall in paper and speech writing occurs after a topic has been selected. The danger is in the failure to sufficiently narrow the broad general topic. The following will help you narrow the subject for writing any paper or speech.

Begin by creating a succession of "working titles", each narrower in focus than the one preceding it. For example, you might choose "George Washington" as a general topic for your American history paper. This is much too broad a topic to be useful. Make your topic more specific.

Take a stack of 3x5 cards and begin by writing down (one item of information per card) everything you can think of pertaining to George Washington. These cards might contain such things as "legends", "honesty", "Valley Forge," "Commander in Chief of the Continental Army", "wooden teeth", "crossing the Delaware", "first President", and "Mt. Vernon".

After writing as many of these subtopics as you can from your personal knowledge, take a reference work such as your history text and look up "George Washington" in the index. Prepare additional subtopic idea cards. They might say "French Indian War", "Annapolis Convention", "banks", "military campaigns", and more. After reviewing indexes in available reference works, check your lecture notes. Skimming Washington biographies in the library completes this stage of the process.

You may at this point have 25 or 30 cards with possible subtopics or working titles. Spread the cards out on a table or desk, face up. Suppose after examining the ideas, you choose to narrow your subject to "military campaigns". Put all cards with subjects related to armies or battles in one pile.

"George Washington's military campaigns" is still too broad a working title for even a long paper. Your stack of cards under military campaigns includes, "French-Indian War", "capture of Fort Dusquesne", "differences between American and European troops", "failure of American cavalry", "guerrilla warfare", "intelligence",

"propaganda", "supply requisitions", "Valley Forge", "uniforms", "strategy".

Looking over the items contained within the general subject of "military campaigns", you might find that one or two topics appeal most to your interests. Perhaps "intelligence" is especially interesting because you like spy stories. "Washington's military intelligence apparatus" is a good working title, but still a bit broad when you discover how

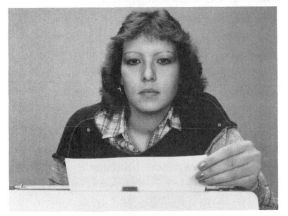

(continued from page 182)

Why this exercise works
Often, what looks to us like several little, nagging problems is only one problem. Sometimes, making one change results in clearing up many problems.

A classic example is the drug addict who is in trouble with the law, about to lose her job, having difficulty in her family relationships, and having trouble paying her bills. She thinks she has a whole basketful of problems. In reality, she has only one.

This is a dramatic example. Less serious problems can also disguise themselves as lots of small difficulties. Difficulty concentrating in class, irritability with the kids, and the annoying squeak in the back door might all be related to a simple thing like not taking enough time to do things around the house. One solution, spending more time at home, can thus solve several problems.

Conclusion
Return to the solutions you generated, and choose one (or several) that you think will work. Write a short intention statement about how you intend to implement the solution.

Exercise #28

Working titles

Using mind maps, 3x5 cards, or other materials you feel comfortable with, create specific, narrowed working titles for the following subjects.
Example:

Subject: Sports
Working Title:
"The effect of the increased popularity of jogging on the health of the population of Little Rock, Arkansas."

Fashion models

Garbage

Space travel

Television

World hunger

American cars

Loud music

much information exists on the topic. One more step is needed in the process.

Thinking over your refined working titles might yield further spontaneous ideas to narrow the topic. Another approach, at this point, is to read about the issue of Revolutionary War spying wherever it might appear in your reference works.

Looking through a bibliography, you may be delighted to find whole books dealing with spies of that era. It gives you an unexpected sense of excitement about your writing project which wasn't there before. This is a common experience.

From this narrowed perspective, you can generate another half dozen possible working titles. At last, you choose "True and untrue military intelligence and its influence on Washington's decision to winter over at Valley Forge in 1778." Of course this is too long, but as a working title it gives direction and structure to research.

Here are some hints for creating good working titles:

1. Be outrageous. If you are stuck, have fun with a working title. Sometimes a crazy title will lead to an imaginative idea concerning an otherwise dull subject. ("George Washington: How he danced his way into the hearts of his troops" might lead to ideas about Washington's personality and his troops.)

2. Look for questions. Questions send research in a definite direction. Even if you don't find the answer, the question may lead to other more fruitful areas.

3. Don't offer the obvious to experts. History instructors know "Washington was important", and biology teachers are aware that "There are many interesting facts about cells." Keep your audience in mind.

4. Don't fall in love with a working title. Be willing to give it up as soon as the data leads you in a better direction.

Collecting data

Not included in this article are the two most important research skills: use of the library (chapter 11, Resources) and effective note-taking (chapter 5, Notes). Presented here are suggestions which can smooth your data collection process.

Handling 3x5 cards

If 3x5 cards haven't found their way into your home by now, joy awaits you. Most students now know the clerk at the stationery store by his first name.

Organize research cards as you create them. Use rubber bands to keep source cards separate from information cards, and to maintain general categories. For a description of these two types of reference cards, see page 129 in chapter 5, Notes. Keeping your 3x5's organized from the beginning saves you time later.

You also save time by making sure you copy all information correctly. Be meticulous with your source cards. Always include the source card code and page number on information cards.

Write legibly. You may not see some of these cards for days or weeks.

Be consistent. Use the same format for all your cards. Don't waste time by reinventing your system of research.

In addition to source cards and information cards, generate idea cards. If you have a thought as you are researching, write it down on a card. Don't trust your memory. Label these cards clearly as your own thoughts. If you already know a lot about your subject, write down each thought on a

3x5 card. Later you can incorporate them in your writing. Information already in your brain is valuable. Don't discount it.

The researcher's frame of mind

Doing quality research asks the best of your master student capabilities. It sometimes calls for a willingness to be frustrated, curious, and always to be alert to all possibilities.

Alertness is especially important. Many times valuable research will seem to happen as if by luck or accident. You stumble across a perfect source, a name in an index just happens to catch your eye, you pick up a magazine during a break and there is an article about the very subject you are researching.

These fortuitous events happen regularly to good researchers. They may not be accidents. Some researchers create their own luck. They do this by being open to information, by having a solid overview of the subject, and by immersing themselves in their work. They pick up clues from the environment and from forbidding, grey pages of type.

There are several methods you can use to get an overview of a subject. Check encyclopedias, other general reference works, even children's books. Make a mind map of the subject before you start researching. Include general areas to research and what you already know about the subject.

Initiate your research by finding a core of four or five major sources on your subject. Compare bibliographies for recurring sources. If a work appears in several bibliographies, it is likely to be important. Read these thoroughly. If you are working on a long project, learn your core materials as if you were to be tested on them. This knowledge will direct your further research and will

act as a magnet for subsequent data. Use current data. If your subject is contemporary, even a source that is a few weeks old can be out-of-date. When you use magazines and newspapers, check the ones that aren't yet listed in indexes.

Look over your collected notes often. Spread them out and practice rearranging them into categories. Think about them. Observe them. This work enables your brain to process the information subconsciously. The benefits will show up two or three days later when an idea suddenly pops into your head.

Another advantage of frequent reflection is that it sharpens your focus. Your working title is only a rough approximation of the final product. Your research will determine the developed form of your paper or speech and the ultimate title.

Writing papers

Every writer has an individual style. The techniques presented here work for most writers. Test them for yourself. Pay attention to what works for you.

Thesis statements

Clarify the purpose of your paper by summarizing it in one concise sentence. This kind of sentence is called a thesis statement, and it is a further refinement of the working title. The first thesis statement you write will not necessarily be your final thesis statement, but it can help you make a good preliminary outline.

For example, in the process of choosing a subject, you might have written a thesis statement such as: "The purpose of this paper is to demonstrate how dubious information supplied by George Washington's spies resulted in his decision to winter at Valley Forge in 1778."

Make your thesis statement clear, detailed, and to the point.

Preliminary outline

Next, write a preliminary outline using your thesis statement as a guide. Start by arranging your 3x5 cards on a table in the order you think best suited to the purpose of your paper. Experiment with the cards. Group them into major categories, then sort each major category into subcategories. Arrange each 3x5 in the proper order within each subcategory. Practice by imagining yourself explaining the whole paper to a friend. Go through the entire outline this way to see if the order is logical. This won't be your final outline; however, it will get you started.

The traditional way is to use the Roman numeral/capital letter style outline.

You can also use a mind map to draw your preliminary outline. Start by writing your working title or thesis statement in the center of a blank page. Then on branches, write down the major sections.

Mind maps are especially useful for papers that don't involve extensive research. For example, if you are writing a short paper on the use of imagery in a particular short story, you can skip the 3x5 cards altogether and simply create a mind map outline of the paper.

Writing at last!

Once you have written a preliminary outline, you are ready to begin writing. Gather your 3x5 cards, arranged in the order they will appear. Now, write about the data on each card.

Don't worry too much about grammar, punctuation, or spelling as you write your rough draft. Write as if you were explaining the subject to a friend. Let words flow. The very act of writing will release creative energy.

Write in paragraphs, one idea per paragraph. If you have organized your 3x5's logically, related facts will appear close to each other. You will revise this rough draft several times, so don't worry if the first draft seems rough or choppy.

A common mistake of beginning writers is to gather a small amount of data, get nervous about a deadline, then hold their noses, close their eyes, and jump into the writing process with both feet (and few facts). Avoid the temptation to start writing without data. Gather more information than you can use.

On the other hand, don't wait until you have finished your research before beginning to write. The act of writing creates ideas. Those new ideas might demand more data. Writing reveals holes in research. If you have gathered data right up to the last minute, hoping to write the paper the night before it is due, you will not have time to fill in the gaps.

As you research, play with your information. Experiment with outlines and thesis statements.

You will know it's time to write when, in the middle of the mind mapping or card sorting process, you see a natural place to begin. Suddenly, you see part or all of your paper as a complete whole. This feeling is characterized by ideas flowing freely and swiftly, sometimes faster than you can write or type.

This is not to say that suddenly the skies will open and your whole paper will appear before your eyes, flanked by trumpeting angels. You may just get a strong sense of how one small section of your paper should be constructed. You may get only one sentence. When this happens, write. You may have to throw away what you write in the early stages of research, but the process itself is beneficial.

Revising

Rewrite. Then, rewrite your rewrite. Then rewrite that one. This is the critical part of writing for 99% of all writers—geniuses included. Paper is cheap.

Schedule time for rewrites before you begin, and schedule at least one day between revisions so you can let the material sit. On

(continued on page 188)

The cheap
word processor

Writing is usually not a matter of finding a clever phrase. It is more often a matter of presenting material in a logical, effective order.

A pair of scissors and a jar of rubber cement are all you need to make that job easy.

First, write a rough draft. Then cut the whole thing into pieces, spread them out, and spend some time fitting the pieces back together, like parts in a puzzle. Once you get used to this process, you'll find that it's faster than trying to get the structure and organization of your writing perfect on the first draft.

Keep your reader in mind as you reorganize the structure. Give your reader information in the order that's easiest to understand, in building-block fashion. It's OK to leapfrog over an important idea in the sequence only if you tell the reader what you're doing. If you don't let them know you skipped something, you'll have their head spinning in the fog.

(The major benefit of electronic word processors is that they enable writers to move ideas around quickly and easily. Cement and scissors do the same thing.)

Use rubber cement rather than library paste or other adhesives. Strips of paper already cemented in place can be peeled off and reglued somewhere else. Rubber cement can be diluted with rubber cement thinner to a fast drying consistency.

Use large, good quality scissors. Short, cheap, dull scissors will blister the hands of industrious writers.

(continued from page 186)

Tuesday night, you might think your writing sings the song of beautiful language. On Wednesday, you will see that those same words, like the phrase "sings the song of beautiful language," belong in the trash basket.

Ideally, a student will revise a paper two or three times, make a clean copy of those revisions, then let the last revised draft sit for at least three or four days. The brain needs that time to disengage itself from the project. Obvious grammatical mistakes, awkward constructions, and lapses in logic are hidden from us when we are in the middle of the creative process. Give yourself time to step back.

One of the best ways to revise your paper is to read it out loud. The eyes tend to fill in the blanks in our own writing. The combination of voice and ears forces us to pay attention to the details. Reading aloud to a friend is even better, and having a friend read your paper aloud to you (if your ego can take it) is the best.

Look for consistency within paragraphs, logical transitions from paragraph to paragraph and from section to section.

Buy a good English grammar book and use it.

Look for excess baggage. Avoid at all costs and at all times the really, really terrible mistake of using way too many unnecessary words, a mistake that some student writers often make when they sit down to write papers for the various courses in which they participate at the fine institutions of higher learning which they are fortunate to attend. (Example: The previous sentence could be edited to: "Avoid using unnecessary words.")

Approach your rough draft as if it were a chunk of granite from which you will chisel the final product. In the end, much of your first draft will be lying on the floor. What is left will be the clean, clear, polished product.

Sometimes the revisions are painful. Sooner or later, every writer invents a phrase that is truly clever but makes no contribution to the purpose of the paper. It is difficult to gun down these phrases. They play to our pride. We all want to demonstrate how witty we are. Those clever phrases look at us with big, watery doe-eyes and beg for life. "I'm cute," they say. "I show everyone how smart you are. Please let me stay in your paper." Grit your teeth and pull the trigger.

Another good revision technique is to have a trusted friend revise your paper. This is never a substitute for your own revision, but a friend can often see mistakes you miss.

When you write, be honest and be yourself. Write the way you talk. For instance, if you attempt to use words that aren't part of your vocabulary, *simply for the sake of using bigger or more obscure words*, the result will be a paper that is difficult to read. Stick with what is natural.

The other side of this coin is that we can't really write the way we speak. The spoken word is accompanied by facial expressions and gestures, as well as changes in voice tone, pitch, and volume. Slang expressions used in everyday speech are not appropriate in academic writing. Compensate for elements peculiar to the spoken language by being clear and concise and by providing smooth, logical transitions from subject to subject.

After you have revised your clean copy, you are ready to begin writing the final draft.

The final product

Take care with the form and appearance of your final product. In a sense, any paper is a sales effort. If you hand in a paper with its shirt tail hanging out, its hair tangled and unwashed, and its face unshaved, your instructor is less likely to buy.

Here are some basic guidelines:

Use the correct format. An instructor may have her own formula for margin width, footnote formats, title pages, and other details, so check with her before you begin to write.

Use a cover page with the title of the paper, your name, the date, the course title, and your instructor's name.

At the risk of saying something that can go unsaid: type your paper.

Double-space. Nothing is more maddening than to make corrections on a single-spaced page. Many instructors will not accept single-spaced papers.

Use ample margins. Use at least one-inch margins all around.

Bind your paper with a paper or plastic cover. A professional-looking paper will indicate that you have taken care with your work.

Include an outline of your paper if appropriate. An outline can make reading your paper easier.

Use a pica (first choice) or elite typewriter. Fancy script types are not appropriate for academic work.

Keep typewriter characters clean. Smudgy, hard-to-read letters degrade the appearance of your paper.

Use medium-inked, black ribbon. Change the ribbon before your copy becomes light.

Use quality paper for your final version.

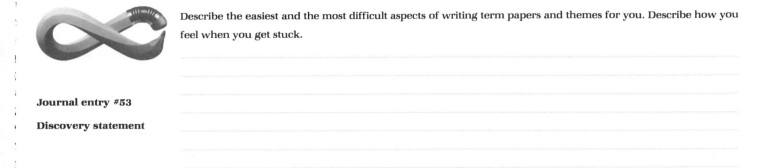

Describe the easiest and the most difficult aspects of writing term papers and themes for you. Describe how you feel when you get stuck.

Journal entry #53

Discovery statement

Preparing speeches

Even if you are certain that public speaking is not a skill you will use after graduation, it is a skill that can help you develop your ability to think on your feet, to think under pressure, and to organize and communicate thought in a clear, understandable way.

Speech organization

It's natural to tune out during a speech. Just think of all the times you have listened to instructors, lecturers, politicians, and others. Think of all the wonderful daydreams you had during their speeches.

Your audiences are like you and tend to react the same way. The way you organize your speech can, in large part, determine the number of people in your audience who stay with you until the end.

Speeches are usually divided into three main parts: the introduction, the main body, and the conclusion.

Introduction

The introduction sets the stage for your audience, ("to tell them what you're going to tell them.") It is the time to make clear to the audience where you are taking them. Unless you are a brilliant presenter such as Billy Graham or Johnny Carson, a rambling speech with no clear internal organization puts your audience to sleep.

The following introduction, for example, informs the speaker's audience of exactly what is going to happen. The speech has been divided into three distinct parts, and each part is presented in a logical order.

"Canary bifurcation is a cruel sport. I intend to describe exactly what happens to the birds, tell you who is doing this, and show you how you can organize yourselves to stop this inhumane practice."

Be precise about the purpose of your speech. Speeches can inform, persuade, motivate, or entertain. Choose what you want to do, and let your audience know what you intend.

Start with a bang!

Compare the following two introductions to speeches on the serious subject of world hunger.

Example number one:

"I'm very honored to be here with you today. I intend to talk about malnutrition and starvation. First, I want to outline the extent of these problems, then I will discuss some basic assumptions concerning world hunger, and finally, I will propose some solutions."

You can almost hear the snores from the audience.

Example number two:

"More people have died as a consequence of hunger in the past five years than have been killed in all the wars, revolutions, and murders in the past 150 years. Yet no one dies of hunger because there is not enough food to go around. I'm honored to be with you today to discuss the problem . . . ."

Most people pay attention to the first few seconds of a speech, so this is a good time to bring out the big guns. Start with dramatic examples, then go into your introduction and outline.

Main body

The main body of the speech is the content—70 to 90% of most speeches. In the main body, you will develop your speech in a logical way, much the way you develop a written paper.

In speeches, transitions are especially important. Give your audience a signal when you change points. ("On the other hand, until the public realizes what is happening to these children in these countries . . .", "The second reason hunger persists is . . .",)

In long speeches, recap from time to time, and preview what's to come.

As in papers, use facts, descriptions, expert opinions, statistics, and other concrete details. A speech that contains only vague generalizations is boring.

Conclusion

At the end of the speech, summarize the points you have made and draw your conclusion ("tell them what you've told them"). You started with a bang, so finish with drama. The first and last parts of the speech are most important. Make it clear to your audience when you've reached the end of your speech. Avoid such trite endings as, "This is the end of my speech," or "Well, I guess that's it." A simple standby signal is, "So, in conclusion I want to reiterate three points: First . . . ." When you are finished, stop talking.

Notes

Professional speakers recommend keeping notes on 3x5 cards. It's easy to keep your speech in order. (Number the cards so that if you drop them, you can quickly put them in order again.) As you finish the information on each card, move it to the back of the pile. Write information clearly and in letters large enough to be seen from a distance.

The disadvantage of the 3x5 card system is that it involves a lot of card shuffling. Mind mapping overcomes this disadvantage. Even an hour-long speech (which is a long speech) can be mapped on a single 8½ by 11 sheet of paper.

Some speakers prefer to use standard outlined notes.

You can also use memory techniques and memorize the outline of your speech. The loci system (chapter 3, Memory) can be especially valuable for organizing speeches. When you practice speeches, experiment with each system.

Subject matter

When the choice is yours, talk about things you know about and are interested in. Include your personal experiences. Your enthusiasm will be transmitted to the audience.

Rehearsal techniques

The key to successful public speaking is practice. This is the one thing most beginning speakers fail to do. The barrier to practice is the same barrier most of us have to recitation—we are embarrassed to talk out loud to ourselves.

Diligent practice relieves you of having to rely heavily on your notes.

When you practice, practice in a loud voice. If possible, practice in the room where you will deliver your speech. Your voice sounds different when you talk loud, and this can be unnerving. Get used to it before the big day.

If you can't practice your speech in the actual room, at least visit the site ahead of time. Become familiar with the seating arrangement, the lighting, and if applicable, the sound system. (It's an especially good idea to hear what your voice sounds like over a sound system before the time of your speech.)

Record your speech and listen to it. Better yet, videotape the presentation. Many schools have video equipment available for student use (check the library). When listening to yourself, listen for repeated phrases like "you know", "kind of", "really", plus any little "uh's" and "ah's."

To get rid of these mannerisms, simply tell yourself that you intend to notice every time they pop up in your daily speech. (Write an intention statement about it.) You will hear yourself every time you say the offending phrase. Don't try to get rid of these phrases. Notice them. When you hear them, stop and tell yourself that you don't use those words anymore. The phrases will begin to sound foreign and out of place to you. Eventually, they will disappear.

Practice your speech in front of a friend. Speaking before one or two friends can be more uncomfortable than talking in front of a large group. The experience of surviving this ordeal makes your actual speech less threatening and is a good way to build your confidence.

Practice by speaking up often in class.

Use stress reduction techniques before and during your speech. Practice them ahead of time.

Make a checklist of materials you will need for your speech, including audio visual aids.

When you practice your speech, don't deliver it word for word. Know your material and present the information in the most natural way.

Delivering the speech

For beginners, the most imposing problem in delivering speeches is nervousness. Hands shake, palms sweat, knees wobble, minds go blank. Give yourself a hand by knowing your material inside out.

Nervousness is a natural occurrence. The best way to deal with it is to notice and experience it. When you get up in front of an audience, pay close attention to how you feel. Tell yourself, "Yes, my hands are clammy. I notice that my stomach is slightly upset. My face feels numb."

Use power process #3: *Love your problems.*

When you notice the symptoms of anxiety and allow them to exist, they will disappear. When you fight them and deny them, they become more persistent.

Also use power process #2: *Be here now.* Be totally in the present moment. Notice all your thoughts about how you feel and gently release them. Notice how the room feels. Notice the temperature and lighting. See the audience. Look at them. Make eye contact.

Another technique you can use to dispel anxiety is to look at your audience and imagine that they are all dressed as clowns. Or, consider the worst, that they will hate your speech. Imagine them booing and throwing fruit at you. Would you survive that ordeal?

Before you speak, visualize yourself in the room successfully giving the speech.

When you speak, talk loud enough to be heard.

Avoid leaning on podiums.

Maintain eye contact. When you look at people, they become less frightening. Remember that it is harder to listen to someone who doesn't look at you. Eye contact keeps your audience with you.

When you look at the audience, don't neglect any part of the room.

Find a few friendly faces around the room and imagine that you are talking to them individually.

Look professional. Your personal appearance communicates a message. Dress appropriately. Don't show up in jeans to speak before the Association of University Presidents, unless it's their Fourth of July pig roast.

Keep track of the time during your speech. Better to end early than run late. The conclusion of your speech is what is likely to be remembered, and you will destroy this opportunity if people are fidgeting and looking at the clock. Pause where appropriate. Beginners sometimes feel they have to fill every moment with the sound of their voice. Let your audience take a mental deep breath from time to time.

If you notice a side conversation in the room, continue speaking and look directly at the people visiting.

Use audiovisual aids, flip charts, and other props whenever possible.

Be enthusiastic. Energy is contagious.

Less than 10% of communication is verbal. Be aware of what your body is telling your audience. Contrived or staged gestures will look dishonest. Be natural. If you don't know what to do with your hands, notice that. Then don't do anything with them.

Lighten up. Friendliness and humor are usually appropriate. Don't take yourself too seriously.

After you speak

Review and reflect upon your performance. Did you finish on time? Did you cover all the points you intended to cover? Was the audience attentive? Did you handle your nervousness effectively?

Welcome evaluation from others. Most of us find it difficult to hear criticism about our public speaking. Be aware that you might be resistant to accepting such criticism, then let go of your resistance. Get feedback.

Participating in class is an excellent way to practice speaking in public. Write an intention statement concerning how you intend to participate in class in order to experience talking to a group of people. Be specific about which class you intend to speak in, how you will set up the opportunity to speak (i.e., having questions ready, sitting in front, etc.), and how you intend to record your observations of the experience.

Journal entry #54

Intention statement

WRITING LETTERS

Personal letters are a great way to practice writing, and they can enrich your life because, generally, the more you send, the more you get.

Here are some techniques you can use to make letter writing easy.

1. Keep a stack of stamped, pre-addressed envelopes handy. Procrastination is the most common curse of would-be letter writers. By pre-addressing envelopes to people with whom you want to correspond regularly, you eliminate one excuse not to write.

A variation of this technique is the pre-addressed and stamped postcard. Keep a stack of them handy for spur-of-the-moment notes.

Think back to a time when you were called upon to speak before a group or called on to answer questions in class. Write down what you remember about that situation. Describe your physical sensations, the effectiveness of your presentation, feedback from the audience, etc.

Journal entry #55

Discovery statement

2. Be brief. You don't have to describe every single event. Sometimes people put off writing because they have so much to say that the job seems overwhelming. If this happens to you, resolve to say just one thing in a letter, say it, and mail it.

3. Visualize the person to whom you are writing. See them sitting across the table from you as you write.

4. Make a mind map of your letter before you write. This is a good way to organize your thoughts.

5. Be aware of the reward. Most people like to get letters. The gift you are giving another person when you send her a letter is the sharing of yourself. Also, know that you are likely to get a letter back for every letter you send.

Be a

A powerful person has the courage to be a fool.

This idea can work for you because you already are a fool. Don't be upset. All of us are fools, at one time or another. There are no exceptions. If you doubt it, think back to that stupid thing you did just a few days ago. You know the one. Yes, that one. It was embarrassing and you tried to hide it. You pretended you weren't a fool. This happens to everyone.

The person who insists that she has never been a fool is perhaps the biggest fool of all. We are all fallible human beings. Most of us, however, spend too much time and energy trying to hide our fool-hood.

But no one is really fooled—not even ourselves. Even worse, whenever we pretend to be something we're not, we miss part of life.

For example, many people never dance because they don't want to look ridiculous. They probably *will* look ridiculous. That's the secret of being a fool. It's OK to look ridiculous dancing. It's OK to be absurd. Absurdity, along with courage and cowardice, grace and clumsiness, is a human characteristic. You might as well be a fool because you already *are* one anyway, and nothing in the world can change that. Why not enjoy it once in a while?

Consider the case of the man who won't dance because he's afraid he'll look foolish. This same fellow will flail away at a tennis ball all afternoon, looking like an idiot. If you tell him so, he even agrees.

"So what? I'm no John McEnroe," he will say. He's right. He isn't John McEnroe. On the tennis court, he is willing to be a fool in order to enjoy the game.

He is no Fred Astaire, either. For some reason, *that* bothers him. The result is that he misses the fun of dancing. (Dancing badly is as much fun as playing tennis badly.)

Power process #7 doesn't suggest that the way to be happy in life is to do things badly. Mediocrity is not the goal. On the contrary, the prerequisite for mastery in most activities is the willingness to try something new, to fail, to correct your errors, to fail again, and so on.

Before you can become a good writer, you must be willing to be a bad writer. Many potential writers quit or, more commonly, never start in the first place, because they are embarrassed by their first products.

Most artists and athletes have learned the secret of being foolish. All of us know, for instance, how it feels to tell a joke and have people react to the punch line by changing the subject. When this happens, we truly look and

fool

feel like fools. Professional comedians risk this every time they perform. Being funny is not enough for success in the comedy business. A comedian must have the courage to face failure.

For a student, the willingness to be a fool means the willingness to take risks, to experiment with new skills, to grow. The rewards are expanded creativity and self-expression.

Here's an experiment that can put you in touch with the joys of fool-hood. The next time you do something silly or stupid, *experience* the feeling. Don't deny it. Don't cover it up. Notice everything about it, including the physical sensations and your inner thoughts. Acknowledge your foolishness. Be exactly who you are. Explore all the emotions surrounding your experience.

And forgive yourself. Know that, at this moment, you are the best that you can be. (At this exact moment, what else can you be but what you are?)

When fully experienced, foolishness loses its power to frighten. It makes room for you to expand and grow.

Be willing to be a fool.

Use this exercise whenever you want to calm your thoughts.

Find a quiet spot where you won't be interrupted. Sit comfortably. Loosen any tight clothing. Relax your entire body, beginning with your feet. Work your way right to the top of your head, telling each part of your body to relax as you go.

Sit quietly for five to ten seconds, letting go of all thoughts as they arise.

Next, imagine a white light entering your feet and flowing up your body, up your legs, through your pelvis and stomach, up your spine, through your arms, and up into your head. Imagine this white light filling your entire body with soothing, healing energy. See your body filled with a white light which gives you power, strength, and confidence.

See and feel this white light as it flows through your body and out the top of your head.

Whenever you feel ready, return to the room, open your eyes, and, like a cat, stretch your body slowly.

Keep going?

Some people keep going, even when they fail again and again. To such people belongs the world.

Consider the hapless politician who compiled this record:

Failed in business	1831
Defeated for Legislature	1832
Second failure in business	1833
Suffered nervous breakdown	1836
Defeated for Speaker	1838
Defeated for Elector	1840
Defeated for Congress	1843
Defeated for Senate	1855
Defeated for Vice President	1856
Defeated for Senate	1858
Elected President	1860

Who was the fool who kept on going in spite of so many failures? See bottom of page 199.

Solving math and science problems

Approach math and science problems the way rock climbers approach mountains. The first part is devoted to preparations you make before you get to the rock. The second part is devoted to techniques used on the rock (problem) itself.

To the uninitiated, rock climbing looks scary and dangerous. For the unprepared, it is. A novice might come to a difficult place in a climb, be unable to figure out the next step, and panic. When a climber freezes, he is truly stuck. Experienced climbers figure out strategies in advance for as many situations as possible. With preparation and training, the sport takes on a different cast.

Sometimes students have the same trouble with academic problems. They get stuck, panic, and freeze. Use the following techniques to avoid that.

Before you get to the rock

1. Practice. Work lots of problems. Do assigned problems and more. Make up your own. Work with a classmate and make up problems for each other to solve.

Set clear goals for practice and write an intention statement about fulfilling those goals.

2. Divide problems by type. Make a list of the different kinds of problems and note the elements of each. By dividing problems into type or category, you can isolate the kinds of problems you have trouble with. Practice those more and get help if you need it.

3. Know your terminology. Mathematicians and scientists often borrow words from plain English and assign new meanings to them. For example, for most of the world, "work" means a job. For the physicist, "work" is force multiplied by distance.

Use 3x5 flash cards to study special terms.

4. Understand formulas. You will be asked to memorize some formulas for convenience. If you understand the basic concepts behind these formulas, you can recall them accurately. More importantly, you will be able to re-create the formulas if your recall falters. Understanding is always preferable to memorization.

5. Use summary sheets for terms and formulas. Mind map summary sheets allow you to see how various kinds of problems relate to one another. You create a structure on which you can hang data, and that helps your recall.

6. Stay current. In math and science courses, understanding the material of week number two depends on what you learned in week number one. Week number three depends on week number two, and so on. Therefore, goofing off for a week in math can have a more serious consequence than goofing off for a week in history. In most math and science courses, falling behind in the first few weeks means the whole course will become effort and struggle. Be very clear about your intentions to stay current in these courses from day one.

7. Notice when you're in deep water. It's tempting to shy away from difficult problems. Unfortunately, the more you do this the more difficult the problems become. Math and science courses present wonderful opportunities to use the first step technique explained in chapter one. When you feel that you're beginning to get in trouble, write a precise discovery statement about the problem. Get it down on paper. Then write an intention statement about what you will do to correct the problem.

8. *When practicing, time yourself.* Sometimes speed counts. Notice how fast you can work problems. That way, when you get to a test, you will know how much time to allot for different types of problems.

9. *Use creative visualizations.* Use the creative visualization techniques described on page 167 to visualize yourself solving problems successfully.

Before you begin a problem-solving session, take a minute to relax, breathe deeply, and prepare yourself for the task ahead.

On the rock

1. *Survey the territory thoroughly.* Read the problem at least twice before you begin. Read slowly. Be certain you understand what is being asked.

2. *Sort the facts.* Survey the problem for all of the givens. Determine the principles and relationships involved. Look for what is to be proven or what is to be discovered. Write these down.

3. *Set up the problem.* Before you begin to compute, determine the strategy you will use to arrive at the solution and plug the data into this framework.

4. *Cancel and combine.* When you have set up a problem logically, you will be able to take shortcuts. For example, if the same term appears in both dividend and divisor, they will cancel each other.

5. *Draw a picture.* Make a diagram. Pictures help keep the facts straight. They show relationships more effectively than words.

6. *Read the problem aloud.* Sometimes the sound of your voice will jar loose the solution to a problem. Talk yourself through the solution. Read equations out loud.

7. *Check results.* Work problems backwards, then forwards. Start at both ends and work towards the middle to check your work.

Another way to check your work is to estimate the answer before you compute it.

CREATE ON YOUR FEET

The latest thing around executive offices these days are "stand-up" desks. These desks are raised so you stand at them instead of sitting.

Standing, as opposed to sitting for long periods, has advantages. You stay more alert and creative when you're on your feet. Standing is great for lower back pains, too. Sitting aggravates the spine and supporting muscles.

You would be joining the ranks of some influential people who spend their days standing rather than sitting on the job. Roger Birk, chairman of Merrill Lynch & Co.; George Shinn, chairman and chief executive officer of First Boston Corp.; C. Peter McColough, chairman of Xerox, along with Xerox's president and at least one vice president, all have switched to standing-style desks. They get more done and are more comfortable doing it.

Thomas Jefferson used a stand-up desk upon which he wrote the Declaration of Independence. Donald Rumsfeld, former Secretary of Defense, used one at the White House and continues to use one in private business.

Winston Churchill, Ernest Hemingway, and Virginia Woolf were fond of standing while working.

Experiment with this idea. Consider setting your desk up on blocks or putting a box on top of your desk so you can stand while writing, preparing speeches, or studying.

Exercise #31

Contra-lateral movement

This is fun. It is based on the notion that physical movement can connect the creative part of your brain to the analytic part. This is done through marching. The trick is to march or do jumping jacks with your arms and legs going in different directions (i.e., when your left knee comes up, your right arm comes up. When your right knee is raised, so is your left arm). Do it like this:

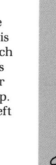

Exercise #32

Master mind map

In this space, create a mind map of the first *six* chapters of this book. Do this without reviewing. (Don't even look up chapter titles.) This exercise is for you to demonstrate to yourself how much material you retain. You might be surprised by the results.

The fool was Abraham Lincoln.

William A. Nolen

From **A Surgeon's World** *by William A. Nolen, M.D. Copyright 1970, 1972 by William A. Nolen, M.D. Reprinted by permission of Random House, Inc.*

In contrast to my four relatively miserable years at Holy Cross, I enjoyed, for the most part, the four years at Tufts Medical School. . . .

For almost the first time in my academic career I was studying material that I knew was going to be of value to me the rest of my life. Anatomy was a course that required mostly brute memory. It wasn't easy to remember where the deltoid muscle began, where it ended, what muscles were next to it, and what blood vessels and nerves nourished it and made it work, but I could see the practicality of having all that information tucked away in my mind. So I studied, not only because I wanted a decent grade but because I wanted to be a knowledgeable doctor.

Like most pre-med students I had resented the time I spent in college on subjects which seemed unrelated to my future as a doctor. I know now that my attitude was based on immaturity. College is a place where a student ought to learn not so much how to make a living, but how to live. In the 1970's we're trying to reduce the time a man has to spend becoming a doctor. Some medical schools will accept students after three years of college—others are combining the fourth year of medical school with the internship. It's possible in some programs to acquire an M.D. degree six years after high school graduation, rather than the usual eight.

The purpose in shortening medical education is to produce more doctors. Personally, I don't think it will work. With every year that passes there is more and more knowledge that a doctor should have. How in the world can we expect students to learn more in less time?

What will happen, I'm afraid, is that we'll start producing pure technicians. If anything is to be eliminated from the would-be doctor's education, it won't be biochemistry, anatomy or pharmacology; it will be the course in Shakespeare, the year of philosophy, the semesters of French. One of the major problems in medicine now is that doctors tend to have depth but not breadth to their knowledge. There is a saying, well known to all medical students, that the General Practitioner is a doctor who learns less and less about more and more, until he eventually

knows nothing about everything; the specialist is the man who learns more and more about less and less, until he eventually knows everything about nothing. This is the age of the specialist, and because their interests are so narrow, the specialists tend to see patients as faceless carriers of diseases, technical problems to be solved, rather than as human beings. What we need in medicine are doctors who are more the artist and less the scientist. I don't think that shortening medical education will produce them.

1. Discuss why allowing the last revision of a paper to sit for three to four days is a good idea.

2. List two "right brain" qualities.

3. Explain why a research paper is more likely to be effective if you begin to write before you have completed all of your research.

4. Describe how you could use discovery and intention statements to sharpen your problem solving skills for math or science courses.

5. Only artists and scientists are creative. True or false.

6. List the three parts of a speech and describe the purpose of each part.

7. List the nine steps of Muscle Reading.

8. In this space, create a short mind map of this chapter.

9. Pick one of the long-term goals you chose in the "Goal Setting Exercise" on page 54. Describe, briefly, how enhanced creativity and self-expression are related to that goal. (If you think they are not related, explain.)

10. Define serendipity.

The following is a list of things I wanted to get from this chapter but didn't.

Journal entry #56

Discovery statement

To get what I wanted from this chapter (but didn't get) I will. . . .

Journal entry #57

Intention statement

Choose two techniques from this chapter and write an intention statement about how you intend to use them in the next week.

Journal entry #58

Intention statement

Think of an innovative, unique, and creative idea. Your idea file from chapter 7 may be useful. Write an intention statement about what you will do this week to start that idea rolling. I intend to . . .

Journal entry #59

Look back

After previewing this chapter, complete the following sentence:

What I want from this chapter is . . .

Journal entry #60

Discovery statement

CHAPTER EIGHT
RELATIONSHIPS

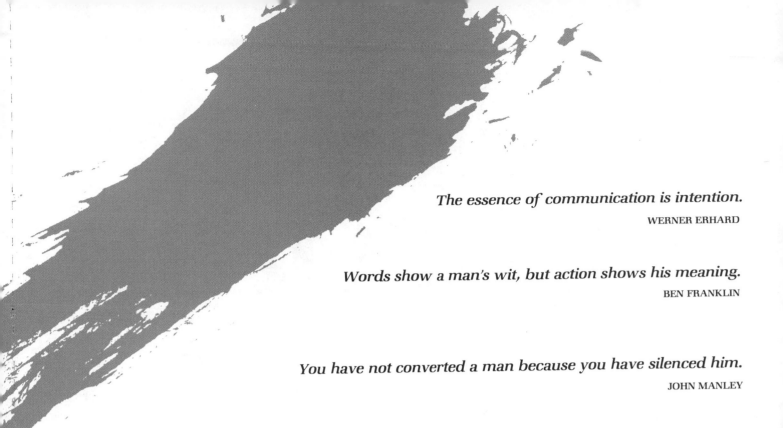

The essence of communication is intention.

WERNER ERHARD

Words show a man's wit, but action shows his meaning.

BEN FRANKLIN

You have not converted a man because you have silenced him.

JOHN MANLEY

In this chapter . . .

At best, communication is difficult. ***Getting your message across*** tells you how to get the job done even in times of love, anger, excitement, and frustration.

A clear understanding of ***The communication loop*** can turn misunderstandings into harmonious celebrations.

Listening turns up the volume on your natural hearing aid by exposing problems like listening with your answer running.

Unless you are a hermit, sooner or later you will appreciate ***Relationships change,*** and the tips included in ***Relationships can work*** could help them change for the better.

All of the debate and confusion surrounding the identity crisis is cleared up. To find out who you really are, read ***Power process #8, You are your word.***

Learn to make distinctions between ***Assertion and aggression.***

Become an armchair expert in ***Observing behavior: A new spectator sport*** and learn an exciting new way to move air in and out of your lungs in ***Limb breathing.***

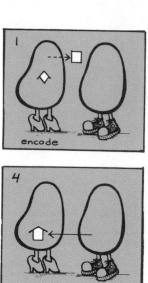

commm la

Communication is often garbled because we try to send and receive messages at the same time. The most effective way to improve your ability to communicate is to be aware of when you are the receiver and when you are the sender.

If you are receiving (listening), then just receive. Don't keep switching into the sending mode. If you are sending (talking), then stick with it until you are done. If the other person is trying to send a message when you want to be the sender, you have two choices. Either stop sending and be the receiver, or stop sending and leave. It is ineffective to try sending and receiving at the same time.

When we talk, we put thoughts into words. Words are only a code for what we experience. Using words, we try to get our internal experience to become another person's internal experience.

We put the thought into a word code. This is called encoding. The person who receives the message takes our words and translates them into his own experience. This is called decoding.

A conversation between two people is like communication between two telegraph operators. One encodes a message and sends it over the wire. The

...e
...nication
...p

operator at the other end receives the coded signal, decodes it, evaluates it, and sends another coded message. The first operator decodes this message and sends another. The cycle continues. The messages look like this:

..--.. --.·.-   --.-- ..---   Operator 1
    --.- ..-..   -..- --.... -. Operator 2

In this encoding-decoding loop you continually switch roles. One minute you send; the next, you receive. It's a problem when both operators send at the same time. Neither operator knows what the other one sent. Neither can reply. Communication works best when each of us has a complete chance to send, sufficient time to comprehend, and plenty of time to respond.

There are other problems in communication. Only a small percentage of communication is verbal. All of us send messages with our bodies and with the tone of our voices. Throw in a few other factors, like a hot room, loud voices, or other people talking and it's a wonder we communicate at all.

Another problem is that the message sent is often not the message received. This process of continually encoding and decoding words can result in the simplest message being muddled. For some, "chair" conjures up the image of an overstuffed, rocking recliner. Others visualize a metal folding chair. More complex ideas can wreak havoc on communication. A "good teacher" can mean someone who is smart, entertaining, easy, challenging, handsome, or none of the above.

To communicate effectively, we must strive to get on the same wavelengths. Even then, it is good to keep checking with each other to be certain we are talking about the same thing.

These difficulties are never fully overcome. They can be partially alleviated by using effective communication techniques and by having a sincere intention to understand one another.

You are y

There are over four and a half billion people on planet Earth. We live on different continents, in different nations, and communicate with different languages. We have diverse political ideologies and enjoy different foods. We choose divergent lifestyles and subscribe to various social and moral codes.

The fundamental element that prevents confusion and disorder despite all these differences is agreement. The world works by *agreement*.

Words, our basic tool of communication, work only because of agreement. A pencil is only a pencil because we all agree to call a wood-covered column of graphite a pencil. We could just as easily call a pencil a ziddle. We would simply need to agree that a wood-covered stick of graphite was to be called a ziddle. We are able to communicate with words only by agreement about their meanings.

Money exists only by agreement. If we find a torn piece of newspaper with ink on it and leave it on a park bench next to a $20 bill (another piece of paper with ink on it), one of them will quickly disappear. The only important difference between the two pieces of paper is our agreement that one is valuable. We agree that one piece of paper can be exchanged for goods and services. Shopkeepers will trade their merchandise for the $20 bill because they trust a continuing agreement.

Society is able to function because of agreement. If agreement is essential to society's working, then it is also essential to our lives working. In fact, our lives work to the degree that we keep our agreements.

If you agree to complete an assignment, and do complete it, your understanding of the subject improves. So does your grade. You also contribute to your self-esteem by experiencing the satisfaction and success of completing another assignment. If you break your word, you create a gap in your learning, a lower grade, and possibly a negative feeling about yourself as a student.

The cost of not keeping our agreements is high. We feel ineffective. We experience psychological upset, interpersonal conflict, and social turmoil. When we break our promise to be faithful to our spouse, to obey traffic laws, to show up after telling a friend we'd help her move, or to pay a bill as we had agreed to, the results are messy. Strained relationships and painful consequences indicate that something in our life does not work.

Keeping our word is enlivening. We experience being effective. Our psychological strength and self-esteem improve. Relationships become

Limb breathing

our word

nurturing and mutually supportive. Our lives work.

Starting with our most intimate personal contacts and moving through levels of family, friends, school, business, community, and nation, keeping our agreements brings satisfaction and harmony.

The person you are right now is a result of all the choices you've made in your life until now. Your future will be determined by the choices and agreements you make from now on.

Be cautious about giving your word. Don't make agreements unless you fully intend to keep them. Keep your agreements as if your life depended on them, because it does.

Be clear about the difference between "I'll try to do it," and "I give you my word that I'll do it." Trying to do something reserves a convenient excuse for not getting it done. "I tried" usually means "I failed." A wide receiver either caught the ball or he tried to catch the ball.

When you break an agreement, examine your intention. A part of you wanted to keep the agreement. Since you didn't keep your word, another part of you must have resisted it. When you genuinely and completely choose to do something, internal resistance disappears.

Everyone breaks agreements. The

only way to be certain you won't break agreements is not to make any. The problem is that relationships are built on agreements. Others know who you are, and what to expect, by your intentions, commitments, and agreements. Your word defines your values and beliefs. You can learn who you are by observing which commitments you choose and which ones you avoid.

Your agreements give life to your purpose and goals. Giving your word is the first step in creating your future.

When you communicate your intentions and purpose, when you give your word, you are engaged in an act of creation . . . literally. Words and language bring your intentions into existence. Until you commit yourself to something by giving your word, there is little chance you will follow through.

Your word and agreement make things happen. Circumstances, events, even attitudes, fall into place. Information and assistance appear as a result of your commitment. Everything starts with your word.

This is an exercise to refresh your whole body.

In a comfortable place, lie down on your back. Close your eyes and relax. Do a quick body scan. Take slow, deep breaths. Focus on the air entering and leaving your lungs. As you inhale, imagine that the incoming air is fresh, clean, and full of invigorating energy. Leaving your body, with the air you exhale, are all your tensions, toxins and frustrations. Do this for several minutes, giving your imagination full rein.

Begin to imagine that the air you inhale comes in through your toes and up through the bones of one leg. When you exhale, the air leaves your chest and travels down your leg and out your toes. Do this three times with each leg. Now imagine breathing through each arm. The air enters your fingertips, moves up your arm into your chest and head. When you exhale, follow the air as it flows down your arms and leaves your hands. Do this three times with each arm.

Finally, do the process with both arms and legs simultaneously.

Listening

Just because a person in a conversation isn't talking doesn't necessarily mean she is listening. She may be preparing her response or daydreaming.

Listening is not easy. Listening effectively requires concentration and energy, and it's worth it.

A good listener is appreciated by friends, family, and business associates. Good listeners make good friends; the best salesmen are the best listeners; so are effective managers. People love a good listener, a receptive audience. Through your listening efforts you gain more than respect. You also gain insight into other people. You can learn about the world and about yourself.

To be a good listener, you must decide to listen. Once you are clear about it, you can use the following techniques to be a more effective listener. These ideas are especially useful in times of high emotional tension.

Nonverbal listening

Much of listening is nonverbal. Here are five guidelines for effective nonverbal listening.

1. Be quiet. Silence is more than staying quiet or not interrupting while someone is speaking. Pausing for several seconds before you start to talk allows the speaker to catch her breath or gather her thoughts. She may want to continue.

If the message is complete, this short break gives you time to form your response and helps you avoid the biggest barrier to listening—listening with your answer running. If you make up a response before the person is finished, you miss the end of the message which often contains the main point.

When someone talks a blue streak, it might be because he fears he will lose the floor if he stops.

Pausing for several seconds may be inappropriate. Ignore this suggestion completely when someone asks in a panic where to find the nearest phone because she wants to call the fire department.

2. Maintain eye contact. Look at the other person while she speaks. It demonstrates your attention and it helps keep your mind from wandering. Your eyes also let you "listen" to body language and behavior. When some of us remove our glasses, we not only can't see, we can't hear!

Don't stare too long; the speaker might think she is talking to a zombie.

Act appropriately.

3. Display openness. You can communicate openness by your facial expression and body position. Uncross your arms and legs. Sit up straight. Face the other person and remove any physical barriers, such as a pile of books.

4. Listen without response. This doesn't mean never respond. It means wait. When listening to another person, we often interrupt with our opinions, suggestions, and inappropriate comments.

"Oh, I'm so excited. I just found out that I am nominated to be in *Who's Who in American Musicians.*"

"Yeah, that's neat. My uncle Elmer got into *Who's Who in American Veterinarians.* He sure has an interesting job. One time I went along when he was treating a cow and . . ."

Watch your nonverbal response, too. A look of "Good grief!" from you can keep the other person from finishing her message.

5. Send acknowledgments.

Periodically, in the midst of so much nonverbal listening, it is important to let the speaker know you are still there. Your words or nonverbal gestures of acknowledgment let the speaker know you are interested and that you are with her and her message. These include "Umhum," "OK," "yes," and head nods.

These acknowledgments do not imply your agreement. If someone tells you what they don't like about you, your head nod doesn't mean you agree. It just indicates that you are listening.

Verbal listening

Sometimes it is necessary to speak to facilitate listening.

1. Feed back meaning.
Paraphrase the communication. Do not just parrot what they said. Briefly summarize. Feed back the essence of what you think the other person said. "Let me see if I got what you said . . ." or, "What I'm hearing you say is . . ."

Often the other person will say, "No, that's not what I meant. What I said was . . ."

There will be no doubt when you get it right. The sender will say, "Yeah, that's it," and will either continue with

another message or stop sending because he knows you understand.

If you don't understand the message, be persistent. Ask the person to please repeat what he said and paraphrase it again. Effective communication involves a feedback loop.

Be concise. This is not a time to stop the other person by talking on and on about what you think you heard.

2. Listen beyond words.
Be aware of nonverbal messages and behavior. You may notice and comment that the speaker's body language is screaming the exact opposite of her words. For example, "I noticed you said you are excited, but you look very bored."

3. Take care of yourself.
People seek out good listeners, and there are times when you don't want to listen. You may be busy or distracted with your own concerns. Be honest. Don't pretend to listen. You can say, "I don't have the time right now." It's OK not to listen.

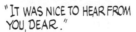
"IT WAS NICE TO HEAR FROM YOU, DEAR."
"THANK YOU. IT WAS NICE TO HAVE SOMEBODY LISTEN TO ME."

DENNIS the MENACE

Dennis The Menace® reprinted by courtesy of Hank Ketcham, and © by Field Enterprises Inc.

Getting your message across

We have been talking for years, and we usually manage to get our message across. There are times, though, when we don't.

Often these times are emotionally charged. Sometimes we feel wonderful or rotten or sad or scared and we want to express it. Emotions can get in the way of the message. Described below are three techniques for delivering a message through tears, laughter, fist-pounding, or hugging. They include: Replacing "You" messages with "I" messages, avoiding questions, and noticing the nonverbal message.

"You" messages

It can be difficult to disagree with someone without his becoming angry or your becoming upset. When conflict occurs, we often make statements about the other person, or "You" messages:

"You are rude."
"You make me mad."
"You must be crazy."
"You don't love me anymore."

This kind of communication results in defensiveness. The response might be:

"I am not rude."
"I don't care."
"No, you are crazy."
"Of course I do, dear."

"You" messages are your own assumptions about someone else. They label, judge, and blame. Sometimes even praise can be an ineffective "You" message. "You" messages don't work. They are hard to listen to, they lack credibility, and they demand rebuttal.

"I" messages

When communication is emotionally charged, consider limiting your statements to descriptions about yourself. Replace "You" messages with "I" messages.

For example:

"You are rude" might become "I feel upset."
"You make me mad" could be "I feel angry."
"You must be crazy" can be "I don't understand."
"You don't love me anymore" could become "I'm afraid we're drifting apart."

An effective "I" message includes at least a few of the following five parts:

1. Observation
2. Feelings
3. Thoughts
4. Wants
5. Intentions

Observation

Describe the facts—the indisputable, observable realities. Talk about what you see, hear, smell, taste, or touch. These are not judgments. Make a distinction between what you observe and your judgment about it.

Feelings

Describe how you feel. It is easier to listen to, "I feel frustrated" than, "You never help me." Talking about how you feel about another's actions can be valuable feedback for that person.

Thoughts

Communicate your thoughts. Use caution. Just because your statement begins with an "I", doesn't qualify it as an "I" message. "I think you are inconsiderate" is a "You" judgment in disguise.

Wants

Communicate what you want. You are far more likely to get it. If someone doesn't know what you want, he doesn't have a choice about helping you get it. Ask clearly. Avoid demanding or using the word "need". Most people like to feel helpful, not obligated.

Intention

The end part of an "I" message is a statement about what you intend to do. Have a plan that doesn't depend on the other person. Communicate your plan.

"I" works better than "You"

Suppose a friend asks you to pick him up at the airport. You drive 20 miles and wait for the plane. No friend. You decide your friend missed his plane, so you wait three hours for the next flight. No friend.

Perplexed and worried, you drive home. The next day, you see your friend downtown.

"What happened?" you ask.

"Oh, I caught an earlier flight."

"You are a rude person," you reply.

Look for the facts, the observable behavior. Everyone will agree that your friend asked you to pick him up; he did take an earlier flight; you did not receive a call from him. But the idea that he is "rude" is not a fact, it's a judgment.

He may go on to say, "I called your home and no one answered. My mom had a stroke and was rushed to Valley View. I caught the earliest flight I could get." Your judgment no longer fits.

When you saw your friend, you might have said, "I waited and waited at the airport. I was worried about you. I didn't get a call. Now I feel angry and hurt. I don't want to waste my time. Next time, call me when you arrive and I'll be happy to come get you."

"I" messages don't create resistance or defensiveness. They don't evaluate or put down. They don't invite the other person to counteract with name-calling or blaming. We alone are responsible for our experiences. "I" messages require us to be honest and genuine with our feelings. Judgment has no place in an "I" message.

Questions are not always questions

We often soft-pedal our values and opinions as questions. We ask questions to get approval for our feelings before owning them publicly. Rather than risk being transparent about our beliefs, we test the water with rhetorical questions. "Doesn't it upset you when you see that?" "Shouldn't we hang the picture over here between the window and the door?" We are hiding behind questions. Our real message is not being expressed. Communication improves when we say, "I'm upset," or, "I want to hang the picture here."

Noticing nonverbal messages

How you say something can be more important than what you say. Your voice tone and gestures can support, modify, or contradict your words. Your posture, the way you dress, how often you shower, and even the poster hanging on your wall can negate your words before you say them.

Most nonverbal behavior is unconscious. We can learn to be aware of and choose many of our nonverbal messages. The key is to be clear about our intention and purpose. When we know what we want to say and believe in it, our inflections, gestures, and words will be congruent.

Barriers to sending your message

Sometimes fear stops us from communicating. We are afraid of other people's reactions, sometimes justifiably. Being truthful doesn't mean being insensitive to others' reactions. Tact is a virtue, but letting fear prevent communication is not.

Another excuse for not communicating is the thought, "She already knows this. I told her once before." You may have sent the same message before, but sometimes people just don't hear. Reminders can be useful.

Sometimes we don't send a message because "he won't listen." If this happens, perhaps the other person might not be listening because of the way we are communicating.

"He'll never do anything about it if I tell him," is another excuse. You limit yourself when you decide beforehand how another person will react. You can never know for sure what someone will do. A five-part "I" message doesn't call for any reactions. Do not allow what you imagine the other person might do to stop you from communicating.

It's easy to make excuses for not communicating. If you have fear or some other consideration about sending a message, be aware of it. Don't expect it to go away. Realize that you can communicate even with your concerns. You can choose to make them a part of the message. "I am going to tell you how I feel, and I'm afraid it will sound stupid."

Don't let barriers to communication run your life. In college, talking to someone when you don't want to could be a matter of educational survival. A short talk with an advisor, teacher, friend, or family member may solve a problem that jeopardizes your education.

Notice your barriers and make choices.

Exercise #34

Write an "I" message

Pick something about school that irritates you. Pretend you are talking to the person who is associated with this irritation.

First, write what you would say as a "You" message.

Now, write the same complaint as an "I" message. Check your "I" message with the suggestions given for an effective "I" message on page 212. Are there any elements you have not included?

I DO TOO TELL YOU. I SAID "I LOVE YOU" RIGHT BEFORE WE GOT MARRIED.

Relationships can work

*S*ometimes relationships don't seem to work very well; sometimes they do. Of all the factors that influence a relationship's workability, the biggest is communication. Here's a list of some other factors that can benefit or damage your relationships.

Do keep agreements. *The quality of your life is affected by whether you keep your agreements.*

Don't make agreements you cannot keep. *Don't make agreements you don't intend to keep.*

Do tell the truth. *Life is complicated when you don't.*

Do support others. *Encourage fellow students to reach their goals and be successful. Respect their study time. Helping them to stay on purpose can help you as well.*

Don't pry. *Being a good listener will be invitation enough for fellow students to share their problems, feelings, and personal goals.*

Don't borrow. *Borrowing a book or a tennis racket may seem like a small thing, but these requests can become a sore point in a relationship. Some people have difficulty saying no and resent lending things. At times it's OK, but keep borrowing to a minimum.*

Do divide chores. *Whether it's a class project or a household chore, do your part. Many frustrations result when you don't sit down with others and agree upon a fair division of work.*

Don't gripe. *There is a difference between griping and sharing problems. Gripers usually don't seek solutions. They just want everyone to know how unhappy they are. Sharing a problem is an appropriate way of starting the search for a solution.*

Do get involved. *Extracurricular activities are a great way to meet people with common interests. If you commute and have little time for these activities, study at the library, eat at the cafeteria, or relax on the campus green. You may be surprised at how many friends you make. It is easy to feel left out. It is also easy to get involved.*

Don't brag. *Other students are turned off by constant references to how much money you have, how great your boyfriend is, your social successes, or your family's accomplishments. There is a difference between sharing excitement and being obnoxious.*

Don't take on other people's problems. *Allow others to accept responsibility. Pitying them, getting upset along with them, or assuming responsibility for solving the problem is not helpful. (Rescue is appropriate when others are in physical danger.)*

Do write a letter. *Sometimes it's not easy to express ourselves face-to-face with another person. If you have something to say and haven't found the right time or the right words, write a letter. Writing can help sort your thoughts.*

Do allow people to be upset. *Trying to joke someone out of their anger, discounting their frustration or minimizing their disappointment invalidates their feelings. You can best support them by allowing them to experience their emotions.*

Don't preach. *This piece of advice must sound funny at the end of a sermon on do's and don't's. Sometimes people ask for advice. It's OK to share your values and opinions. It's not OK to pretend you know what's best for someone else. Don't try to reform the world.*

Relationships change

Relationships change, and the changes can be painful. Be prepared. If you came to college directly from high school and are away from home for the first time, forget about buying broken heart insurance. You are too high a risk. In fact, anytime you choose to care about another person you risk a painful, but rarely fatal, broken heart. Love relationships grow and die. Pain is part of living and can be dealt with in ways that work.

When an important relationship ends and you feel bad, don't resist it. It is appropriate to be miserable when you are. It's normal to cry and express your feelings. Also realize that it is possible to go to class, study, work, eat, sleep, get your laundry done, and feel miserable at the same time.

Sometimes emotional pain is intense. If you feel absolutely rotten, useless, ugly, and unlovable, look in the mirror and tell yourself over and over again how rotten, useless, ugly, and unlovable you are. It may be hard to do this for very long and keep a straight face.

If you are determined to feel sorry for yourself, go all the way. Punish yourself by studying a few extra hours. This method works especially well on a Saturday night. You can get the most out of being depressed and deprived while everyone else is out having fun.

It might go like this: You get some extra studying done and start feeling like a good student. Maybe you are more worthwhile than you thought. You fight it, but you can't help feeling pleased with yourself. The pain subsides.

Feeling good about yourself has an interesting side effect. Usually others start feeling good about you, too.

Another way to work through this kind of pain is to do something. Do anything. Mop the kitchen floor, clean out your dresser drawers, iron your shirts. This sounds ridiculous, but it works. Keep busy with a task.

When you feel ready, start doing things with other people. Include old friends. Make new friends. Don't become a hermit.

Emotional pain usually doesn't last forever. Often it ends in a matter of weeks. One case disappeared in four hours and 12 minutes.

If you get severely depressed and stay that way, talk to someone. If friends and family can't help, most colleges and communities have counselors available.

Depression can affect your health, and it can be alleviated. Take action.

Don't let a broken heart stop your life. You can find buckets full of advice on the subject. The best advice to remember is, "This, too, shall pass."

RELATIONSHIPS
WITH • INSTRUCTORS

Instructors are people. They are an integral part of your education. Here are some suggestions for forming a good working relationship with them.

Avoid excuses. Instructors know them all. Most teachers can see a snow job coming before you finish thinking it up. Be honest, accept responsibility for mistakes and failures, and don't con yourself into thinking you can fool the professor.

Submit professional work of high quality in both content and form. Prepare papers as if you were submitting them to an employer. Imagine that a promotion and raise will be determined by your work.

Form your own opinion about each instructor. Students talk about teachers, and you may hear conflicting reports. Decide for yourself.

We all have pictures about instructors. Perhaps they are unapproachable, brilliant, boring, demanding, bearded, eccentric, etc. Assume nothing. Get to know your teachers firsthand. Take advantage of their office hours. Some teachers best express their love and enthusiasm for their subject in private conversations rather than lectures.

Be attentive. Daydreaming, sleeping, or having side conversations in class will

Journal entry #61

Discovery/intention statement

Think about one of your relationships for a few minutes. It might be with a parent, sibling, spouse, child, friend, hairdresser, etc.

Next, write all the things that are not working in the relationship. What bugs you? What do you find irritating or unsatisfying?

_____

_____

_____

_____

Now, think for a moment, what do you want from this relationship? More attention, less nagging, more openness, trust, security, money, freedom, what?

_____

_____

_____

After deciding what you want from the relationship, describe a suggestion from the chapter you could use to make the relationship work.

_____

_____

_____

_____

_____

insult your instructor. Besides, you miss what's happening. Side conversations also disturb other students.

Arrive early for class. You can visit with your instructor or classmates, review notes, or spend a few minutes relaxing. Being on time demonstrates your commitment and interest.

Participate in class discussions. Ask questions. Provide answers. Be ready to debate and discuss. Your instructor will know you are interested and prepared. Asking questions to sidetrack your teacher or just to get noticed, however, wastes everyone's time.

Accept criticism. Learn from your teacher's comments on your work. It is a teacher's job to correct. Don't take it personally.

Many instructors have special hours around exam time. Most are delighted to talk to students. That's why they are teachers. Talking to one student allows them to focus on the area that's critical to that student, and their enthusiasm can be contagious. What sounded incomprehensible in class may become clear in a one-to-one exchange.

A conference with your teacher may be necessary at some time. Difficulties can arise over grades, attendance policies, lecture styles, term papers, or personality conflicts. Here are some specific suggestions for this situation.

Set up a meeting. Don't try to solve a serious problem in the few minutes before or after class. The instructor might feel uncomfortable or may not think it is appropriate to handle the problem in front of the other students.

Don't begin your meeting by saying, "Are you crazy? This paper was brilliant and you gave me a C. You don't like me, do you?" Judgments like this limit the possibility for effective and open communication. Instead, use "I" messages. Consider "I worked hard on this paper and feel disappointed about my grade. I expected a higher grade. I want to know how I could have improved this paper to get a better grade." It is easier to listen to a complaint about a specific problem than to a personal attack.

Listen without judgment to your instructor's comments. Discuss the issue openly, and be assertive. Ask for what you want.

If after this meeting, you and your instructor still don't agree, you have options. One is to forget it. Another is to talk to the department head or the next level of administration. If you are still unsatisfied and feel your cause is just, go higher. Go to the president of the school if necessary.

You are a consumer of education. You have a right, and even a responsibility, to complain if you think you have been treated unfairly or if your needs are not being met.

Exercise #35

V.I.P.'s (Very Important Persons)

Step 1

Under the column titled "Name", write the names of 12 people who have influenced your life. They may be relatives, friends, teachers, or perhaps someone you have never met. (Complete each step before moving on.)

Step 2

In the next column, rate your gratitude for this person's influence. (From 1 to 5: 1—a little grateful, 5—extremely grateful.)

Step 3

In the third column, rate how fully you have communicated your appreciation to this person. (Again, 1 to 5: 1—not communicated, 5—fully communicated.)

Step 4

In the final column, put a "U" beside the persons with whom you have unfinished business (important communication that you have withheld).

	Name	Grateful (1-5)	Communicated (1-5)	U?
1	paul	1	2	
2	walter	1	4	
3	Gregg	1	2	
4	shange	1	2	
5	Scott	1	3	
6	erin	2	3	
7	Brain	2	3	
8	pete	1	2	
9	andy	1	2	
10	Jason	3	3	
11	Ronda	3	2	
12	amber	3	2	

Step 5

Now, select two persons with U's beside their name and write them a letter. Express the love, tenderness, and joy you feel towards them. Tell them exactly how they have helped change your life and how you are glad they did.

Step 6

You also have an impact on others. Make a list of people whose lives you have influenced. Consider sharing with these people why you enjoy being part of their lives.

Journal entry #62

Discovery statement

There are things we think about telling people, but don't. Examine your relationships and complete the following statements.

I realize that I am not communicating about _____

_____ with _____

I haven't because _____

I realize that I am not communicating about _____

_____ with _____

I haven't because _____

I realize that I am not communicating about _____

_____ with _____

I haven't because _____

ASSERTION and AGGRESSION

To get what we want, we must communicate. Whether we want to order a chicken salad sandwich, convince someone of the merits of a democratic form of government, or request a reevaluation of a test grade, we must express it in a way that will get results. To do this, we can use either assertive or aggressive behavior.

"Aggressive" is a dirty word, except in football. Aggressive behavior is not generally effective in relationships. People who act aggressively are domineering. They get what they want by putting other people down. They win. The other person loses.

Assertive behavior is a sign of a healthy, strong personality. Assertive people are confident and respectful of others as well as themselves. They ask directly for what they want without feeling embarrassed or inadequate. When they don't get what they want,

their self-esteem does not suffer.

Here are five guidelines for acting assertively:

1. Ask specifically for what you want.
2. Know that you are worthy, and so are your opinions and desires.
3. Be open-minded and tolerant. Others' opinions and desires are also worthy.
4. Use the effective communication techniques contained in this chapter.
5. Expect to get what you want. Don't act apologetically.

Many people don't act assertively for fear they will appear aggressive. Passive behavior, behavior that is neither assertive nor aggressive, gets us nowhere. By remaining quiet and submissive, we allow others to infringe on our rights. When others run our lives, we lose contact with our own self worth.

They made me do it

Write down all the activities you have completed in the last 24 hours, from making the bed to going to class. List these activities in the proper column: the activities you chose to do and the activities that other people required you to do. If there was a particular person requiring you to do something, write that person's name after the activity.

Activities I chose	Activities others chose for me

Of the activities others chose for you, which ones did you really want to do? If you discover you did some things that you didn't want to do, consider not doing them in the future. Write how you feel about the activity and why you don't want to do it. Consider sending this communication to the person who "made" you do the activity.

HANDLING

Complaints

Sometimes we have complaints. Whining, blaming, pouting, kicking, and spitting usually don't get results. Here are some guidelines for complaining effectively.

1. Go to the source. Start with the person who is most directly involved with the problem.

2. Present the facts without blaming anyone.

3. Go up the ladder. If you don't get satisfaction at the first level, go to that person's direct supervisor. Requesting a supervisor's name will often get results. Write a letter to the company president.

4. Ask for commitments. When you find someone who is willing to solve your problem, get him to say exactly what he is going to do and when.

5. Use available support. There are dozens of groups, as well as government agencies, willing to get involved in resolving complaints. Contact consumer groups or the Better Business Bureau. Trade associations can sometimes help. Check out the state legislature or even your U.S. Senator or Representative.

6. Take legal action if necessary. Small claims court is relatively inexpensive, and you don't have to hire a lawyer. These courts can handle cases involving small amounts of money ($1000 to $2000 usually). Legal aid offices can sometimes answer questions.

7. Don't give up.

Criticism

Although criticism is rarely fun, it is often educational. Here are some ways to get the most value from it.

1. Don't criticize the criticizer. When your mind is occupied with finding fault in others, you aren't open to hearing constructive comments about yourself.

2. Take it seriously. Some people laugh or joke to cover their anger or embarrassment. Humor can be mistaken for a lack of concern.

3. React to criticism with acceptance. Most people don't enjoy pointing out another's faults. Denial, argument, or joking make it more difficult for them to give honest feedback.

4. Keep it in perspective. Don't blow the criticism out of proportion. The purpose of criticism is to generate positive change and self-improvement. Don't beat yourself with it.

5. Don't respond with defensiveness. You can't hear the criticism if you're busy building your case.

HE FOUR C's

Conflict

Conflict can lead to anger, hostility, and further conflict. Or, it can be used as a powerful problem-solving opportunity.

Conflict can be resolved by denying the problem exists, smoothing it over, or using power. This leads to win/lose situations. When conflict is resolved through collaboration and compromise, you can achieve win/win solutions. Here are six steps to transform a conflict into a solution in which both parties win.

1. State the problem. Using "I" messages, explain the problem. Allow the other person to state his perception. You may have different problems. This is the time to clearly define the conflict. It's hard to fix something before you both know what's broken.

2. Brainstorm solutions. Dream up as many solutions as you can. Be outrageous. Don't evaluate them. Quantity, not quality, is the key. If you get stuck, restate the problem and continue brainstorming.

3. Evaluate the solutions. Discard the unacceptable ones. This step will require time and honesty. Talk about which solutions will work and how difficult they will be to implement. You may hit upon a totally new solution.

4. Choose the solution. Choose the one most acceptable to all. Be honest.

5. Implement. Decide who is going to do what by when. Keep your agreements.

6. Re-evaluate. Review the effectiveness of your solution. If it works, pat yourselves on the back. If not, be open to making changes or implementing a whole new solution.

Compliments

For some people, compliments are more difficult to hear than criticisms. Here are some hints for handling compliments.

1. Don't sabotage the compliment. We sometimes respond to praise with, "Oh, it's really nothing." This undermines both you and the sender.

2. Don't automatically return a compliment. It can appear suspiciously polite and insincere.

3. Don't fish for more. "Do you really think so?" questions the integrity of the message.

Accepting compliments is not the same as being conceited. You are worthy and capable. Allow people to acknowledge that.

Observing behavior: a spectator sport

Brainstorm behaviors you have observed in others in stressful situations. List them below.

Look back at your list and decide if some of the behaviors you noted are actually judgments. For example: anger, rudeness, jealousy, or meanness are judgments—not behaviors.

A behavior is something factual, observable. For instance, yelling, arriving 10 minutes after the movie starts, or pulling a dog's tail are all observable behaviors.

Fran Worden Henry

. . . I went to my desk and wrote out a few pages of notes to remind me of why I wanted to get an MBA. I needed some special support and validation that wasn't to be found in my professors or my classmates or the things I was learning.

I reviewed the whys again. Why did I want an MBA? Why from Harvard? I recalled knowing years before that I wanted a useful graduate degree, one which gave me practical tools I didn't already have. I remembered hearing about how MBA's could telescope years of business experience into a few months of learning. I remembered, too, that when I had called the Harvard admissions office for the application, I was scared that they would reject my voice over the phone, knowing as they must that I wasn't qualified, that I hadn't taken math since high school.

Then I remembered an event that was a kind of turning point in my decision to apply. It had occurred during a business trip in 1979. I was on a plane, flying from London to Bangkok. I flew First Class as there were no coach seats left by the time I booked my flight. While I liked the comfortable seats in First Class, I was dismayed to find the only other women in the cabin were waiting on the men. I had thought I would have my row to myself on the flight, but just before the door closed a stout, balding man in a dark blue pinstriped suit eased himself into the seat next to me.

After we had been flying for a while, he asked about my T-shirt. It was dark blue with a sun and it said NO NUKES. I explained that I had bought it at a demonstration in Washington, D.C. a few weeks before. And I went on to say the demonstration was to support solar and other alternative energies so that we wouldn't put ourselves and our children at risk with nuclear power. He looked at me with his head tilting one way and his eyes slanting another. I know he thought I was, at the very least, strange.

"And what about you, where are you going?" I asked.

"I'm flying from London to Dubai," he said. "I'm an executive for an oil firm and I've just come from my annual holiday."

Dubai is the capital of the United Arab Empirates.

It was at least eight hours away, so I decided to talk. We chatted about the oil situation and about living abroad. He asked where I was going and whether I was on vacation.

"No, I'm traveling to Bangkok for my company. It's a firm in Washington, D.C. that supports the efforts of developing countries to use appropriate technologies. That usually means, for poor countries, labor-intensive rather than capital-intensive projects. You know, like building many small village hand pumps with community workers instead of building huge dams which benefit only a few."

Well, no, it was clear that he didn't understand. But we discussed these concepts for a good two hours. Basically, he saw things in a way that was diametrically opposite from mine. After a while he gave me a smug grin and stopped talking. A few hours later he spoke to me again, when we were flying over Turkey, and he asked about our meal, which was outstanding. It was clear that he was no longer interested in my opinion of serious topics.

More to be pleasant, I believe, than anything else, he said, "And what will you do with your career?"

I told him just exactly what was on my mind. In the coming year I planned to apply to Harvard and Stanford business schools and get my MBA.

From that moment on he never stopped talking. He asked me at least a dozen questions about politics, about Carter, about the U.S. dollar, about personnel problems. He and I talked for the rest of the trip, and when he got off at Dubai, I was greatly relieved not to have to bend my neck in that direction anymore. I thought and thought about his reaction. How could an English oil executive who worked in the Mideast value an American MBA so much that it overshadowed his distaste for my point of view?

Back in my dorm room with my thoughts, I was exhausted from the strength of my emotions. But I wasn't finished writing or finished with the subject of why I was at Harvard Business School, struggling to fit in against what seemed like impossible odds. I remembered one aspect of the incident on the airplane that was so important to all of my feelings about being in graduate school. It was the power to influence people, the power to be listened to and taken seriously . . . .

I would try to stay at Harvard. I didn't want to be better than anybody else and I knew that earning the degree wouldn't make me better. But it certainly did feel good to be equal, and that was worth some pain.

QUIZ

1. The usual result of "You" messages is: (choose one)
   a. understanding
   b. defensiveness
   c. compromise
   d. agreement

2. List the five parts of an "I" message.

   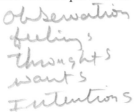
   Observation
   feelings
   Thoughts
   wants
   Intentions

3. What you say is always more important than how you say it. True or false.

4. Discuss the meaning of listening beyond the words.

5. Define "paraphrase."

6. Contrast griping and sharing problems.

7. What is an interesting side effect of feeling good about yourself?

8. What is the difference between assertive and aggressive behavior?

9. Putting our thoughts into words is called _____.
   Hearing another person's words and forming our own perceptions
   of what she said is called _____.

10. Using effective communication strategies, you can communicate
    your internal experience directly to another person. True or false.

List below things you wanted to get from this chapter but didn't.

Journal entry #63

Discovery statement

Describe below steps you intend to take to get what you wanted.

Journal entry #64

Intention statement

Tomorrow, I intend to use the following communication techniques when I talk to

Journal entry #65

Intention statement

Journal entry #66

Look back

After reading *You are your word* in chapter eight, have you become more careful about making promises?

Do you question the sincerity of other people's quick promises?

Take a few minutes to list what doesn't work in your life and how these problem areas may be related to broken agreements.

Journal entry #67

Discovery statement

What I want to get out of this chapter is . . .

CHAPTER NINE
HEALTH

Emotion, which is suffering, ceases to be suffering as soon as we have a clear picture of it.

SPINOZA

Disease is not only suffering, but also the body fighting to restore itself to normal. A sort of healing source within.

HIPPOCRATES

In this chapter...

Your *First step in health* exercise demands excruciating honesty. See how a comprehensive program for health makes the best sense in *Take care of your machine.* Suggestions include how to *Feed it, Move it, Rest it, Protect it,* and *Fix it.*

Emotional pain is not a sickness makes a case for not fixing what ain't broken.

Alcohol, tobacco and drugs—the truth rolls out "just the facts, ma'am." Peer into the looking glass.

Find out what evil lurks in the hearts of men in *Advertising can be dangerous to your health.*

Power process #9 invites you to test a novel way to handle problems—*Surrender.* So often the energy we spend resisting is what keeps "the enemy" going. When you surrender to your problem, you leave it nothing to gain by fighting you.

You are a whole community. Members of the community include your central nervous system, circulatory system, muscular system, digestive system, and endocrine system. You are the micro-organisms in your intestinal tract and the electrical impulses leaping your synapses. You are your pancreas, liver, and lungs. You are your five senses. You are a soul, a spirit. Far more than a brain, you are a lively society of processes, all interconnected in both obvious and subtle ways. Get the whole community involved when you study. You will get results when you all work together. Ways to take care of your community are suggested in this chapter.

Take care of your machine

Some people are offended by the notion that a body is a machine. This analogy is made with great respect for our bodies and with the understanding that we are more than our bodies. We have a mind and a soul that are certainly separate from our body even though they are connected. And, in order to house the mind and soul, we have a body—a fantastic machine.

It is possible to abuse this machine terribly and it will still operate. You can pollute it, dent it, run it too hard, let it sit idle for years, even wreck it, and it will usually continue to run. Interestingly, it is also possible to take excellent care of it, and then have it quit on you just when you need it.

The following suggestions are the tried and true ways to take care of your machine. These are the suggestions accepted by almost all experts in the health field. If you follow these, you are on your way to health.

When we buy a car or a new appliance, we generally look at the owner's manual. We study it to find out just how this new machine works. We make sure we understand all the features and what is needed to properly maintain the equipment. The following suggestions are like an owner's manual. Study them as if they described a priceless object, one that can't be replaced, one that your life depends on.

To an extent greater than most people imagine, we choose the level of health we have. The best way to ensure health is by taking positive action. There are definite steps you can take to minimize the risk of becoming sick.

Feed it

It is a cliché, but true, you are what you eat.

There have been hundreds of books written about nutrition. One says don't drink milk. Another says buy a cow. Some say load up on 5000 milligrams of vitamin C a day. Others say avoid oranges. This debate can be confusing. There is, however, some agreement among nutritional scientists.

The following recommendations were developed by a committee of experts and published by the U.S. Senate. While this doesn't mean you couldn't do better, it does mean you won't go wrong eating this way.

Weight control

Self-starvation is as much a problem as obesity. Both conditions are dangerous and can be controlled. Working with others who have similar problems brings good results. Look for support groups.

If you are overweight, don't go for fast remedies. Avoid people, groups, diets, or chemicals that claim a quick fix. To lose weight, you must burn more calories than you eat. The best way to do this is with a combination of exercise and decreased eating. To lose one pound, you need to eat 3,500 calories fewer than you burn. Don't try to lose more than two pounds a week. Local newspapers and the yellow pages list dozens of classes and support groups that will help you to reduce and to maintain your ideal weight.

If you want to lose weight, be careful not to go overboard. Bulimia is a serious illness that runs in cycles of excessive eating and forced purges. A

person with this disorder might gorge on a large pizza, 14 donuts, or a gallon of ice cream, then force himself to vomit. Or, he might compensate for the overeating by using excessive laxatives, enemas, or diuretics. Anorexia nervosa is an illness typified by starving through extended fasts or by eating only one food for weeks at a time. Both these illnesses are life-threatening and require a doctor's care.

Move it

Some people are out of shape, overweight, or underweight and unattractive. They feel they cannot change. The human body *can* change. Inside even the most dilapidated body there is a trim, healthy, energized body that wants to escape into the world.

After the first step of admitting the problem and realizing the desire for change, real progress can be seen in a matter of weeks. If you stick to an exercise schedule for just three weeks, you will be rewarded.

This is not about the Boston Marathon. This is about exercise and people who don't do it.

The world used to run on muscle. Until very recently, human bodies did nearly all of man's work. Now, machines do the work and our bodies are attempting to adjust. In order to be fit and well, our bodies don't need to go out and kill a woolly mammoth every few days, then drag it back to the cave by hand, uphill.

If that is your job, you get plenty of exercise. Most students have to make other arrangements. The fact is, lean muscles absorb nutrients more efficiently than muscles marbled with fat. The best reason to get in shape isn't to improve how you will look in designer jeans. With lean muscles, you

function better at whatever you do.

The heart is a muscle that can get fat, too. A fat belly may be unattractive. A fat heart can be lethal.

Dieting alone doesn't create lean muscles and a strong heart. The only way to get lean is by moving.

A 10-mile run every day isn't necessary. It's not even smart, unless you're in great shape. Divide and conquer, and do something you enjoy. Start with 15 minutes a day. If that's overwhelming, break the fifteen minutes into three five-minute periods.

Here are some ways to move your body. Pick something that looks fun and do it regularly.

1. Aerobics. Take a class that gets you moving. Group spirit might get you going at 6:30 in the morning when part of you is screaming, "Sleep!" Aerobics classes usually work out to music. That can make your inactive body more fun to move.

2. Swim. This is one of the best exercises when water is available. Otherwise it is hard on the knees.

3. Walk. No equipment is needed and training time is minimal. This is a great way to get started if you haven't exercised for a long time. Walk when you do errands. Walk up stairs instead of taking the elevator. Go for a daily walk. Gradually increase until you are walking briskly at least 20 minutes a day.

4. Jog. Some people swear by it. Others swear at it. If you have never tried running, and if you don't shudder at the thought of pounding pavement, give it a shot. It is a fast, effective way to get your pulse and breathing elevated.

5. Sports. If you like competition, this might be the way to get you moving. Teams are always forming for various sports. Your ability, high or low, can be matched. Select from tennis, handball, racquetball, soccer, ping-pong, bowling, hacky-sack, volleyball, softball, basketball, hockey, golf, polo, or other sports.

6. Horseback riding. Rentals are available even in the city.

7. Skate. The popularity of roller skating has made this form of movement an option even in climates that don't produce ice.

8. Jump on a trampoline. For less than $100 you can get a mini-tramp for bouncing and jogging your way to fitness.

9. Bike. An indoor exercise bike is particularly good for the TV addict. Put on several miles while mystery unfolds or love blossoms. You can also ride outside and watch scenery unfold and flowers blossom.

10. Row. If you don't have a boat, use a machine.

11. Jump rope. For a few dollars you can buy the equipment, and, if you have high ceilings and no one living below you, you can do it indoors.

12. Ski. Do it summer or winter, on land or on water. It can be very inexpensive when done with rented equipment on a snow-covered field.

13. Lift weights. The idea is to get your muscles working. You can do this with fancy machines, inexpensive weights from a discount store, or bags of sand from a lumberyard.

The experts recommend

SIX DIETARY GUIDELINES

1. Eat a variety of foods every day. Include fruits, vegetables, whole grains, breads, cereals, milk, cheese, yogurt, meats, poultry, fish, and eggs in your diet.

2. Maintain your weight. Overweight people tend to develop chronic disorders such as high blood pressure. To lose weight, you don't have to buy dozens of diet books or pills, or make a profession of the endeavor. Increase your physical activity and eat less sugar and fat. Avoid alcohol. Eat slowly. Avoid second helpings. Eat smaller portions.

3. Decrease fat and cholesterol consumption. This is a good idea even if you are not overweight. High blood cholesterol is a health risk. Eat lean meat. Eat fish, poultry, dry beans, and peas. Limit your intake of eggs, organ meats, butter, cream, shortening, and oil. Broil, bake, or boil rather than fry. Cut off excess fat before cooking meat.

4. Increase starch and fiber consumption. Complex carbohydrates contain fewer calories than fats. These include fruits, vegetables, whole grains, beans, peas, and nuts.

5. Decrease sugar intake. Obesity, impaired circulation, tooth decay, and other problems relate to excessive sugar in the diet. Almost all prepared foods contain sugar. Look at product labels. Do not select foods that list sugar as a major ingredient. (Major ingredients are listed first. If sugar is a major ingredient, it will appear first, second, or third on the list. Sometimes it is called corn syrup, dextrose, fructose, or sucrose.)

6. Reduce salt intake. Americans use too much salt, a common cause of high blood pressure. Limit your intake of salty foods like pretzels, potato chips, cheese, salted nuts, and popcorn. Pickled foods have lots of salt.

Your body does need sodium chloride (salt). However, our food generally contains so much that we get enough, even if we try to avoid it.

14. Climb mountains. Throw a frisbee. Garden. Sail. This list could go on. Find something that involves movement and fun, and do it regularly.

Eventually work up to an exercise program that will get your lungs pumping and blood flowing rapidly for at least 20 minutes a day at least three times a week. It is this type of movement that will lead to a trim, healthy, and alive body.

Rest it

Human bodies have a need for rest built into their design. Resting your body can take place in the form of sleep, meditation, or relaxation.

Sleep and how to get it

It is possible to drive a person crazy or even to kill him by depriving him of sleep. Don't do this to yourself. All-nighters are common in college.

You may participate, and advice won't change that. If you find you are doing it often, read chapter two, *Time*, once again. Depriving yourself of sleep is a choice that can be avoided.

Sometimes getting to sleep isn't easy, even when you feel tired. If you have trouble falling asleep, experiment with these suggestions:

1. Exercise daily to help tire the body.
2. Keep your sleeping room cool.
3. Take a warm bath, not a shower, just before bed.
4. While lying in bed, practice relaxation techniques.
5. If you can't fall asleep after 30 minutes, get up and study or do something else until you're tired.
6. If sleeplessness persists, see a doctor.

Fatigue, depression, irritability, and other emotional problems sometimes result from lack of sleep. Get a good night's sleep.

Meditation and how to do it

The word "meditate" came from the Sanskrit word *medha* which means, literally, "locating your center, your inner wisdom." Meditation is now being taught and endorsed by everyone from gurus in long white gowns to medical

(continued on page 234)

Crazed glazed donut runs amok

Bill Harlan

PANCREAS CITY, IOWA—A glazed donut, apparently out of control, caused a multiple-sugar pileup here early yesterday. The entire state is reeling in lethargy and the governor is reportedly considering calling in extra fatty tissue.

At approximately 9 a.m., a slowdown in the state's energy level caused assistant brain cells at the Capitol to phone the state procurement office in Right Hand with a request for a glazed donut. Procurement officers, who this morning insisted that they were merely following orders, delivered the donut to Mouth, two miles north

of Throat, at 9:01.

Records indicate the energy level throughout the state did rise for more than a half hour. However, about 45 minutes after the donut was delivered, things began to slow down. Within an hour, the situation was serious.

When the donut reached Stomach, the town was deserted. It raced on through Duodenum Gap right into Intestine County. The whole state was in a frenzy when the bottom fell out. No energy.

Officials in Pancreas are alleging that the donut was pure glucose, the kind of sugar which causes an immediate energy boost.

By that time,

Pancreas was in a state of utter confusion. The donut burned out in a glucose spree. Cells everywhere were demanding more sugar, but only traces of glucose could be found. It was then, officials believe, that terror-stricken cells near Stomach began screaming, "Send down a candy bar."

For the rest of the day, the state was reeling under an assault of caffeine and sugar. Three candy bars in all. Four soft drinks.

By evening, the governor's office had called up alcohol reserves.

"We have been recommending proteins and carbohydrates since Tuesday," said a highly

placed source, vacationing at the Isle of Langerhans in Lake Pancreas. "They release glucose gradually, to be used all day. An egg, some cereal, a piece of fruit, and this tragedy could have been avoided. Heck, a burger would have been better. This donut thing has got to stop."

This morning, a saddened state lies under a layer of fat. "I'm guessing it will take at least a hard 10-mile run to get this mess cleaned up," said one administrative assistant in Cerebellum.

Officials in East and West Leg could not be reached for comment.

Journal entry #68

Discovery statement
First step in health

If you look and feel healthy, a greater awareness of your body will let you know what you're doing right. If you are not content with your present physical or emotional health, you may discover some ways to improve.

This exercise is a structured discovery statement that allows you to look closely at your health. As with the first step exercise in chapter one, the usefulness of this exercise is determined by your honesty and courage.

1. Draw a simple outline of yourself. You have positive and negative feelings about various internal and external parts of your body. Label the parts, and include a short description of the attributes you like or dislike. For instance: terrific straight teeth, fat thighs, clear lungs, strong heart, etc.

2. The body you drew substantially reflects your past health practices. To discover how well you take care of your body, complete the following sentences.

Eating

1. The truth about *what* I eat is . . .

2. What I know about the *way* I eat is . . .

3. The thing about my diet that I would most like to change is . . .

4. Because of my eating habits I am . . .

Exercise

1. The way I usually exercise is . . .

2. The last time I had 20 minutes or more of heart/lung (aerobic) exercise was . . .

3. As a result of my state of conditioning, I feel . . .

4. And I look . . .

5. It would be easier for me to work out regularly if I . . .

6. The most important benefit for me in exercising more would be . . .

Harmful substances

1. My history of cigarette smoking is . . .

2. An objective observer would say my use of alcohol is . . .

3. In the last ten days I have had exactly ____ alcoholic drinks . . .

4. The thing I know about my use of coffee, colas, and other caffeine drinks is . . .

5. I have used the following controlled substances (non-prescription, illegal drugs) in the past nine days:

6. When it comes to drugs, what I am sometimes concerned about is . . .

7. I take the following prescription drugs . . .

Relationships

1. Someone who knows me fairly well would say I am emotionally . . .

2. The way I look and feel has affected my relationships by . . .

3. My use of drugs or alcohol has been an issue with . . .

4. The best thing I could do for myself and my relationships would be . . .

Sleep

1. I sleep . . .

2. On weekends I normally sleep . . .

3. I have trouble sleeping when . . .

4. Last night I . . .

5. Night before last I . . .

What concerns me more than anything about my health is . . .

Alternative health care

Health care is a controversial issue. This chapter presents suggestions accepted by almost every health care professional. There are dozens of other techniques, and many philosophies of health care.

Explore and experiment with alternatives. Some of the methods you may wish to investigate are listed below. It may be advisable to consult your doctor before trying them.

Macrobiotic diets—longevity through a diet balanced in accordance with Far Eastern philosophy of positive and negative energy.

Fasting—one or two days without food is thought by some to have a cleansing effect. It may also provide valuable insights into your behavior regarding food and eating.

Mega-vitamin therapy—based on the theory that body chemistry (and nutritional needs) vary tremendously from one person to the next.

Vegetarian diet—a healthy diet does not need to include meat.

Acupressure—trained therapists apply intense pressure to specific points on the body and limbs to relieve discomfort and increase blood circulation and flow of energy.

Rebirthing—a theory of re-experiencing your birth through guided breathing and suggestion in order to release long-held tensions and feelings from the body.

Massage—touch is critical to our well-being. Skilled massage relaxes and soothes the entire body.

Reflexology—practitioners manipulate and massage the feet in order to restore health in other areas of the body.

Rolfing—deep tissue massage may be a way to release trapped emotions and restore balanced health and posture.

Acupuncture—insertion of needles at critical places on the body can have anesthetic effect and help prevent diseases.

Chiropractics—adjustment of the skeleton, particularly the vertebrae of the back and neck, is done to relieve pain and numbness.

Biofeedback—learning to regulate such "automatic" life processes as heart rate and brain waves by connecting with a monitoring device.

Iridology—mapping the state of health of all the body's organs and glands revealed by examination of the iris (colored portion) of the eye.

Herbal medicine—curing disease and maintaining health by administering compounds derived exclusively from plant substances.

Laugh therapy—industrial-strength funny stuff may shake out cancer cells.

Music therapy—soothing the souls and calming the behavior of hyperactive, super-stressed people.

Psychic healing—effecting cures by focusing spiritual energy.

Hair analysis—tracing body chemistry and nutrition by measuring trace elements and compounds found in hair.

(continued from page 231)

Exercise #38

Setting your bio-alarm

Sometimes, after only a few hours of sleep, we wake up feeling miserable. Other times, we bounce out of bed feeling terrific. How we feel in the morning often depends on how we program our bio-alarm clock the night before.

After a long night of studying, you may go to bed with the thought, "I shouldn't have stayed up so late. I'll be exhausted tomorrow. I hope I hear the alarm in the morning." The next morning, you oversleep and miss class.

To wake up refreshed, experiment with this exercise.

Before going to bed, decide what time you want to get up in the morning. Now say aloud, "I am going to get up at seven," (or whatever time you chose).

Next, lie in bed and allow your body to relax. Imagine feeling heavy and sinking into the bed. Now softly say (out loud if possible), "I will wake naturally at seven feeling refreshed, rested, and ready to start my day."

Do a body scan by relaxing each part of your body starting with your feet, then ankles, legs, lower back, and so forth until you are completely relaxed and asleep.

You will probably wake up feeling great, at exactly the time you chose. Experiment with this exercise a few times while setting your alarm clock five minutes later. After a while, you'll never have to hear the buzz again.

doctors. Our contemporary ills—tension headaches, high blood pressure, insomnia, anxiety, irritability, lack of self-confidence, blocked creativity—have made the art of achieving calmness and one-pointedness more attractive than ever.

Meditation can provide a deeper form of relaxation than sleep. Pulse rate and oxygen consumption may drop as much as 20%. Meditation restores energy and promotes self-healing. It is a way to achieve inner peace, the value of which can be easily overlooked when advancing toward other goals.

There is no right or wrong way to meditate. Here are a few guidelines:

1. Make a commitment. Meditation is about being here and now with yourself. You can learn a lot from yourself. You can learn to relax at will. The results will be directly proportional to your intention.

2. Set a specific time and place. When you are consistent about doing an activity in one location, at one time of day, your body and mind know what to expect. If you don't have a special place to meditate, set up other signals, like wearing a special shirt, lighting a candle or incense or playing a certain tape or record. Meditate for at least 20 minutes a day.

3. Pay attention to your breathing. Sit in a comfortable position with your spine erect. Notice your breath as it flows gently in and out of your body. Imagine yourself breathing in calmness, relaxation, and well-being. Visualize yourself breathing out frustrations, tensions, and negative emotions.

4. Clear your mind. Concentrate on something to lessen distractions. Repeat silently a word or phrase (love, God, yes, om), or stare at a candle flame. Allow your mind to be blank. Each time a thought enters, gently let it go. Another thought will soon enter; let it float away.

5. Consider taking a class. Local meditation centers, YMCA's, and community education programs teach a wide variety of meditation styles. You can learn meditation that involves movement (tai chi), breathing and postures (yoga), or science and ceremony (transcendental meditation).

Relaxation and how to have it

Stress results from pleasant experiences as well as unpleasant ones. You may be a bundle of nerves and tense as a frozen garden hose even when your life is going great. Excitement is perceived by your body in almost the same way

that fear is perceived. Both emotions produce rapid heart rates, increased adrenaline flow, and muscle contractions. Both emotions produce stress.

Whatever the reason causing stress, the cure is the same: relax. That is easy to say. It is also easy to do when you develop a few simple techniques. Use the techniques for handling test anxiety from chapter six, *Tests*. The tension and worry which develop around tests require the same relaxation as the stress from a job promotion, an upcoming wedding, a long-awaited graduation, a move to a better place, or the excitement of a new relationship.

If the relaxation techniques in chapter six don't work within a few weeks, get some help. There are trained relaxation therapists in every city. Ask a doctor, counselor, or school dean for a referral. Stress management is a developed field and much is known. There is no need to continue to have a pain in your neck, a knot in your stomach, cold feet, or a dozen other symptoms of tension. Relax.

Protect it

It makes sense to protect our bodies from unnecessary injury or illness. Part of this protection can be preventive as suggested in *Feed it*, *Move it*, and *Rest it*. Some of the protection is more active. You probably already follow many of the suggestions given below. Read them all with an eye for what you don't do. Those are the ideas that can help you protect yourself.

Against accidents

More than four million disabling injuries occur every year in the haven called home. Each year over 27,000 people die of accidents in their home. Almost twice that many die in their car. You can greatly reduce the odds of this happening to you.

1. Don't drive after drinking alcohol or using psychoactive drugs.
2. Drive with the realization that other drivers are possibly preoccupied, intoxicated, or careless.
3. Put poisons out of reach of children

and, for adults, label them clearly. Poisoning takes a larger toll on people ages 15 to 45 than on children.

4. Keep stairs, halls, doorways, and other pathways clear of shoes, toys, newspapers, or other debris.

5. Don't smoke in bed.

6. Don't leave burning candles.

7. Keep children away from hot stoves and turn pot handles inward.

8. Check electrical cords for fraying, loose connections, or breaks in insulation. Don't overload extension cords.

9. Have a fire extinguisher handy.

10. Watch for ways that an infant or toddler could suffocate—small objects that can be swallowed, old refrigerators or freezers that can act as air-tight

Exercise #39

Auto-suggestion

This exercise can be used to prepare your mind, body, and spirit for any activity that requires being relaxed and centered.

Sit or lie down in a comfortable position. Close your eyes. Imagine your forehead relaxing so much that it begins to melt and flow over the rest of your head and face, spreading deep relaxation as it goes. Relax the muscles of your jaw so that it hangs limp and loose. Your mouth will be slightly open. Now begin to regulate your breathing using the following counting cycle:

Inhale to the count of one; exhale to the count of two;
Inhale to the count of two; exhale to the count of four;
Inhale to the count of three; exhale to the count of six.

Continue increasing your count, exhaling twice as long as you inhale, up to inhaling for six counts and exhaling for twelve.

Now, beginning with inhaling for six counts and exhaling for twelve, reverse the cycle and shorten your breaths. Inhale six, exhale twelve, inhale five, exhale ten, and so on until you inhale one and exhale two.

After this breathing warm-up, you can learn by suggestion to experience a variety of sensations throughout your body. Here is a routine which begins by inducing the feeling of heaviness in your arm.

Repeat each of the following phrases several times silently. Do this with purpose and meaning.

"My right arm is getting limp and heavy"—six to eight times.
"My right arm is getting heavier and heavier"—six to eight times.
"My right arm is completely heavy"—six to eight times.
"I feel supremely calm"—one time.

Then open your eyes, shake off the heaviness, start over with the breathing cycle, and repeat the above auto-suggestions again.

If you do this for several days, you will begin to experience a wonderful feeling of heaviness in your arm. Then you can begin the same process with your left arm.

Auto-suggestions can be used to experience the following:

Heaviness and warmth in your arms and legs.
Your chest feeling warm and pleasant.
A clear and steady heartbeat.

Calm and clear breathing.
Your stomach feeling soft and warm.
A cool forehead.

Always end your auto-suggestions with "I feel supremely calm."

One by one, you can add new sensations to those you already experience. Your final auto-suggestion might be:

"My arms and legs are heavy and warm."
"I feel supremely calm."
"My heartbeat and breathing are calm and steady."

"My stomach is soft and warm, and my forehead is cool."

Mastering these exercises to achieve the desired sensations can help you enjoy a peaceful state of relaxation. A relaxed state is useful before you take tests, do affirmations and visualizations of success, participate in sports, or meditate. Deep relaxed states have also been used to sharpen attention, gain conscious control of physiological processes, control moods, and enhance abilities in everything from schoolwork to pain control and self-healing.

prisons, unattended or unfenced swimming pools, kerosene heaters in tightly-closed rooms, plastic kitchen or clothing bags.

Against venereal disease

Venereal diseases do not discriminate on the basis of moral character. Plenty of nice people get them. They are extremely contagious.

Herpes is epidemic. It appears as sores on the genitals and can be painful. The symptoms usually subside and disappear for a time, then flare up periodically.

Gonorrhea is usually experienced as painful urination. It is treatable with antibiotics.

Syphilis develops in three stages, and treatment is critical before the illness has a chance to progress. If you get it, it will not go away without treatment. It can result in death. An early symptom is an open sore on the genitals.

AIDS (Acquired Immune Deficiency Syndrome) is the newest and perhaps most deadly sexually-transmitted disease. The disease causes a breakdown in the victim's ability to fight infections that otherwise would not threaten the individual's life.

AIDS is most often transmitted through anal intercourse. It has also been linked to the sharing of injection needles by intravenous drug abusers and occasionally by blood transfusion.

Massive efforts are underway to find out how the disease works and how to treat it.

Although not considered a venereal disease, AIDS (Acquired Immune Deficiency Syndrome) is a fatal disorder that is loosely linked to sexual contact. It is transmitted through the blood. Symptoms include a series of unusual, recurring viral infections. Treatment, cause, and infectiousness are all unknown at this time.

If you suspect you might have a venereal disease, go to a doctor or public health clinic immediately and find out. Early treatment is usually effective, and infecting others isn't nice.

Prevention is a function of discrimination or abstinence. Know people well enough to trust them to tell you the truth, and ask directly. If your relationship is intimate enough to allow sexual contact, it is intimate enough for straight talk about venereal diseases. Condoms can help protect against most sexually transmitted illnesses.

Brainstorm for three minutes ways to increase your chances to be safe. (For example, use seat belts.)

1. Write your ideas here:

Journal entry #69

Intention statement

2. Circle the ideas you plan to implement this week.

Against unwanted pregnancy

There are more ways to avoid pregnancy now than ever before. This can make the choice confusing. Some people evade the responsibility of contraceptive use by hoping that pregnancy won't happen to them. Sixty percent of sexually active teenagers don't use birth control. Here is some information that can help you avoid unwanted pregnancy.

The "pill" is a synthetic hormone that tells a woman's body not to produce eggs. To be effective, it must be taken every day for 21 days a month. Different women require different types and doses, therefore birth control pills must be prescribed by a doctor. Side effects sometimes include slight nausea, breast tenderness, weight gain from water retention, and moodiness. Some women should not take the pill. It is about 98% effective in normal use.

An IUD (intrauterine device) is a small metal or plastic device that is inserted in the uterus and left there for months at a time. It prevents fertilized eggs from developing. Side effects may include heavier menstrual flow, anemia, pelvic infection, perforation of the cervix or uterus, or septic abortion. IUD's must be prescribed and inserted by a physician. They are about 95% effective.

A diaphragm is a shallow rubber dome that is covered with sperm-killing cream and inserted in the vagina. It fits over the cervix, the opening of the uterus, and prevents sperm from getting to the egg. A doctor must measure and fit the diaphragm. It must be inserted before intercourse and left in place for 6 to 8 hours. It is more than 80% effective.

A sponge contraceptive works something like a diaphragm. It is effective for 24 hours. It can be purchased over the counter at drug stores. Side effects might include odor, difficult removal, or allergic reactions. Sponges are more than 80% effective.

Foams, creams, tablets, suppositories, and jellies are chemicals that are placed in the vagina before intercourse and prevent sperm from getting to the egg. They are about 85% effective when used consistently.

Condoms (rubbers) are thin membranes which are stretched over the penis prior to intercourse and prevent semen from entering the vagina. When used properly and consistently, condoms are over 95% effective.

The rhythm method involves avoiding intercourse during ovulation. The problem with this method is that it's difficult to know for sure when a woman ovulates. An organization called Natural Family Planning teaches women how to monitor their bodies to determine fertility. If done with skill and care, this method can be over 95% effective. Normally it is less than 80% effective.

Douching is flushing the vagina with water or other liquid after intercourse. Don't use it for birth control. Even if you douche immediately, sperm are quicker than you are.

Withdrawal is the act of removing the penis before ejaculation occurs. This is ineffective. Sperm can be present in pre-ejaculation fluid. Don't rely on this practice.

Sterilization is a permanent form of birth control and should not be used by people who might someday want children. It is almost 100% effective. The procedure involves surgery to tie the Fallopian tubes which carry eggs from the ovary to the uterus in women, or to cut the vas deferens (tubes which carry semen) in men.

(continued from page 237) Abstinence is choosing not to have intercourse. It is 100% effective. Sexual intercourse, contrary to popular belief, is not necessary for a happy existence. You may feel pressured to change your mind about this choice. Remember, abstinence is only guaranteed when it is practiced without exception.

Fix it

You are the expert on your body. You live with it every day, and you are right there when even the smallest change occurs. Pay attention to these changes. They are often your first clue to the need for repair.

Watch for these signs:

1. Weight loss of more than ten pounds in ten weeks with no apparent cause.
2. A sore, scab, or ulcer in the mouth or on the body which doesn't heal in three weeks.
3. A skin blemish or mole that bleeds, itches, or changes size, shape, or color.
4. Persistent or severe headaches.
5. Sudden vomiting that is not preceded by nausea.
6. Fainting spells.
7. Double vision.
8. Difficulty swallowing.
9. Persistent hoarseness or nagging cough.
10. Blood that is coughed up or vomited.
11. Shortness of breath for no apparent reason.
12. Persistent indigestion or abdominal pain.
13. A big change in normal bowel habits such as alternating diarrhea and constipation.
14. Black and tarry bowel movements.
15. Rectal bleeding.
16. Pink, red, or unusually cloudy urine.
17. Discomfort or difficulty in urinating.
18. Lumps or thickening in a breast.
19. In women, vaginal bleeding between menstrual periods or after menopause.

If you are sick, get help. Even if you think it might not be serious, check it out. Untreated illness or injury can often cause problems much more serious than would occur had you received prompt treatment.

The

Alcohol, tobacco and drugs— truth.

The truth is, they are fun. In our culture, high has become synonymous with having a good time. Even if you don't smoke, drink, or take drugs every day, you are certain to come in contact with people who do.

We are in a drug-using society. Drugs (legal and illegal), alcohol, tobacco, and caffeine are acceptable and sought-after answers to practically any problem anyone has. Do you have a headache? Take a drug. Is it hard for you to fall asleep? Take a drug. Is it hard to stay awake? Take a drug. Are you depressed? Are you hyperactive? Are you nervous? Are you too skinny? Too fat? Too weak? Do you have a hard time being comfortable in a group? Would you like to really have fun at a party? Want to meet new people? Want to impress your friends? Are you too inhibited to ask for a date? There is a brand of liquor, a particular wine, a certain cigarette, or a stronger, faster acting drug that can help.

There is a big payoff in using alcohol, tobacco, caffeine, cocaine, heroin . . . or else people wouldn't do it. The payoff is sometimes direct—relaxation, self-confidence, comfort, excitement, pleasure. At times, the payoff is not so obvious—avoiding rejection, masking emotional pain, peer group acceptance, rejecting authority.

People enjoy using drugs and alcohol so much they often push these substances on to others. "Here, have another drink. Loosen up. Enjoy yourself." "I can't believe this stuff. Here, try some." "The insights I had into my life were incredible. I realized for the first time that . . ." "Come on, try it. Are you some kind of a lightweight?"

In addition to the payoff, there is a cost. For many people, the cost is much greater than the payoff. Yet they continue to abuse.

Lectures about why not to abuse alcohol or drugs are pointless. Ultimately, we don't take care of our bodies because we "should". We might take care of ourselves when we see that using a substance is costing us more than we're getting for our trouble. You choose. It's your body. So here are facts that can help you make choices about what you put in your body.

1. One in ten adult Americans is an alcoholic. Most experts define an alcoholic as a person whose life is not working well and who regularly drinks alcohol. Many more people have, at some time, a problem with alcohol. Alcohol is a powerful chemical. Addiction to it is a serious illness.

2. In 1972, the Boston Drug Surveillance Program found that the risk of a heart attack increased by 50% for persons drinking 5 cups of coffee daily and by 100% for those having six cups or more each day.

3. The death rate of cigarette smokers in the United States at all ages is higher than that of non smokers. It climbs in proportion to the number of cigarettes smoked, the number of years smoking, and how early in life smoking was started.

4. One of every four teenagers is a problem drinker. The problem is not only that they drink to excess, but that they use alcohol as a method of coping with problems. This form of coping prevents them from developing effective ways to deal with life's challenges. Adolescence is the time for development of life-coping skills, but this growth doesn't occur when problems are artificially fixed with alcohol or drugs.

5. Using drugs (or alcohol) leads to an initial feeling of euphoria (a high). This is followed by a slump (even a mild hangover) which seems like a good reason to repeat the use.

This can result in a downward spiral like this:

low self-esteem —
drug or alcohol use —
brief euphoria —
low emotional state —
use — brief euphoria —
low emotional state —
more use —
personal failures —
lower self-esteem —
more use —
longer euphoria —
lower emotional state — . . .

6. In a study of 36,705 pairs of American men, smokers of a pack or more per day were computer-matched with non smokers. The 19 factors used to match the pairs included race, height, age, and national origin. After three years, there were 110 lung cancer deaths among cigarette smokers and only twelve lung cancer deaths among the non smokers.

7. 80% of all deaths in fires are linked to the use of alcohol. 65% of all drownings are linked to the use of alcohol. 22% of all home accidents are linked to the use of alcohol. 36% of all pedestrian accidents are linked to the use of alcohol. 55% of all police arrests are linked to the use of alcohol.

8. Recent research at the University of Georgia at Athens showed that women who drink two cups of coffee per day are twice as likely to have cancer of the ovaries or pancreas than those who do not drink coffee.

9. Persons who drink six to ten cups of coffee per day are likely to exhibit one or more of the following: euphoria followed by depression, feelings of ineffectiveness, worry over performance, insomnia, nervousness, excitement, headache, ringing in ears, fatigue, trembling muscles, heart fluttering, rapid heart rate, fast and deep respiration.

(continued on page 243)

Choose one negative habit or action that you will begin to eliminate today. Write an intention statement about changing this health deterrent so your healthy body can break out of its shell.

I intend to . . .

Journal entry #70

Intention statement

Exercise #40

Alcoholism, how do I know . . .

People who have problems with drugs or alcohol are great at hiding the problem from themselves and others. It is also hard to admit that a friend might have a problem.

The purpose of this exercise is to give you an objective way to look at your relationship to drugs or alcohol. This exercise is also useful in looking to see if a friend might be addicted. Addiction can be emotional and not physical. These are signals that let us know when drug or alcohol use has become abusive.

Answer the following questions quickly and honestly. If you are concerned about a friend, replace each "you" in the following questions with your friend's first name.

Yes or No

_____ Are you uncomfortable discussing drug abuse or alcoholism?

_____ Are you worried about your drug or alcohol use?

_____ Are any of your friends worried about your drug or alcohol use?

_____ Have you ever hidden from a friend, spouse, employer, or co-worker the fact that you were drinking? (Pretended you were sober? Covered up alcohol breath?)

_____ Do you sometimes use alcohol or drugs to escape lows rather than produce highs?

_____ Have you ever gotten angry when confronted about your use?

_____ Do you brag about how much you consume? "I drank him under the table."

_____ Do you drink or do drugs when you are alone?

_____ Do you store up alcohol, drugs, cigarettes, or caffeine (in coffee or pop) so you're sure you won't run out?

_____ Does having a party almost always include alcohol or drugs?

_____ Do you try to control your drinking so that it won't be a problem? ("I only drink on weekends now," "I never drink before 5 p.m.," "I only drink beer.")

_____ Do you often explain to other people why you are drinking? ("It's my birthday," "It's my friend's birthday," "It's Veteran's Day," "It sure is a hot day.")

_____ Have you changed your friends to accommodate your drinking? ("She's OK, but she isn't excited about getting high.")

_____ Has your behavior changed in the last several months? (Grades down? Lack of interest in a hobby? Change of values or what you think is moral?)

_____ Do you drink to relieve tension? ("What a day! I need a drink.")

_____ Do you have medical problems that could be related to drinking? (stomach trouble, malnutrition, liver problems, anemia)

_____ Have you ever decided to quit drugs or alcohol and then changed your mind?

_____ Have you been high in the morning during the last year?

_____ Have you had any fights, accidents, or similar incidents related to drinking or drugs in the last year?

_____ Has your drinking or drug use ever caused a problem at home?

_____ Do you envy people who go overboard with alcohol or drugs?

_____ Have you ever told yourself you can quit at any time?

_____ Have you ever been in trouble with the police after or while you were drinking?

_____ Have you ever missed school or work because of alcohol or drugs?

_____ Do you feel uncomfortable at a party if you don't drink or get high?

_____ Have you ever done badly on a test because you had a hangover?

_____ Have you ever had a blackout (a period you can't remember) after drinking?

_____ Do you wish that people would mind their own business when it comes to your use of alcohol or drugs?

Now count the number of questions you answered "yes." If you answered "yes" more than five times, talk with a professional. Five "yes" answers do not mean that you're an alcoholic or that you have a serious problem. They do point out that drugs or alcohol are adversely affecting your life. It is very important you talk to a counselor with alcohol and drug abuse training. ***Do not rely on the opinion of anyone without such training.***

If you answered this questionnaire about another person, and you answered "yes" more than five times, your friend may need help. You probably can't do it alone. Seek out the help of a counselor or a support group such as Al-Anon. (Call the local Alcoholics Anonymous Chapter for an Al-anon meeting near you.)

(continued from page 241)

10. 65% of all murders, 40% of all assaults, 35% of all rapes, 30% of all other sex crimes, 30% of suicides, 55% of fights or assaults in the home, and 60% of all cases of child abuse are associated with the use of alcohol.

11. In a study of twelfth graders in Dallas, Texas, those who used the largest amounts of caffeine and sugar had the lowest grade point average.

12. It is estimated that up to 90% of all auto fatalities and injuries are related to drinking and driving. At least 26,000 Americans are killed every year by drunk drivers.

13. A University of California study of 25,000 persons showed that those who drank two or more cups of coffee daily had a 70% greater chance of ulcers than those who drank no coffee.

14. People with drinking problems are seven times more likely to get divorced.

15. Cigarette smokers have 70% more heart attacks than non-smokers. Other risk factors related to heart attacks include high blood pressure, obesity, and high blood cholesterol.

16. Suicide among alcoholics is 58 times higher than for non-drinkers.

17. Families and friends of alcoholics or drug addicts often have equally serious problems. They are known as co-addicts, and they rationalize, deny, excuse, and cover for unacceptable behaviors. They often walk around pretending something that is obvious (the drug or alcohol abuse) doesn't really exist. Drug and alcohol treatment programs treat co-addicts right alongside the addicts.

18. Cirrhosis of the liver, one of the many known conditions related to alcoholism, is the cause of over 30,000 deaths/year.

19. One in four people report there has been a problem in their family due to alcohol.

20. Over five billion dollars per year are spent on medical services and property damage due to drunk driving. The total cost of alcoholism to the nation is nearly 43 billion dollars per year due to absenteeism, health and welfare services, property damage, and medical expenses.

21. Alcohol use is the number one cause of death for people between the ages of 15 and 24.

22. Skid row derelicts account for less than five percent of U.S. alcoholics today.

23. Men who smoke less than half a pack a day have a death rate about 60% higher than that of non-smokers; one to two packs a day, about 90% higher; and two or more packs a day, 120% above non-smokers.

24. Low self-esteem is a crucial factor in addiction. This lack of self worth is usually masked or concealed by the drug or alcohol use, but it is basic to almost every person who abuses drugs, cigarettes, caffeine, or alcohol. One way to cope with feeling worthless is to bury those feelings in a mood-altered state.

25. If cocaine, heroin, and other drugs don't make you broke, they can make you crazy—not necessarily the kind of crazy where you dress up like Napoleon. Recreational drugs can make you the kind of crazy where you care about little else except finding more drugs; friends and family be damned. The personality changes that occur with regular drug use are masked to the user but readily apparent to friends and associates. Facts are plentiful, see the chart in this book titled *Contemporary drugs of choice* on page 250.

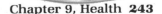

What to do

If you have a problem with alcohol, drugs, cigarettes, or caffeine, it can be solved. Your problem may be your own abuse of one of these substances or perhaps the behavior of someone you love. In any case, these problems can be handled. Consider implementing several of these suggestions.

1. Admit the problem. Drug and alcohol abusers are a varied group—rich and poor, young and old, successful and unsuccessful—but they do have one thing in common; they are masters of denial. Alcoholics have great difficulty admitting their disease. They deny they are unhappy. They deny that they have hurt anyone. They are convinced they can quit drinking anytime they want. They sometimes become so adept at hiding the problem from themselves that they die.

2. Use consciously. If you drink, use drugs, smoke, or drink caffeine, do it with awareness. Do it with deliberate decision rather than out of habit or because of pressure from another person or group. Use of these substances is so acceptable that we often do it without decision. It becomes automatic.

3. Look at the costs. There is always a trade-off. You may feel great after ten beers, and you will probably remember that feeling. No one feels great the morning after ten beers, but it seems easier to forget pain. Often, people don't notice how badly drugs, alcohol, or cigarettes make them feel.

4. Don't blame yourself. Nobody plans to be an alcoholic. Alcoholism and drug addiction are diseases, like flu or cancer. There is evidence that alcoholism is inherited. If you have pneumonia, you go to a doctor, get treatment, and recover without guilt or shame. Approach a drug or alcohol problem in yourself or others the same way.

5. Get help. Alcoholism and drug addiction are not diseases you can treat yourself. The drinking or drug abuse are symptoms of an illness that needs treatment. Self-control doesn't work for very long.

Alcoholics Anonymous is listed in most phone books. These are people who understand the problem of alcohol (and drug) abuse. They have a systematic approach to living without it. With over a million members, this is one of the oldest and most successful self-help programs in the world.

Every chapter of AA welcomes people from all walks of life. You don't have to be an alcoholic to attend most meetings. These people are open about dealing with drinking problems. They take a frank look at how it feels and what it means to be in trouble with alcohol.

Narcotics Anonymous is a similar organization; its focus is drug addiction. Local treatment programs are available in almost every community. They may be residential (you live there for weeks or months at a time) or outpatient (you visit several hours a day). Find out where these treatment centers are located by calling a doctor, mental health professional, or a local hospital. Alcohol and drug treatment are now covered by many health insurance programs. If you don't have insurance, it is usually possible to arrange some other payment program. Money is not a good reason to avoid treatment.

The American Cancer Society (see the phone book) has excellent pamphlets on how to stop smoking. Private stop-smoking programs are present in most cities. They use a variety of techniques, from education and behavior modification to

(continued on page 246)

Exercise #41

Watch it

A common theme running through many suggestions in this book is to observe yourself. This is particularly important with health.

As human beings, one of our greatest weaknesses is selective perception. We tend to see only what we would like to see. Monitoring can give us objective data that isn't apparent from mere observation.

Chart your behavior. Pick something you do and make a careful record of it over time. You can chart food you eat (sugar, calories, meat), what you drink (coffee, soft drinks, beer, wine, liquor), exercise (running, swimming), smoking, sleeping, or anything you want to change.

On the attached "Watch It" form, fill in the time line and the behavior line. There are several examples to follow. As the hours, days, or weeks go by, fill in the form. Record your observations and self-discoveries.

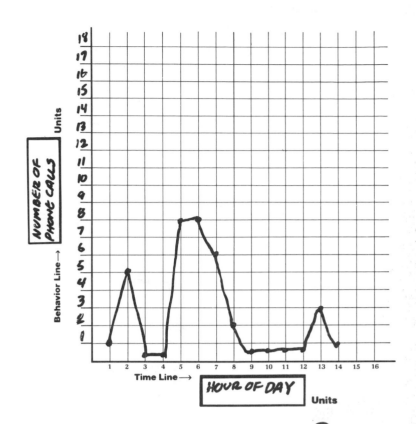

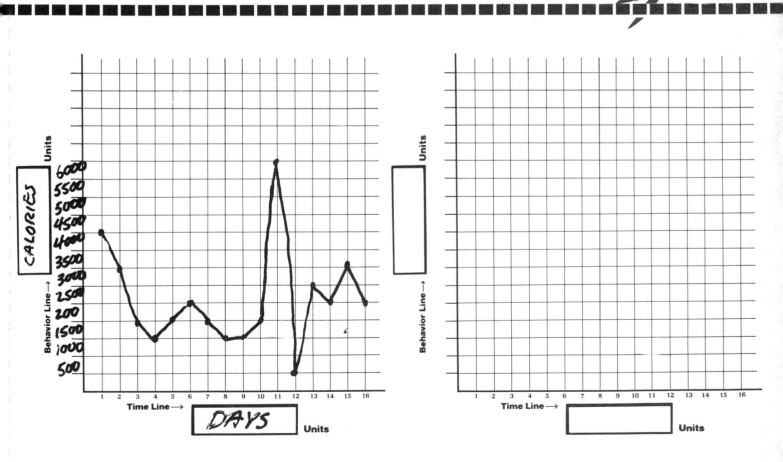

(continued from page 244)

hypnosis. It is not easy to quit, but 30 million people have done it. Some people don't quit because they feel the damage has already been done. The fact is that after one year of not smoking, there is a significant decrease in the risk of heart attack. After ten years, the death rates of ex-cigarette smokers, from all causes, is as low as for those who have never smoked.

National Council on Alcoholism Publication Division at 733 Third Avenue, New York, NY 10017, has easy-to-read, up-to-date information. Write for it.

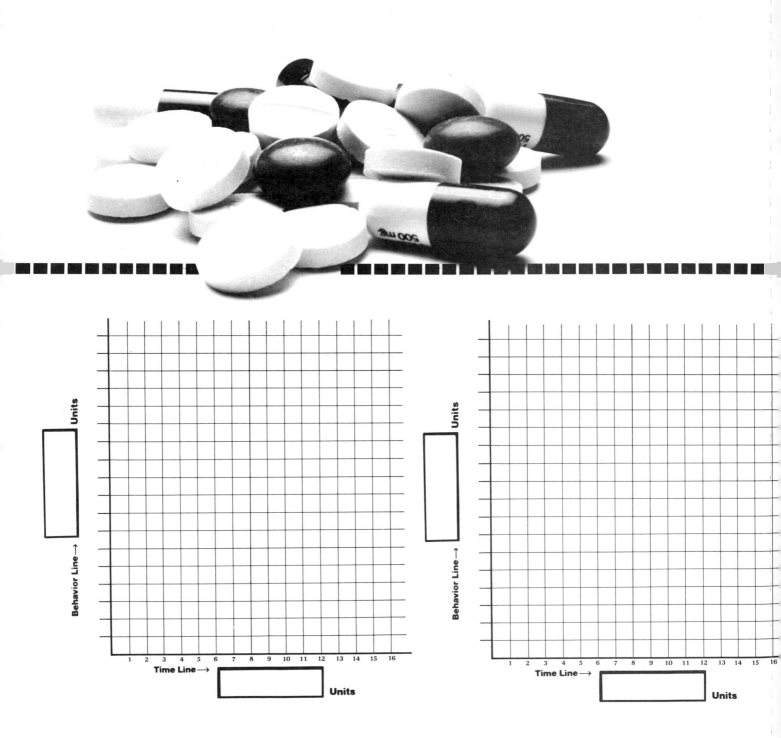

Advertising can be dangerous to your health

The average American is exposed to thousands of advertising messages per day. The United States, with six percent of the world's population, receives 57% of the world's advertising. Unless you are stranded on a desert island, you are affected by commercial messages, and probably more than you know. Advertisers spend tens of billions of dollars a year applying their best strategies to convince you to buy, buy, buy.

Advertising serves a very useful function. We live at a time when there is a huge variety of products and services. Every day we make choices about spending money. Advertising helps us decide among cars, kitchen appliances, health clubs, books, plants, groceries, home builders, dog groomers, piano tuners, locksmiths, movies, amusement parks, and the list is endless. Advertising informs, and that is valuable. Advertising also convinces, and that can lead the unaware into harm.

Be aware of what the advertiser wants to accomplish. Ask yourself if the ad is trying to inform or manipulate. If you see or hear an ad, and the purpose is unclear, don't just dismiss it as a mistake by the advertiser. Space to advertise is very expensive and the messages are very carefully crafted.

Ads for alcohol glorify drinking. The illusion is that there is a difference among products and that commercials are designed to help you choose which brand of liquor, beer, or wine to consume. Without the label, very few people can tell the difference between one brand and another. The real message is "drink."

Alcohol advertising confronts a special problem. It needs to convince heavy drinkers that the amount they drink is normal. Twenty-seven percent of all people who drink consume 93% of the alcohol sold. Advertisers appeal to this group by implying that daily drinking is the norm, pleasant experiences go with drinking, holidays naturally include alcohol, parties are a flop without it, and everybody drinks.

Advertising alcohol, tobacco, and pain relievers is big business. Newspapers, magazines, radio, and TV depend on these products for much of their revenue. It is estimated that over half of all commercial periodicals would go out of business without the money they are paid by cigarette and alcohol advertisers. Alcohol taxes are the second biggest source of income to the federal government.

Advertising also affects our self image. The typical advertising message is, "You are not OK. If you buy our product, you will be OK." These messages are painstakingly programmed to get you to buy clothes, makeup, lotions, creams, hair products, and contact lenses to make you look OK; drugs, alcohol, and food to make you feel OK; perfumes, mouthwash, toothpaste, and deodorant to make you smell OK; and lots and lots of stuff to make you seem OK.

Television most directly manipulates by linking an emotion (aroused by sight and sound) to a product. TV pervades our culture. By graduation from high school, a typical student has spent about 11,000 hours in classes and 25,000 hours watching television. The money spent for one minute of TV advertising far exceeds the cost to conduct several hours of class.

Advertising affects what we eat. In 1977, a U.S. Senate committee made several recommendations about the American diet. It advised the average person to reduce her overall intake of sugar, salt, cholesterol, and fat, and to increase consumption of complex carbohydrates such as fresh fruit, vegetables, and whole grains.

There wasn't a stampede to health food stores. Consider how the other side of the story was told.

Three billion dollars, or one fifth of advertising money in the United States, is spent promoting food items. A U.S. Department of Agriculture study revealed that the least nutritious foods receive the most advertising money. Soft drink advertisers alone spend $285,000,000 every year. A similar amount is spent advertising candy, ice cream, and other desserts.

Perhaps the biggest problem of manipulative advertising is the image it portrays of women. The basic message has been that women are inferior to men and are either stupid or sex objects. The woman presented in most ads either spends her day discussing floor wax and laundry detergent, or sits around looking sexy.

These images are demeaning to women and damaging to men. Women lose if they accept as self-image either picture portrayed by the ads. Men lose when they expect real-life women to be as dumb or as beautiful as portrayed. Many men pointlessly search for a woman who looks like the ones they see on TV and in magazines. Advertising photography creates illusions. Next time you're in a crowd, notice how few people look like the ones on TV.

Advertising serves a very useful purpose when it merely informs. It can be dangerous when it manipulates. Don't be brainwashed. Be an informed self-determining observer. Be aware of how a multi-billion dollar industry threatens your health and well-being.

Surr

A Zen parable says the Garden of Truth, the grand place everyone wants to enter, is guarded by two monsters— Fear and Paradox. Most of us see how fear keeps us from getting what we want. A paradox is two ideas that seem contradictory or absurd but may actually be true. *Surrender* seems inconsistent with power process #5, *You create it all.* Suspend the sovereignty of logic. However paradoxical, both these processes are valuable.

Life can be magnificent and satisfying. It can also be devastating. Sometimes there is too much pain or confusion. Problems can be too big and too numerous. Life can bring us to our knees in a pitiful, helpless, and hopeless state. A broken relationship with a lover, a diagnosis of cancer, total frustration with a child's behavior problem, or even the prospect of four long years of college are situations that can leave us feeling overwhelmed and powerless.

The first thing you can do is admit that you don't have the resources to handle the problem. Humble yourself. No matter how hard you try and no matter what skills you bring to bear, some problems remain out of your control. When this is the case, tell the truth. "It's too big and mean. I can't handle it."

Once you have acknowledged your lack of control, all that remains is to surrender. Formal religions say surrender to God. Buddhists say surrender to the "Self." Luke Skywalker would surrender to The Force. Agnostics might suggest surrendering to the ultimate source of power and love in the universe. To whomever or whatever you surrender, it works. The process of surrender has a consistent charm for life's major barriers and its insignificant hassles.

You might say, as you struggle to remember a name that's just not available to your conscious mind, "It's

ender

on the tip of my tongue." Then you surrender (give up trying so hard) and say, "Oh well, it will come to me later."

After trying unsuccessfully for years to have a baby, a couple finally surrenders and applies for adoption. She conceives the following week.

After finding out she has terminal cancer, a woman shifts between panic and depression. Nothing seems to console her. Finally, she accepts the truth and stops fighting her tragedy. She surrenders. Now at peace, she invests her remaining time in meaningful participation and communication with the people she loves.

Surrender is not a suggestion to simply quit and do nothing about your problems. You have many skills and resources. Use them. You can apply all your energy to handling a situation and surrender at the same time. Surrender is doing whatever you can in a positive, trusting spirit. Giving up is fatalistic and

accomplishes nothing. So let go, keep going, and know that the true source of control lies beyond you.

Desperately struggling to control a problem can easily result in the problem controlling you. Surrender is letting go of being the master in order to avoid becoming the slave.

Watching yourself with detachment can facilitate your ability to surrender. Pretend that you are floating away from your body, and then watch what's going on from a distance. Witness the drama of your life unfolding objectively, as if you were watching a play. When you see yourself as part of a much broader perspective, surrender seems obvious and natural.

For surrender to happen, you must trust. Trust dawn to follow darkness. Trust that you will come out on the other side of your problem with new strength and wisdom. Trust that your life is turning out exactly as it should. Trust the process. Surrender.

SATIATION

Drug	Street Names	Effects	Withdrawal Symptoms	Adverse/Overdose Reactions
Narcotics: Heroin	H, hombre, junk, smack, dope, horse, crap	Apathy, difficulty in concentration, slowed speech, decreased physical activity, drooling, itching, euphoria, nausea	Anxiety, vomiting, sneezing, diarrhea, lower back pain, watery eyes, runny nose, yawning, irritability, tremors, panic, chills and sweating, cramps	Depressed levels of consciousness low blood pressure, rapid heart rate, shallow breathing, convulsions, coma, possible death
Morphine	Drugstore dope, cube, first line, mud			
Codeine Percodan Demerol Methadone	Perks Meth			
Sedative Hypnotics: Nembutal	Yellow jackets, yellows	Impulsiveness, dramatic mood swings, bizarre thoughts, suicidal behavior, slurred speech, disorientation, slowed mental and physical functioning, limited attention span	Weakness, restlessness, nausea and vomiting, headache, nightmares, irritability, depression, acute anxiety, hallucinations, seizures, possible death	Confusion, decreased response to pain, shallow respiration, dilated pupils, weak and rapid pulse, coma, possible death
Seconal Tuinal Phenobarbital Quaaludes	Reds Tueys Ludes, 714's			
Valium Librium Equanil	V's			

Contemporary Drugs of Choice

Reprinted from *Psychology Today Magazine* Copyright 1983 American Psychological Association

AROUSAL

Drug	Street Names	Effects	Withdrawal Symptoms	Adverse/Overdose Reactions
Benzedrine Dexedrine Desoxyn Biphetamine, Ritalin Preludin Cocaine	Speed Speed Speed, crystal methedrine Black beauties, speed Coke, blow, toot, snow, lady	Increased confidence, mood elevation, sense of energy and alertness, decreased appetite, anxiety, irritability, insomnia, transient drowsiness, delayed orgasm	Apathy, general fatigue, prolonged sleep, depression, disorientation, suicidal thoughts, agitated motor activity, irritability, bizarre dreams	Elevated blood pressure, increase in body temperature, face-picking, suspiciousness, bizarre and repetitious behavior, vivid hallucinations, convulsions, possible death

FANTASY

Drug	Street Names	Effects	Withdrawal Symptoms	Adverse/Overdose Reactions
Hallucinogens: LSD	Electricity, acid, quasey, blotter acid, microdot, white lightning, purple barrels	Fascination with ordinary objects, heightened esthetic responses to color, texture, spatial arrangements, contours, music, vision and depth distortion, hear colors, see music, slowing of time, heightened sensitivity to faces, gestures, magnified feelings of love, lust, hate, joy, anger, pain, terror, despair, etc., paranoia, panic, euphoria, bliss, impairment of short-term memory, projection of self into dreamlike images	Not reported	Nausea, chills, increased pulse, temperature, and blood pressure, trembling, slow deep breathing, loss of appetite, insomnia, longer, more intense "trips", bizarre, dangerous behavior possibly leading to injury or death
Mescaline	Peyote buttons, (natural form)	Similar to LSD but more sensual and perceptual, fewer changes in thought, mood, and sense of self,	Not reported	Resemble LSD, but more bodily sensations, vomiting
Psilocybin	Mushrooms, shrooms, rooms	Similar to LSD but more visual and less intense, more euphoria, fewer panic reactions	Not reported	Resemble LSD, but less severe
Cannabis Marijuana Hashish Hash Oil	Bhang, kif, ganja, dope, grass, pot, smoke, hemp, joint, weed, bone, Mary Jane, herb, tea	Euphoria, relaxed inhibitions, increased appetite, disoriented behavior	Hyperactivity, insomnia, decreased appetite, anxiety	Severe reactions are rare, but include panic, paranoia, fatigue, bizarre and dangerous behavior
Phencyclidine	PCP, angel dust, hog, rocket fuel, superweed, peace pill, elephant tranquilizer, dust, bad pizza	Increased blood pressure and heart rate, sweating, nausea, numbness, floating sensation, slowed reflexes, altered body image, altered perception of time and space, impaired immediate and recent memory, decreased concentration, paranoid thoughts and delusions	Not reported	Highly variable and possibly dose-related, disorientation, loss of recent memory, lethargy/stupor, bizarre and violent behavior, rigidity and immobility, mutism, staring, hallucinations and delusions, coma

Emotional pain is not a sickness

There is nothing wrong with feeling bad. There seems to be someone going around giving emotional pain a bad name. This type of slander is undeserved. It's OK to feel miserable, depressed, sad, upset, angry, dejected, gloomy, or unhappy.

It may not be pleasant to feel bad, but it can be very good for you. Often, the appropriate thing to feel is bad. When you leave a place you love, sadness is just the thing to feel. When you lose a friend or lover, miserable might be in order. When someone does you wrong, it is probably appropriate to feel angry. Leaving home for the first time calls for a little homesickness. Many people don't let bad feelings happen.

Everyday, in many ways, we are told not to feel bad. Even when we feel bad. "Oh, cheer up!" "Sleep on it. You'll feel better in the morning." "Drink _____. A great way to perk you up." "Take two of these pills and you'll feel great." These messages usually come from well-meaning people who don't want you to feel too bad. That's the catch—*too* bad.

It is not possible to feel *too* bad, and, it is possible to feel bad for *too* long. If depression, sadness, or anger persist, get help. Otherwise, allow the feelings. They are usually appropriate and necessary for personal growth. When a loved one dies, it is necessary to grieve. The grief might appear in the form of depression, sadness, or anger. That is OK. The sadness might feel out of control. That is OK. There is nothing wrong with extreme emotional pain. It is natural, and it doesn't have to be fixed.

When feeling bad becomes a problem, it is usually because you didn't allow yourself to feel bad. So, next time you feel rotten, go ahead and feel rotten. It will pass; and it will probably pass more quickly if you don't fight it or pretend it doesn't exist.

How to feel bad

1. Give yourself permission. Most of us have been taught, from the time we were little, not to feel bad. Send yourself a reverse message. Say to yourself, out loud if you can, "It's all right for me to feel the way I do," or "I feel bad and that is good."

2. Don't worry about reasons. Sometimes we allow ourselves to feel bad if we have a good reason. "Well, I feel very sad, but that is because I just found out my best friend is moving to Cleveland." It's all right to know the reason that you are sad, and it is fine not to know. You can feel bad for no apparent reason. And, the reason doesn't matter.

3. Set a time limit. If you are concerned about feeling bad, if you are worried that you need to "fix it", give yourself a little time. Before you force yourself not to feel the way you feel, set a time limit. Say to yourself, "I am going to give myself until Monday at noon, and if I don't feel better by then, I am going to try to fix myself." Sometimes, it is very appropriate to fix a bad feeling. There might be a problem that needs a solution. You can use feeling bad as your motivation to solve the problem. And, sometimes you just need to feel bad for awhile.

4. Tell others. Often, other people (friends, family) have a hard time letting us feel bad. They are usually worried that they did something wrong, so they want to make it better. They want you to quit feeling bad. Tell them you will. Assure them that you will feel good again, but for now you just want to feel bad.

Sometimes students think this whole idea of allowing yourself to feel bad is a joke, reverse psychology, or something. It isn't. It is a suggestion that is based on the notion that good mental health is only possible if you allow yourself to feel bad as well as good. So, have a rotten day.

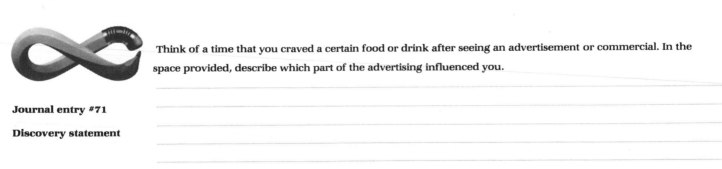

Think of a time that you craved a certain food or drink after seeing an advertisement or commercial. In the space provided, describe which part of the advertising influenced you.

Journal entry #71

Discovery statement

May Lemke

Excerpts from "The Miracle of May Lemke's Love" by Joseph Blank, Reader's Digest, October, 1982. Reprinted with permission from Reader's Digest.

The Milwaukee County General Hospital had a serious problem: a six-month-old infant named Leslie. Mentally retarded and without eyes, the baby also had cerebral palsy. He was a limp vegetable, totally unresponsive to sound or touch. His parents had abandoned him.

The hospital staff didn't know what to do—until a pediatrician mentioned May Lemke, a nurse-governess living nearby. A nurse telephoned May and explained that in all likelihood Leslie would die in a short time. "Would you help us by taking care of him while he lives?" the nurse asked.

"If I take him he certainly will not die, and I will take him," May replied . . .

. . . When May accepted the baby, she accepted him as just that, a baby—no different from the others—to be taught and loved . . .

. . . She bathed him, cuddled him for hours, talked to him, sang to him. He never moved or uttered a sound.

Year after year she cared for him, but there was no movement. No smile. No tears. No sound . . .

. . . The Lemkes then had a chain-link fence erected along the side of their property, and May stood Leslie next to it, thrusting his fingers through the openings. After several weeks he finally got the idea of letting the fence support him. He stood. He was 16. . . .

. . . One day she noticed Leslie's index finger moving against a taut piece of string around a package, as if plucking it. *Was this a sign?* she wondered. *What did it mean?*

Music! she exclaimed to herself. *That's it. Music.* From then on the Lemke house was filled with music from the record player, the radio and the TV. Hour after hour the music played. Leslie gave no indication that he was listening.

May and Joe bought an old upright piano for $250 and placed it in Leslie's bedroom. Repeatedly, May pushed his fingers against the keys to show him that his fingers could make sounds. He remained totally indifferent.

It happened in the winter of 1971. May was awakened by the sound of music. It was 3 a.m. Someone was playing Tchaikovsky's *Piano Concerto*

No. 1. She shook Joe. "Did you leave the radio on?" she asked.

"No," he said.

"Then where's the music coming from?" She swung out of bed and turned on a living room light. It dimly illuminated Leslie's room. Leslie was at the piano. May saw a smile glowing on his face.

He had never before gotten out of bed on his own. He had never seated himself at the piano. He had never voluntarily or deliberately struck the keys with his fingers. Now he was actually playing a concerto—and with deftness and confidence.

May fell to her knees. *Thank you, dear God. You didn't forget Leslie. . . .*

. . . "Coming out" musically opened the door for all kinds of emotions and developments. Occasionally a single word popped from his mouth. Then one afternoon some children were playing on the other side of the chain-link fence, and May asked them what they were doing. One of them answered, "We're having fun." Leslie took a few steps along the fence. "I'm having fun," he said in a thick but understandable voice. It was his first complete sentence, and May grabbed him and hugged him . . . .

. . . Two years ago, at the age of 28, Leslie began talking in earnest. Although he cannot hold a give-and-take conversation, he makes statements and can ask and answer questions. Sometimes he expresses an opinion. While listening to TV one night Leslie got fed up with the dialogue in a situation comedy. "Better get that off," he said. "They're all crazy."

As news of Leslie's talent traveled, groups requested him for concerts. May pondered the invitations; then she decided that public appearances would be valuable to Leslie. The music would give him a sense of participating in society. "And those people sitting out there, watching and listening, might get a sense of wonderment and a feeling of hope that they might never have had. They would see what can happen to a human being thought to be absolutely hopeless and helpless. . . ."

. . . There are still many things that Leslie cannot do. Those fingers that perform so brilliantly at the keyboard cannot use a knife or fork. Conversation does not flow easily. But ask what music means to him and he replies with a voice that is firm. "Music," says Leslie, "is love."

1. List the six dietary guidelines recommended by the U.S. Senate.

2. Eventually working up to an exercise program of at least _____ minutes a day at least _____ times per week (fill in the blanks) will lead to a trim, healthy, and alive body.

3. Discuss one stress-reducing technique from chapter 6, *Tests.*

4. Name eight alternative health care ideas from this chapter.

5. Describe the difference between bulimia and anorexia nervosa.

6. Most lethal poisoning occurs in children under 14. True or false.

7. How do most experts define an alcoholic?

8. The word "meditate" comes from the Sanskrit word *medha*. What does this mean?

9. What is the term for family or friends of an alcoholic who deny or rationalize the problem?

10. Name four possible effects of valium.

Journal entry #72

Discovery statement

The things I wanted from this chapter but didn't get include...

_____
_____
_____
_____
_____
_____
_____
_____
_____
_____
_____

Journal entry #73

Intention statement

I intend to get the things I wanted and didn't get from this chapter by...

_____
_____
_____
_____
_____
_____
_____
_____

Journal entry #74

Intention statement

Choose one health-related activity you can increase today or do for the first time. Write an intention statement about doing this activity today so that your healthy body will begin to emerge.

I intend to...

_____
_____
_____
_____
_____
_____
_____
_____

Review the First Step exercise in chapter 9, *Health*. What did you discover about yourself as a result of completing that exercise?

Journal entry #75

Look back

Think about your relationship to money. Remember a time when you were broke. (For many students, that time was a few seconds ago.) Write about what you would like to get from this chapter that can help you deal with money.

Journal entry #76

Discovery statement

CHAPTER TEN
MONEY

So much is a man worth as he esteems himself.

FRANCOIS RABELAIS

Develop a plan of control over your spending. Then you will make progress toward the kind of living which means the most to you.

SYLVIA PORTER

In this chapter . . .

"I can't afford it," is the most frequent reason given by students dropping out of school. It would probably be more accurate to say, "I don't know how I am going to pay for it," or "I don't think it is worth it." Both of these excuses for leaving school invite a further look.

It's worth it is a look at the value of education. It is a way to consider for yourself whether the payoff justifies investing a lot of money in school.

If you aren't sure that money is available for school, *You can pay for it* may turn you around. It's almost always possible to pay for school if you get involved in the search.

Money in—money out is a straightforward look at how to handle money so that money does not handle you. It is possible to manage your money without being a Scrooge and without making accounting your hobby.

Power process #10 suggests that *The process is always the same.* The way you relate to money may be the way you relate to the other parts of your life. People who think money is scarce ("There's never enough") may approach love, jobs, friendships, and time in the same way, ("There is just not enough to go around, so I can't get all I need.")

Exercises in this chapter include: *What are you worth?* which is an easy way to figure out your financial worth. *Where does all the money go?* shows how to monitor your money. *Monthly budget* and *Long-term budget* take the mystery out of spending. *Education by the hour* figures out how much you pay to sit in one class one time (the results are surprising) and other exercises and journal entries that help you see your relationship to money.

Money in— money out

Money produces more unnecessary conflict and worry than almost anything else, regardless of how much money a person has. People who earn $5,000 a year never have enough. That seems understandable. Those who earn $15,000 a year never have enough. And people who earn $50,000 a year say they don't have enough, either. "Not enough" seems to upset people no matter how much money they have, but it is usually unnecessary.

Money worries result from spending more than is available. Simple. We do everything we can to make it complicated.

The solution is also simple: Don't spend more than you have. This idea has never won a Nobel Prize in economics, but you can't go broke applying it.

There is a big payoff in making money management seem more complicated than it really is. The payoff is that if we don't understand it, we don't have to be responsible for it. If you don't know how to change a flat tire, then you don't have to be the one responsible for fixing it. If you never learned to cook, then you get to let someone else make dinner. It works the same for money. If you never learned

how to manage money, you have an excuse for not facing the truth about what is available to spend. The responsibility gets to belong to someone else.

That doesn't work when you admit the truth about money. It doesn't work to spend more than you have. Follow that suggestion and your money worries will be almost nonexistent. The techniques in this chapter can help you spend no more than you have, and they can help you stop worrying that "I don't have enough."

Budget
This process is easy because it is mechanical once you get started. The idea is to set up a projection of how much money is coming in and how much is going out.

Budgets are most useful when you have one for the next month and one for the long-range (a year or more). The monthly budget will include usual income and expenses such as paycheck, food costs, and housing that vary little from one month to the next. It will also list unusual income and expenses such as loan money for school, tuition, and trips. The long-range budget shows the big picture and helps you make realistic choices about how to make or spend money now so that you have what you need in the future.

The budget system in this chapter is set up on a cash basis. That means you consider the money that you are actually getting or spending that month. Businesses often budget and keep financial records using a different method, the accrual basis. This means that they consider as income money they haven't actually received but that has been billed (accrued on their books). They also consider as expenses money that has not actually been spent (bills received but not paid). The latter form of accounting is unnecessary for most individuals as long as bills are kept up-to-date.

Complete Exercises #43 and #44, and you will have a budget system in place. Monitor your money each month (Exercise #42), and you will then have a cycle of budget-monitor-budget-monitor. This cycle allows you to continually refine your money management process. Within a month or two, you can be free of money worries.

When what comes in is less than what goes out, you have three alternative solutions: You can increase money in, decrease money out, or both. Generally, it is easiest to do both.

Increase money in

Several ways to increase the amount of money you have each month are described in the article entitled *You can pay for it*. These include grants, loans, savings and part-time work. Other ways to increase your money supply include investments and theft. These alternatives are risky and can easily distract you from your life as a student.

Decrease money out

There are many ways to decrease the amount of money you spend. Pick from the following list those ideas which best fit your situation and see what works for you. By continually monitoring your money flow, you can determine how to decrease what you spend.

1. Use the telephone to save time and travel expense. Find out in advance if the store has what you want at the right price.

2. Comparison shop to find the best deal. If you wait, a sale on almost everything comes along sooner or later. Make sure sales are really sales. This is a good way to control impulse buying. If you plan to buy a big item such as a stereo, don't take your checkbook with you. Look at all the possibilities, then go home and decide in a nonpressure atmosphere. Compare warranties, too.

3. Be aware of quality. The cheapest product is not always the least expensive over the long run. Sometimes, the cheapest item is the best buy. Realize that value is sometimes inversely proportional to advertising. Inspect your purchase very carefully. See if it is well-made.

4. Keep receipts. If the product turns out to be defective, your complaint carries more weight when you have proof of purchase.

5. Complain when you don't get your money's worth. Start with the person who sold you the item and work your way up until you are satisfied. Don't be afraid to go to the top. If you have been treated unfairly, *contact your Better Business Bureau*. If you can't find it in the telephone book, call the local Chamber of Commerce for a telephone number for the Better Business Bureau. Make your complaint specific: date, amount, location, problem.

6. Use coupons. Newspapers and magazines carry clip-out coupons. Beware of misleading coupons—ones that offer widgets for $11.95 when

Where does all the money go?

It's not easy to know where all the money goes. It seems, at times, to grow wings and fly away on its own. This exercise is a way to watch how you get and spend money.

The idea is to write down all money received and spent for a month at a time. This is no small task. It requires commitment to carry a pen and a Money Monitor, and to use them even when it's not very convenient. The results will be worth it.

When you are aware of your money, you can control it. Otherwise, it is likely to control you. This is a way to gain awareness.

1. (This first step is the same as Exercise #43 where you completed a Budget Worksheet. Even the form is the same.) Tear out a Money Monitor and put categories across the top that represent the general ways you get and spend money. Group all of the categories that represent money coming in on the left of the page. If you need additional space, continue on the back of the form. Keep the categories general. There are a few common categories printed on the form, and you can refer to the example.

2. For the next 30 days, write down all the money you either receive or disperse. If you can't figure out what category it fits in, start a new

(continued on page 260)

category. For each entry, write a date and a note indicating whether the money was cash, check, or credit card. You could use these abbreviations: $ = cash, ck = check, cc = credit card.

3. At the end of the month, add up all of the columns. Use these totals to help you plan a budget or revise one. Partway through the month, you could also add the columns to determine how well you are sticking to your budget.

This Money Monitor is a form that you can complete every month. You may want to round all entries to the nearest dollar, and eventually you may only want to keep track of purchases made by checks and credit cards. Total cash expenses can be recorded by keeping track of all cash received as income and cash you get from cashing checks. This total can then be divided into the separate expense categories by estimating.

down the street you can buy generic widgets for $8.95.

7. *Shop for nutrition and food value.* Fresh produce, whole grains, and other foods are not only better for you than processed food, they cost less. Plan your meals in advance and cook for yourself.

8. *Plan your wardrobe in advance.* Stick to one or two color schemes. Find items that fit with other items. That maroon sharkskin disco belt looks fantastic in the store, but what can you wear with it? And when?

9. *Conserve fuel.* Keep windows and doors closed in winter. Avoid loss of cool air in summer. When you wash dishes or take a bath in winter, leave the hot water in the sink or tub until it is cool. The heat is exchanged in the room rather than warming the sewer for half a block. Turn out the lights. Dress warmly and keep the house at 68 degrees or less.

10. *Don't pay too much for rent.* Sometimes a place a little farther from campus will be much less expensive. Carefully compare the cost of living when utilities are not included in the rent. Look for opportunities to house-sit. Some people will pay a responsible person to live in their house when they are away. At the least, you may get free rent. Be a good tenant. *Treat rental property with respect.* Landlords appreciate good tenants and will often give a break in rent or deposits to someone they trust.

11. *Avoid credit purchases.* Deal in cash. If you don't have the cash, don't buy. When you're on a tight budget, keep close track of what you have spent so you don't spend more than you have. Buying on credit makes the process difficult. You can easily bust next month's budget with this month's credit purchases.

12. *Fix things yourself* whenever you

can. Many repair or service jobs are easy when you take the time to look into them. Ask friends for help. It's cheaper (and more fun) to buy a friend lunch or treat her to a movie than to pay a repair shop.

13. *Don't let pleasurable pastimes become burdensome habits.* Blowing your money on fun is fun. It is also a fast way to ruin your budget. Old whiskey and fast horses have wrecked some of the best financial plans. Free entertainment is abundant in the world. Search it out. It can't be heavily advertised.

14. *Use public transportation.* A car can be the biggest financial burden in a student's budget. The purchase price is often only the tip of the iceberg. Be sure to include the cost of parking, insurance, repairs, gas, oil changes, maintenance, and tires.

15. *Postpone purchases.* When you are ready to buy something, wait a week. What seems like a necessity today may not even cross your mind day after tomorrow. If this seems like a hardship, give yourself a small reward for waiting and write yourself a reminder note to reconsider the purchase in a week.

16. *Don't shop on an empty stomach—for anything.* Being hungry for food is not just an enticement to buy food. We tend to "want" when we're hungry, and that wanting can extend to anything that is for sale.

17. *Avoid snacks.* This may sound like a suggestion from a prison guard in northern Siberia. It's not. It is sound advice for the person looking for ways to decrease spending. Snacks typically cost more per nutritional unit than any other food. It is easy to spend several dollars a week, a quarter at a time.

18. *Don't carry cash.* If you see money every time you open your wallet, you get the impression you have money to spend.

Money / Budget
Monitor / Worksheet

Categories

DATE/NOTE	AMOUNT	DATE/NOTE	AMOUNT	DATE/NOTE	AMOUNT	DATE/NOTE	AMOUNT	DATE/NOTE	AMOUNT	DATE/NOTE	AMOUNT	DATE/NOTE	AMOUNT	DATE/NOTE	AMOUNT

Categories

Money / Budget
Monitor / Worksheet

DATE/NOTE	AMOUNT	DATE/NOTE	AMOUNT	DATE/NOTE	AMOUNT	DATE/NOTE	AMOUNT	DATE/NOTE	AMOUNT	DATE/NOTE	AMOUNT	DATE/NOTE	AMOUNT	DATE/NOTE	AMOUNT

Categories

Money / Budget
Monitor / Worksheet

DATE/NOTE	AMOUNT	DATE/NOTE	AMOUNT	DATE/NOTE	AMOUNT	DATE/NOTE	AMOUNT	DATE/NOTE	AMOUNT	DATE/NOTE	AMOUNT	DATE/NOTE	AMOUNT	DATE/NOTE	AMOUNT

Money / Budget
Monitor / Worksheet

DATE/NOTE	AMOUNT	DATE/NOTE	AMOUNT	DATE/NOTE	AMOUNT	DATE/NOTE	AMOUNT	DATE/NOTE	AMOUNT	DATE/NOTE	AMOUNT	DATE/NOTE	AMOUNT	DATE/NOTE	AMOUNT

Budget

For month(s) _____

Money in from:

1 _____ $ _____
2 _____   _____
3 _____   _____
4 _____   _____
5 _____   _____
6 _____   _____
7 _____   _____
8 _____   _____
9 _____   _____
10 _____   _____

Total cash income $ [   ]   Total in
(Add 1-10)

Money out to:

11 _____ $ _____
12 _____   _____
13 _____   _____
14 _____   _____
15 _____   _____
16 _____   _____
17 _____   _____
18 _____   _____
19 _____   _____
20 _____   _____
21 _____   _____
22 _____   _____
23 _____   _____
24 _____   _____
25 _____   _____
26 _____   _____
27 _____   _____
28 _____   _____
29 _____   _____
30 _____   _____
31 _____   _____
32 _____   _____
33 _____   _____
34 _____   _____
35 _____   _____
36 _____   _____
37 _____   _____
38 _____   _____
39 _____   _____

Total cash expenses $ [   ]   Total out
(Add 11-39)

Money left $ [   ]   From Total In
Subtract Total
out

Budget

For month(s) _____

Money in from:

1 _____	$ _____
2 _____	_____
3 _____	_____
4 _____	_____
5 _____	_____
6 _____	_____
7 _____	_____
8 _____	_____
9 _____	_____
10 _____	_____

Total cash income $ _____   Total in (Add 1-10)

Money out to:

11 _____	$ _____
12 _____	_____
13 _____	_____
14 _____	_____
15 _____	_____
16 _____	_____
17 _____	_____
18 _____	_____
19 _____	_____
20 _____	_____
21 _____	_____
22 _____	_____
23 _____	_____
24 _____	_____
25 _____	_____
26 _____	_____
27 _____	_____
28 _____	_____
29 _____	_____
30 _____	_____
31 _____	_____
32 _____	_____
33 _____	_____
34 _____	_____
35 _____	_____
36 _____	_____
37 _____	_____
38 _____	_____
39 _____	_____

Total cash expenses $ _____   Total out (Add 11-39)

Money left $ _____   From Total in Subtract Total out

Exercise #43

Monthly budget

Use this exercise to develop a plan for spending your money month by month. Complete the Money Monitor (Exercise #42) before doing this exercise. This monthly budget should be completed prior to doing the long-term budget. Figures from month to month will change because of periodic payments such as tuition, so revise this as needed.

1. (This first step is the same as Exercise #42 where you completed a Money Monitor. Even the form is the same.) Tear out a Budget Worksheet and put categories across the top that represent the general ways you will get and spend money. Group all of the categories for money coming in on the left side of the page. If you need additional space, continue on the back of the form. Keep the categories general. There

Exercise #44

Long-term budget

The long-term budgeting process works very much like the monthly budget (Exercise #43). Do the monthly budget exercise before you do this one.

1. Take out a budget worksheet and divide it into several months to get a grasp of the big picture. (See the example.)

2. Label the categories—you can use the same categories as in the monthly budget.

3. Under each category, put items and amounts that represent unusual expenses for a particular month. Amounts that don't change month to month can be brought from the monthly budget as totals (e.g., utilities).

are a few common categories printed on the form, and you can refer to the example.

2. Take your Money Monitor (Exercise #42), old receipts, canceled checks, or checkbook record and write down what you are likely to spend next month. Round figures to the nearest dollar. Under each category, list expenses that will occur.

3. Total the categories and move those totals to the form titled Budget.

4. On the Budget, total the Money In and the Money Out. Subtract Money Out total from Money In total to see how much is left. This is your monthly surplus.

Each month, examine the previous month's Money Monitor and use that information to refine your budget. Be realistic about what is likely to come in and go out. Then stick to the budget.

Money Monitor / Budget Worksheet

Categories

Entertainment		Car - gas, repair		Clothing		Laundry		Food		Phone	
DATE/NOTE	AMOUNT	DATE/NOTE	AMOUNT	DATE/NOTE	AMOUNT	DATE/NOTE	AMOUNT	DATE/NOTE	AMOUNT	DATE/NOTE	AMOUNT
2/1 Lounge	5.00	2/4 gas	4.00	2/13 sweat suit	12.68	2/5	2.00	2/4 pop	.50	2/8	9.58
2/5 6-pk	3.50	2/11 gas	4.50			2/14	2.00	2/5 Peggsim	7.50		
2/16 movie	4.00	2/18 gas	2.25			2/21 soap	4.00	2/20 pop	.50		
2/19 cards	3.00	2/19 oil	1.50			2/27	4.00	2/20 m&ms	.40		
2/21 movie	4.00	2/23 gas	4.00					2/22 JB's	3.62		
2/27 fun	3.00	2/27 gas	3.75					2/26 chips	.40		
								2/26 pop	.50		
	22.50		20.50		12.68		12.00		13.42		9.58

4. Total each category, transfer the numbers to the Budget, and figure out how much money is left.

It is common in long-term budgeting to have more money going out than coming in the first time you complete the form. The effectiveness of this exercise may be finding out that you are spending more than you have. If that is the case, try it again. Rework your Budget until Money Out is less than Money In. But be realistic, don't cut necessary expenses.

Budget

For month(s) Jan - Apr

Money In from:

1	Mom & Dad	$ 500
2	Grant	350
3	Tax refund	300
4	Job	200
5	Uncle Jim	500
6	Loan	1000
7		
8		
9		
10		

Total cash income $2850.   Total in (Add 1-10)

Money out to:

11	Entertainment ($20/mo)	$ 80
12	Car - gas, oil, tune-up (Apr)	138
13	Clothing	75
14	Laundry ($8/mo + soap)	36
15	Food ($15/mo)	60
16	Phone ($10/mo)	40
17	Household	45
18	Tuition	868

What are you worth?

Net worth is an accounting term that refers to the difference between what you own and what you owe. The goal of most companies is to have their net worth increase even when they take on more debt. This is a reasonable goal for individuals as well.

1. Under assets, list everything you own that is worth anything. This can include money you have in the bank in checking, savings, bonds, certificates of deposit; money owed to you; the value of your car, house, stocks, boat, and personal property including clothes, jewelry, appliances, hobby equipment. Don't list as value the amount you paid, what you think it's worth, or its replacement cost. List the value as what you could get for it if you had to sell it quickly. (This is often a fraction of what you paid.)

2. Under liabilities, list everything that decreases your worth. This includes money and interest you owe to others, money you owe to credit card companies, and school or car loans.

3. Total the assets first and then liabilities. Compute your net worth by subtracting total liabilities (Total 2) from total assets (Total 1). This is your financial worth as seen from a banker's point of view.

This exercise can be repeated every few months for a picture of how your financial worth changes.

Financial Statement

As of __2 / 21__
(date)

Assets

1	Checking	37.48
2	Savings	250.00
3	1972 Nova	800.00
4	Clothes	150.00
5	Jewelry	25.00
6	Stereo	50.00
7	Camera (new)	75.00
8	Weights	25.00
9	Bicycle - 10-speed	50.00
10	Textbooks ($10/ea - 10 books)	100.00

Total assets $ 1562.48   Total 1 (Add 1-10)

Liabilities

11	Uncle Jim + interest	1050.00
12	Student loan	2000.00
13		
14		
15		
16		
17		
18		
19		
20		
21		
22		
23		
24		
25		
26		
27		
28		
29		

Total liabilities $ 3050.00   Total 2 (Add 11-29)

Net worth $ -1487.52   From Total 1 Subtract Total 2

Financial Statement

As of ____/____/____
(date)

Assets

1 _____   _____
2 _____   _____
3 _____   _____
4 _____   _____
5 _____   _____
6 _____   _____
7 _____   _____
8 _____   _____
9 _____   _____
10 _____   _____

Total assets $ [_____] Total 1 (Add 1-10)

Liabilities

11 _____   _____
12 _____   _____
13 _____   _____
14 _____   _____
15 _____   _____
16 _____   _____
17 _____   _____
18 _____   _____
19 _____   _____
20 _____   _____
21 _____   _____
22 _____   _____
23 _____   _____
24 _____   _____
25 _____   _____
26 _____   _____
27 _____   _____
28 _____   _____
29 _____   _____

Total liabilities $ [_____] Total 2 (Add 11-29)

Net worth $ [_____] From Total 1 Subtract Total 2

Financial Statement

As of _____/_____/_____
(date)

Assets

1 _____   _____
2 _____   _____
3 _____   _____
4 _____   _____
5 _____   _____
6 _____   _____
7 _____   _____
8 _____   _____
9 _____   _____
10 _____   _____

Total assets $ [   ]   Total 1
                                      (Add 1-10)

Liabilities

11 _____   _____
12 _____   _____
13 _____   _____
14 _____   _____
15 _____   _____
16 _____   _____
17 _____   _____
18 _____   _____
19 _____   _____
20 _____   _____
21 _____   _____
22 _____   _____
23 _____   _____
24 _____   _____
25 _____   _____
26 _____   _____
27 _____   _____
28 _____   _____
29 _____   _____

Total liabilities $ [   ]   Total 2
                                           (Add 11-29)

Net worth $ [   ]   From Total 1
                                   Subtract Total 2

Free fun

Sometimes, it seems that the only way to have fun is to spend money. Not true. Aside from free entertainment available to you through the community or college, your imagination is the only limitation on what you can do for fun with no money. Most of these ideas sound crazy. Pick a few that might be fun for you and experiment. Add your own ideas.

Exercise
Visit a pet store
Ride elevators
Take a candlelight bath
Grow a beard
Start a club
Write a letter
Play board games
Have an egg toss
Give a massage
Reread old letters and journals
Sing loudly
Climb trees
Test drive new cars
Look at the babies in the maternity ward
Kick a rock down the street
Paint scenes on your windows
Write a poem
Give a haircut
Learn to juggle
Adopt a grandparent, little brother or sister, etc.
Bicycle
Play cards
Throw a popcorn and TV movie party
Window shop
Arm wrestle
Write to Ann Landers
Donate blood
Go puddle stomping
Make yourself breakfast in bed
Hike
Watch sunrises or sunsets
Skip
Kiss
With a stranger and without conversation, start a game of tic, tac, toe
Build a snowman
Call a friend (not long distance)

Floss your teeth
Tickle
Pillow fight
Plan a slumber party
Sleep outside
Read
Start a water balloon fight
Bird watch
Dress up
Open all your cabinets, doors, and drawers, then close them
Look at old photographs
Draw
Make wildflower crowns
Sunbathe
Roast marshmallows
Listen to music
Dance
Catch fireflies
People watch
Whittle
Whistle
Stretch
Take a nap
Fill a friend's car with balloons
Have a goofy scavenger hunt
Peel an orange, keeping the peel in one piece
Star gaze
Shortsheet the beds
Skip stones
Play tag
Weed a garden
Wash & wax your car
Giggle
Scratch a back
Race frogs
Go fishing
Fly a kite

Part-time jobs

Working while you go to school may be a great idea. It provides money, variety, work experience, and references. A part-time job now will demonstrate your work patterns. Future employers will ask, "Where have you worked in the past?" They don't expect you to have been on the President's Cabinet, but they do like to know that you can get along with co-workers and arrive on time every day.

The money you make from a part-time job can be a big boost to a lopsided budget. Regular income, even at minimum wage, will quickly add up, and taxes are minimal when you don't earn big money. Look at your monthly budget to see how it would be affected if you worked just 15 hours a week (times 4.3 weeks a month) for only $3 an hour.

Variety is the spice. . . . College is often a closed social system that contains few old people and almost no one under 15. Children are fun. Old people are rich with life. A part-time job may provide contact with people who are otherwise unavailable.

Much about life has nothing to do with money. Brainstorm a list of areas in your life that are unaffected by money. Remember, a brainstorm is a quick, long list of whatever comes to mind.

After the brainstorm, circle those items that really don't have anything to do with how much money you have. Then write a discovery statement concerning money.

Journal entry #77

Discovery statement

List brainstorm here:

Concerning money in my life, I learned that I . . .

How to find one

Some of the best part-time jobs are never advertised. Don't rely on one to just come along. Search out possibilities. Ask around. Tell everyone that you want a job. Particularly, tell people who might be able to create a job for you.

Make a list of several places that you would like to work. (Include places that have advertised jobs and those that don't.) Then go to each place on your list and tell someone there you would like a job. They will probably say they don't have a job or that it is filled. Don't stop at that.

Ask to see the person in charge of hiring and tell her you want to work. She will probably say she doesn't have a job. Tell her you are a student. Explain why you would like to work there. Briefly tell why you would be an excellent employee (trustworthy, loyal, courteous, kind, obedient, cheerful, thrifty, brave, clean, reverant,...), and offer to start work anytime ("Today, if you need me"). Ask to fill out an application or leave a resume. Remember to check back in two or three days!

A resume is a summary of your work history, education, and references. More than that, it is a calling card. It is something you leave with the employer so she remembers you. Make it memorable. For just a few dollars, a local print shop can proof for spelling, typeset, and print your resume. Have it printed on heavy, rich-looking paper. Don't get too fancy, but let the printer set some small headlines.

The interview is the most important part of a job search. When speaking to the prospective employer, remember that people like to talk about themselves. Ask questions. Also respect the other person's time. You want her to know that you know time is money. Don't ramble. *Ask* for the job.

People recall about 20% of what they hear in a conversation. They recall about 90% of how they feel. The impression you leave at an interview will depend much more on how you act (relaxed, confident, eager...) than what you say. Lighten up, enjoy yourself. If you do, so will the interviewer, and that will increase your chance for a job. Many jobs are created right on the spot because a person showed up who would be an asset to the company.

Job hunting is like prospecting for gold. You have to dig a lot of holes, uncover a lot of rocks before you can expect success. Eventually, you will find work. Before you start your search, set a quota. Tell yourself you will continue the search until you have spoken to at least 100 people—or some other number you can live with.

After two or three interviews you may get tired of hearing people say, "We don't have an opening," or "We already filled that job." At this point, consider your quota—a number chosen before you had your first few rejections. Remember, if you ask enough people, someone will say, "Yes!" Each time you hear, "No," silently thank the person for putting you one "no" closer to the "yes" you are bound to hear.

How to find another

The first job you get may not be the one you want. If it doesn't conflict with school, consider taking it anyway. Work hard, make a good impression, and look for another job. It is easier to find a job when you have a job, and you can earn money while you wait for the "right" job.

Your new job may not be the "executive position" you originally had in mind. Make a list of the benefits of the job (it's a job, it pays $3.80 an hour, it's close to where I live,...) and the disadvantages (too much work, grouchy boss, dry cleaning fluid makes me sick,...). If the disadvantages outweigh the benefits, continue your search.

Use the quota system. Make a list of people you will contact and tell everybody you are looking. Keep up the good work at your present job. You will need the reference.

Keep it in perspective

The purpose of a part-time job, when you are a student, is to earn money to support your education. If the job is in your career field, great. If it is meaningful and contributes to society, great. If the job involves working with people you love and respect, fantastic. If not, well, remember its purpose.

It is easy to let a job eat up time and energy that you need for your education. Don't let this happen. Remember its purpose.

It's worth it

An education beyond high school is the most durable and worthwhile investment you can make. It's one of the safest investments possible. When you are clear about what you want, education is usually the surest way to get it.

Education is a unique purchase. It is the only thing you can buy that will last your lifetime. It can't rust, corrode, break down, or wear out. Education can't be stolen, burned, repossessed, or destroyed. Education is a purchase you store in your head. Once it's there, no one can take it away.

Investing money in your training, in your skills, in your abilities, in yourself is a sure bet. Money invested in land, gold, oil, or stocks can easily be lost. When you invest in yourself, you can't lose. Investment in education pays off directly in salaries and job promotions. It pays off indirectly in career satisfaction and self-esteem.

Higher education has been suggested as the source of everything from better health to happier marriages. The list continues:

> *Learning will continue.*
> *Personal growth occurs.*
> *Social status improves.*
> *Self-confidence improves.*
> *You more easily grasp world events.*
> *You will have more economic and social opportunities.*
> *You will be better equipped to be a parent.*
> *You will enjoy more physical comfort.*
> *You will enjoy increased flexibility on the job (with tight supervision less likely).*
> *You will enjoy improved retirement benefits.*
> *You will save more money.*
> *You will enjoy greater travel opportunities.*
> *Your spouse is likely to earn more.*
> *And your children are more likely to get farther in their education.*

In short, education is a good deal.

Exercise #46

Education by the hour

Determine exactly what it costs you to go to school.

Fill in the blanks. Use totals for semester, quarter, or whatever system your school uses.

Tuition:	_____
Books:	_____
Fees:	_____
Transportation:	_____
Clothing:	_____
Food:	_____
Housing:	_____
Entertainment:	_____
Other (insurance, medical, etc.):	_____
Subtotal:	_____
Salary you could earn per term if you weren't in school:	_____
Total:	_____
	(total A)

Figure out how many classes you attend in one term. This is the number of your scheduled class periods per week multiplied by the number of weeks in your school term. Put that figure here:

_____
(total B)

Divide the number of classes (total B) into the total cost (total A) and put that amount here:

_____

This is what it costs you to go to one class.

You can pay for it

Financial aid is almost always available. Sometimes you have to look in different places. Where you get help depends on your background and needs. It is always possible to receive assistance in paying for school when you can't pay for it yourself. Play an active role and stay interested until you find the best financial arrangement.

Don't just turn the job over to someone else. Investigate your options and you will find a way to pay for your education.

Taking an active role in financial aid means that you determine total costs (tuition, fees, living expenses, travel, books, supplies); actively search for all types of funding (part-time work, savings, relatives, scholarships, loans, grants); understand everything before you sign; complete forms accurately and on time; notify your school or lender of changes in address, financial condition, or attendance; and are aware of refund policies.

Set up a strategy

Financing your education is best done with a master plan. Don't just look at one term. Consider the entire time you will be in school and plan for the big picture.

Having a plan for paying the cost of your entire education makes staying to

Check to see what you want from an education that makes it worth the investment. You are likely to spend several thousand dollars, maybe even tens of thousands of dollars getting educated. Write about what's in it for you.

Journal entry #78

Discovery statement

Spending money on education is worth it for me because I will get . . .

I will also get . . .

(continued from page 275) the end seem more realistic. If you start every term wondering where you are going to get the money, it is much more likely that you'll drop out. A master plan consists of a clear picture of your income and expenses. It is a long-term budget of how much you need to complete your education and where you will get the money. Use the budgeting system described in this chapter.

Sticking to a budget is particularly important if you receive a large grant or loan at the beginning of the school year. It is tempting to spend the money on something besides education. Hundreds of dollars in financial aid for your education could go a long way toward buying a car, stereo, clothes, camera, video equipment, parties, and ski vacations. Not only would you be short for the next term, you might have to pay back the money without benefit of a completed education.

Once you know precisely how much you need, get help in finding the money. Every college has someone to assist with this. Make sure you and your counselor look at financing your entire education.

You can also get help from publications in financial aid offices and most public and college libraries or by writing for the following information:

The Student Guide: Five Federal Finanical Aid Programs or
 The Pell Grant Formula
    Both are free. Write to:
Federal Financial Aid
Box 84
Washington, DC 20044

Need A Lift? (A list of sources of Financial Aid)
$1.00
American Legion
P.O. Box 1055
Indianapolis, Indiana 46206

Exercises #42, #43, #44, and #45 all dealt with you and your money. You were given a chance to look at your financial worth, your current spending habits, getting and spending money, and short- and long-term budgets. Write about what you learned concerning each area.

Journal entry #79

Discovery statement

Having completed the financial statement that listed my assets, liabilities, and net worth, I learned that I . . .

I also discovered that I . . .

Having completed the Money Monitor, giving a picture of how I deal with money, I learned that I . . .

I also learned that I . . .

Having completed the long-term budget, I learned that I . . .

Having completed the monthly budget, I learned that I . . .

A Selected List of Higher Education Opportunities for Minorities and Women: Annotated Selections, 1984, Publication #065-000-00226-4
$3.00
Superintendent of Documents
Government Printing Office
Washington, D.C. 20402

Find money

You can find money for your education from the Federal Government, most state governments, parents, other relatives, banks, and the college or school you attend. The programs vary and are available for students with differing needs. Look for money in the following places.

1. *National Direct Student Loans* are available directly from a school that has received money for this purpose. These are long-term loans based on financial need and have very low interest rates. You repay the loan after you complete your education.

2. *Pell Grants* are based on need, are awarded by the school you attend and are financed by the Federal Government. This is the largest federal student aid program. Money received through a Pell Grant does not have to be repaid.

3. *Supplemental Educational Opportunity Grants* (SEOG) are designed to add to other forms of financial aid. SEOG's differ from Pell Grants in how the money is awarded to the school. Money is limited and application deadlines are critical.

4. *College work-study* is financial aid in the form of jobs with non-profit organizations. There is a limit on how much can be earned. The limit is based on need. A large part of your wage is paid by the Federal Government.

5. *Scholarships are available* through most colleges for outstanding performance in athletics, academics, or the arts. Fraternal, service, educational, and social societies (American Association of University Women, Elks, Rotary, Kiwanis, Sertoma, Lions for example) often provide grants for local students that don't have to be repaid.

6. *Guaranteed Student Loan Program* (GSLP) is a government agency that insures loans you get directly from a bank, credit union, or savings and loan association. The interest is low, and you must show financial need. The loans are repaid starting six months after you complete your education.

7. *PLUS loans* are also government guaranteed low-interest loans. They differ from GSLP loans because you don't have to show need, and repayment begins right after the loan is made.

8. *The Veterans Administration* has money available to some veterans and their dependents. The War Orphans Educational Assistance, Air Force Aids Society, and Army Educational Assistance programs are set up for children of military personnel.

9. *Social Security payments* are available up to age 22 for unmarried students with a deceased parent or a parent who is disabled or drawing Social Security benefits.

10. *State vocational rehabilitation offices* usually have financial assistance for people who are visually impaired, have hearing or speech difficulties, or are otherwise handicapped.

11. *The U.S. Bureau of Indian Affairs* has

available financial aid for Native American students.

12. *The local branch of your state employment* office provides information about two government programs which are set up to train the unemployed. These programs are CETA (Comprehensive Employment Training Act) and WIN (Work Incentive). They both provide money for going to school.

13. *Relatives* often provide financial help for a dedicated student. Someone who would be reluctant or unwilling to lend you money for a car, a new business, or a trip to the South Pacific might be honored to help you get an education. A sincere, straightforward request is never insulting.

14. *Personal savings* account for a bulk of the money spent on higher education. Use money from savings accounts, bonds, stocks, or trusts set up by others to support your education.

15. *Part-time employment* is another way students can get additional money. Working in a job related to your future career can supplement your education as well as provide money.

16. *Sell something.* Find something you need less than an education and sell it. This may be an option of last resort, but it *is* an option. Don't overlook the money you have tied up in a car, a motorcycle, a horse, a piano, a house, a hobby, or a rare, priceless, cherished family heirloom. "Gee, I don't remember seeing Great Grandmother's china anywhere, either!" (Check first with others who may have an interest.)

If you're in trouble

Financial problems are common. You can handle money problems in a way that minimizes other people's concerns and protects a good credit rating. If you get in over your financial head, here is a strategy.

1. *Get specific data.* Complete a financial statement (Exercise #45), summarize your Money Monitor (Exercise #42) and set up a budget for the month and for the year (Exercises #43 and #44). If you are having trouble getting this information together, get some help. A bookkeeper or an accounting student can usually help.

2. *Be honest with creditors.* It is best to let people know in advance if you aren't going to be able to pay them. They may not be happy, but they will appreciate knowing about the problem. Suggest a payment schedule. Determine the amount you are sure you could pay every month and ask if that would work for them. Usually, creditors would rather have something each month than risk never getting paid.

3. *Go for credit counseling.* Most cities have agencies with professional advisers that will help you straighten out your financial problems. They may even contact creditors for you. Go prepared. Take all your bills, loans, and other obligations. Take the data mentioned in step one above.

4. *Review the money in—money out exercise.* Look at how you can change your spending patterns. Spending money is a habit similar to eating food. It is not easy to change. If you have a history of overspending (or under-earning), know that change is possible and sometimes slow. Congratulate yourself on small improvements and stick to techniques of money management that you know will work.

We live like kings

"But I really don't have enough. If you had my bills, you wouldn't be so quick to say that eliminating my money worries is easy. You don't know what it's like to struggle and try to get by on what I make."

The suggestion that money worries are unnecessary upsets some people. It is not intended to make you angry. The purpose of the suggestion is this: Your frustration about not having enough money will not get you more money nor will it help you to spend less.

So, if you want to eliminate money worries, keep reading. This chapter is full of ways to handle money problems. This book is full of ways to handle frustrations in general. The power processes can all be applied to your relationship with money. You can ease the frustration by being here now, detaching, surrendering, letting go of your pictures of how much money you ought to have, loving your frustration to death, or looking at how you create your money woes. It is all hard work and requires the courage to look inward.

You can also consider alternatives to the thought, "I don't have enough." You can find a positive thought or series of thoughts to replace your negative mental programming of, "Money is scarce."

Here are some alternatives: "I have money I haven't even spent yet," "I deserve money and I will have as much as I need," "I am rich", or "I live like a king." These thoughts, when repeated constantly, can have the effect of changing how you feel about money, and consequently, they can affect how much money you actually have.

Some people can't say to themselves, "I live like a king." They believe it is a lie. They are so locked into scarcity as a way of life that they can't see the riches they possess. They truly do create it all by their selective perceptions, only they are choosing to create scarcity.

Step back in time just 100 years and imagine how a king might have lived. He would have enough to eat. Several times a year, he would have a feast. In his food there would be spices from the four corners of the earth. There would be so much delicious food that he would be stuffed when he was finished. Good drink would abound.

This king of a century past would have entertainment at his fingertips. If he wanted music, a clap of his hands would bring him dozens of songs. If he wanted humor, he could summon the court jester. If he wanted variety or drama, he could watch the actors of the court.

Transportation was no problem for the king. He could go anywhere he wanted. Horses were always ready and a driver would chauffeur him from kingdom to kingdom in a matter of days or weeks.

Dress was lavish. He wore the finest cloth. It was smooth and colorful and cleaned frequently. Unlike lesser mortals, his clothes kept him dry and warm. He got new clothes at least once a year and never had to wear anything that was full of holes.

His house was a castle. It was clean, dry, and had warm fireplaces in many rooms. He was safe from nature and the weather and was relatively safe from intruders.

In short, he lived like a king. He didn't have it nearly as good as almost everyone in the United States today, but he lived like a king.

Planning

INVESTMENTS

Investing is risky. It is best to invest only after you have saved several thousand dollars. If you do have money to invest, consider something safe (blue chip stocks or bonds), or plan to spend a lot of time studying investment alternatives.

Sensible investing requires extensive homework. Don't take a friend's advice on how to invest your hard-earned money. Don't risk money that, if lost, would force you to spend more than you have. Don't invest the grocery money.

A good rule of thumb: Don't invest money until you have enough savings in the bank to meet your expenses for six months, even if you lose your job.

INSURANCE

Medical costs are astronomical. If you think that is an overstatement, call the hospital and get a quote on removing an appendix, having a baby, fixing a broken leg or getting a nose job. The cost of a few days in the hospital is often more than the cost of a new car. Most of us can't pay for that without help.

Medical insurance is usually available through your school. If you are under 21, you may qualify under your parents' insurance. If neither option is available, shop around. Buy health insurance with high deductibles (you pay the first few hundred dollars of the claim) to save money on premium payments. Buy from an agent you trust.

Once you have insured your health or your life, it's usually possible to stay insured even if you develop a major illness. For that reason, it is a wise investment for the future to insure yourself now.

There are basically two kinds of life insurance: term and whole life. Term insurance is the least expensive. It pays if you die, that's it. Whole life is more expensive. It is a savings and investment plan in addition to paying if you die. Under a typical whole life policy, you could collect a pension when you retire in addition to having your life insured. There are some new policies, called "universal life," that combine features of both plans.

All insurance is *not* alike. Shop more than one agent before you decide. Ask questions about anything you don't understand. If the agent can't answer your questions to your satisfaction, get another agent.

Insurance is available for your possessions even if you don't own a house. Check the cost of renter's insurance. It will cover your belongings against fire or theft.

If you drive at all, car insurance is a must. Shop around, premiums vary considerably.

CONTRACTS

Be careful. Before you sign anything, read the fine print. If you are confused

ior

about a point, ask. Be leery of someone who says, "Oh, this is just the standard lease arrangement. I wouldn't try to pull the wool over your eyes. You look too smart for that." After you sign a contract or lease, read the entire thing again.

If you think you have signed something that you will regret, back out quickly and get your release in writing. Purchase contracts in many states are breakable. The buyer is allowed three days in which to back out, and there is no penalty. If you can't get out, get legal help right away. If you have little money, inquire at any attorney's office or look in the phone book for the phone number of the legal aid office in your community. This is free legal help for people who can't afford a lawyer.

Be particularly careful of long-term purchase agreements, "This is a great deal for you; you don't have to pay a thing until you graduate," or "How can you live without this beautiful cookware? Look, there's no down payment, and it will cost only 72 cents a day." That adds up to more than $785 in the three years of the contract.

Don't join book or record clubs or buy magazine subscriptions in a package deal without first determining the total cost and how it will affect your budget. Multiply the monthly payments or minimum purchase requirements to get a total cost. Those record clubs don't give you the first ten albums for a penny out of the kindness of their hearts.

CREDIT

A good credit rating is a worthy objective. If you don't already have one, you can begin to establish a credit rating now. Borrow some money and pay it back on time. Consider borrowing for the next major purchase you make. Go to a bank, savings and loan association, or credit bureau. Start now to establish a relationship that demonstrates you can be trusted to make all of your payments, and that you will make them on time.

Credit cards are also a way to establish a credit record. Get a bank credit card, an oil company credit card, or a major department store card. Use it only for necessary items that you have enough cash to buy anyway. Keep track of how much you spent and save the equal amount in cash. Pay off the entire balance each month. An unpaid balance is a sure sign that you are spending more money than you have.

Utility companies also influence your credit rating. Pay your telephone, gas, electric, and water bills on time. The temptation is to let big companies wait for their money. Don't do it. Develop a credit rating that will support your borrowing large amounts of money if you need it (new business, house, car, marriage, catastrophe, school).

the future

The pro always

When you carefully observe one part of your life, you gain insight into the way you conduct other parts of your life. And if you change your behavior in one small area, your behavior automatically begins to change in several other areas.

This idea is true in biology, physics, sociology, and management, as well as in individual human behavior. In biology, the chromosomes in each cell are the blueprints for that entire organism. Careful study of any one cell will show a plan for the entire body.

In physics, holographic film produces three-dimensional pictures using laser light. One small section cut from the film can be used to reproduce the entire picture. Each piece of the film contains all the elements of the whole picture.

In sociology, a few members of a group are studied to discover how the entire group behaves. Public opinion is determined by polling a few chosen people. Marketing experts test new products and advertising campaigns on a few hundred people. The response to these tests is all the marketers need to know. They can then confidently spend millions of dollars in a national campaign, knowing how the product is going to sell.

In management, it is known that the philosophy of a company can be determined by interviewing only a few of the employees. If they are courteous and respectful to customers, it's a good bet that the company places a high value on treating customers well.

Many large companies now hire graphologists (handwriting experts) to help select potential employees. Complete personalities are revealed in a few handwritten sentences. Small actions, even how you form letters, indicate much about how you conduct your life.

Use this principle to look at your personal life. How you handle yourself in one situation can reveal a pattern of behavior that occurs everywhere in your life. The process is always the same, though usually it is easier to see when you observe it in others.

When you see a stranger in the checkout lane yell at her child, jerk him by the arm, and swat him on the seat, you can be fairly certain she has done the same thing countless times. You can anticipate her reaction in similar situations, even though you saw but one brief glimpse of her behavior.

A student who appears in English Literature class without having read the assignment very likely will not be prepared for the next class, either. If he

cess is
he same

hasn't prepared for any of the last three classes, you can be certain that he will be unprepared for the rest of the term.

If a person meticulously balances her checkbook, she probably is very conscientious about paying her bills. When preparing for a camping trip, you could reasonably expect her to be methodical and thorough. She probably makes detailed lists of things to do. We can also expect to make fairly accurate predictions about the life of a woman who never balances her checkbook.

At the extreme, how a man ties his shoes might indicate the kind of mechanic he would be. How someone reacts in a traffic jam might tell how she handles stress in general. If a man is attentive and thorough in washing the dinner dishes, he is probably detail-oriented at work.

This natural tendency to live in repetitious patterns, to act out of habit, greatly expands our opportunities for self-knowledge.

The discovery statements in this book are intended to help you learn more than is immediately obvious. Look beyond the specific study technique and see your whole life reflected in how you react to an exercise or a suggestion. See what that small insight tells you about other ways you operate.

A critical, objective look at one item in your personal catalog of behavior can be like putting your eye to a keyhole. Suddenly, a whole new room appears, and what you see is you.

When you discover something you don't like in your behavior program, you can rearrange the whole pattern by changing one small part of your life. If you have a habit of being late for class, and if you want to change that process, be on time to one class. As soon as you change the old pattern by getting ready and going on time to one class, you will find yourself arriving at all of your classes on time automatically. You may even start arriving everywhere else on time.

The joy of this process is watching one small change ripple through your whole life.

If you know that you are usually nervous, you don't have to try to change how you react in all situations at all times. Just change your nervous behavior in one setting. Like magic, watch the rest of your nervousness disappear.

Look closely at the little things you do, and you can discover yourself. Modify little things you do, and watch your whole life change.

Fred Smith

A Business Visionary—Federal Express, *excerpted by permission from* Nation's Business, November, 1981. Copyright © 1981 by Nation's Business, Chamber of Commerce of the United States.

Frederick W. Smith may have a common last name, but he is a most uncommon man. What other American business leader of today had a revolutionary idea and converted it into a company that, starting from scratch and with heavy early losses, passed the $500 million revenue mark and had a 10% net profit margin in a few years?

Or founded such a company in his 20's and is guiding it toward a distant maturity at the ripe old age of 37?

What other American business leader with so brilliant an idea first wrote it out in a college paper that was graded C? Or says that the people with the greatest impact on him have been a poorly educated sergeant whom he led in combat and a science professor who liked to buzz a university stadium in a fighter plane?

What other . . . ?

This could go on and on.

Fred Smith is chairman and chief executive officer of Memphis-based Federal Express Corporation, an air cargo firm that specializes in overnight delivery door-to-door, using its own planes. Its success has confounded not only the unappreciative grader of that college paper but also rival package-delivery companies, which used to ship air freight only via scheduled airlines.

To put it another way, Fred Smith is Federal Express.

Smith, a Memphis native whose father became a millionaire after founding a bus company and whose grandfather was a Mississippi riverboat captain, got his revolutionary idea in the '60's while majoring in economics and political science at Yale.

Technological change had opened a radically new transportation market, he decided. The proliferation of computers and similarly intricate equipment—and the impracticality of stocking multitudes of expensive and rapidly obsolescent parts at offices and plants all over the country—posed an enormous logistics problem.

"Steamboats and trains were the logistics arm of the Industrial Revolution's first stage," he says. "Trucks became a good logistics arm later—and still are because of their flexibility. But moving the parts and pieces to support the Electronics Age requires very fast transportation over long distances. I became convinced that a different type of system was going to be a major part of the national economy . . . ."

Smith spelled it out in an overdue economics paper. To cut cost and time, packages from all over the country would be flown to a central point, there to be distributed and flown out again to their destinations—a hub-and-spokes pattern, his company calls it today. The flying would be late at night when air lanes were empty. Airports used would be in sizable cities, and trucks would carry packages to their final destinations, whether in those cities or in smaller communities. Equipment and documents from anywhere in the U.S. could be delivered anywhere in the U.S. the next day . . . .

For the benefit of business history, it would be nice to have that college paper today. But who saves college papers, particularly those done in one night and branded mediocre? Smith says the professor—he doesn't name him—apparently didn't think much of either his concept or the way he laid it out. "Anyway," he says, "to a ne'er-do-well student like myself, the grade was acceptable."

He says one reason he was no scholastic superstar was that many courses he had to take didn't interest him. Other things did. He and two faculty members resurrected a long-dormant flying club at Yale. One of his cohorts was Prof. Norwood Russell Hansen.

"Russ taught the psychology of science—how science was developed," Smith says. "I was a friend of his, not one of his students. He had a big impact on me because of his outlook on life. He was a great singer and a pianist of virtual concert talent. He rode a motorcycle, and he had a World War II fighter plane that he flew all over the place. He buzzed the Yale Bowl from time to time. He marched to the beat of a different drummer . . . ."

Smith went to Vietnam as a platoon leader . . . .

"A lot of the people in my platoon had an influence on my life," he says. "The one who made the strongest impression was my platoon sergeant, Jack Jackson, a black guy who had been in the Marines about 14 years and was not very well educated. He lost his life in Vietnam later.

"Sgt. Jack was probably the wisest man I have ever met. He had wisdom about what people who aren't officers think and want. That has stood me in good stead since as a manager.

"Ordinarily, kids who go to Yale—some of them work on construction gangs for the summer; big deal!—don't really get to know the kind of people who fill your gas tank."

Such people, Smith says, are "enormously important" to a company's success, and at Federal Express, to make sure they realize he realizes it, he has done some "iconoclastic things . . . ."

"I spend much time trying to find out what our employees think," Smith says . . . .

Will he be successful in future undertakings? Says Arthur C. Bass, vice chairman: "A few years ago, some of us used to let off steam in the afternoon by playing basketball on a court behind an apartment house. It was amazing—no matter who had the ball and no matter where Fred was on the court, if Fred's side needed to score to win, he would get the ball and make the winning basket. That's the way he is in the business world."

1. What is the simple solution to money problems?

2. Businesses that consider money they haven't actually received (but have sent bills for) as income are keeping financial records on an _____ basis. Fill in the blank.

3. Name the three alternatives you have if the money that comes in is less than the money that goes out.

4. List five ways to decrease the amount of money that you spend.

5. Which of the following forms of financial assistance must be repaid?

a. National Direct Student Loan
b. Pell Grant
c. Supplemental Educational Opportunity Grant (SEOG)
d. College work-study

6. Describe the hub-and-spoke pattern used by Fred Smith and Federal Express.

7. "I can't afford it," is the most frequent reason given by students for dropping out of school. True or false.

8. A person earning $15,000 a year is more likely than a person earning $50,000 a year to say she doesn't have enough money. True or false.

9. List two ways to increase the amount of money you have.

10. What is the payoff for making money management seem more complicated than it really is?

List the things you wanted to get from this chapter but didn't get.

Journal entry #80

Discovery statement

To get what I wanted from this chapter, I intend to . . .

Journal entry #81

Intention statement

Your self-discoveries revealed in journal entry #79 concern your relationship to financial worth, spending patterns, earning patterns, and budgeting. What changes will you make as a result of these discoveries or the work you did in Exercises #42, #43, #44 and #45?

Journal entry #82

Intention statement

I intend to . . .

I intend to . . .

I intend to . . .

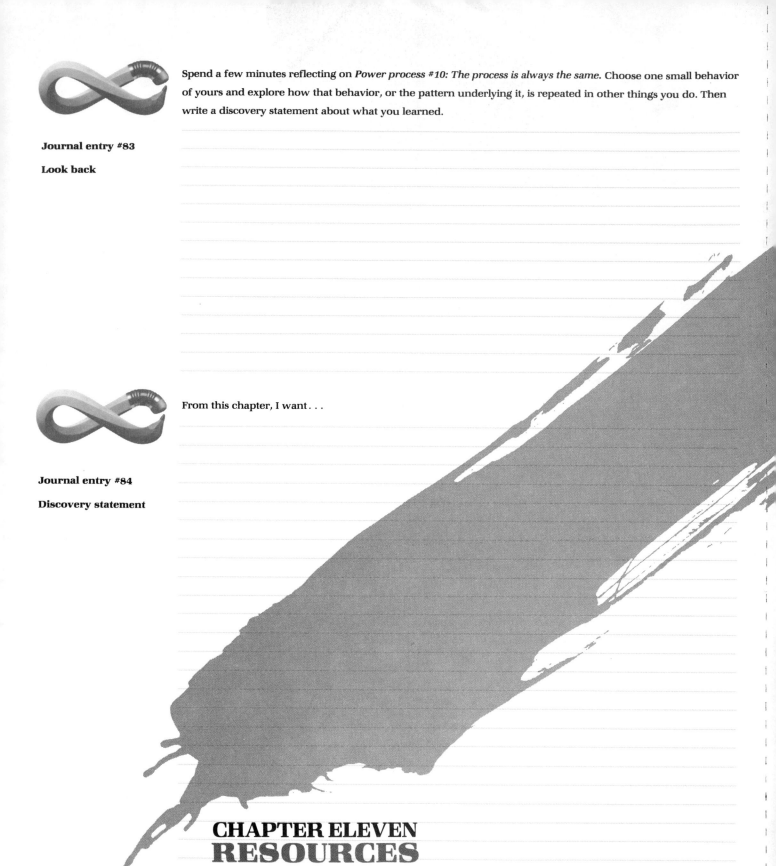

Spend a few minutes reflecting on *Power process #10: The process is always the same.* Choose one small behavior of yours and explore how that behavior, or the pattern underlying it, is repeated in other things you do. Then write a discovery statement about what you learned.

Journal entry #83

Look back

From this chapter, I want...

Journal entry #84

Discovery statement

CHAPTER ELEVEN
RESOURCES

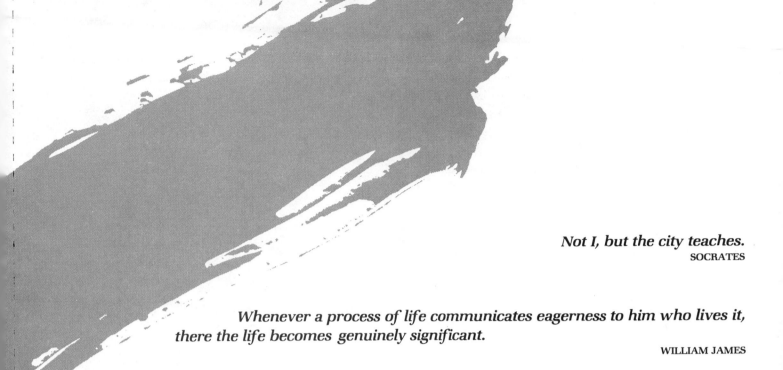

Not I, but the city teaches.
SOCRATES

Whenever a process of life communicates eagerness to him who lives it, there the life becomes genuinely significant.

WILLIAM JAMES

In this chapter...

There are mountains of gold located nearby that most people don't know exist. This chapter is about how to find them.

Campus resources points the way to people who come to work everyday just to serve you. They want to give you what you already paid for.

Community resources have also been paid for; they are supported by personal and business taxes and they are available, free, to you.

The most valuable resource for students, the center of education, is the ***Library.*** You may be surprised by all the gold in this mountain of information.

A hidden resource is uncovered in ***Contributing—the art of selfishness.*** The suggestion is that when you contribute to others, you will get back more than you give. Contributing is a selfish activity.

Test the water and ***Magic machine*** suggest other ways to get more out of what you have already purchased.

Forty-seven miles from the next town and you're out of gas? Six chapters of analytic geometry to comprehend before tomorrow's midterm exam? Don't sweat the small stuff—use ***Power process #11: Find a bigger problem.***

Exercises in this chapter direct you to the mountain of resources available to every student.

PART ONE   GETTING READY TO SUCCEED
PART TWO   LEARNING IN LECTURES
PART THREE WORKING WITH TEXTBOOKS
PART FOUR   TAKING TESTS

LIBRARY
The buried treasure

Books. That's what most people imagine when a library is mentioned. Books occupy a lot of space in a library, but they are only a small part of what is really there.

Most libraries have books. They also have, for your use, records, art work, maps, telephone directories for major cities, audio-visual equipment, microfiche, slide programs, film strips, magazines, dictionaries and encyclopedias of all varieties, research aids, computer searches, and people.

Libraries range widely in size. Most have the same purpose. They exist to help you find information—facts, opinions, or ideas that might have been buried for years.

The best resource is not made of paper

People who work in libraries are trained explorers. They know how to search out information that might be located in several different places. They can also act as a guide for your own expedition into the data jungle. Their purpose is to serve you. Ask for help.

Most libraries have a special reference librarian who can usually let you know right away if the library has what you need. He may suggest a different library or direct you to another source, such as a business, community agency, or government office.

You can save hours by asking.

Any book you want

Most libraries now have nearly every book you could ever want through a service known as interlibrary loan. This sharing of materials gives even the smallest library access to millions of books on any subject you could imagine. Just ask that the book be ordered from another library. It often takes only a few days.

Periodicals

The magazines and newspapers a library carries depends mostly on the location and purpose of the library. A neighborhood branch of a public library may have copies of the local paper and magazines right from the grocery store aisle. A library in a business school is more likely to have the *Wall Street Journal* and trade journals for accountants and business managers. Law libraries subscribe to magazines that would probably bore the socks off a veterinarian.

Reference material

The card catalog lists books available in that library and their location. It is an alphabetical listing that is cross-referenced by subject, author, and title. Each card carries the author's name, the title, the publisher, the date of publication, the number of pages and illustrations, the Library of Congress or Dewey decimal system number (for locating the book), and sometimes a brief description of the book.

Books in Print is a list of most books currently in publication in the United

States. Like the card catalog, it is organized by subject, author, and title.

The Reader's Guide to Periodical Literature catalogs articles found in most magazines. By subject, you can find titles of articles from a wide variety of magazines. The magazine name, date, and page numbers will be listed. If you want an older magazine, many libraries require that you fill out a form requesting the magazine so it can be retrieved from storage in closed stacks.

Other guides to what has been recently published include: *New York Times Index, Business Index, Applied Science and Technology Index, Accountants' Index, General Science Index, Education Index, Humanities Index, Art Index,* and many others. These indexes help you find what you want in a hurry.

Abstracts are publications that summarize current findings in specific fields. You can review condensed versions of specialized articles by reading *Chemical Abstracts, Psychological Abstracts* or *Education Abstracts.*

Pamphlets and clippings are usually stored in file cabinets organized by subject. This section contains information from the U.S. Government Printing Office, state and local governments, and newspaper and magazine clippings.

Facts about virtually anything you can imagine are waiting in almanacs and publications from government departments such as Labor, Commerce, and Agriculture.

The U.S. Government Printing Office is the largest publisher in the world. *The Monthly Index* of its printings takes up several feet of shelf space.

Resources listed in indexes or *Reader's Guide* but not available at a particular library are usually available through interlibrary loan.

General and specialized encyclopedias are found in the reference section. Find what you want to know about individuals, groups, places, products, words, or other books. Specialized examples include: *Encyclopedia of World Authors, Encyclopedia of Music and Musicians, Encyclopedia of Religion and Ethics, Encyclopedia of Associations, Thomas Register of American Manufacturers,* and *Encyclopedia of the Arts.*

Dictionaries of all sizes and specialties are also available in the library. Technical disciplines (medicine, computer science, engineering) often have their own dictionaries. Of special value to your writing projects is the thesaurus, a type of dictionary. You will find single words that have a very similar meaning to the word you look up (synonyms). Instead of standard definitions, a thesaurus provides fast relief when you just can't think of the word you want.

Computer networks now provide information and resource materials to most libraries. DIALOG, ORBIT, and BSR are the three major electronic information vendors, and each contains several dozen data bases. Up-to-the-minute reports (stock prices set in the past 15 minutes, yesterday's *New York Times* stories) can be retrieved almost instantly on a video terminal.

Gaining familiarity with all these resources and services is crucial to the success of most students. And to some, even more valuable than access to information is the convenient, comfortable, quiet, and dependable atmosphere for study to be found in a library.

Exercise #47

Find it

Most libraries have the answers to the following questions. Go exploring. If you search for the answer and can't find it on your own, ask one of the librarians for help.

1. What are a dozen words that mean about the same thing as the word "power"?

2. How many students were graduated from high school in 1980? _____ How many of them continued their education?

3. What is the Library of Congress number (which is used to locate books in many libraries) for the novel *1984* by George Orwell? (Give the Dewey decimal number if that is the system used in your library.)

4. Is the book *Lazy Man's Guide to Enlightenment* still in print? _____ If so, who is the publisher?

5. What are three magazine articles, published since last year, that discuss methods to prevent or treat cancer?

6. Who manufactures nails and tacks? List three companies you could contact if you wanted one million nails made to your specifications.

7. What computer search capabilities are available at two libraries you can use? List the names of the two libraries and briefly describe information they can access directly by computer.

Contributing

the art of selfishness

This book is about contributing to yourself—about taking care of yourself—about being selfish. The techniques and suggestions in this book focus on how to get what you want out of school and out of life. The net result of all of this successful selfishness is the capacity for contribution, for giving to others.

People who are satisfied with life can share that satisfaction with others. It is not easy to contribute to another person's joy until you experience joy. You can't contribute love without being filled with love yourself.

This book is about filling yourself, taking care of yourself. As you do that, contribute also to others. Contributing is the one thing left, and it completes the process.

The earth really is very small. We are dependent upon one another for our lives. Every day we stake our lives on the sensibilities of other people. When you drive, it's easy to see that you depend on other drivers for your life. If a driver in the on-coming lane of traffic decides to cross into your lane, you are likely to die. In fact, you depend as much for your safety upon the sensibilities of world leaders as you do upon the driver in the next lane.

People everywhere are growing more interdependent. This small planet works something like a human being. Sprain the ankle and the body limps. Neglect the eyes and the entire system will be inefficient. Remove the liver and the body dies.

In this interdependent world, the only way to win (to get what we want in life) is for others to win also. If they lose, their loss will directly affect us. If we lose, we cannot contribute to others. There is no such thing as win/lose. We either all win or eventually we all lose.

The idea of contributing is not the same as knowing what is best for other people. We can't know. There are people, of course, who go around "fixing" other people. "I know what you need. Here, do it my way." That is not contribution. It can cause more harm than good and can result in dependence on the part of the person we are "helping."

True contribution occurs after you have first found out what another person wants or needs and, second, determined if you can lovingly support him to have it. Only then is the act of contribution possible. You can give your money, your time, your talents, and yourself.

Read *Campus resources* and *Community resources.* Look for ways you can contribute to the organizations mentioned. You can also consider the following organizations to see how you might add to their contributions. Getting involved with any one of these organizations, or a dozen others, is also a way you can "break the ice" in a new community and meet people with interests similar to your own.

The American Cancer Society raises money for research and helps educate people on ways to detect and prevent cancer.

Big Brothers and Big Sisters provide friendship and guidance to children who have only one parent.

Blood services in every community provide an opportunity to donate blood desperately needed by hospitals and clinics.

Girls Club, Boys Club, Girl Scouts, and Boy Scouts of America all need large numbers of volunteers.

Hospitals often depend on volunteer help to supplement patient care provided by the professional staff.

Museums and art galleries need interested people to conduct tours and provide supervision.

Nursing homes welcome visitors who are willing to spend time listening and talking with lonely people.

Political parties, candidates, and special interest groups need volunteers to stuff envelopes, gather petition signatures, and distribute literature.

The American Red Cross provides disaster relief. It needs volunteers.

Service organizations like Cosmopolitan, Zonta, Jaycees, Jayceettes, Altrusa, Kiwanis, Lions, American Association of University Women, Sertoma, Business and Professional Women, and Rotary want members who are willing to serve others.

Tutoring centers offer opportunities for competent students to help non-English-speaking people, grade school and high school students, and illiterate adults.

Churches of all denominations want volunteers to assist with on-going projects for the community and the world.

World hunger projects want your assistance to help feed starving people and to educate all of us to the problems of malnutrition, food spoilage, and starvation.

Recall a time when you contributed to a person or a group of people. Recall a time when you volunteered your time for an important cause or a worthy group. Write details of the contribution you made and how you felt afterwards.

Journal entry #85

Discovery statement

Review the list of places in the article *Contributing—the art of selfishness*. See if there is some organization which deserves your assistance. Also, think about people in your life to whom you could give time, money, or something of yourself.

Make a commitment to contribute. Keep the commitment small and time-specific.

Journal entry #86

Intention statement

I intend to contribute. . .

Test the water

If you are concerned about a course you will have to take in a future term, if you are worried that it might be too hard, if you think you might not be able to pass it, test the water. Audit the course.

Most colleges and schools have an audit policy that allows you to sit through a course without paying full tuition. You will not get credit for it, and you may not be able to take the tests or receive grades. However, you will be exposed to all the lectures, and you can study the material and ask questions. You can learn as much as if you were taking the course for credit.

The advantage to auditing the course before you take it for credit is that it diminishes the risk of failure. The audit is like a test drive or a practice game. This is also a great way for a business major to take an art or philosophy course, but not pay for credit she doesn't need or worry about a grade.

Campus resources

Colleges, universities, technical schools, business colleges and schools of all types offer services that students often don't even know about, let alone use. Here is a brief description of things that are often available.

As you read this, look for resources that you might use someday.

1. The school catalog is an often overlooked resource. It is the rule book of the game of education. It usually contains course descriptions, requirements for graduation, faculty, financial aid, accreditations, goals and objectives, history, student services, admissions policies, grading practices, student organizations, and academic calendars.

2. Student organizations can be a source of information as well as companionship and fun. Explore fraternities, sororities, service clubs, veteran's organizations, religious groups, sports clubs (bowling, cards, skiing, tennis), and political groups. Most schools also have some type of student government that can be a place to contribute or a group that can help you get something done.

3. Placement offices help students find jobs. They often help with part-time employment while you are in school, as well as career placement upon graduation.

4. Counseling centers or deans' offices offer academic or personal counseling, usually at no cost. If they are not equipped to deal with your personal needs, they can refer you to the appropriate community agency.

5. The registrar is responsible for school records. This is the office to see about transcripts, grade changes and how to add or drop classes, change majors, or transfer credits.

6. Financial aid can be confusing, and there is usually one office that handles all of the paperwork and can answer your questions.

7. Alumni organizations offer information to current students as well as graduates.

8. Tutoring is usually available through academic departments or special tutoring centers.

9. A health clinic or nurse's office provides free or inexpensive treatment of minor problems.

10. Chapels are open to students of any religion. They are quiet places to pray or meditate.

11. Child care may be provided on campus through an early childhood education department or as a separate service.

12. Car pooling maps show who wants to go, and who is going, to different parts of the country.

13. A college's print shop may provide services to students in addition to the work they do for the school.

14. The school newspaper is a place to advertise and to find out about local entertainment, school policy changes, or other resources.

15. Campus security . . . radio station . . . television station . . . museum . . . art galleries . . . music practice rooms . . . observatory . . . computer center . . .

Review *Campus resources,* and place a check by the resources that are available where you attend school. Put a line through those not available at your school.

If you're not sure, great. The purpose of this exercise is for you to discover your campus resources. Ask around, call someone, find out which you can use. If you are aware of resources not listed, write them in the margin of the book.

This campus resource list will be the place to look when you need to find help you haven't needed in the past.

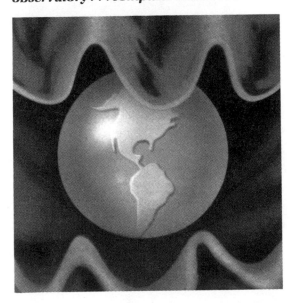

Community resources

You can be an explorer without going to the North Pole. Your community is rich with culture, diversity, and fun. People who have lived in one place all their lives often have not visited nearby spots that tourists come hundreds of miles to see. Likewise, people often travel hundreds of miles and spend thousands of dollars looking for something that is free five blocks from their home.

Know your community. Explore and be surprised.

Review this list with two questions in mind. "How can I use this resource now or in the future?" and, "In what way can I contribute to this resource?"

Chambers of Commerce and Tourist Bureaus provide pamphlets and information on local attractions and the economic condition of the city.

Churches and synagogues offer social programs as well as places to worship.

Clubs and organizations promote the development of skills in speaking (Toastmasters), skiing, flying, gardening, conservation (Sierra Club), photography, bird watching (Audubon Society), scuba diving, etc. A list of local organizations and clubs is usually available from the Chamber of Commerce.

Consumer credit advice is provided free in many communities for people with severe financial problems.

Counseling for career or personal problems is available through local Job Service offices, rehabilitation offices, church agencies, private clinics, and social service agencies or area mental health clinics.

Day care for children is provided by private and public organizations. Some places charge for child care based on your income.

Girls Clubs and Boys Clubs offer child care, guidance, and recreation opportunities for young people.

Handicapped people are often provided special transportation services, unique library privileges, or individual nursing care.

Health care centers provide inexpensive birth control, gynecological exams, venereal disease diagnosis and treatment, vaccinations, and care for pregnant women and sick children.

Hot lines are available for people to call during crisis situations involving child abuse, suicide, or rape.

Humane societies and animal shelters offer help for animals and may be the source of an inexpensive pet.

Legal advice is provided free or inexpensively to low income people at legal services offices in many communities.

Locals, people who have spent their lives in your community, often know the best restaurants, the most fascinating second-hand stores or the secluded hiking spots close to town.

Money for emergency situations is sometimes available through churches, Red Cross or county relief agencies.

Newspapers list community events and services which are free or inexpensive. These include outdoor concerts, art showings, hobby and craft shows, amateur sporting events, auctions, etc.

Public transportation (buses and subways) is a money-saving alternative to owning and operating a car.

Recreation departments, YWCA's, and YMCA's provide free or inexpensive ways to exercise and have fun.

Seminars offered to the public teach everything from nutrition to transformation. You can find programs for improving your marriage, your looks, communication, shyness, assertiveness, self-defense, child raising, or your career.

Subcultures and ethnic communities are part of most cities. They often have fairs, festivals, or celebrations that are entertaining and inexpensive.

Support groups exist for just about everything. You can find people with problems similar to yours who meet every week to share suggestions, information and concerns. These include groups for the overweight, for single parents, for abusive parents, for parents with twins, for newly-widowed people, for alcoholics, drug addicts, terminally ill people, women who have had a breast removed, people who have had open-heart or colon-rerouting surgery, families of drug addicts or alcoholics, women who are abused, nursing mothers, Vietnam veterans, and parents who have lost a child.

United States Senators and Representatives usually have local offices. If you have exhausted other resources, they can generally help you. Be exact in your letter. Give as much specific information as you can. List people, places, and dates, and be straight about what you want. Put your home address on the letter as well as the envelope.

Address your letter to either:

Honorable (Senator's name)
Senate Office Building
Washington, D.C. 20510

or

Honorable (Representative's name)
House Office Building
Washington, D.C. 20515

If you are not sure of the name of your U.S. Senator or Representative, call the mayor's office, the local office of the Republican or Democratic party, the Chamber of Commerce, your local newspaper, the news department of your local TV station, or find the information at the library.

You can also write directly to the government offices. On page 302 is a list of Federal Government offices and telephone numbers.

Exercise #49

Catalog reconnaissance

Look at every page in your school catalog— quickly. Notice what is new, interesting, or puzzling.

Locate your major program description and notice the courses you are required to take for graduation. Find out more about courses you know nothing about. If you see that you have to take Macro Economics to graduate, find out how that differs from Micro Economics and Accounting.

Locate the major program that is most different from yours. Look through the courses students in that major are required to take. Pick out a course that looks interesting, even though it is different from anything you have ever thought you'd take. Find out more about that course.

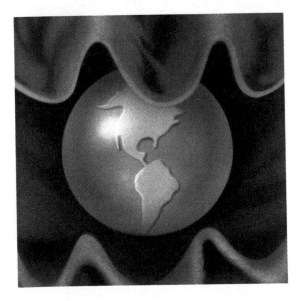

Find a big problem

Most of the time we see problems as barriers. They are a source of inconvenience and annoyance. They get in our way and prevent us from having happy and productive lives. When we see problems this way, our goal becomes the elimination of problems. This point of view is futile. It is impossible to live a life without problems. Besides, they serve a purpose.

Problems are opportunities to participate in life. If there were none, our lives would be meaningless and boring. When we don't have a problem to work on, we are likely to create one. Problems stimulate us and move us forward.

When problems are seen this way, the goal becomes not the elimination of problems, but rather the creation of more. Then the challenge is to tackle problems (create opportunities) which will make the most difference.

Problems seem to follow the same law of physics that gases do. They expand to fill whatever space is available. If your only problem for the entire day is to write a follow-up letter to a job interview, you can spend the whole day finding paper and pen, thinking about what you're going to say, writing the letter, finding an envelope and stamp, going to the post office, and then thinking about all the things you forgot to say.

If, on that day you also need to shop for groceries, the problem of the letter shrinks to make room for another problem. If you also want to buy a car, it's amazing how quickly and easily the letter and the grocery shopping are finished. One way to handle little problems is to find bigger ones.

Bigger problems are not in short supply. Consider world hunger. Every

minute of every day, 21 people die because they don't have enough to eat. Each day, 35,000 people starve. Each year 13 million people die because they don't have enough food.

Consider alcoholism. One of every four people in the United States is directly affected by his own drinking or the alcoholism of someone in his family. Consider nuclear war that threatens to end life on the planet. Child abuse, pollution, drug abuse, street crime, energy shortages, poverty, and wars throughout the world await your attention and involvement. You can make a contribution.

Perhaps your little voice is saying, "That's crazy. I can't do anything about those kinds of problems," or "Everyone knows that hunger has always been around and always will be, and there is nothing anyone can do about it." These thoughts prevent you from taking on bigger problems.

Realize that you can make a difference. Investigate the facts and find out who's doing something about it. Get involved. Take a stand.

This is your life. It's your school, your city, your country, and your world. Own it. Treat it with the same care you would a new stereo or a new car. You are no less worthy or less valuable than anyone else. Your thoughts and actions can change the quality of life on the planet.

The surest way to flatten your own problems, no matter how large, is to take on a bigger one. Your own bruises are easily ignored while you are saving someone else's life. Take responsibility for problems that are bigger than you are sure you can handle. Watch your other problems disappear.

Directory of Federal and Congressional Offices

Department of Education
Office of the Assistant
Secretary for
Human Rights
330 C Street SW,
Switzer Bldg.
Washington, D.C. 20202
Info: (202) 732-1213

Department of Education
400 Maryland Ave., SW
Washington, D.C. 20202
Info: (202) 245-3192

Postsecondary Education
7th and D Street SW
Room 4082
Washington, D.C. 20202
Info: (202) 245-9274

Internal Revenue Service
1111 Constitution
Ave., NW
Room 3005
Washington, D.C. 20224
Info: (202) 566-2111

Department of Labor
200 Constitution
Avenue, NW
Washington, D.C. 20210
Info: (202) 523-7316

Equal Employment
Opportunity Commission
2401 E Street, NW
Washington, D.C. 20506
Info: (202) 634-6930

Office of Federal
Contract
Compliance Programs
200 Constitution
Avenue, NW
Washington, D.C. 20210
Info: (202) 523-9475

Federal Trade
Commission
Pennsylvania Avenue &
7th, NW
Washington, D.C. 20580
Info: (202) 523-3830

Senate Labor and Human
Resources Committee
428 Dirksen Senate
Office Building
Washington, D.C. 20510
Info: (202) 224-5375

Senate Subcommittee on
Education, Arts
and Humanities
428 Dirksen Senate
Office Building
Washington, D.C. 20510
Info: (202) 224-5375

Financial Assistance
Office of Student
Financial Assistance
ROB 3, 7th & D
Streets, SW
Washington, D.C. 20202
Info: (202) 245-8595

Department of Education
Student Financial
Assistance
Room 4680, FOB #6
400 Maryland Avenue
Washington, D.C. 20202
Info: (202) 245-3192
(202) 472-5080
Student Financial Aid

House Committee on
Education and Labor
2181 Rayburn
House Building
Washington, D.C. 20515
Info: (202) 225-4527

U.S. Postal Service
475 L'Enfant Plaza
Washington, D.C. 20260
Info: (202) 245-4034

House Subcommittee on
Postsecondary Education
320 Cannon Building
Washington, D.C. 20515
Info: (202) 225-8881

U.S. Department of Labor
Office of Information
and Consumer Affairs
200 Constitution
Avenue, NW
Room C 4331
Washington, D.C. 20210
Info: (202) 523-8743

Veteran's Administration
810 Vermont
Avenue, NW
Washington, D.C. 20420
Info: (202) 393-4120

White House
1600 Pennsylvania
Ave., NW
Washington, D.C. 20006
Info: (202) 456-1414

Review *Community resources,* and select at least 10 services that you might use in the next year or that you might volunteer for or contribute to. Using a phone book, a library, and/or your ingenuity, find the name, address, and phone number of the local organizations that offer those services.

For example, if you think you might use day care for your child, find out where day care centers are located in your community. If you think you might want to donate some time to the Big Brothers/Big Sisters organization, put it on your list and find out the address and phone number.

Magic machine

There is a magic machine very close to you. You can use it as often as you like. It has miraculous qualities.

This machine can send a part of you to almost any place in the world, almost instantly, for only a few cents. You can go to Japan, New Zealand, Peru, or India. You can go to Chicago, Ft. Lauderdale, Portland, or Denver. These machines are available to nearly everyone and you see them everywhere.

Don't neglect the power of the phone. It can save you hours of shopping, miles of walking, and reams of paper. A call can give you information, advice, comfort, or friendship.

The white page directory and the Yellow Pages are detailed guides to your community. The Yellow Pages are indexed to quickly locate the nearest pizza parlor or the closest dog groomer. Find out who sells fire extinguishers or fertilizer. In a snap you can discover who will complete your tax return or paint your car. If you can't find it yourself, call information and ask for help.

Businesses and government agencies receive calls every few minutes. If they didn't want you to call, they wouldn't put their number in the book. Call before you go. Take advantage of this device that will take part of you to other places, almost instantly.

This magic machine is a marvelous resource.

Lauren Elder

From **And I Alone Survived,** *copyright 1978 by Lauren Elder with Shirley Streshinsky. Reprinted by permission of the publisher, E.P. Dutton, Inc.*

Good Lord. He wasn't even sure if his ten-year-old daughter knew he was going flying today. Didn't he make any contingency plans for her? It all seemed so haphazard, so slipshod. No flight plan. Nobody knows where we are. I don't even know where we are, I thought. There was nobody to sound the alarm.

It hit me then: *I am on my own.* Jay couldn't take care of me, and I couldn't expect him to. We were in this together. We could help each other, but there had to be a balance . . .

. . . *So much for Plan A*, I said to myself. *What is Plan B?* Clearly, I would have to settle for an alternative course of action. Then I remembered the second line of defense—the rocks. What we had was a pile of very hot granite rocks that would give off heat for a time, maybe for a long time. The heat would last longer if I could get the rocks into a small, protected space out of the wind. I decided to load them into the tail section of the plane, the part that had partially split off from the main body. It was a small aluminum cone just big enough for two bodies and a store of heated granite.

"If we get in there," I said to Jay, "I mean, if we pile some rocks into the tail of the plane—" I knew I had asked him the question several times before, but clearly the idea bothered me. "If we pile in all those rocks and ourselves in after," I started over again, "do you suppose we might tip it over?" I could imagine the plane tumbling down the mountain.

"It's okay," he said with unconcealed annoyance. "It's anchored. The wingtip is dug in. The wheels too." He answered as if by rote. There was a tape-recorded quality to his voice, and it gave me the bizarre feeling that in some way he wasn't there.

The thought crossed my mind: Is he leaving? Leaving, slipping away. Could something be wrong with him that I didn't understand?

No, I told myself firmly. I had survived the crash and so had Jay. All I had to think about was keeping warm. Jay said the plane was solidly anchored. I sincerely hoped he was right.

I squeezed sideways throught the tiny baggage door and kicked out some flimsy plastic dividers used to separate the compartment. Our feet would be near the bottom, where the fuselage narrowed at the tail of the plane, and our heads would be at the top. The roof had split open, exposing the rear passenger seat; but if we curled as low as we could, we would be well enough protected.

"We've got to pile as many rocks into the tail as we can," I ordered as I climbed back out. "There's enough room for the two of us, and we've got to fill the leftover space with stones. Maybe they'll get us through what's left of the night."

Jay said nothing, and he did not move. I resisted the urge to say something cutting. It would take too much energy, and I had to gather the stones.

I began to grope in the dark, feeling for the hot, oil-blackened stones. I smelled flesh singeing, felt the stinging rocks. *The hotter the better,* I thought. My left arm was of little use, but I managed to get several rocks into the tail. A fingernail bent back and broke off, and my fingers were smashed and charred; but it was the price I had to pay, I told myself. The rocks were all the insurance we had . . . .

It seemed forever, but it was worth it, because the added heat was immediately noticeable. The air in the section was almost warm, and I was content that I had done all I could do. With that thought I pulled my silk scarf over my face and curled into a fetal position. *Lauren,* I congratulated myself, *you really are smart.*

That is how I felt—smart. I don't mean intelligent or bright or any of the usual meanings of the word. I mean, simply, that given a certain set of conditions, I had chosen the proper sequence, I had made optimum use of the possibilities presented. I had put the puzzle together in the time allotted.

1. Most libraries now have nearly every book you could ever want through a service known as _____.

2. An abstract serves the purpose of: (choose one)
   a. listing all books currently in publication.
   b. cataloging articles found in most magazines.
   c. summarizing current findings in specific fields.
   d. organizing information from the U.S. Government Printing Office, state and local government agencies, and newspaper and magazine clippings.

3. What is a thesaurus?

4. List five campus resources.

5. There is no such thing as win/lose. True or false.

6. Where would you call to find the name of your U.S. Senator or Representative?

7. Describe auditing a course.

8. In what way is contributing to others a selfish act?

9. Which library resource would you use to find a magazine article about a specific subject?

10. Which campus office is responsible for school records, handling transcripts, grade changes, and adding or dropping classes?

I wanted, but didn't get, these things from this chapter.

Journal entry #87

Discovery statement

To get what I wanted from this chapter, I intend to . . .

Journal entry #88

Intention statement

Of the dozens of resources reviewed in this chapter, pick one or two you will use. Consider various resources in the library, at your school, or around your community, and make an intention to use something you haven't used in the past.

Journal entry #89

Intention statement

I intend to . . .

Review the intention statements throughout this book. They appear at the end of every chapter as well as throughout each chapter. See if you have been keeping agreements with yourself. See if you have been getting what you said you wanted.

If you are consistently not doing what you said you would do, if you are not getting what you said you wanted, examine what you have been saying. You might be saying you want one thing, while you actually want something else.

On reviewing past journal entry/intention statements, I learned that I . . .

Journal entry #90

Look back

From this chapter, I want . . .

Journal entry #91

Discovery statement

CHAPTER TWELVE
WHAT NEXT?

*Learning is not a task or a problem—it is a way
to be in the world. Man learns as he pursues goals
and projects that have meaning for him.*

SIDNEY JOURARD

*Live as if you were to die tomorrow. Learn as if you were to
live forever.*

GANDHI

*Whatever you can do or dream you can, begin it. Boldness has genius, power
and magic in it.*

GOETHE

In this chapter . . .

What you have learned so far is wonderful, significant, and
commendable. Everything you have learned from this book about how to
learn, and everything you have learned to this point in your life, is
insignificant compared to what is available.

The universe of learning is never-ending. Becoming a master student
is a lifelong adventure. This chapter is about continuing that adventure.
What next? suggests how you can program your life so personal
discovery and growth will be a habit.

Knowing clearly what you intend to do in your career lets you know
with equal clarity why you are in school. And when you know that, you
are a force to be reckoned with. ***Careers and goals*** gets down to it.

Start believing you can be and have anything you want, because here
comes ***Attitudes, affirmations and visualizations*** and ***Power
process #12: Be it.***

Some of our attitudes stand squarely between us and our desires,
and they deserve to go on the scrap heap. ***Attitude replacements*** will
clarify that for you.

The journal entries in this chapter invite you to complete your
experience of the book, see what you did and didn't get, and surprise
yourself some more. You get to ***Write yourself a letter, Do
something you can't*** and ***Reprogram your attitudes.***

What next?

If you *used* this book, if you actively participated in reading the contents, writing the journals, doing the exercises, and applying the suggestions, then you have had quite a journey. You are on a path of growth toward becoming a master student. Now what? What's the next step?

The world is packed with opportunities for master students. If you excel in adventure, exploration, discovery, and creativity, you will never lack for possibilities. If you want to continue to grow, continue to learn how to learn, the choices are endless.

You are on the edge of a universe so miraculous and full of wonder that your imagination at its most creative moment cannot encompass it. Paths are open to lead you to worlds beyond your wildest dreams.

If this sounds like a pitch for the latest recreational drug, it may be. The drug is adrenaline, and it is automatically generated by your body when you are growing, risking, and discovering new worlds inside and outside of your skin.

This book has started a process of discovery and intention which can be a powerful tool in assisting you to get exactly what you want in life. Following are several ways to reinforce that discovery and intention process.

1. Keep a journal. Go to a stationery store and buy a bound notebook that will hold your private reflections and dreams for the future. Get one that will be worthy of your personal discoveries and intentions. Write in this journal daily. Record what you are learning about yourself and the world. Write about your hopes, wishes, and goals. Keep account of significant events.

2. Take a seminar. Workshops start each week in most cities that can help you discover yourself and your intentions. Research the options, and consider taking a Dale Carnegie course, psychodrama (a process of role-playing life events), assertiveness training, The Forum (a personal transformation seminar developed by Werner Erhard), meditation, Effectiveness Training (a communication workshop developed by Thomas Gordon), yoga, or a martial arts program.

3. Read. Dozens of books are recommended in the bibliography at the back of this book. If these don't look interesting, go exploring for good books. Ask friends. Talk to a librarian. Talk to the owner/operators of small bookstores. Ask teachers. Great treasures await your discovery.

4. Take an unrelated class. Sign up for a class that is totally unrelated to your major. If you are studying to be a secretary, take a physics course. If you are going to be a doctor, take a bookkeeping course. You can discover a lot about yourself and your intended future when you step out of old patterns.

5. Travel. See the world. Visit new neighborhoods. Travel to other countries. Explore. Find out what it looks like inside buildings you normally have no reason to go into, museums you think you have little interest in, cities that are out of the way, forests and mountains that lie beyond your old boundaries, and far-off places that require planning and saving to reach.

6. Get counseling. Solving emotional problems is not the only reason to visit a counselor, a therapist, or a psychologist. They are excellent resources for personal growth. You can use counseling to look at yourself and talk about yourself in ways that may be uncomfortable for anyone except a trained professional. It is a chance to talk about nothing but yourself without anyone thinking you are rude.

7. Redo this book. You may not want to reread every page. You may believe that you already know what it says. Redo a chapter and see if you are surprised. Redo the quizzes. You can use the quizzes to test your ability to recall. Redo the exercises. Most of the exercises in this book will produce a different result after a few months. The discovery wheel can be particularly useful to reveal techniques you have actually put into practice. Redo the journal entries. If you keep a journal, refer to the suggested journal entries whenever you are stuck about what to write.

Journal entry #92

Intention statement

Consider the value you could produce for yourself if you redid this book one year from now. Imagine what you could gain by rereading the material, rewriting the journal entries, and redoing the exercises.

Also consider the cost of redoing the book. You would spend hours reading, writing and experimenting. You would probably get uncomfortable looking at some aspects of yourself or looking for ways that you created circumstances you would like to blame on others.

Once you have thought about the potential costs and benefits of redoing this book, write down your intention. Be specific about completion dates and the extent of your review. If you know that you only intend to redo chapter 8, then write that.

I intend to . . .

_____

_____

_____

_____

Attitudes, & affirma & visualiz

"I have a bad attitude." People say this as if they were saying they have the flu. An attitude is certainly as strong as the flu, but it isn't something you have to accept.

Some people see their attitudes the way they see their height or their eye color. "I may not like it, but I might as well accept it."

Acceptance is certainly a worthwhile approach to things you cannot change. Acceptance is not necessary when it comes to attitudes. If you have an attitude that you don't like, change it. You may have to go through life being too short or too tall. You don't have to live your life with an attitude that doesn't work.

Attitudes are powerful because they create behavior. If your attitude is that you're not very interesting at a party, then very quickly your behavior matches your attitude, and you act like a bore. Likewise, if your attitude is that you are fun at a party, then your behavior matches, and soon you are the life of the party. All that has to change is attitude.

You can change your attitude by regular practice with affirmations and visualizations.

Affirm it

If you want something to be a certain way, start with an affirmation. An affirmation is a statement describing what you want. It needs to be personal, positive, and written in the present tense.

The power of affirmation is almost magical. It is used successfully by athletes and actors, businessmen and ballerinas, and tens of thousands of people who have succeeded in their lives. Affirmations can change your attitude and your behavior.

To use affirmations, first determine what you want, then write down a description of yourself as if you already had it. For example, if you decide you want a relationship with a wonderful man, you might write: "I, Susan Webster, have a wonderful man in my life. I see him four times a week and each visit is exciting and comfortable. He is sensitive and funny and he absolutely loves me." Or, if money is your desire, you might write: "I, John Henderson, am rich. I have more money than I can spend. I have everything I want including a six-bedroom house, a new sports car, a 200-watt stereo system, and a video tape recorder with a satellite dish receiver."

What makes the affirmation work is detail. Use brand names, people's names, and your own name. Keep it in the present and word it in a way that

ions
ations

describes your wish as reality. Word it in the positive. For example, instead of saying, "I am not fat," say, "I am slender."

Once you have written the affirmation, repeat it. Practice saying it aloud several times a day. It works best if you say it at a regular time, perhaps right before you go to sleep or right after you awaken. Sit in a chair in a relaxed position. Take a few deep and relaxing breaths, and then repeat your affirmation with emotion. It is also effective to look in a mirror while you are saying it. Keep looking and repeating until you are saying your affirmation with conviction.

Visualize it

It would be difficult to grow up in our culture without hearing that practice improves performance. The problem is that most of us limit what we consider practice. Effective practice can actually occur when you are not moving a muscle.

You can improve a golf game, a tennis serve, or your skiing ability while lying in bed. You can become a better driver, speaker, or cook while sitting silently in a chair. In line at the grocery store, you can improve your ability to type or take tests. This is all possible through visualization—the art of seeing yourself be successful.

Here's how. Decide what you want to improve, and write down what it would look like, sound like, and feel like to have that improvement. If you are learning to play the piano, write down briefly what you would see, hear, and feel if you were playing very successfully. If you want to improve your ability to communicate with your children, write down what you would see, hear, and feel if you were successfully communicating.

Once you have a sketch of what it would be like to be successful, practice in your imagination. Rehearse in your mind. Include as many details as you can. Always have your practices be a success. Each time you toss the basketball, it will swoosh through the net. Every time you invite someone out, she will say yes. Every test will have an A on the top.

Practice at least once a day.

You can also use visualizations to replay errors. When you make a mistake, replay it in your imagination. After a bad golf shot, stop and replay it in your head. Imagine yourself making that same shot again very successfully. If you just had a discussion with your lover that turned into a fight, replay it successfully. Get all your senses involved. See yourself calmly talking it over together, hear the words, and feel the pleasure of a successful interaction.

Visualization and affirmation restructure your attitude and your behavior. Be clear about what you want and then practice.

Exercise #51

Reprogram your attitude

Affirmations and visualizations can be used to successfully reprogram your attitudes and behaviors. Use this exercise repeatedly to restructure your approach to dozens of situations in your life.

Step 1
Pick something in your life that you would like to change. It can be about relationships, work, money, personal skills, or self-esteem. Write a brief description of what you choose to change.

_____
_____
_____
_____
_____
_____
_____
_____
_____
_____
_____
_____
_____
_____
_____

Step 2
Write how you would like your choice in step 1 to change. Be outlandish. Write down your greatest wish about how you would like it to be. Imagine you are about to ask your fairy godmother for a wish you know she will grant. Be detailed in your description of how you want it to be.

_____
_____
_____
_____
_____
_____
_____
_____
_____
_____
_____
_____
_____
_____
_____
_____

Step 3
Here comes the fairy godmother. Use affirmations and visualizations to start you on the road to creating exactly what you wrote about in step 2. Below, write at least two affirmations that describe your dream wish. Also, briefly outline a visualization that you can use to picture your wish.

_____
_____
_____
_____
_____
_____
_____
_____
_____
_____
_____
_____
_____
_____

Step 4
Put them to work. Set up a schedule of practice. Determine a time and place when you will practice your new attitudes. Set the first time to be right now, then set up at least five other times that you intend to practice your affirmations and visualizations.

I intend to relax and practice the affirmations and visualizations for at least five minutes on the following dates and at the place(s) given.

	Date—Day—Approximate time	Location
1.		
2.		
3.		
4.		
5.		

Attitude replacements

Affirmations can be used to replace a negative attitude with a positive thought. Imagination and practice will be your only roadblocks to having the attitude you want. Here are some ideas to stir your imagination. Modify them to suit your individual hopes and dreams, and then add practice. The article, *Attitudes, affirmations, and visualizations,* explains how to use these attitude replacements.

I, _____, am healthy.
I, _____, have abundant energy and vitality throughout my day.
I, _____, exercise regularly.
I, _____, eat wisely.
I, _____, plan my days and use time wisely.
I, _____, have a powerful memory.
I, _____, am a great speller.
I, _____, fall asleep quickly and sleep soundly.
I, _____, am smart.
I, _____, learn quickly.
I, _____, am creative.
I, _____, am aware of and sensitive to people's moods.
I, _____, have relationships that are mutually satisfying.
I, _____, work hard and contribute to other people through my job.
I, _____, am wealthy.
I, _____, know how to play and have fun.
I, _____, am attractive.
I, _____, like myself.
I, _____, am liked by other people.
I, _____, am now a worthwhile person even though I am _____.
I, _____, have a slim and attractive body.
I, _____, am relaxed in all situations including _____.
I, _____, make profitable financial investments.
I, _____, have income that far exceeds my expenses.
I, _____, live a life of abundance and prosperity.
I, _____, always live my life in positive ways for the highest good of all people.

Exercise #52

I have to . . .

This exercise is about obligation and limitations. We often limit ourselves because of what we think we have to do or what we think we can't do.

Part 1

Take a look at all aspects of your life (family, friends, school, work) and complete each of the following sentences with whatever comes to mind.

I have to . . .
I ought to . . .
I should . . .
I can't . . .
I really must . . .
I just couldn't . . .
I am not able to . . .
I have to . . .
I can't . . .
I shouldn't . . .

Part 2

Review each of the previous sentences, cross off the first two or three words, and replace them with one of the following groups of words:

"I want to . . ."
"I don't want to . . ."
"I choose to . . ."
"I choose not to . . ."

The reason many people go to school is to get a better job. A satisfying, worthwhile, and lucrative career is often the ultimate goal of education. If that is true for you, then it is important to clearly define your career so that your education is indeed leading toward your goal.

If you're undecided

Set up a plan for career exploration. Many people know when they're eight years old what they are going to be when they grow up. They stick to their dream, and it often serves them well. Choices made early in life can be very wise, and they serve to focus energy and set a path for growth. However, many people get to middle age and still don't know what they want to be.

If you are undecided about your career, set a strategy for exploring the possibilities. Decide how many hours you are going to spend looking at alternatives, what specific steps you are going to take in your search process, and when you will reach a tentative decision. The time limitations on your plan are important. Big decisions are easy to postpone. A plan to which you are committed will set limits on procrastination and indecision.

Realize that the deadline you set is for a tentative choice—a career decision that will let you plan other aspects of your life. You can even set a time, several months in the future, when you will return to your search strategy and reconsider other careers.

When you are developing your plan for selecting a career, set aside at least 25 hours to consider the options and make a choice. Actually schedule this time into the next few weeks.

Steps outlined in your career exploration plan might include reading, interviewing, testing, counseling, and brainstorming. Use all that you have learned about creativity and come up with novel ways to help yourself determine your future.

Reading can include trade and technical journals for careers that interest you or books written especially to help people make career choices. Check the library. *The Dictionary of Occupational Titles* and *The Occupational Outlook Handbook* are two government publications located in most libraries. They summarize thousands of career choices.

Interviewing can include visiting with teachers, professionals, and people that come to campus to interview graduates. Ask them what it's like to work in various occupations. Call and make an appointment to visit with someone who is spending each day doing what you might like to do. Generally, people will take a few

ers

minutes or a coffee break to tell you about their job.

Testing can help you determine your interests and abilities. The Strong-Campbell Interest Inventory is a computer-scored test that matches your interests with those of thousands of people in dozens of different careers. You are then shown the careers enjoyed by people with interests similar to your own. Aptitude tests give you an idea of the jobs you are best suited for. Both types of tests are usually available through colleges, counseling offices, or state employment agencies.

Counseling is available specifically to help people make career choices. If you don't think you will make a decision on your own, get some help. When you make the appointment, let the counselor know that you want help specifically in choosing a career. Some counselors specialize in that type of work.

Brainstorming is one creativity technique mentioned in chapter 7, *Creativity*. It is particularly helpful in selecting a career. First, spend ten minutes brainstorming all of the jobs that you are almost sure you don't want. Second, spend ten minutes listing quickly all the careers that might be a possibility. Third, evaluate your lists. Pick a few possibilities to explore further. The list of what you don't want to do can be very helpful. It shows that

you really have made lots of career choices. You know a lot about what you don't want.

Follow your plan; take all of the steps; spend the time you allocated; and keep your deadline. Once you've made a tentative choice and lived with it for a few months, other options will become clear. You will know that you are on the path to your career.

If you know

Describe in detail what you want in your career. Clarify your goals. If you have known for years what your career will be, or if you just settled on it, it is useful to clearly define your life's work.

Talk to people who work in the career you have chosen. Find out how they spend their days. What do they like about their work? What don't they like? Ask them for ideas on how to prepare for the career. Find out more about what you are working toward.

Get a related job. Even scrubbing the floor of an operating room can be valuable experience, if you are thinking about becoming an operating room technician, a nurse, or a surgeon. Get the feel of where you will be spending your time. Look around. Listen to what goes on in your career.

Match yourself

Make sure your career matches your

Careers

(continued from page 317)

values and desires. Ask yourself if your personal values will fit the job requirements. Does the required travel fit into the type of family life you want? Does the salary range match what you expect to earn? How much free time will you have? Will you have the amount of responsibility you want? Can you live where you want?

Look at the costs of careers as well as their benefits. You want a career which will fit with your other important life goals.

Success is different things to different people. To some, it is having time to fish in the Canadian wilderness; for others, it is building a small business. Some find success at the top of a corporate ladder. Others find it in the city slow-pitch softball championship.

Whatever your definition of success, you can find a career that supports you. You might even consider a back-up profession.

Sometimes, your first choice may indeed be impractical. If you are absolutely committed to becoming a great actor, painter, or novelist, then work on that goal. In the meantime, you might need to have something that will feed and support you. Authors sometimes work in advertising. Commercial designers often paint in their spare time.

Career fields that need people now include medicine, data processing, secretarial, engineering, and technical vocations. The job market, however, is constantly changing. Pick an area that fits you and your goals.

Keep it in mind

A clear picture of your career can make all your goals come into focus. It is easy to spend three hours reading your cost accounting text when you keep in mind the C.P.A. designation that you want after your name. The fifth time you rewrite your English paper won't seem as frustrating when you clearly visualize yourself writing for a city newspaper.

Post reminders of your career choice. Advertise your goals to yourself the way Madison Avenue pitches soap. Advertising is not always done to tell you something new (everyone knows they need soap); its purpose is often to reinforce the image of their product in your mind. Create advertisements that remind you that your goals are worth the time and energy you spend.

Be creative in the way you keep your goals in mind. Posters, photographs, daily visualizations, notes on refrigerators, study groups, professional organizations, and career-related jobs can all serve to remind you of your purpose.

When you remember your purpose, it is easy to make the moment-to-moment choices which will take you to the career you want.

Journal entry #93

Intention statement

If you are not sure of your career choice, make a commitment to plan to determine the kind of work you will do. This plan is a written strategy for exploring career possibilities. It will be a list of steps you will take, hours you will spend, and a date on which a tentative choice will be made.

Write about your intention to get that plan written. Include in your intention statement when you will have the plan finished and what your reward will be for setting up this strategy for choosing a career.

I intend to . . .

_____

_____

_____

_____

_____

_____

_____

_____

_____

_____

_____

_____

_____

_____

_____

_____

Exercise #53

Write yourself a letter

You can send yourself advice, greetings, gossip, love, news, or an invitation. Write a letter and mail it. On the outside of the envelope write a message, "Do not open until _____." After you get the letter, don't open it until the date you specified. Better yet, give the letter, in a stamped envelope, to a trusted friend who will hold the letter and mail it on the date you request.

If your letter contains advice, make it the best you have. Advise as if you knew it all and were writing to a very important person.

If your letter contains greetings or love, make it mushy. Overdo it. Write as if you really wanted the reader to know how much you care.

If your letter is an invitation, make it for something you really want to do. It can be an invitation to something concrete (a play, a party, an evening out) or abstract (success, wealth, love).

If your letter is full of gossip or news, make it interesting even if you have to make it up. Remember, you will read this letter sometime in the future, and you don't want to be bored.

Exercise #54

Do something you can't

You can accomplish much more than you probably think you can. Few significant accomplishments have resulted when people stuck to doing what they knew they could do. Risk yourself.

Pick something that you don't know how to do and do it. Pick something you may think you can't do and do it.

Be smart. Don't pick something that will hurt you physically, such as flying from a third-floor window.

This exercise has three parts.

Part 1

Select something that you are going to do, that you have never done before, that you don't know how to do, or that you think you probably can't do. Describe below the thing you have chosen.

Part 2

Do it. Of course this is easier to say than to do. This exercise is not about easy. It is about discovering capabilities that stretch your self-image.

In order to accomplish something that is bigger than your self-perceived abilities, use all the tools you have. Develop a plan. Divide and conquer. Be willing to be a fool. Stay focused. Use all available outside resources. Let go of self-destructive thoughts.

Part 3

Write about the results of this exercise in your journal if you choose to start one.

This book shouts:

use me

Becoming a Master Student is designed to be used for several years. The success strategies presented here don't become habits overnight. There are more suggestions given than can be put into action immediately. Some of what is discussed may not apply to your life right now, but it may be just what you could use in a few months.

If you plan to keep this book and use it again, imagine this: Your book has a mouth. (Visualize the mouth.) Your book has arms and legs. (Visualize them.)

Now, picture your book sitting on a shelf that you see every day. Imagine a time when you are having trouble in school. Visualize yourself struggling with being successful as a student. Now, imagine your book jumping up and down, tugging at your sleeve and shouting, "Use me! Read me! I may have the solution to your problem, and I know I can get you started solving it yourself."

This is a memory technique to remind you to use a resource. Sometimes, when you are stuck, all you need is a small push or maybe just a list of possible actions. At those times, hear your book shout, "Use me!"

Be it

BE   DO   HAVE

"Be it" is the ultimate power process. All of the techniques in this book depend on your using this process. The idea is that getting where you want to *be* by what you *do* or by what you *have* is like swimming against the current. It's much easier to go the other direction. To get what you want, *be* it.

We usually work against nature by trying to *have* something or *do* something before *being* it. That's the hard way. All of your deeds (what you *do*) won't get you where you want to *be*. Getting all the right tools (what you *have*) won't get you there either.

If you can visualize yourself where you want to be, if you can go there in your imagination, if you can *be* it, then you have achieved most of your goal. You will soon *have* and *do* what you want. This is true because, as human

beings, we *subconsciously create* whomever we *think* we are.

Frequently we hear about people that *had* everything necessary and *did* everything right, yet they still didn't make it. Life didn't work out to their expectations. What went wrong is usually very subtle. "He lost the match but he sure played a good game. Something seemed to *be* wrong. His technique was fine, but each swing was just a little off."

Two people tell the same joke in what seems to be the same way, yet one person brings a smile, and the other person has you laughing so hard your muscles hurt. The difference in how they *do* the joke telling is imperceptible.

The successful comedian still goes through the actions of telling a joke. He does it, however, from his experience of

already *being* funny. Laughter results from *being* funny, not from *doing* anything. And that's the difference.

This last power process contains the same message that began the book. "This book is worthless." Only now, the idea is carried a step further. The techniques in this book are indeed worthless, no matter how often you use them, *if* you operate from the point of view that you are an ineffective student. Even if you consciously and conscientiously apply all the techniques presented, you are likely to subtly sabotage your success.

For example, if you consider yourself stupid in math, you are likely to fail at math. If you are convinced you have a poor memory, chances are that no matter how much you practice memory techniques, your memory won't improve much.

Great achievements happen as the result of very subtle actions that are often unconscious. If you want to succeed, reach to the source of those subsconscious choices that determine your future. Do this by starting from *be*.

Starting from *be* doesn't guarantee anything; it is still necessary to use action to get what you want. But when you start from a mind-set of *being*, your actions become much more natural and on target. That's because your body is not fighting your subconscious idea of what is possible.

Begin your journey toward becoming a master student by being a master student. Get what you want naturally. Use your subconscious powers.

If you want it, be it.

Exercise #56

Did this book work?

By now you know the answer to this question. This book doesn't work. It is worthless. Only you can work. Only you can make a difference. A more appropriate question is, "Did you use this book to become a more effective student?"

The purpose of this book is to give you the opportunity to change—your behavior, not your mind. Something may seem like a good idea, but that doesn't mean you will put it into practice.

This exercise gives you a chance to see what you have put into practice.

Answer each question quickly and honestly. Record your results in the discovery wheel, and then compare it with the wheel you produced in chapter 1.

The score on this evaluation indicates your current strengths and weaknesses in becoming

1. _____ I start each school term highly motivated, and I stay that way throughout the term.

2. _____ I know what I want to get from my course of study.

3. _____ I enjoy learning.

4. _____ I have a clear idea of the benefits I expect to get from my education.

5. _____ I have a clear idea of myself using what I am learning.

6. _____ I study even when I'd rather be doing something else.

7. _____ I get excited about the courses I take.

8. _____ I put in long hours of studying when necessary.

_____ Total score **(1) Motivation**

1. _____ I am confident of my ability to remember.

2. _____ I remember people's names.

3. _____ At the end of a lecture, I could give a friend a short speech about what was presented.

4. _____ I use a regular strategy to remember things.

5. _____ I remember under pressure.

6. _____ Remembering lots of facts about one subject is easy for me.

7. _____ I can jog my memory when I'm stuck and can't recall.

8. _____ I remember formulas, equations and similar material.

_____ Total score **(3) Memory**

1. _____ I set aside regular periods of time to review and refine my long-term goals.

2. _____ I set aside regular periods of time to review and refine my short-term goals.

3. _____ I assign priorities to each day's list of things to do.

4. _____ I plan my review time so I don't have to cram at the end of a course.

5. _____ I write a schedule for my week in advance.

6. _____ I plan regular recreation time.

7. _____ I decide for each course how much time I will devote to it.

8. _____ I have enough time during the day to accomplish everything I want to.

_____ Total score **(2) Planning**

1. _____ I feel comfortable reading textbooks.

2. _____ I generally need to read a textbook only once to get what I need.

3. _____ When I read, I ask questions about the reading.

4. _____ When I read textbooks, I am alert and awake.

5. _____ I relate what I read in textbooks to my life.

6. _____ I select my reading strategy to fit the kind of book I'm reading.

7. _____ I take effective notes when I read a textbook.

8. _____ When I don't understand a concept I'm reading, I make a note of my question and ask the instructor.

_____ Total score **(4) Reading**

1. _____ When I am in class, I keep my attention in the room.

2. _____ I take notes in class.

3. _____ I can still read my notes a week after I take them.

4. _____ My notes are valuable for review.

5. _____ I review class notes within 24 hours.

6. _____ I notice when an instructor uses key phrases that might indicate later test questions.

7. _____ I copy material the instructor writes on the board.

8. _____ I take notes in my own words.

_____ Total score (5) Observation

1. _____ I have flashes of insight, and solutions to problems appear to me at unusual times.

2. _____ I find it easy to select a subject for a paper or speech.

3. _____ When I get stuck on a creative project, I have a way to get unstuck.

4. _____ When I get a great idea, I follow up on it and develop it.

5. _____ I am a good problem-solver in math and science.

6. _____ I am confident when I speak before others.

7. _____ I see problems as opportunities for learning and personal growth.

8. _____ I trust my intuition.

_____ Total score (7) Creativity

1. _____ I feel confident and calm during an exam.

2. _____ I plan my time and work fast enough so that I answer every question I am capable of answering.

3. _____ I feel alive and energetic during exams.

4. _____ I feel secure about myself no matter what my grade on an exam.

5. _____ My test scores reflect my knowledge of a subject.

6. _____ I adapt my test-taking strategy to the kind of test I'm taking.

7. _____ I can examine essay questions in light of what I know and come to a new and original conclusion during a test.

8. _____ I receive the grades I want on tests.

_____ Total score (6) Test-taking

1. _____ I develop and maintain relationships which help me to get what I want.

2. _____ I say what I feel and let people know who I am when I talk to them.

3. _____ Other people have reported to me that I am a good listener.

4. _____ I value time alone.

5. _____ I enjoy contributing to the lives of others and do it regularly.

6. _____ I get along with my instructors.

7. _____ I have the ability to make friends and create valuable relationships in a new place.

8. _____ I am open to being with people I don't especially like in order to learn from them.

_____ Total score (8) Relationships

a master student. The last page of this chapter provides space for intended changes. As you complete this self-evaluation, ask yourself how you want to improve, what you want to change. Your commitment to self-improvement will allow you to get all you want and to contribute to others.

5 This statement is always or almost always true of me.

4 This statement is often true of me.

3 This statement is sometimes true of me (about half the time).

2 This statement is seldom true of me.

1 This statement is never or almost never true of me.

1. _____ At the end of the day, I have energy left to study.

2. _____ My physical health helps me to concentrate.

3. _____ My emotional health supports my ability to learn.

4. _____ If the situation calls for it, I have enough reserves to put in a very long day or a series of long days.

5. _____ I accept my body the way it is.

6. _____ I am responsible for the way I look.

7. _____ I am in control of the alcohol and drugs I put into my body.

8. _____ The food I eat contributes to my health.

_____ Total score (9) Health

1. _____ I have control of the money in my life.

2. _____ I have enough money to get the education I want.

3. _____ I have a clear picture of financial resources available to students.

4. _____ I have the ability to make a little money go a long way.

5. _____ My education supports my financial goals.

6. _____ I repay my debts.

7. _____ My sense of personal worth is independent of my financial condition.

8. _____ I know where my money goes.

_____ Total score (10) Money

5 This statement is always or almost always true of me.

4 This statement is often true of me.

3 This statement is sometimes true of me (about half the time).

2 This statement is seldom true of me.

1 This statement is never or almost never true of me.

1. _____ I feel comfortable and at home in libraries.

2. _____ I am involved in community activities.

3. _____ I use my job as a learning experience.

4. _____ I learn by contributing to others.

5. _____ I know where to get help in my community for a variety of problems.

6. _____ I have a group of friends with whom I meet for mutual support toward our educational goals.

7. _____ I use my own imagination as a resource.

8. _____ I see the world's problems as an opportunity for me to contribute.

_____ Total score (11) **Resources**

1. _____ I relate my learning process to what I plan to do for the rest of my life.

2. _____ I relate the subjects I study to my personal goals.

3. _____ I see learning as a lifelong process.

4. _____ I can experience myself growing every day through the learning process.

5. _____ I am clear about my purpose in life.

6. _____ I know that I am responsible for my own education.

7. _____ I am the creator of my experience.

8. _____ I recognize that I never stay the same, that I am always learning and growing.

_____ Total score (12) **Purpose**

Shade in each section's slice of the pie to the appropriate level. Use the scores from each section of the discovery guide.

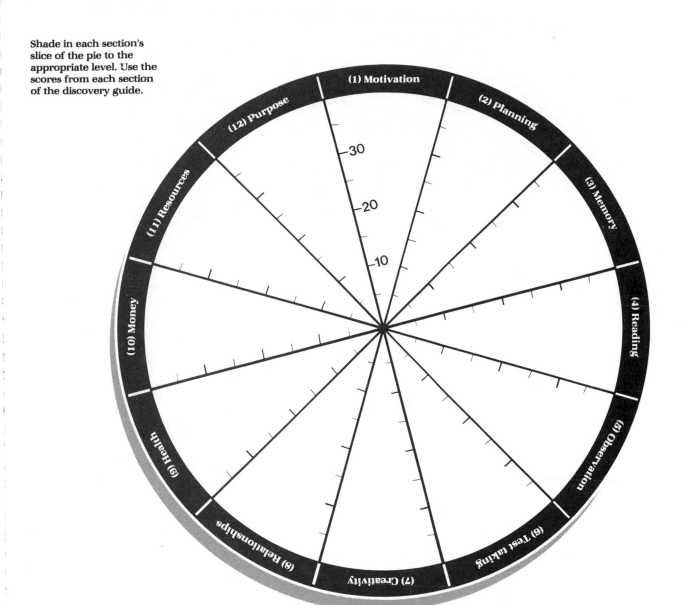

Compare the discovery wheel you produced in chapter 1 with the one you created in this chapter.

By comparing the two discovery wheels, I learned that I...

_____

Journal entry #94

Discovery statement

_____

I also learned that I, . .

_____

Lincoln Steffens

Now I like history: I had neglected it partly because I rebelled at the way it was taught, as positive knowledge unrelated to politics, art, life or anything else. The professors gave us chapters out of a few books to read, con, and be quizzed on. Blessed as I was with a "bad memory," I could not commit to it anything that I did not understand and intellectually need. The bare record of the story of man, with names, dates, and irrelevant events, bored me. But I had discovered in my readings of literature, philosophy, and political economy that history had light to throw upon unhistorical questions. So I proposed in my junior and senior years to specialize in history, taking all the courses required and those also that I had flunked in. With this in mind I listened attentively to the first introductory talk of Professor William Cary Jones on American Constitutional history. He was a dull lecturer, but I noticed that, after telling us what pages of what books we must be prepared in, he mumbled off some other references "for those that may care to dig deeper."

When the rest of the class rushed out into the sunshine, I went up to the professor and, to his surprise, asked for this memorandum. He gave it to me. Up in the library I ran through the required chapters in the two different books, and they differed on several points. Turning to the other authorities I saw that they disagreed on the same facts and also on others. The librarian, appealed to, helped me search the bookshelves till the library closed, and then I called on Professor Jones for more references. He was astonished, invited me in, and began to approve my industry, which astonished me. I was not trying to be a good boy; I was better than that: I was a curious boy. He lent me a couple of his books, and I went off to my club to read them. They only deepened the mystery, clearing up the historical questions, but leaving the answer to be dug for and written.

The historians did not know! History was not a science, but a field for research, a field for me, for any young man, to explore, to make discoveries in and write a scientific report about. I was fascinated. As I went on from chapter to chapter, day after day, finding frequently essential differences of opinion and fact . . . I hunted far enough to suspect that the Fathers of the Republic who wrote our sacred Constitution of the United States not only did not, but did not want to, establish a democratic government, and I dreamed for a while—as I used to play I was Napoleon or a trapper—I promised myself to write a true history of the making of the American Constitution. I did not do it; that chapter has been done or well begun since by two men: Smith of the University of Washington and Beard (then) of Columbia (afterward forced out, perhaps for this very work). In all my courses, in ancient, in European, and in modern history, the disagreeing authorities carried me back to the need of a fresh search for (or of) the original documents or other clinching testimony. Of course I did well in my classes. The history professors soon knew me as a student and seldom put a question to me except when the class had flunked it. Then Professor Jones would say, "Well, Steffens, tell them about it."

Fine. But vanity wasn't my ruling passion then. What I had was a quickening sense that I was learning a method of studying history and that every chapter of it, from the beginning of the world to the end, is crying out to be rewritten. There was something for Youth to do; these superior old men had not done anything finally . . .

Nothing is done. Everything in the world remains to be done or done over. "The greatest picture is not yet painted, the greatest play isn't written (not even by Shakespeare), the greatest poem unsung. There isn't in all the world a perfect railroad, nor a good government, nor a sound law." Physics, mathematics and especially the most advanced and exact of the sciences, are being fundamentally revised. Chemistry is just becoming a science; psychology, economics, and sociology are awaiting a Darwin, whose work in turn is awaiting an Einstein. If the rah-rah boys in our colleges could be told this, they might not all be such specialists in football, petting parties, and unearned degrees. They are not told it; however, they are told to learn what is known. This is nothing, philosophically speaking.

1. Lincoln Steffens was inspired by his independent reading because he could find the answer to any question by looking in the right book. True or false.

2. Compare and contrast visualization and affirmation.

3. Once you have decided on a career, put those thoughts aside so you can devote more time and energy to your school work. True or false.

4. Does this book work?

5. List the three steps in exercise #54, *Do something you can't.*

6. Suggestions for continuing your journey in growth, discovery, and intention include:
   a. keep a journal
   b. get counseling
   c. travel
   d. take an unrelated class
   e. all of the above

7. Attitudes are powerful because they affect your _____.

8. Select the most effective affirmation:
   a. I don't snack between meals.
   b. Within three months I will be slender.
   c. I am not fat.
   d. I am slender and weigh 120 lbs.

9. You can become a better basketball player while sitting quietly in a chair. True or false.

10. Name three of the five suggestions that were given for a career exploration plan.

At the beginning of each chapter in this book, you were asked to describe what you wanted from the chapter. In the introduction, you were asked to list what you wanted from this book. Review each of those journal entry/discovery statements and describe below what you did not get.

Journal entry #95

Discovery statement

Devise a plan for getting what you want and then make some commitments about what you will do.

Write your strategy here.

Write your commitments here.

I intend to . . .

Intention statement

Hundreds of tools, techniques, hints, processes, and suggestions for being a successful student have been presented in this book. At the end of each chapter you have been asked to make a commitment to experiment with a suggestion or two.

Quickly review this book and choose a few more techniques that you can be counted on to use. Make sure your promises are time-limited and achievable and include a reward.

Intention	Time/Date	Reward
I will . . .		
I will . . .		
I will . . .		

Bibliography

PERSONAL DEVELOPMENT:

Bach, Richard. *Illusions: The Adventures of a Reluctant Messiah*, New York, NY: Delacorte, 1977.

Bandler, Richard & Grinder, John. *Frogs into Princes: Neuro-Linguistic Programming*, Moab, UT: Real People Press, 1979.

Benson, Herbert & Klipper, Miriam Z. *The Relaxation Response*, New York, NY: Avon, 1976.

Bloomfield, Harold, et.al. *How to Survive the Loss of a Love*, New York, NY: Bantam Books, 1977.

Buber, Martin. *I and Thou*, New York, NY: Scribner, 1970.

Castaneda, Carlos. *Separate Reality*, New York, NY: Pocket Books, 1981.

Castaneda, Carlos. *The Teachings of Don Juan: A Yaqui Way of Knowledge*, Berkeley, CA: University of California Press, 1968.

Castaneda, Carlos. *Journey to ixtlan*, New York, NY: Pocket Books, 1981.

Corey, Gerald. *I Never Knew I Had a Choice*, Monterey, CA: Brooks-Cole Publishing, 1982.

Emery, Stuart. *Actualizations: You Don't Have to Rehearse to Be Yourself*, Garden City, NY: Doubleday & Company, Inc., 1978.

Frankl, Victor. *Man's Search for Meaning*, New York, NY: Simon & Schuster, 1970.

Gawain, Shakti. *Creative Visualization*, Mill Valley, CA: Whatever Publishing, 1978.

Golas, Thaddeus. *The Lazy Man's Guide to Enlightenment*, Palo Alto, CA: Seed Center, 1972.

James, Muriel and Jongeward, Dorothy. *Born to Win*, Reading, MA: Addison-Wesley, 1971.

Keyes, Ken, Jr. *Handbook to Higher Consciousness*, Berkeley, CA: Living Love Center, 1974.

Kopp, Sheldon. *If You Meet The Buddha on the Road, Kill Him!*, New York, NY: Bantam, 1976.

Maltz, Dr. Maxwell. *Psycho-Cybernetics*, New York, NY: Pocket Books, n.d.

Maslow, Abraham. *Toward a Psychology of Being*, New York, NY: Van Nostrand Reinhold, 1968.

Miller, William A. *You Count-You Really Do!*, Minneapolis, MN: Augsburg Publishing House, 1976.

Pirsig, Robert. *Zen and the Art of Motorcycle Maintenance*, New York, NY: Bantam, 1976.

Rajneesh, Bhagwan S. *Journey Toward the Heart*, New York, NY: Harper & Row, 1980.

Rhinehart, Luke. *The Book of est*, New York, NY: Holt, Rinehart & Winston, 1975.

Satir, Virginia. *Peoplemaking*, Center City, MN: Hazelden, n.d.

Waitley, Denis E. *The Psychology of Winning*, cassette, Chicago, IL: Nightingale-Conant Corp., n.d.

Williams, Paul. *Energi*, New York, NY: Warner Books, 1980.

Zimbardo, Philip G. *Shyness—What It Is, What To Do About it*, Reading, MA: Addison-Wesley, 1977.

Zukav, Gary. *The Dancing Wu Li Masters*, New York, NY: Bantam, 1979.

LEARNING TOOLS:

Barzun, Jacques & Graff, Henry F. *The Modern Researcher*, New York, NY: Harcourt, Brace, Jovanovich, 1977.

Blanchard, Kenneth & Johnson, Spencer. *The One Minute Manager*, New York, NY: William Morrow, 1983.

Buzan, Tony. *Use Both Sides of Your Brain*, New York, NY: E. P. Dutton & Co., Inc., 1974.

Gilbart, Helen W. *Pathways: A Guide to Reading and Study Skills*, Boston, MA: Houghton Mifflin Company, 1982.

Higbee, Kenneth L. *Your Memory—How It Works and How to Improve It*, Englewood Cliffs, NJ: Prentice-Hall, Inc., 1977.

James, William. *Talks to Teachers on Psychology and to Students on Some of Life's Ideals*, New York, NY: Norton, 1958.

Lucas, Jerry, & Lorayne, Harry. *The Memory Book*, New York, NY: Ballantine Books, Inc., 1975.

Matheson, Maureen, ed. *College Handbook*, New York, NY: The College Board, 1983.

Pauk, Walter. *How to Study in College*, Boston, MA: Houghton Mifflin Company, 1974.

Ries, Al and Trout, Jack. *Positioning: The Battle for Your Mind*, New York, NY: McGraw Hill, 1980.

Rogers, Carl. *Freedom to Learn*, Columbus, OH: Charles Merrill Publishing, 1982.

GOALS:

American Personnel and Guidance Association. *Career Decisions*, Washington, D.C.: American Personnel and Guidance Association, n.d.

Bolles, Richard Nelson. *What Color is Your Parachute?*, Berkeley, CA: Ten Speed Press, 1983.

Lakein, Alan. *How to Get Control of Your Time and Your Life*, New York, NY: New American Library (Signet), 1974.

Satir, Virginia. *Making Contact*, Berkeley, CA: Celestial Arts Publishing, 1976.

U.S. Department of Labor. *The Directory of Occupational Titles*, Washington, D.C.: Government Printing Office, n.d.

U. S. Department of Labor. *The Occupational Outlook Handbook*, Washington, D.C.: Government Printing Office, n.d.

REFERENCE:

Davies, Peter, ed. *The American Heritage Dictionary of the English Language*, New York, NY: Dell, 1982.

Department of Energy. *The Car Book*, Pueblo, CO: Consumer Information Center, n.d.

Strunk, William, Jr. & White, E. B. *The Elements of Style*, New York, NY: Macmillan Publishing, 1979.

CONSUMER AND HEALTH:

Cousins, Norman. *Anatomy of an Illness As Perceived by the Patient*, New York, NY: Bantam Books, 1981.

Johnson, Vernon E. *I'll Quit Tomorrow*, New York, NY: Harper Row Publishers, 1980.

Porter, Sylvia. *Sylvia Porter's New Money Book for the 80's*, New York, NY: Avon, 1980.

Ryan, Regina Sara and Travis, John W., M.D. *Wellness Workbook: A Guide to Attaining High Level Wellness*, Berkeley, CA: Ten Speed Press, 1981.

Vickery, Donald M. and Fries, James F. *Take Care of Yourself: A Consumer's Guide to Medical Care*, Reading, MA: Addison-Wesley Publishing Co., 1981.

RELATIONSHIPS:

Driekurs, Rudolf & Soltz, Vicki. *Children: The Challenge*, New York, NY: E. P. Dutton, 1964.

Gordon, Thomas. *Parent Effectiveness Training: The Tested New Way to Raise Responsible Children*, New York, NY: New American Library (Thomas), 1975.

Keyes, Ken, Jr. *A Conscious Person's Guide to Relationships*, Coos Bay, OR: Living Love, 1979.

Keyes, Ken, Jr. *The Hundredth Monkey*, Coos Bay, OR: Vision Books, 1982.

Index

Index

(continued)

BECOMING A Master STUDENT

Quiz answers

Chapter 1 Quiz answers

1. False. The ideas in this book are merely tools. If they work for you, use them.

2. Telling the truth about yourself and admitting what you want to be.

3. Franklin admitted (after it was pointed out by his father) that his writing style was less elegant than Collins's and he determined that he wanted to change it. Also, when Franklin compared his writing to that in the *Spectator* he admitted when his was not as effective and chose a course of action to improve it.

4. Human beings are designed to both learn and resist change, and learning involves change.

5. The purpose of this book is to set a stage upon which students can create their own dramas, bring into being their own learning experiences.

6. The desire to be right. The master student is a person who, like Maslow's self-actualizing person, is oriented toward reality rather than oriented toward protecting his self-image. The master student is willing to be wrong.

7. You might have written:

   a. Franklin was energetic, as evidenced by his willingness to get up early and stay up late to practice the art of writing.

   b. Franklin was creative in his approach to learning how to write prose. He did it by writing poetry.

   c. Franklin was self-directed in his studies.

8. First step is the first chapter because, for any student, learning the process of learning is the most important objective, and self-examination is the beginning of the process of learning.

9. The aircraft is constantly telling itself the truth about where it is and where it wants to go.

10. The Discovery and Intention Journal System starts with a first step. You tell the truth about where you are and what you want (Discovery Statements). After a time, when you look at whether you accomplished what you intended, you complete another first step. A time passes and you complete another.

Chapter 2 Quiz answers

1. Now

2. The seven ways listed in this chapter are:

   Agree with roommates on study time.
   Notice when you are losing your concentration.
   Avoid noise distractions.
   Get off the phone.
   Use a "do not disturb" sign.
   Notice how others abuse your time.
   Learn to say no.

3. False. The purpose of managing time is for the student to plan for times when frustration and discomfort are likely, not to avoid them.

4. False. A items are those which require immediate attention.

5. False. You can't force thoughts to do anything for very long. Besides, there are times when being in the here and now means being with daydreams or thoughts.

6. Two.

7. After you have used a regular study area several times your body will begin to respond to it automatically. You will more quickly be able to get into the proper frame of mind for studying.

8. Perhaps perfection on these papers isn't

necessary. If your instructor does not require a flawless paper, your time might be better spent on another task.

9. Now. (The only possible answer).

10. False. The time plan helps you see the big picture for the week, while daily "to do" lists allow you to focus on specific tasks.

Chapter 3 Quiz answers

1. To give you an opportunity to discover your powerful memory and to give you an opportunity to develop methods you can use to tap into it.

2. Short-term memory has a limited capacity. It only lasts a few moments.

3. Animals never leave the forest. This law represents the idea that we never really forget anything.

4. Be organized. Be physical. Be clear. Be smart.

5. A man is pushing down on a bicycle pump as a pressure gauge rises. The man is becoming "boiling" angry as he does it.

6. Interaction, vividness, and concreteness.

7. Reciting aloud engages thought and two kinds of physical activity, hearing and vocalizing, in the learning process. The effect is synergistic, in that the combination of senses is greater than the sum of the effects of the individual senses. When you use a combination of your senses, you wear a deeper neural trace, making recall easier.

8. Most of us feel silly when we talk aloud to ourselves. That barrier prevents us from using recitation, a guaranteed-to-work memory technique.

9. In situations where material must be learned in order.

10. Usually, when introduced to someone, we don't hear the name. Our minds are occupied with thoughts about ourselves.

Chapter 4 Quiz answers

1. POQ RUA RRR

2. Be organized
   Preview
   Outline
   Question
   Be Physical
   Recite
   Visualize material
   Make a storyboard
   Use gestures when you recite
   Be Clear
   Answer
   Underline
   Review
   Review again
   Be Smart
   Tailor reading technique to material
   Distribute review periods
   Engage in a dialogue with the text

3. Absolutely false. This question is a giveaway. Even a student with a poor vocabulary and weak grammar skills can be an effective reader if that student approaches the task intelligently, admits shortcomings and uses all the muscle reading techniques.

4. Charts, diagrams, chapter titles, paragraph headings, summary statements.

5. Relate questions to your goals. Turn section titles into questions. Create questions that relate material to what you already know.

6. Synergy is the combined action or force of several elements. Recitation combines auditory and kinesthetic (touch and motion) stimulation with repetition.

7. Students who review material within 24 hours demonstrate significantly increased ability to recall information.

8. Read it again, look for essential words, read it aloud, use your instructor, find a tutor, use an alternate text, pretend you understand and explain it, stand up.

9. Decrease regressions by improving concentration and awareness, and/or move eyes faster.

10. With pencil and pad, he copied the entire dictionary.

Quiz answers

(continued)

Chapter 5 Quiz answers

1. Complete outside assignments. Conduct a pre-class review. Clarify intentions about your observation in class. Arrive early. (Also: bring necessary materials and sit front and center).

2. False. Fighting daydreams is useless. Notice them and gently let them go.

3. When you notice your attention drifting, you can sit up in your chair. If you find that you are having difficulty concentrating, return your consciousness to class by running your hand along the side or top of the chair, paying close attention to the feel of the wood, metal or plastic. In other words, pay close attention to your environment.

4. If you allow yourself to judge while you are observing and recording in class, the internal noise created by your judgments is likely to drown out information being presented.

5. Sit as if the lecture were interesting. The position of your body will quickly change your mind, sit front and center. Make eye contact with the instructor. Look as if you're interested. (The teacher may react to you as a person who is excited by the lecture and act as if his presentation mattered, rather than delivering what a bored-looking class expects.) In your thoughts, substitute the word "interesting" for the word "boring" when you describe to yourself what's going on. Prepare for the lecture by doing your assignments. Take very detailed notes. (Generally "boring" instructors have dry presentations but the material has been well thought out. They have spent more time developing what they're going to say than how they're going to say it.) Make up test questions while listening to the instructor. Participate actively in class exercises, ask questions, relate what you're listening to to your own life . . .

6. Use first step, intend to improve, visualize success, watch your pen, demonstrate excellence, fix problems immediately, use quality materials, take a calligraphy course, dot i's, notice letters, print, and appreciate value of legibility to improve your handwriting.

7. It's more difficult to fall asleep at the front. The instructor's voice is louder. At the front you can make eye contact with the instructor more easily. (And she can see you more easily. It's harder to doze when the risk of discovery is high.)

8. Most people fail to recall 80% of material learned within 24 hours, unless the material has been reviewed.

9. Preview, outline, question, read, underline, answer, recite, review and review again

10. One important quality for the keen observer is intention. Sherlock Holmes looked at potential clues with the intention of extracting all that they had to offer. He was committed to observation. Your intention to get everything you can from the classroom is more valuable than any techniques you learn.

Chapter 6 Quiz answers

1. The daily review is a short follow-up of reading and lecture notes to improve recall in the critical 24 hours following initial learning. It is also used to set the stage for the next lecture or reading assignment.

   The weekly review is a longer structured study session designed to deepen understanding, command and recall of the subject.

   Major reviews are to integrate the information presented throughout the term and to prepare for exams.

2. An outlined review uses linear, logical sequences, while a mind map review reveals patterns. A mind map can show relationships graphically as well as verbally, while traditional outlines rely mainly on words. Outlines list subjects in order, whereas a mind map starts with a central subject and branches out to subordinate subjects.

3.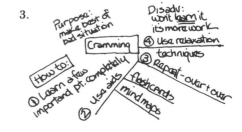

4. Use flashcards for formulas, definitions, theories, key words, axioms, dates, foreign language phrases etc. from your notes.

5. The brain works on material subconsciously. Concepts, problems or theories that confuse you at first can become clear if you give yourself enough time to reflect on the problem. By conducting major reviews well before a test, you give your brain a chance to work on the ideas.

6. A. The eyes. If an instructor goes to his notes for a particular point, that might indicate a future question.
B. Anything written on the board.
C. When an instructor repeats a point several times. Extra points if the instructor says, "This will be on the test."

7. Compatibility, shared academic goals, seriousness of purpose, availability.

8. When she is seated, she relaxes completely in her chair, taking a few seconds to do a body scan for tension and a breathing exercise. When she gets her test, she scans it from beginning to end, noting the point value and difficulty of each section. Then she outlines a brief time plan in the margin of her test booklet. She turns to the easiest section and begins.

9. False. There is a difference between healthy desire and addictive need. Addictions are emotion-backed demands that control your behavior.

10. When we express our worst fears in specific, detailed terms, those fears often turn out to be less disastrous than we imagined.

Chapter 7 Quiz answers

1. By allowing a paper to sit for a few days, you give yourself time to step back from the project. Often it is difficult to see obvious mistakes when you are deeply involved.

2. Intuition, creativity.

3. Writing will stimulate your thought processes. You will see holes in your research, and new research areas will be suggested. If you budget time for research to be done as you write, you will be able to fill in the gaps and/or explore new ideas.

4. Discovery statements can be used to identify the types of problems that you have trouble with. You can also use discovery statements to monitor the amount of time you spend practicing problems. Intention statements can be especially valuable in math classes because falling behind in math can be dangerous. You can use intention statements to set short, achievable goals for practicing problems.

5. False, everyone is creative.

6. Introduction—tell the audience what you're going to tell them; get their attention.
Body—tell them (70-90% of the speech)
Conclusion—wrap up; tell them what you told them.

7. Preview, outline, question. Read, underline, answer. Recite, review, review.

8.

9. Whatever you wrote is the correct answer. Carl Rogers, Abraham Maslow, and many other wise people have suggested that self-expression is a human need, not a luxury. If you had difficulty describing how your long-term goal was related to your self-expression, you might consider reevaluating that goal.

10. Serendipity is discovering important, valuable or pleasant things when you aren't looking for them.

Chapter 8 Quiz answers

1. b. defensiveness. "You" messages label, judge and blame. They are hard to listen to.

Quiz answers
(continued)

2. Observations, feelings, thoughts, wants, intentions

3. False. How you say something can be more important than what you say. Your tone of voice and gestures can support or contradict your words.

4. Listening beyond the words means being aware of nonverbal messages and behavior. A person's body language and actions may be screaming the exact opposite of his words. For example, he may say he's very excited but he looks and acts very bored.

5. Paraphrase means to summarize in your own words and feed back the essence of what you think the other person said.

6. Griping is usually not intended to be a part of finding solutions. Sharing problems is an appropriate way of starting the search for a solution.

7. An interesting side effect of feeling good about yourself is that others start feeling good about you, too.

8. Aggressive behavior is domineering and based on a win/lose point of view. Assertive behavior signifies a healthy personality. It is confidently asking directly for what a person wants without feeling embarrassed or inadequate. It respects other people and their values and opinions.

9. Encoding; decoding

10. False. You can never communicate your internal experience directly to another person. Words are not the experience.

Chapter 9 Quiz answers

1. Eat a variety of foods every day, maintain your weight, decrease fat and cholesterol consumption, increase starch and fiber consumption, decrease sugar intake, reduce salt intake.

2. Twenty; three.

3. Possible answers include: Relax with a sigh or do other breathing exercises; daydream or substitute a pleasant image for a negative thought; detach yourself; consider the worst; visualize success; do a body scan; focus your attention on an object or meditate; tense your muscles then relax them; use guided imagery; do aerobic exercises; focus on your anxiety.

4. See the alternative health care article for a complete list of answers.

5. Bulimia is a gorge and vomit cycle. Anorexia nervosa is starving oneself. Some victims have a combination of these illnesses. They go through a bulimia cycle and then don't eat for days or weeks before gorging again.

6. False. More poisonings occur in people aged 15 to 45.

7. An alcoholic is a person whose life is not working well and who regularly drinks alcohol.

8. Medha means "locating your center, your inner wisdom."

9. A co-addict.

10. Impulsiveness, dramatic mood swings, bizarre thoughts, suicidal behavior, slurred speech, disorientation, slowed mental and physical functioning, limited attention span.

Chapter 10 Quiz answers

1. Don't spend more than you have.

2. Accrual

3. Increase money in, decrease money out, do both.

4. Use the telephone
   Comparison shop
   Keep receipts
   Search out free entertainment
   Plan your wardrobe
   Don't shop on an empty stomach
   Use public transportation
   Avoid snacks
   Complain when you don't get your money's worth
   Use coupons
   Conserve fuel

Avoid credit purchases
Postpone purchases
Don't carry cash
Be aware of quality
Watch rent costs
Shop for nutrition and food value
Fix things yourself

5. a. National Direct Student Loan

6. Packages from all over the country are flown to a central point, then sorted and distributed and flown out again to their destinations.

7. True.

8. False.

9. Financial aid programs, part-time work, sell something, ask relatives for assistance, invest (can be risky), steal something (not recommended).

10. If we don't understand it, we don't have to feel responsible for it.

Chapter 11 Quiz answers

1. Interlibrary loan.

2. c. Summarizing current findings in specific fields.

3. A thesaurus is a type of dictionary that gives synonyms (words that have the same or similar meaning) for the word you look up.

4. The school catalog
Counseling center
Alumni organizations
Chapel
College print shop
Campus radio station
Art gallery
Computer center
Student organizations
Registrar's office
Tutoring center
Child care services
School newspaper
Campus TV station
Music practice rooms
Placement office
Financial aid office
Health clinic
Car pooling sign up sheets
Campus security
Museum
Observatory

5. True. Since we are so interdependent, either we all win or eventually we all lose.

6. City mayor's office, the local offices of the Republican or Democratic party, the Chamber of Commerce, the newspaper, the news department of your local TV station or the library.

7. You can sit through a course without paying full tuition. You will not receive credit but you can study the material, ask questions and be exposed to all the lectures.

8. In an interdependent world, the only way to live a prosperous, safe and satisfying life is to ensure that people you depend upon (everyone else) are also prosperous, safe and have the chance to be satisfied.

9. *Readers' Guide to Periodical Literature.*

10. The Registrar's office.

Chapter 12 Quiz answers

1. False. He was inspired because he found discrepancies and unanswered questions.

2. Affirmations are written or spoken. Visualizations are imagined. Both are ways to restructure your attitudes and behavior to get what you want.

3. False. When you remember your purpose, it is easy to make the moment to moment choices needed to reach your goals.

4. No. Only you can work.

5. Select something, do it, write about it.

6. e. All of the above.

7. Behavior.

8. d. "I am slender and weigh 120 lbs," is in the present tense, is positive and is specific.

9. True. Visualization and affirmation work.

10. Reading, interviewing, testing, counseling, and brainstorming.

This book was designed
on a five column matrix
with vertical breaks
based on 11 and 14 point
leading. Typography is in
most cases either 12/14
Zapf book light, 10/11
Zapf book light or 8/11
Zapf book medium.
Manuscript was
composed and edited on
a word processor and
transmitted electronically
to the typesetter.